All hell broke loose before we'd moved fifty yards into the village. The firing we'd been hearing in the distance erupted violently upon us, and we were suddenly in a mess of fighting. I remember the chattering dialogue of bullets from rifles, machine guns, and burp guns, and the flares that blossomed endlessly in the dark sky. I remember a new and strange enemy weapon from which a tail of flame lashed malevolently, and my skin crawled because we'd never before faced a flamethrower. It turned out to be not a flamethrower but a bazooka. They were firing at us with bazookas, and this was a fantastic and outrageous thing, to fire bazookas at *men*.

And there was shouting and many dark figures darting across the road and no way of knowing whether they were friends or enemies. . . .

ROLL ME OVER

An Infantryman's World War II

Raymond Gantter

IVY BOOKS • NEW YORK

Ivy Books
Published by Ballantine Books
Copyright © 1997 by The Estate of Raymond Gantter

http://www.randomhouse.com

Library of Congress Catalog Card Number: 96-94893

ISBN 0-8041-1605-9

Manufactured in the United States of America

First Edition: July 1997

10   9   8   7   6

To the Infantry—
the Queen of Battles

Roll me over
In the clover;
Roll me over, lay me down,
And do it again!

A song of the infantry

Foreword

People keep talking about another war as though it were inevitable and only the moment of its coming uncertain, tomorrow, or maybe next week. Self-appointed prophets of doom, all of us. We talk a lot about it, but we don't really think about it because it doesn't bear thinking on: We know (and hide the knowledge from ourselves) that when it comes, if or when this "cold war" becomes a blaze, it will ravish the world. Atomic warfare, biological warfare, the swift murder of cities and civilians—warfare to make a mockery of the conventions of war, transforming armies into bewildered huddles of uniformed men who scamper crazily to catch up with an adversary who struck ten minutes ago and is now gone and away.

Yet I believe that the next war, like the last one, will require the foot soldier. New weapons and new techniques there will be, new devices to blast and devastate with laudable efficiency, but when the weapons and devices have finished their work, the battered target, the precious, battered inches of ground, will have to be secured and held, and that's a job for the infantry.

This book, then, is at once a tribute to all former infantrymen, a personal narrative for my family, and a rough notebook of sorts for the young men who will be the foot soldiers of the next war.

My original purpose in writing was nothing so lofty. I started to write because I was scared. Most of the time I was scared—not by bullet and shell alone, but by the huge and brutal impersonality of the whole business. Writing about it gave me a measure of control over my fears.

Some of the material in this book is taken from letters written to my wife, Ree. Most of it, however, is drawn from rough notes jotted during the combat months, hastily scribbled observations that, for reasons of security, could not be included in letters home. I started those notes on the day I finished with the homeless misery of the Replacement Depots and joined an outfit, became a member of a family. I wrote as the circumstances permitted, employing whatever material was at hand—the backs of envelopes, paper bags, even the wrappers from our miniature packets of GI toilet paper. I carried the notes between my underwear and my shirt to protect them against the weather.

A lot of war books have been written, and perhaps there's nothing in this one that someone hasn't already said. But now that it's over and a degree of perspective becomes possible, a couple of things have hit me hard and hit me fresh. One concerns heroism and heroes. It's a commonplace to say that heroes, most of them, are accidental. The thing that surprised me is that a guy can be a hero and a bastard at the same time. I'm talking about true heroes, of course, not guys who wear decorations. A lot of phonies are wearing ribbons they never earned, and that's no secret. But I mean a man who does something truly gallant, something that rings inside you like the surging memory of Hector before the walls of Troy. And yet you don't like him. If you didn't like him before, you're surprised to find you don't like him any better now, even though you recognize the magnitude of his act and are awed by it. He's a hero, sure, but he's still a jerk. That contradiction belongs to war. War is a marriage—almost a rape—of giant opposites. It's everything and all things and all at the same time: bad and good, heroism and cowardice, terror and serenity, feast and starvation, gallantry and bestiality. The wonder is that you can continue to be surprised.

Something that always angered and frightened me was the small horizon of the man in the ranks. Most of the time you don't know what's happening, or why. You don't even know where you are. It's something you force yourself to accept—the big picture is for the brass, but it's none of your damn business. You have a job to do, a town or a hill to take, and you do your job. Sometimes you know the name of the town; sometimes it remains forever in your memory only as That Place Where. I puzzle yet over maps, striving to find certain villages that were significant in my odyssey, but they are like cities on the moon, having no geographical context.

If I were concerned with trying to show you the sweep of war, I'd have to do a lot of research, and then I'd be able to tell you that on such and such a day, when we'd been ordered to take such and such a town, the strategic picture was this and this, and we did what we did because of its relationship to the big plan. But I leave all that for the memoirs of generals. My purpose is to show you the dark side of the medal: how it was to be fumbling and blind, moving because we'd been ordered to move, but not knowing where or why. If some faint tingle of that unreality touches you, you will understand how it was that we were sometimes overwhelmed by black and crawling fear.

You'll find errors, possibly some misinformation in this. I'll try to avoid them and give the true and accurate story, but I'm not going to worry much about a few errors of fact. If you at home lived in a world ruled by rumor and misinformation, so did we. You ought to know something about that rumor world of ours.

In marshaling my notes and letters and memories together to form some semblance of continuity, I have frequently been nudged by the disturbing reflection that portions of this book would seem false or distorted or incomplete to many of the men who shared these experiences with me. To all those familiar voices, raised in reproach, incredulity, or shock, I plead only that men, sharing a common experience, saw different things and saw them differently. My view was not complete nor even accurate necessarily, but it was mine.

One last thing: War is supposed to be a young man's business, and maybe it is. And though the age of thirty doesn't usually indicate senility, it's not what you'd call springtime, either. What I'm getting at is this: I went in with a group of men my own age. High school, even college, were long past, and we left wives and children behind us and well-used marriage beds. Because of these circumstances, we saw some aspects of war rather differently from younger men. I'm not implying a moral judgment: I say only that we saw some things differently. Sometimes, listening to the talk of the younger men, watching them, I felt old and sagging. They had sap in their veins, which I was aware had run a little thin in mine. But I did all right. I have no complaints.

Raymond Gantter
September 1944–June 1949

CHAPTER ONE

". . . they were still picking up bodies from D Day."

September 1944.

I made the crossing on the *Queen Elizabeth*. There's nothing to say about it except that we were too damn crowded, and our quarters were deep in the belly of the ship. We were so hot that we slept naked and dripped waterfalls of sweat through the thick canvas of our bunks. Sometimes we tried to sneak up to the decks to sleep, but always the guards would discover us and make us go back down. The food was lousy.

A few days before leaving Camp Shanks, I'd been named an "acting noncom" (noncommissioned officer) to serve as assistant to the orientation officer of our shipment. The assignment made me pretty happy because I thought it was a little more up my alley than toting a gun in the ranks, and I attended the three-day orientation school at Shanks with zest. I believed ardently in the importance of finding out what we were fighting for, and I thought I knew some of the answers. Unfortunately, the orientation officer on the *Elizabeth* shared neither my ardor nor my convictions. He was a fuzz-faced college boy, not yet twenty-one—I was painfully conscious of my seniority in age and his seniority in rank—and he didn't believe in books, didn't believe in theories that fell short of a solid, unequivocal QED, and thought the entire Orientation Program of the army a lot of damn-fool nonsense. In fumble-tongued bluster he stated that unless a book contained "facts that you could prove"—he named a text on engineering as an example—or was written for amusement only (like the Thorne

1

Smith novel he was reading), it served no legitimate purpose and might better be burned or thrown away. I tottered away and sat in the latrine with my head in my hands, cursing the army and bemoaning my lot in life.

We landed in Scotland, boarded a train, and sped to the south of England. At the first letter-writing opportunity I tried in oblique fashion to tell my wife, Ree, about my journey thus far. But the censor, canny man, caught the giveaway word "moors," and snipped it out with a nail scissors, spoiling a lush bit of prose. However, he missed "rowan berries," "crofts," "heather," and "Black Angus cattle," and she guessed correctly after all.

October 2–7, 1944. Warminster Barracks, England.

A depressing interlude. We pitched tents in the middle of a muddy clay field and endured the raw cold and the rain with as much noisy self-pity as our officers would tolerate. At least once a day we'd have to strip to the buff, don overcoats and shoes, and march in long, shivering lines to some barn of a barracks where the medics waited. Sometimes it was to get a "shot" of something, although we never could figure out why it was necessary to strip naked in order to have a needle stuck in our arms. But most of the time the trip meant another short-arm inspection. Since the short-arm consisted of shuffling along in the line until you reached the medic, opening your coat for a second—shyly or with bravado, depending on how much cause for pride you had—whipping it close again and shuffling along, it seemed time wasted. We'd been short-armed just before boarding the *Elizabeth* on the other side of the Atlantic, short-armed *on* the *Elizabeth*, herded from a dock in Scotland to this bleak camp in England without more than a glimpse of a female ankle, and denied pass privileges to town since arriving at Warminster. We began to feel that the army was taking an unnecessarily heavy interest in keeping us pure.

In spite of these cloistered and hygienic precautions, the army pressed prophylactic kits and contraceptives upon us in such profusion that, lacking more purposeful use for them, the men treated the latter as toy balloons. And many a sweating officer, conducting a training film lecture, was forced to pause and chew ass for a while because the screen would be obscured by the floating shadows of air-filled, grossly distended contraceptives. I have a low sense of humor: the spectacle always made me laugh like hell. Some grotesque and telling effects were achieved by the skillful tying together of three balloons in strategic arrangement. The army is a wonderful place.

Something very disturbing occurred before we ended our brief stay in England and sailed for the Continent. One day our entire package was ordered to assemble before the captain's tent. We shifted from foot to foot in the mud and wondered what was up. We found out fast. An officer whose duties included the censorship of our letters strode from the captain's tent, thrust his jaw fiercely in our direction, and delivered a vicious and blindly hot diatribe about the anti-British sentiments we were expressing in our letters home. The official attitude was, and I quote: "It will not be tolerated!"

The incident had grave implications, it seemed to me. In the first place, I was baffled by the accusation of prejudice. I'd heard a few wisecracks, a few sour comments, but I dismissed them as the escape-valve griping of men who were frightened, homesick, and ill at ease in a foreign land. It hadn't occurred to me that anti-British feeling was truly bitter or widespread. Why should it be? All of us were fresh from the States, new to Europe, and new to the army. We'd been in England but five or six days, had met possibly a dozen English men and women—most of them workers in the canteens of Warminster Barracks, and kindly folk—and yet, according to the officer admonishing us, an anti-British wave of serious proportion had engulfed our group.

Another aspect of the incident that bothered me was the official attitude as expressed by the lieutenant—who was a schoolteacher in civilian life. "It will not be tolerated!" Will not be tolerated? Were these words to speak to a civilian army, to free Americans? (Remember, I hadn't been in the army very long! I learn slowly.) I felt my hackles rise and yearned to wave old battle flags and yell old battle cries: "Don't tread on me!" . . . "54–40 or fight!" . . . "Remember the *Maine*!"

The prejudice I heard expressed in the army was often provoking and sometimes silly, but I maintained (silently, of course) that the men had every right save the right of intelligence to speak their piece. If they believed what they said, no matter by what subterranean groping they'd reached their conclusions, then by God, they had a right to *say* it, even as those who would disagree had a right to argue about it. So long as wartime rules of security were observed, no officer had any goddamn right to stand in front of us and tell us that certain things we were saying in our letters "will not be tolerated."

My final judgment, expressed frequently and with a great display of indignation, was: Why the hell didn't the army do something intelligent about it? During training we'd been fed a lot of pap about the value of orientation, the importance of education in this, the most honest and necessary war in all history. Yet, faced with a situation that could be cured only through the techniques of education, our officers were turning their backs on intelligence and open sincerity and giving arbitrary orders for the governing of our thinking. Logically, there could be only one result: the grievances would be driven underground, to fester unseen and grow poisonous.

Thus ran my complaint, unheard save by a close circle of friends. And feeling as I did that this war would be the same bloody waste as the last unless we emerged from it with increased understanding and tolerance, the "this will not be tolerated" incident made me pretty sick for a while.

October 1944. Normandy, somewhere near Le Mans.

We had our first casualty as we transferred gingerly from the ship in which we'd crossed the Channel to the LST that would deliver us to the coast of France. One of our officers, a grinning and likable guy, was crushed to death between the LST and the Channel steamer. Climbing down the landing net hung over the side of the larger vessel, he hesitated a moment too long before leaping for the LST. A bad omen.

We landed on Omaha Beach, scene of the D Day invasion. Attempts had been made to clean it up, discipline it into some kind of order, but dead vessels still thrust gaunt fingers from the tossing water, rusty barbed wire was snarled in vicious tangles on the sand, and the beach was littered with broken and abandoned equipment. One of the guards on the beach said they were still picking up bodies from D Day. Every day a few were washed ashore or uncovered by the vagrant sand. We looked with frightened eyes at that grinning, naked beach and the sheer cliffs leaning over it, studded with the vast wreckage of German pillboxes. We muttered in profane gratitude our deep thanks that we'd been safe in the States on D Day.

It was a helluva long hike up the hill from the beach to an apple orchard flanked by neat hedgerows where we pitched tents, in the rain again. Then more waiting.

Just before we left Warminster to board ship for France, our sergeant toured our area, stopping at every tent to give the occupants a generous supply of contraceptives. (I don't really have a fixation on the subject of birth control or sex hygiene, but don't let anyone kid you that this was a pure war.)

The next appearance of the safeties was in a kind of parade of virility. With skies that opened and flooded us every day and every night, it was something of a problem to prevent the bore of a rifle from rusting. So, with true Yankee ingenuity— and after all, there had been no occasion thus far to put the prophylactics to the use for which they'd been designed—the men utilized them as rubber caps on the muzzles of their rifles. I feel that there was a certain insouciance to our marching columns, although I've often wondered what the French villagers thought, if it seemed to them the most arrogant kind of boasting.

* * *

Sometimes the mud in Normandy has the thick, rich creaminess of melted milk chocolate, a quality so smoothly silken that you walk through it with a kind of dreamy pleasure in the lazy gulping and gurgling created by your moving feet. But most of the time it's just plain mud, and you curse it and flounder and splash, and yearn for a comfortable, dry desert.

CHAPTER TWO

"... a kind of dull struggle to keep warm and get enough to eat."

November 1944. A pine forest, three miles from Bastogne, Belgium.

It took the ruined villages of France and Belgium to teach me a proper humility before civilians. My stateside experience with civilians had been a little embittering, and it didn't help much to tell myself that my point of view was lopsided. I didn't like the army; I didn't like the infantry. I resented the separation from my family and the interruption of my career. By God, if I had to endure all these miseries, it seemed to me that the least civilians could do to repay me for my sacrifices (however reluctant) was to stand at attention as I went by, and buses and streetcars stop and the passengers get out and bow.

Seriously, it frequently angered me to see civilians doing business as usual, with careless unconcern or open rudeness for the men in uniform. Since the war had broken into my life and kicked me around and forced me to recognize its existence, I felt that all these civilians should indicate by some small sign that they also recognized the enormity of the cataclysm that had swallowed me. After all, I argued, it was their cataclysm, too! Life should stop for them or be vastly changed because it had stopped or been vastly changed for so many of us.

But when I saw the gray-faced peasants of France and

7

Belgium stand for motionless moments staring at the gutted wreckage of their homes; when I saw them kneel and start patiently to separate the whole tiles from the broken, the good timbers from the useless splinters; when they turned from their labors to smile at us and run smiling to pin flowers on our jackets—I woke up. I saw that life goes on, and that's a good thing. It was right that the pattern, whenever broken, be patiently started once more by the brave at heart, and not abandoned in despair. It was right that when one of us dropped out, the gap should close up or be filled and life kept flowing, the complex structure maintained by any means because its units were so interdependent. Armies and wars were extracurricular: the basic structure remained always the same. And I knew that it was because *I* was now involved in this extracurricular activity—a bloody luxury for which I had no taste—that I had become so acutely conscious of the gap between myself, wearing a uniform, and the civilian. The peasants taught me the validity of that gap, the justice of it. Once I accepted that bitter condition, I was able (some of the time, at least) to shake off the numbing sense of estrangement from the world.

We'd barely settled ourselves, tents up and slit trenches dug, before the kids started drifting out from Bastogne. "Goom?" they'd say. "Choong goom?" One of them, a freckle-faced youngster about eight years old, sidled up to me. After a solemn exchange of the amenities, we discovered to our mutual delight that we enjoyed the same first name. Secretly I felt that such a bond ought to put me off limits, spare me the customary appeal. Noblesse oblige, I thought. But no! He opened up by asking for shoes *pour Papa*. I assured him no dice; I had no shoes *pour Papa*. Then brightly, as though he had only that moment thought of it, "Cigarillos? Cigarettes?" Registering shock, I said, *"Pour toi?"* Grinning, he answered, *"Oui ... et mon papa!"* I was low on cigarettes and rations were erratic, so I decided Papa had better fend for himself awhile longer and Junior was better off without them. I gave him some candy, we exchanged solemn smiles, and presently he wandered off and I heard his voice at the next tent. "Goom? Choong goom?"

Time moved on mud-heavy feet in the Bastogne woods. We slept, we huddled around tiny fires and tried to get warm, we wrote letters, we talked idly and passionately about anything and nothing and sweated out the next chow time. Sometimes we sang, and the songs we chose offer an interesting commentary on the "popular" music of wartime.

Early in the war I had started a collection of war songs, just for the hell of it. It soon became apparent that all war music fell roughly into three categories.

The first category was the straight love theme, the tearjerker: the gallant hero off to meet the enemy, and the true-blue sweetheart left behind, who apparently divided her time evenly between praying, weeping, and (judging from the number of promises it required) trying like hell to remain faithful. There were some ingratiating melodies in this group; it was the lyrics that gagged.

The second category was the real *nux vomica* section. It contained the songs that made capital of honest feeling and attempted to cash in on patriotism. Consider such nauseous messes as "We've Gotta Slap the Dirty Little Jap" and "Goodbye Mama, I'm Off to Yokohama." Mawkishness was a staple in this trade, and the offensively creamy use of good phrases: "This Is Worth Fighting For"..."Comin' in on a Wing and a Prayer." Absolute zero was reached by a little gem called "Send This Purple Heart to My Sweetheart."

Subheading A in this group was the "religion cum patriotism" school, including such things as "I Had a Little Talk with the Lord," and "We've Got the Lord on Our Side." No comment.

The third group was made up of songs that were real attempts to create music for the men in service, music designed for the singing and marching of men, rather than the lucrative weeping of the folks at home. Songs like "In My Arms," "Praise the Lord and Pass the Ammunition," and "What Do You Do in the Infantry?" Oddly, the two most popular songs in my outfit were British in origin: the rollicking "I've Got Sixpence," and "Bless 'em All." The Australian "Waltzing Matilda" was well-liked, too, but I never met anyone who knew all the words. And perhaps the most popular of them all was the German "Lili Marlene," a particular favorite of American and British troops who'd seen service in Africa.

Perhaps there ought to be a fourth category, one closely related to the third by virtue of a tough and humorous acknowledgment that war is not all beer and skittles, heroic heroes and faithful females. Songs in this group were written with a courteous bow to the serviceman's point of view, but they did not lend themselves easily to unison singing or to marching. Here, with a C rating, I'd list "Three Little Sisters." I'd give a B rating to "Don't Sit Under the Apple Tree." And here, marked with a triple-A rating in purest gold, I'd list "G.I. Jive" and "They're Either Too Young or Too Old."

All this is only the prelude to my discovery that most men in uniform were left cold by ninety percent of the musical crap that, theoretically, was dedicated to the war effort. (And *that's* a lousy phrase, too: "The war effort!") On those rare and sentimental times when it was safe to sing and we were drunk enough to feel like it, there was an occasional chorus of a tune that had been popular when we left the States. But for the most part our sentimental yearnings were best satisfied by older music, music antedating the war by many years and minus the phony war flavor. Songs like "In the Evening by the Moonlight," "Home on the Range," "I Want a Girl," "Drifting and Dreaming," "Moonlight Bay." Locker-room favorites, songs from summertime front porches in Kansas and Vermont and Jersey and Texas. And the ageless favorite of all males, "I've Been Working on the Railroad."

As for war songs per se, we sang the kind with which soldiers from time immemorial have cheered themselves. Dirty songs, songs that reflected with rough, brutish humor our intense need for women and our hunger for the soft world of women. I am stoutly convinced that when Achilles sallied from his tent to avenge dead Patroclus, the drinking song of the night before that still roared in his ears was an old Greek version of "Roll Me Over in the Clover." And Beowulf and his hairy crew, carving the white swan road, bellowed the Scandinavian equivalent of "Mabel, Get Off the Table." The old army promise, "An old soldier never dies!" is peacetime talk, barracks talk, but there is a larger truth implied here: soldiers are deathless, and war is forever. The terrain shifts, the weapons evolve beyond recognition, the uniforms and slogans change, but some things lie beyond the power of the centuries to alter, and there are aspects of modern army life and modern war that a centurion of Caesar's army would find nostalgically familiar. Soldiers lying down each night with sudden death their bedmate are concerned with five things only. Three of them are physical: food, sleep, shelter. The other two, though physical at source, are heavily charged with emotional implications.

Men complain about the first three; they piss and moan endlessly. Yet without them they can endure for incredibly long periods of time, finding new reserves of strength each time it seems the end has been reached. But the other two, home and sex, eat inward, and the secret preoccupation with them strips off in unguarded moments the tough, protective, masculine sheathing, lays bare the soft places in men. It is a nakedness too revealing to contemplate, and only the unperceptive are shocked or outraged to hear a weary man say hoarsely, "By Christ, if my wife was here now, right now, I'd clip her in the jaw, just a little tap, just to remind her I'm still boss, an' then I'd throw her in bed so goddamn fast she wouldn't even have time to get her shoes off!" The words are crude, but the hunger of the voice hints at all the loveliness men have surmised in women and sanctified with music and poetry and high art.

(There will be many references to the soldier and sex in this journal, but I draw a line between the raw license that came on the heels of V-E Day and the hunger during the combat months, the hunger that sometimes was rape, orgy, or satyriasis, hunger born of the hovering presence of death and the wild desire not to die unsatisfied, with a body still fierce and full and unused.)

To return to war music and dirty songs: several were more obscene than "Roll Me Over," but I heard none that seemed as witty. And Kate Smith, Irving Berlin, and the American Legion notwithstanding, I heard "God Bless America" not a single time while I was overseas, an aesthetic deprivation that distressed me not at all.

Maybe all this talk about sex and dirty songs gives the impression that men in wartime have one thought only in their inflamed minds. That's not true, of course. There was a lot of talk about sex, sure, but so is there in a clubhouse locker room or a fraternity house bull session. We did talk about other things, honest! We even thought about other things.

Food was a major topic of conversation. We bitched a lot about the quality and quantity, mostly the quantity, of army food, and sometimes with reason. Here's a sample of our breakfast menu while we lay in the woods near Bastogne: one-half ladle of hot cereal, one-third canteen cup of coffee, one small teaspoon of sugar (you could choose: either in your coffee or on your cereal), one tablespoon of milk (same choice), four dog biscuits (hardtack about the size of graham crackers), and one slice of bacon. I admit that this menu represents one of the bad days and often we ate better. But sometimes we ate worse, and there were many days when even the daintiest eaters wholeheartedly agreed with the wit who said, "In this goddamn army you don't get enough to eat in a week to have one good bowel movement!"

Neither Supply nor our field kitchens and mess sergeants should be blamed for the food situation, by the way. They did an admirable job under trying conditions. I don't blame anyone, as a matter of fact, because I don't know where the blame should lie. It was just one of those things, and I mention it only because food and the lack of it was so important to us.

We'd sit around our daytime fires—fires at night were not permitted because of the danger of air raids—and talk about food, talk about the things we'd like to be eating. There was plenty of time to write long letters home, and when our wives received them and tore them open, looking eagerly for words of love and comfort, they found us drooling about the things we wanted to *eat* when we came home! Here's a sample, taken from one of my Bastogne letters:

> I have been thinking long, tender thoughts of the dishes you cook that I'm particularly fond of: rich, dark chocolate cake, heavy with fudge icing . . . grilled kidneys and bacon . . . that favorite menu of ours—roast pork, accompanied by red cabbage that has been cooked with red wine and apples . . . shrimp curry . . . strawberry shortcake and cherry pie . . . steak, two inches thick, and new potatoes, glazed and browned in the oven . . . pumpkin pie, with the extra tang that a shot of good liquor gives it . . . our favorite omelette with that special liver sauce . . . those Swedish cookies that you roll in powdered sugar while they're still hot . . . apple pie with cream, hot mince pie—why the hell am I doing this?

Why indeed? All I know is that it passed many long hours almost pleasantly, and it was even possible to sustain a glow of anticipation while trotting through the mud with clanging mess gear, en route to what was sure to be another unsavory arrangement of Spam and green beans.

Another fireside discussion that took place at least once a day always started the same way. Some sorehead would start to burlesque FDR's famous and easily mimicked voice: "I don't like waw! Eleanaw doesn't like waw!" Then, the mimicry having served its purpose as introduction, he would say in his normal voice, "Why, that sonofabitch!" And we'd be off again. I know now that much of it was bitching just for the sake of bitching, a safety valve that relieved other pressures. My judgment was not so charitable at the time, but I learned discretion; those of us who protested the easy blindness of this standard gripe were regarded as the close relatives of the Antichrist. After a while we just shrugged and let the stuff roll off our backs.

Thinking about the bull sessions in the Bastogne woods

reminds me of an incident at Camp Shanks a day or two before we sailed. We had been alerted, and were confined to our barracks. We were tense and restless, talkative because we were frightened. I stretched on my bunk and tried to read, but soon dropped the book and eavesdropped on a conversation a few bunks away.

In the main it was a diatribe directed against the Negro. The biggest mouth of them all was telling the others of an argument he'd had during basic training with "some nineteen-year-old college bastard" who was apparently so stupid that he couldn't see the difference between a white skin and a black. All the weary old chestnuts were dragged out: "Would you let your sister go out with a Negro? Would you eat outta the same plate, use the same fork?" (An absurdity that always makes me yearn to reply, "No, and I never share my toothbrush with my wife, either!") Encouraged by approving grunts, the gabby one spouted on and on, ever more loose-mouthed, and my anger rose in pace with his clichéd eloquence. With each moment that passed and no protest raised, I grew a little more sick inside, too, because if that was the way these men felt, then we weren't in the same war, we weren't fighting for the same things. We were enemies, not sharers in a common hazard. And yet I knew I didn't really believe that, because these were good Joes, fundamentally. Most of them. It was just that they had accepted the easy solution of label-sticking, and the label had become their stock answer to bothersome questions. The label was the important thing and not what was hidden under it, and the army was doing a lousy job of teaching them to be more careful with the labels.

So I lay in my bunk and got sicker and madder, and finally decided there was no other way out. I'd have to get in that discussion, even though I'd certainly end up by having a label slapped on me—not to mention a possible poke in the jaw. I swung my legs over the edge of my bunk, and as I did so, a Jewish boy with whom I'd become acquainted walked over to my bunk, leaned an arm on it, and looked up. Neither of us spoke, and after a moment he turned away, murmuring, "I guess I don't have to say anything." I glanced down the length of the barracks and saw another man sitting erect on his bunk, listening. He looked over, flashed a smile of warmth and understanding, and there was another ally. Turning, I glanced at the sergeant who slept on the upper next to me. He opened one eye, grinned, and put his finger warningly to his lips. And I lay down again, heartened beyond belief. Democracy was saved! Jack Dalton Rides Again! Maybe in the entire barracks there were only four of us opposed to that hot little group up the row, but that was a better ratio than us radicals usually got. We'd make out.

One final note on Camp Shanks. For many years I've concealed a degenerate interest in latrine interior decoration. By artistic standards it may be primitive, even infantile, but there are real finds occasionally, flashes of genuine wit. The latrine at Shanks was decorated from ceiling to floor, and since it was a large one—a thirty-holer, at least—the representation of "art" and "literature" was sizable.

The common quality that made these testimonials unique was that they had been scrawled by men in the army, most of whom were about to ship for whatever unknown awaited them overseas, a few days or weeks away. The prevailing note was sexual, of course, but sex with a difference, sex plus nostalgia, sex with overtones of despair because the delights of the flesh were ended for a time. Or forever. There were dithyrambs of praise for the special glories of "New York tail"; there were also the bitter comments of those who had been disappointed, those who had found New York only a glorified clip joint and all the women lecherous and greedy. Most of these men had already been touched by a sense of transiency, the cold warning of danger and death and decay. There was poignancy in their farewells to shapely breasts and warm thighs. And in their boasts of unique sexual development and prowess in bed there was something frightened, something that informed with what desperate premonitions they hugged the comfort of their own maleness to themselves.

There was something else on those walls, too, something new and sobering in latrine literature: a devout consecration of self to God. Prayers for protection, statements of simple belief, protestations of faith and innocence, vows of future purity, oaths of vengeance for brothers or cousins already fallen in action. More than a third of the messages on those wooden walls were like that, the world of the flesh already behind and only the world of the spirit holding hope of life and return. It was a curious and moving juxtaposition. But it was logical and simple and not incongruous.

This is as good a place as any to give a well-merited plug to the Editions for Armed Services, Inc., a nonprofit organization established by the Council on Books in Wartime, composed of American publishers, librarians, and booksellers. Through their efforts we were kept supplied with a truly catholic selection of current best-sellers, old live-forevers, westerns, short stories, mysteries, and an excellent variety of nonfiction.

No one who has ever known the slow acid of waiting, day after weary day, for something to happen can appreciate how important those books were to us. They were particularly precious through the long weeks we spent in replacement depots, and again when the war was ended and we had time on our hands. But even during combat we valued them and carried them in our packs until the moment when even those few ounces had to be pared from loads grown suddenly too heavy. I abandoned my pocket-size Shakespeare one weary day in the cellar of a ruined farmhouse and regretted my hastiness for weeks afterward.

My thanks and gratitude to the Editions for the Armed Services. I think the bread they cast upon the waters will someday return to them as a fully equipped bakery: many men thus discovered the world of books for the first time. Not all of them will forget it when they're civilians again.

Nothing important happened while we were in the Bastogne woods. The days passed in a kind of dull struggle to keep warm and get enough to eat. After we'd been there awhile, occasional three-hour passes were granted and we'd walk the railroad tracks to Bastogne, get a meal in a restaurant, buy souvenirs and fruit and pastry at shocking prices. We would chisel some bread from a baker—we lacked the necessary bread coupons, and the bakers drove hard bargains, trading bread for cigarettes or soap—get a little drunk, and gloomily trudge back to the woods.

Life in our pine woods camp was like life in a hobo jungle. It was a marking-time period, lax and empty, held together loosely by a few organizational activities: calisthenics in the morning, rare mail calls, formations for meals three times daily, and the so-called orientation periods, badly run and ineptly taught but our only source of news. All of us soon reached the point where we'd have preferred combat to this slow death of monotony. There were a few small luxuries that helped, helped out of all proportion to their actual worth. And there was gaiety at times, and high spirits and horseplay.

From a letter written in the Bastogne woods on November 9, 1944, which illustrates the morale value of quite small comforts as well as the kind of hilarity that sometimes infected us:

Something new has been added: the kitchen now serves hot coffee every evening at 7:30 to anyone interested in going after it. It's a kindly gesture and there are only two things wrong with it: one, drinking coffee at that hour and then hitting the sack for eleven hours means that you have to get up at least once during the night to relieve yourself. Two, the kitchen is a helluva long way from our company area, and the only two routes are a bad proposition at night. Route 1 is the road, ankle deep in slimy, treacherous mud. Route 2 is a path through the woods, where the hazards are the stumps and the trees, the slit trenches and the straddle trenches. Neither Walt nor I have a flashlight, of course. (Walt Dunn is my current tentmate.)

Last night Walt and I went down for the coffee and the evening turned into something crazy and hilarious. The captain and two lieutenants were there for coffee, too, and when they started for home, we decided to tag along because they had a light. They elected to travel by the woods route, and we plunged along gallantly in their rear.

But there's a funny thing about traveling single file at night when the only light is in the hands of the leading man. The head of the line begins to pull away from the rear elements, forgetting that the men in the rear are compelled to move more slowly. (This is especially true, of course, when the head of the line is an officer and the rear is a buck private.)

That's the way it was last night. The captain, closely followed by the other two officers, moved quickly through the woods, which were draped with wet, clinging snow, the kind of snow that slumps from the trees in heavy clots whenever someone passes below. I've made a careful study of that phenomenon and I'm convinced that a tree can hold an immeasurable quantity of snow without complaint: the moment of discharge is coincidental with the appearance of a human.

I am always at a disadvantage in night movements. Anyone who wears glasses has special hazards. Trees appear where there were none a moment ago, branches claw in vicious ill-humor, the man ahead of you inevitably stops without warning and his rifle or bazooka hits you between the eyes. When I walk at night, I have learned to sling my rifle and travel with my arms curved before my head like the bumper on a car. I can't see where I'm going, of course, but I don't break my glasses getting there.

The officers and their light quickly outdistanced us and we were alone in the woods, and lost. Then it started.

WALT: Where are you, Ray?

ME: Here!

WALT: Where's that?

ME: Over—ugh! That goddamn tree! Here!

WALT: Oh . . .

ME: Where are you?

WALT: Right over—owww!—here! On the right!

ME: Well, which way is that? If we don't happen to be going in the same direction (and I don't think we are), *your* right may be Germany and mine may be France.

WALT: Well, I'm right here. Follow my voice.

ME: Okay. Keep talking and I'll get to you.

WALT: Mary had a little lamb

Her fleece was white as snow,

And everywhere that Mary went—

ME: (This is real anguish) Owooooooo! How the hell did you get through this tree to get where you are?

WALT: (Icily) I didn't go through it. I went around it.

ME: Well, why the hell didn'tcha say so? Okay, here I am. Let's go.

WALT: Which way?

ME: Let's try this way. It looks different.

Four wet feet later, we figure we must be nearly home. By this time we have been walking long enough to be near the Siegfried line.

ME: We're nearly there now. I can see the clearing—I think!

WALT: Yeah. Hey, where are the latrines? The straddle trenches?

ME: Jeez, I forgot all about 'em! But they're right along in here somewhere. We'd better go slower.

WALT: No, wait a minute! (A pause. Then confidently): I know where we are now.

ME: (Suspiciously) Ya sure?

WALT: Sure I'm sure! We're nowhere near the latrines: they're way on the other side. This is all clear sailing —ugh!

ME: (Innocently) What's the matter, Walt?

WALT: (In anguished tones) I stepped in one!

BLACKOUT

A floundering quarter hour later we finally arrived at our own tent. No sooner had we dropped our rifles and belts inside than we realized, almost simultaneously, that we had to go back to the straddle trenches on pressing business.

(I ought to explain that Belgian pine forests, being a

money crop, are planted in precise, equidistant rows. We have been digging our straddle trenches between the rows, moving farther and farther into the woods as a trench is filled and closed up and a new one dug. To be prepared for nighttime emergencies, I keep a mental count of how many rows of trees from the clearing the current latrines are located.)

I said to Walt, "They're easy to find—just ten rows in from the clearing. Follow me!" Fifteen minutes later we found them and stood teetering on the brink of a straddle trench, wondering why in hell we had gone through all this just to take a leak.

Returning to our tent, we climbed in and began the nighttly contortions necessary when two men try to undress in a space designed for a single undernourished midget (a maneuver that was doubly complicated last night because the tent was wet and to touch it meant a leak at that spot all through the night). At last we were between the blankets, our feet slowly getting warm, and our numbed hands just strong enough to hold a cigarette.

We talked for a while, began to get sleepy, and were engaging in amiable argument over whose turn it was to warm whose back when I became aware that the 7:30 coffee was exerting uncomfortable pressure and I'd better get up. I told myself sternly that I didn't *really* have to go, but all the time I knew I would and I groaned inwardly at the prospect of crawling from the warm blankets, slipping wet, icy shoes on my feet, unbuttoning the frozen tent flap and going out to face the cold wind we could hear in the treetops. When Walt saw me getting up, he laughed heartlessly and curled deeper in the blankets, making rude and vulgar comment on the riotousness of a past which had so devastated my kidneys. Just as I was struggling into my second shoe he sat up and said in deep disgust, "Damn it, I think I've got to go, too!" This last felicitous circumstance convulsed us, and we burst into howling laughter, pummeling each other and careless of the sides of the tent. Let the bitchin' thing drip, what the hell do we care?

You can see from this that our life here is not always keyed to the darker pages of Chekhov or Turgenev. Today, in the middle of a training march through the rain and mud, a cold wind cutting the flesh from our bones like ribbons, I thought: "It's my birthday, I haven't seen Ree or the kids in months, I haven't had a word from home in forty-nine days, I'm cold, I'm wet and hungry, I don't think I'll get any mail today, I don't like the army and I'm not very fond of Belgium! And yet, dammit, I'm not as miserable as I *ought* to be with such a burden of woes!" And I wasn't.

I have been thinking: when I get home, people will ask me, "What was it like?" [Note: They didn't. Damn few people at home were interested in the war once the war was over.] And I'll have to say, "It was muddy. It was cold and it was muddy. It was wet and it was cold and it was muddy. It was altogether unpleasant and it was cold and wet and it was muddy. It was not a good time." And then I'll hesitate and look for the words that will tell them what it was really like, and finally I'll turn in despair to anecdotes. Because I can't find the words to tell even you what the unceasing cold is like, or what the special quality of the mud is and how it is forever and everywhere, or how it is to be always so numbed by the wet coldness that your body feels like someone else's, or what the combination of everything adds up to. It's a fourth dimension of sorts, beyond the definitive terms of shape, proportion, color, taste, smell, or touch. You'll come closest to understanding, I know. As for the others . . . well, there are anecdotes.

There was a challenge in the physical discomfort, which most men answered, and they were cheered and strengthened by the proof of their ability to answer. A few men didn't—a few cowered and whimpered ceaselessly and never squared up to this adversary. Everyone bitched, of course, but the bitching was automatic, and for most of the men there was an obscure zest in this life some of the time. It was a male world and far from the upholstery that padded what we had known as normal life. Once my face got dirty and I found it wasn't so bad, I was pretty proud of the men around me. Even a little proud of myself.

One demonstration of spirit that heartened me every time I saw it was the little Christmas tree that a couple men had erected in front of their tent. The decorations included a long strip of white tape, bits of tinfoil from gum and candy, a comb with most of the teeth missing, a clip of German ammunition, an empty Bull Durham sack, a few sprays of holly, the tops of several C-ration cans with the long, silvery "curl" still attached where it had been peeled off the can, the red cellophane tapes from packs of cigarettes, and a few scraps of Christmas wrapping paper and ribbon. (Some of the men had already received Christmas boxes.) It was a gay and brave sight in our mudhole.

So the long days passed and turned to weary weeks, and we began to wonder what the hell was the rush in getting us over here if they weren't going to use us? The sense of homelessness that afflicts replacements, casuals, is very acute. Unattached and belonging to no outfit, you are lost and forlorn. And it's an unhappy life from the practical point of view, too, because there are no ratings for a replacement. You are an "acting" sergeant or "acting" corporal—we called such gratuitous ratings "acting gadgets." But you remain what you were when you became a replacement, whether it be buck private, master sergeant, or buck private doing the work of a master sergeant. All through my brief career in the army I had been an "acting gadget," and I was getting a little browned off at the extra responsibilities that carried no extra pay or privileges. Lacking a rating, a man could be an "acting" platoon guide (as I was) and be responsible for running a guard shift (as I was), and two days later, in his real capacity of buck private, be assigned to K.P. or latrine-digging detail.

But the days went by, and we assembled daily for the orientation talks and the news, sparse as it was, and we laid wild and hopeful bets on the end of the war. I remember betting one guy everything I had in my pocket—it happened to be the staggering sum of eighteen Belgian francs, but he didn't know that—that the war in Europe would be over by Christmas,

1944. I never paid the bet: we were assigned to different outfits and I learned much later that he was killed the following February.

Even our officers were optimistic and assured us that our chances of seeing combat were slim. One officer volunteered to bet six months' pay on that. And so we wagered and planned and dreamed of Christmas at home, until November 18.

Up to this point I have used only my letters for reference. From here the source will be twofold: letters, and the rough notes I started to write on November 22 and continued through May 13, 1945. I repeat the admonition I offered earlier: don't look too closely for historical or geographical accuracy. I know damn well that some of my facts are dubious. But, I submit, if I have not checked and verified those physical details, it's because they are unimportant to the purpose of this report. It may be a slipshod way of writing, but my aim is not the recording of facts. The official publications of the War Department will give you those. I'm trying to capture a sense of some of the things less easily pinned down and tested by the rules of science. If you're a perfectionist, if you haggle over strict accuracy, I suggest you regard this journal as fiction. You will then be able to swallow what passes for fact without flinching.

When I started these rough notes I was impelled by panic. My uncomfortable but safe little world in the Bastogne woods had been kicked out from under me and I was plunged into the immediacy of war overnight. It did no good to tell myself that this, after all, was what I'd been trained for, what I was here for. My reason had accepted that eventual destination from the day I was inducted. But emotionally I was still unprepared. I lived in a "but it can't happen to me" state that had been vastly encouraged by the false security created by our weeks of inaction. All at once it was swept away: our sedate and uneventful existence, our reasonably adequate shelter, our fantastically hopeful bull sessions around the campfire. I seized the first opportunity after we reached the front to write it down—the turmoil, the speed, our fear and confusion—and thus purge myself of a part of my panic. All I can tell you is that it worked. I used the device from then on, partly to maintain my grip on fear that might otherwise run away, partly because the desire grew to tell Ree, and my children Geoff and Sukey, about it someday, and I knew I could not trust memory alone.

The opening paragraphs of my rough notes were flamboyant with melodrama, ominous with a sense of the untimely death I was certain would soon cut me down. Pruned of the purple verbiage, I said that I was writing down all the things I could not say in letters, that I hoped to deliver these notes in person, and in the event of my death, would the censors please permit Ree to have them? I'll pick it up from there.

CHAPTER THREE

"A helluva lot of firsts."

November 21, 1944. Germany.

Four days ago we lay in our dugouts near Bastogne and tossed an enchanted phrase back and forth like a shuttlecock. "Moving to winter quarters!" The captain had announced that soon we'd be quitting the woods and moving to a village, possibly into buildings. We'd have stoves, even! Maybe cots! At the very worst, we could count on pyramidal tents, stove-heated. Oh joy! Oh happy November 17!

On the morning of November 18 we were alerted, not for a move to a village, but for immediate duty on the front. We were numbed by the news, we couldn't quite believe it. We left the assembly area slowly, soberly, trying to pretend our hearts were not pounding thunderously. We were moving up.

We spent the day in a rush of silent activity, covering slit trenches and straddle trenches, filling the dugouts we had so laboriously excavated and lined with straw for warmth. We threw away old letters, examined and cleaned our rifles with studious care. When the day passed and the expected order had not yet come, we pitched tents where our dugouts had been and spent a wet, sleepless night, our weapons and ourselves tucked between the blankets against the damp. In the quiet darkness the familiar flashes on the horizon seemed nearer, and our interest in the buzz bombs that rumbled overhead became abruptly personal.

We pulled out on the following morning, twenty-three men to a truck. It wasn't a long ride, and by one P.M. we had reached our destination, another pine forest—but this one was in Germany. To our surprise, the setup here was far

25

more luxurious than at the Bastogne camp behind us. Board-walks and corduroy roads protected our feet against the muck; we were quartered in pyramidal tents, stove-equipped, and the latrines had seats! They were high, wooden thrones, open-frame in construction and thus a little drafty, but you could sit down, that was the thing. The high seat was a little conspicuous—you saw some remarkable silhouettes against the skyline as you came through the woods—but after weeks of tortured crouching over a straddle trench, any kind of a seat was luxury, and modesty be damned!

The food seemed delicious to us: real potatoes, canned vegetables, and we commented with some bitterness on the dehydrated and tasteless sawdust that had been our daily rations in Belgium. After a moment's sober reflection, we admitted the justice of this difference: it was right that the best food go to the men at the front, even if rear area groups ate less well as a result.

Blackout was strictly enforced. Setting out for home after an hour in the special services tent, I stepped into blinding darkness and was lost before I'd gone ten paces. After staggering over unfamiliar paths and falling at last into a slit trench filled with water, I called in desperation for a tentmate to be my bellwether and ring me home with his voice.

In spite of my bed of dry straw and the glowing stove nearby, I didn't sleep well. None of us did. A ceaseless barrage of neighborhood artillery kept us tense and alert. Once, a passing buzz bomb came so low that its muttering became a roar that shook the sides of the tent like a strong wind. The sound hushed abruptly just after the bomb passed overhead—the sudden silence warned of an impending hit—and we froze in anticipation. The gut-walloping explosion seemed only yards away, but we learned the next morning that the bomb had landed three miles from us.

Up early on November 20, a slippery march through knee-deep mud, and a truck ride eastward, in the direction of Aachen. We bivouacked in the woods near a village called Walheim. I pitched my tent with a chap named Dempsey who raised dalmatian dogs (Walt and I had already been separated), and we smoked endless cigarettes during the night, listened to the artillery barrage, and tried to estimate how near a certain 105mm gun was. The war seemed very close.

The next morning, November 21, we were assembled in a little clearing in the woods and our names and assignments were read from a roster by an officer. At last I had a home and a family, Company G, 16th Infantry Regiment, 1st Infantry Division. We were mildly lectured on our good fortune in being assigned to such an outfit, and we were properly impressed; we knew something of the 1st Division record. However, we were more impressed, and less happily, by the discovery that the 1st was up front, in the Hurtgen Forest and engaged in what was called the "Big Push."

We were told it might be several days before we would be called up and that we'd better find ourselves some shelter until that time: the Jerries had an unfortunate habit of lobbing shells into our area on occasion, just for luck. Dempsey had been assigned to another unit and I was alone again. I wandered about forlornly and finally found a one-man prone shelter, dug by an earlier doggie in these woods. It was well-covered with logs and dirt, but small and cramped. I enlarged it, moved my pack inside, and felt the honest pride of the pioneer who has just completed his first log cabin. I didn't want to think about the man who had first sheltered himself here and where he was now.

After chow, which was cold C rations, we got our call. We picked up and packed up, waded through mud a little deeper than before, mounted our trucks, and "Hi-yo, Silver!"

Already it's hard to remember some of the things I wanted not to forget, the things I saw, because I was raw and new and would never see them again in just this way: the careful unconcern of the few German civilians we encountered . . . the pleasured surprise of discovering that the vaunted "dragon's teeth" concrete tank barriers are tinted a soft green . . . the signs of battle—blown bridges and shrapnel-scarred walls . . . the German helmet lying mutely on the top of a thorny hedge,

a jagged hole torn significantly through the front and rear . . .
the empty C- and K-ration containers that marked the progress
of American troops . . . the faint sickness in my stomach when
I saw a house with a shell hole in the wall large enough to
drive a tank through, and my sense of shock, as at something
improper, that a house should be so used . . . the five dead
Americans in the woods near Walheim, lying in a neat row by
the side of the road. They'd been brought back from the front
in a truck, lifted out—not gently but not carelessly, perhaps
unfeelingly is the word, as though it were habitual and there
was more to do and so little time—and placed there. Several
hours later someone covered them with a blanket, and later
another truck came up from the rear and took them away.
Many of the men went over to look at the bodies, drawn by a
horrible fascination. We hadn't seen any dead men yet. Most
of them came back looking very ill. I didn't go over.

We arrived at the Hurtgen Forest on the afternoon of November 21. The company was at the front, on line, and no
officers were there, only the supply room and cook-tent personnel. There was no one to tell us what to do or where to
go. We stood about helplessly, feeling lost and unwanted
again.

One of the supply room NCOs told us we were six miles, by
road, from our front line, and Cologne was twenty-eight miles
away. There were two ridges between our front and the broad
plain that lay before Cologne. Several days ago our outfit had
taken the first of these ridges, and once the second was captured, the Armored was to take over and push across the plain
to Cologne. Accompanied by the infantry, of course. One of
the cooks told us (rumor! rumor!) that the division had been
promised a rest when Cologne fell. I cheerfully admit I was a
reluctant warrior, and thought a rest at that point would be
dandy.

All afternoon we huddled in uneasy groups, talking in
undertones and asking timid questions of the veterans in the
kitchen and supply tents. The seventeen weeks of basic
training that had once been so interminable now seemed scant

indeed, and knowing how soon we were to put that training to a test in which our uniquely precious lives were involved, we felt unprepared, awkward, and exposed. As dusk drew on, a noncom appeared and told us to make up combat packs in preparation for going up that night. Silently, nervously, we set to work—breaking our ponderous bedrolls in the mud and rain and assembling combat packs: small compact units holding one blanket, a raincoat, and whatever small items the individual man feels impelled to take for his private solace. The seasoned soldier, we soon learned, takes only the essentials. The rest of our personal belongings and equipment we rolled in a shelter half, marked the bundle with our name and serial number, and added it to the growing pile under a tree. In the gathering dusk the mound of bedrolls loomed grimly, and in our mind's eye we saw each one stamped "Personal Effects." We worked in silence. There was no joking now; the time for humor was past.

After we'd completed our task, the supply sergeant issued extra ammunition: three bandoliers and two hand grenades to each of us. We handled the grenades awkwardly, having had only limited experience during basic training with these tools of war, and even that seemed far away and inadequate. Then we stood around and waited, huddling in small groups of five or six, impelled by the need to feel someone else near at hand.

It grew darker. It had been raining steadily all day and we were soaked to the hide. There were no shelters except the cook and supply tents, and we'd been forbidden them because there were too many of us. Chow time came, and still no further orders concerning us. Our spirits slipped another three notches. Going up was bad enough, but going up in the dark, unable to see where we were going or what it was like ... How could they do this to us, and how many of us would make it, and would I, would I?

The artillery barrage continued, the guns never stopping altogether, and German shells screamed back in spiteful answer, some of them landing in the trees near us.

In the late dusk we assembled for chow, and as night fell

some of us sought shelter from the rain in an empty GI truck parked near the cook tent. (As I record this, I am sitting in that truck, my raincoat stretched over my paper to protect it from the water that drips steadily through the leaky tarpaulin.) We talked in undertones. We were bewildered and unhappy. There was the usual pointless cursing of Eleanor Roosevelt.

Then a jeep pulled up and an officer jumped out. He had just come from the front and he was weary and unshaven and caked with mud. He said there had been a change in orders and we weren't wanted up there until the present push had been completed. We were so green and there were so many of us that we'd be more hindrance than help to the seasoned veterans on the line.

We were pathetically, shamefully grateful for this reprieve. It seemed like the greatest good fortune in the world. (I still think so. I learned later what the battle of the Hurtgen Forest had been like.)

Now we were confronted with the milder problem of where to spend the night. We had one blanket apiece, and having turned in our shelter halves, we had no tents. Some of the men elected to sit in the truck all night, but the rest of us set out to find dugouts in the woods. (The Germans had been here before us, and they had been well dug in.) With a man named Nelson, a former seaman who was now unaccountably in the infantry, I began the search for a two-man dugout we'd discovered earlier in the day, deep in the woods. We begged two extra blankets from the supply room and smugly contemplated a warm and comfortable night.

The dugout had appeared to be large and dry, but we learned it was neither. Scooped shallowly from the rain-soaked earth, it was less than two feet deep and roofed over with a framework of logs that rested on the surface of the ground and were covered with mud. The entrance was a mere slit, an opening so small that we had to lie flat on the ground and wriggle through on our stomachs. Nelson went in first and I handed our "bed linen" in to him: first our raincoats, then our overcoats, and finally a blanket on top of the overcoats. That left three blankets for cover over us. At last the bed was made, and I slid in.

It was pretty bad, too short and too narrow, and we were forced to lie facing the same way, our knees drawn up and our bodies curled one inside the other. Turning over in bed was a dual operation, requiring inch-by-inch maneuvering and much panting. A puddle quickly formed under us and grew wider and deeper, soaking through our raincoats, our overcoats, and the single blanket. Water dripped from the roof, tapped on our blankets, splashed icily on our faces. The roof was so low that straggling roots touched us like cold fingers.

I had a moment of near panic after Nelson fell asleep and the comfort of his voice had ceased. The sense of being trapped grew more frightening every moment, the choking fear of being locked within a grave. In the dark, the severed roots of trees glimmered phosphorescently on the earth walls with a green and unholy light. And the never-ceasing drip of water hammered maddeningly. I couldn't sleep and the night was long: a nap of a few minutes and I would be waked by the agony of my cramped legs. I smoked a lot, struggling to pull a cigarette from my pocket, making it last as long as possible, putting it out by holding it under one of the streams that dripped from the ceiling. And the guns pounded on, sometimes a lonely single report, more frequently thunderous barrages that shook the earth and sprinkled our blankets with dirt. I thought long, aching thoughts of home and wondered bitterly what I was doing there.

But the night passed at last. The final misery was to miss breakfast because I was catnapping when the cook yelled, "Come and get it!" and Nelson, of course, had slept angelically all night long.

A minor mystery: one of the replacements in our bunch, known as "Chesty" because of his magnificent but exaggerated torso, disappeared during the night. His rifle and pack and all his equipment were still by the tree where he was seen to have placed them, but Chesty was gone. The men who knew him best insisted it wasn't desertion. They believed that his somewhat simpleminded curiosity to find out what it was like on the front led him to make a personal reconnaissance in that direction. At any rate, he was gone.

(Note: The disappearance of Chesty is still one of the mysteries of Company G. When I sailed for home in December 1945, Chesty was still missing, and he was still carried on the company books as a case of "desertion." I wonder what did become of him. It's possible that he wandered up to the front that night and was killed, perhaps so mangled that he was unrecognizable and his dog tags lost. Or a German sniper or straggler may have killed him and concealed his body in Hurtgen Forest . . . or he may have stumbled on a mine or booby trap . . . or perhaps he'd spent the night in a dugout that collapsed on him, burying him alive. It remains a mystery, and not a pleasant one.)

November 22, 1944. The day before Thanksgiving.

We've been sitting around all day trying to get warm, trying to get dry. It's a raw, rainy day.

Ree, I wish I could make you *feel* what it is like to be here, only a few miles from a battle that is likely to be regarded as one of the worst of the war. A jeep driver who just came back has been telling us about it. He says the Germans are drunk and singing, and he tells of attacks and counterattacks in which they rush from their positions, singing as they come, firing until their ammunition is gone, then throwing down their useless weapons and still coming on, still singing. German or not, enemy or not, there is a magnificent and barbaric carelessness in the gesture that is spine-tingling. There is tragic waste, too. Perhaps it's my own Germanic origins that make me thrill to such grandiose extravagance . . . the Wittelsbach madness that tainted all Bavaria.

And the guns, our guns, continue to thunder, and we wonder how long the Germans can hold out . . . *and when will we go up?* We wait here, our imagination running loose and wild

... frightened and willing to admit it, sick with longing for home and wishing desperately that the whole bloody mess were over.

Last night and the night before, the usual spells failed. I couldn't bring you and the children close to me, couldn't hold you. For the first time since I've been in the army, you are not here; you are someone in a book I read somewhere and a long time ago. You are more than miles from me.

I am aware of fear, compounded with a curiosity to see what "it" is like and how I will react. I am conscious only of my cold, wet, dirty, aching body, and yet I am impersonally curious to discover how much punishment it can take.

November 23, 1944. Nearly eleven A.M., Thanksgiving Day.

Two thousand miles from me you're sleeping still, while I, miserably awake in this rain-drenched German forest, sit with a leaky raincoat pulled over my head and try to write myself out of my misery.

Yesterday afternoon we looked for new quarters, as it seemed likely that we would be here for another night. Found a sturdy but unfinished log cabin, lacking a roof and open at one end. It's not as safe as a dugout in the event of a shelling, but we're going to take the chance. Nelson and I constructed a log roof, covering it with strips of linoleum I found in the woods and piling pine branches on top for camouflage. Wandering in the woods, I came upon a straw mattress, very damp, and threw that in for a bed. We finished our dream castle with burlap bags to stop up the chinks in the walls, thus ensuring blackout when we wanted to smoke. We hung a German shelter half over the open end, and the finished product impelled us to link arms and bleat one quavering chorus of "My Blue Heaven." At chow I invited another homeless waif to bunk with us, and that night the three of us slept warm and almost dry, in spite of leaks that appeared in the roof during the night.

I'm sitting in our mansion now and the leaks have increased

a thousandfold because it's raining hard at the moment. If it stops raining this afternoon, Nelson and I are going to tear the roof off and start from scratch one more time.

And still we have had no word on when we'll be sent up. Last night our barrage was heavy and the Jerries retaliated in some strength with their own guns, trying to feel out and blast the artillery positions in our rear. We huddled in our blankets, listening to the shells moaning through the air over our heads, wondering if the Jerries would shorten the range and drop a few in our neighborhood or if there would be any accidental short rounds from our own guns. Not a pleasant way to spend an evening.

They say we're to have turkey for chow today. It will take more than turkey and fixings to make this seem a day of Thanksgiving. And yet it is, in one very real sense, a day on which to give thanks: I'm still alive. But oh, darling—being a soldier is being a wet, dirty, miserable creature, one dubious step removed from the animal. And I'm not sure whether the step is up or down!

There is no news from the front on the progress of the push. Stories have come back, however, of the capture of eleven- and twelve-year-old German guerrillas. One twelve-year-old boy had seven notches on his rifle, which he boasted were his American "kills." I cannot entirely credit such stories, but there is overwhelming evidence that there *are* harassing guerrilla forces of teenage and under-teenage boys. And girls. It would seem that Hitler's plea for a "people's war" is being answered exclusively by the German bobby-sox set. Last night I talked to some machine-gunners from another company, lately returned from the front. In shamed and bitter revulsion they spoke of cutting down scores of tender-faced young German soldiers, boys of sixteen, seventeen, and eighteen who would advance in fanatical fervor, deaf to all orders, to all entreaties to throw down their arms and surrender.

Cologne is reputed to be only a mass of rubble. Yet we have heard only an occasional plane for the past several days. The weather is bad for flying.

I miss you with a curious detached misery. You are still dreamlike, Ree—and my physical discomfort continues to be prime in my thoughts. Last night I lay awake in my almost comfortable bed and thought in terror and panic of days and weeks to be spent on the front lines, lying in muddy foxholes, standing in icy water. Curious, isn't it, that I should be more concerned over these pedestrian miseries than I am about the threat of wound or death? Perhaps it's because I willfully repudiate the possibility of death. My reason, insisting on cold logic, tells me "maybe," but emotionally I reject it entirely. My equanimity has not yet been shaken, and I ponder much and naively on how I shall react under fire, in the immediacy of danger. I am sourly amused at my sneaking suspicion that if I crack, it will be from sheer physical discomfort, from too much mud and snow and water. I'm a tender blossom, all right!

November 24. Still in Hurtgen Forest.

It's a clear day at last, after a night of rain, and it is expected that the Air Corps will give the Jerries hell today.

A month from tonight will be Christmas Eve. That's a thought that doesn't bear much dwelling on. It's just occurred to me, as an ironic underscoring of my premature Christmas homesickness, that my childish delight in Christmas has its origin in the holiday customs observed in my family when I was a youngster. And those customs were German. This reflection puts me and my current task strangely at odds. I don't mean that I'm slipping into any apologia for the German state, or even for the German people. I'm convinced that the very qualities in the German national character from which burgeoned the lovely Christmas customs also nurtured and richly fed the vigorous and rank growth that became Nazism. The ecstatic emotionalism that saw symbols in trees, fairy tales in rivers and rocks, holy legends in falling snow— the same emotionalism that transmuted these gentle miracles into song and story, also gave birth to the myth of the Aryan super race, spawned the bizarre Gothic tale of a German superculture, and in monstrous abortion spewed the nightmare of concentration camps and genocide. I'm no scientist, surely, and perhaps there is no scientific validity in the attributing of "national characteristics" to a group of people, but if there is, I would list an openmouthed childishness among the outstanding German characteristics, a naive and credulous belief in the painted and hollow shams that wiser people readily identify as canvas, cardboard, and gilt paint.

I got through Thanksgiving somehow. We did indeed have turkey and dressing and giblet gravy and mashed potatoes. And a dab of cranberry sauce on a slab of bread. The food was cold when we got it, and we stood in a pouring rain to eat, but it *was* Thanksgiving. The calendar said so. And by the time you were eating Thanksgiving dinner, I was already in bed, listening to the artillery, which was worse than usual, and wondering how long it would be until my socks dried and my feet got warm.

We have been unable to write any letters since our arrival here. Only officers may censor letters, and our officers are up front. Of course, mail pickup is a little irregular here, also. I get panicky at the realization that the last letter you will receive from me will only tell you that I'm in Germany. After that there will be days, perhaps weeks, of silence. I know how bad those days will be for you, and there is nothing I can do to ease them. I have had no mail since leaving Bastogne, but that's a minor discordancy in a world completely out of tune. It's harder for you.

The German paper on which I have been writing these notes has a tendency to dissolve in moisture, like flour and water paste. I've been keeping these scribbled pages inside my shirt, between shirt and woolen underwear, in the hope of keeping them dry. Even so, I have no real hope that they will survive the coming weeks and get home to you eventually. I keep writing because it's something to do.

We are told that before we're assigned to positions within our particular platoons as scouts, antitank grenadiers, BAR men (Browning automatic riflemen), and so on, we will be interviewed individually by the captain. This is a sop to our still-civilian habits of mind, and I am becoming armywise at last. A month ago my hopes would have soared at the possibility of finding a niche tailor-made to fit my special talents. The "interview" news today left me unmoved and . . . ? Reconciled, is the word, I guess. All I want now is for this to be over so I can go home and feel my kids tumbling over me like fat puppies . . . see you smiling serenely from the green chair. I'll do any kind of dirty job that will help bring that about.

November 25, and it's still the Hurtgen Forest.

Another clear day, although colder, and our planes appeared in strength this morning to blast the German artillery positions. It's believed that given a few days of clear weather, we'll be in Cologne within a week.

It's a weary and anxious time for us. Having nothing to do, we stand around and talk, hopefully exchanging the latest rumor or inventing a new one, hanging breathlessly on every word uttered by the occasional "old" men who drift back from the front for a few hours' rest and a hot meal. We learn that the line has advanced four times in the past few days and the battle has settled down to dull waiting. There is little small-arms fire at the present time; casualties are mainly from mortar and artillery fire.

Trying to determine the exact front is very confusing because we have guns all around us. The heaviest barrages are at night, and lying in bed, I feel the ground shake and wonder if our reeling log hut will collapse upon us. The concussion is so great that our internal organs quiver and dance. It's hard to describe the exact sensation. It's as though heart and lungs, stomach and liver and lights, were suspended in Jell-O, and the bowl being shaken violently. It's not too unpleasant after you get used to it, but sleep is frequently difficult.

The men who come back from the front for brief rests or to be treated for trench foot or other army ailments tell us not to be disturbed by the wild tales we may occasionally hear. Very rarely we meet a man who takes cruel delight in filling our credulous ears with reports of conditions on the front as even worse than they are, a death rate even more appallingly high than it is, and false and misleading tips on what to take with us when we go up, what to do when we get there, et cetera. We haven't met many like that. Most of them treat our ingenuousness with grave and elderly regard and give us honest and sound advice. It's bad, they say, but not as bad as we might imagine. And even when we are told of some horror we had not suspected, still it is comforting to be *told*, to *know* a little of what it is and what we may expect. It's the not-knowing that is hard to bear.

Talking to one of those veterans today, I was struck by how old he seemed. Not in physical appearance—in spite of his heavy beard, his haggard eyes, and all the evidences of great weariness, he was still a young man in his early twenties. Nor, in spite of what's written in war novels, was his age heavily implicit in the tragedy of his eyes. No, it was in the way he spoke of life and death and mutilation, in his calm acceptance of transiency and impermanence, his serene willingness to receive whatever would come instead of the Quixotic rebellion against fate that every young man has a right to enjoy. I felt young and naive before his mature and unbegging resignation.

These woods testify mutely to all that preceded us here. In the holly thicket a few steps from my hut are two baby carriages, abandoned by fleeing civilians who left the road to avoid strafing. I have found three oil lamps, two of them of fine porcelain, decorated with hand-painted roses. And there is all manner of equipment that has been discarded as nonessential by GIs: money belts, tubes of toothpaste and shaving cream, a case of C rations that we raid between meals, a blanket, a gas mask, playing cards, books and magazines, stationery and ink—a motley and pathetic array of small possessions. The dregs of German passage are here, also: army blankets of coarse gray wool (we add all blankets, whether GI or German, to our bed), German gas masks, envelopes of "protective clothing" for use in gas-contaminated areas. (Like us, the Germans have apparently decided that poison gas will not be employed in this war.)

The question on everyone's tongue, repeated a thousand times a day, is: "How long can they hold out?" We're sure that it can't last much longer; we're confident it's only a matter of days. No real reason for that confidence, it's what we want to believe.

November 29 now.

Haven't written for two days. Two reasons for that, one for each day. I spent November 27 trying to dry my clothing over a small fire, and yesterday we moved up and joined our outfit. We're a couple of miles behind the front. The outfit was pulled out of the line for a few days in order to reorganize, but we'll be going back up shortly. I'm now officially at home—a member of the first squad, first platoon, Company G, 16th Infantry Regiment, 1st Infantry Division, 1st Army. A helluva lot of firsts.

There is much to tell you. But before I bring you up to date I want to report on two things I had almost forgotten:

(1) We do have fresh meat occasionally. One of our cooks has fallen into the habit (deplorable, but praise the Lord for it!) of wandering off every now and then with an M-1 cradled in his arm and knocking off a stray cow—German, of course, and therefore incontrovertibly enemy. The dead animal is loaded on a trailer and brought back to camp where we skin it, butcher it, and eat it. We've had steak four times in the past week.

(2) You've probably wondered how effective the "Volksturm" is. From all I can discover, it's not effective at all. It doesn't even seem to exist, so far as adult Germans are concerned. (I have already mentioned guerrilla bands of teenage boys and girls, but if they are the "Volksturm," may God have mercy on Germany!) However, we find an increasing number of young German boys, sixteen to eighteen years, in the regular German army. That is, they are in uniform and legitimately a part of the Wehrmacht.

Now for November 28, my day of matriculation. The order to pack up came without warning at nine-thirty A.M. By 9:45 we were ready to go, and at ten we were on the way. (I recall with wonder those Sunday mornings at home when a sudden desire to spend the day at the lake cottage meant two or three frenzied hours of packing food, diapers, bassinets, sweaters, bathing suits, toys, playpens, children, and dogs into the car before setting off at last in a sweaty and Bumpsteadian hugger-mugger.)

We marched about seven miles. After weeks of inactivity we were soft and it was tough going, especially when the roads dissolved into a single flowing stream of mud. Someday someone will write a book about war and tell the truth about the mud . . . how you live in it, sleep in it, eat it and drink it, absorb it through your pores, comb it from your hair and shave it from your face, smell of it, wear it like a skin and like a rose in your lapel. I am tempted to paraphrase Bliss Carman:

> There is something in the army that is native to my blood—
> I think it's mud . . . !

Despite the mud, it was a good day to march. Clear, crisp, and fitfully sunny. The briskness of our pace soon warmed us, and excitement added its own special glow to the temperature of our bodies.

It was a vivid and memorable day, and I want to write down what I can remember of it because I'm pretty damn sure there will be many memorable days in the future. The near future . . . maybe tomorrow.

We moved steadily in the direction of Cologne through towns that were torn to pieces, littered with household goods and the broken wreckage of ancient buildings . . . through fields so thickly dotted with shell holes that they seemed scarred as though by the pox. Scores of dead cows lay in the fields and ditches, most of them unwounded. Concussion is apparently more deadly to livestock than shrapnel. (The sight became commonplace in later weeks, and always the majority of casualties were adult cows: young calves by the dozen trotted homeless and hungry about the countryside.) Many of the cattle had been dead so long that they'd begun to collapse into the earth, the ragged pelts and awkward skeletons hugging closer and closer against the ground as though for shelter too late. Once we saw a dead goat, and the small body was somehow more pathetic than that of an equally dead cow, or score of cows. (Why, I wonder? Because the goat is a more personable animal?)

Everywhere was the litter of German retreat—helmets, gas masks, belts, packs, blankets, mess gear. Occasionally an unexploded hand grenade, either the potato-masher concussion type or the more deadly fragmentation variety, in shape like our own hand grenades. Once I saw the hilt of a German knife protruding from the bank, but I dared not go after it because the shoulders of the road had not yet been cleared of mines. German mines were freely in evidence, heaped on the edge of the road as they'd been discovered and rendered harmless by our engineers.

In the ditches flanking the road were foxholes and prone shelters at intervals of only a few yards, striking evidence of the kind of fighting it had been—advancing a little, digging in, advancing a little more, digging in. Backbreaking, heartbreaking labor. The woods on either side of the road were splintered matchwood, with not a single tree standing for thousands of yards at a stretch.

In the towns the churches were pretty badly damaged. That surprised me until I was told that the church steeples, being the highest points in any village, had been used by the Germans as artillery observation posts and such employment of churches made them legitimate targets for our artillery.

The sky was filled with our planes. I've just realized that I have not yet seen a German plane. Where the hell *is* this much vaunted Luftwaffe, anyway? Except for ack-ack, our own planes are unmolested. Today, flight after flight of our bombers and fighter escorts swarmed over, dropped their eggs on

Cologne, and sped homeward. I did not see any of our aircraft fall, though surely there must have been some casualties.

The evidence of civilian tragedy is sometimes too poignant for easy dismissal. My heart lurched when I saw a toy automobile, just Geoff's size, hanging drunkenly by one wheel from the shattered window of a ruined building. It was painted red. And a sick taste filled my mouth when I saw a Sukey-size teddy bear peering with one blue yarn eye from under a pile of broken stone—all that was left of a home. And there were books and china and home-canned fruits and vegetables, and embroidered tablecloths and doilies and all the female frip-frap so beloved of the German hausfrau, now spilled on the dirty cobbles, half buried under the ruins. In the few habitable houses we passed, GIs were at work, trying to get the stoves to function. Mattresses and quilts padded broken windows and the shell holes in the walls. Once, I saw a green satin comforter in a deserted bivouac area, abandoned to the mud. A little startling.

All of the villages seemed to be occupied by our troops, and we encountered no civilians. As we passed one house, a shell hole in the roof and side revealed an American jeep placidly resting in the dining room, its blunt nose nudging a large and garish lithograph of Christ blessing the loaves and fishes.

We moved along steadily, a ten-yard interval between men as a precaution against enemy shells. In the fields that stretched between the little villages were sugar beets, rotting in the ground for lack of hands to harvest them. Once, we passed a bed of white chrysanthemums, cool and undisturbed, that stretched a hundred yards in length. At one end of this floral exclamation point an immense shell crater made an emphatic period. Affirmation and rebuttal.

We reached our destination about midday, a cement factory near Eschweiler. It was a new and modern building and not severely damaged, barring shell and bullet holes. Two dead Germans lay beside one of the buildings. Someone had covered them carelessly with their own overcoats, from which their feet protruded awkwardly. Their shoes were very muddy and very large.

Following chow we were assigned to platoons and squads. The few old men in the company seemed like good Joes. I liked the look and manner of the captain, and the way the men spoke of him, the shy understatement that revealed their love for the guy. (Note: This was the famous and well-loved Captain Shelby.) Looked like a good setup.

And that brings me up to date. What happens next is what I've been in the army eight months for. I'm scared, but at the same time keyed up with a kind of eagerness for an experience that is now so common that I feel poor lacking it. That sounds like comic book or Horatio Alger dialogue, but you will understand what I mean. I think any man not in this business, or in it but rotting helplessly back in the States and thus not a part of it, will understand that feeling, too.

The captain told us that there is one wooded section between us and the plains of Cologne. It's not in our sector, so it may not be our job. And he repeated what I have heard countless times from other sources: General Eisenhower has stated that the 1st Division is through when it hits the Rhine. We have less than twenty miles to go.

December 1.

A sunrise so beautiful this morning that I am persuaded it's a good omen. We're still in the cement factory, but we were alerted last night and are prepared to move out on a moment's notice.

Day before yesterday, I had a shower. I mean a real shower, not standing naked in a rainfall. Twenty of us piled into a truck, drove sixteen miles to the rear, had hot showers, and were issued clean clothing. I'm cold without my dirt.

Yesterday we walked to a makeshift range for a practice session with the bazooka. There was a tragic footnote to this semblance of basic training days. One of the men in another company was carrying a hand grenade in his hip pocket, and when he reached for his handkerchief, he accidentally pulled the pin. He was unable to get the grenade from his pocket in time and the explosion tore his hip away. He bled to death very quickly, lying in the mud on the side of the road.

To our incredulous disgust, we had a session of close order drill this morning. Shades of Camp Wheeler, is *that* what we're in Germany for?

Noon chow is just over, served today with an unscheduled aperitif to stimulate digestion. We had finished eating and were standing in the wash-up line, waiting to clean our mess gear, when a Jerry plane suddenly screamed down upon us. We broke and hit for cover like a bunch of big-assed birds. (That's a favorite army phrase that delights me.) Expecting strafing, we were sure it was upon us when we heard machine-gun fire. But it turned out to be our own guns, firing at the plane from defense emplacements in the field. Our ack-ack opened up at the same time, and to us, new and very green, it really seemed like war for a moment. The plane did not return the fire. It came over the factory twice, then fled.

Today was a day for disappointment, too, so bitter that I wanted to hide in a dark corner. We had a mail call, the first one, and there was no mail for me. "Shorty" Fennell and Bill Dillon—two names I'll mention frequently from here on—got big bundles, but not even a postcard for me. There is a special pang to my grief because we are likely to move out at any time and no one can guess when the next mail call will be. I won't dwell longer on my unhappiness. You know how it feels when the postman passes your door without even glancing up.

The two dead Germans I mentioned earlier have not yet been buried. Their bodies lie very near the place where we line up for chow three times a day, and we squat beside them on upturned helmets to eat our meals. No appetite seems impaired by the presence of these silent guests. Fortunately, the weather remains cold.

The old men of the company have received us, the new replacements, with understanding tolerance. As you probably have surmised from the bitching in my letters, a replacement's lot is not an 'appy one, and we've been kicked around a helluva lot. So, as we approached our final assignation, we felt a certain trepidation; we expected a supercritical appraisal from the old men, a look of scorn as if to say, "Oh, my Christ, look what they sent us!" Appraisal there has been, but thus far no scorn. We've had the sensation of being welcomed, and that is so rare an experience after eight months in this damn army that it's like coming home. Combat will tell the tale, of course, but at least we have no feeling of being here on sufferance, even if in fact we are. The old men have been patient with our ignorance, kindly in their tutelage, and generous in their sharing of experience. It's pretty damn wonderful, the way they've greeted us.

Note: In one of the letters I wrote Ree from the cement factory, I enclosed a clipping from *Stars and Stripes* that had made me sick and angry. My letter crossed one of hers, mailed at the same time, which contained the same news item, as it had appeared in one of the local papers, datelined November 29, 1944, St. Joseph, Missouri:

> The little bakery shop was crowded and a woman was clearly heard to say, "I hope this war lasts awhile longer so we can pay off our mortgage."
>
> Another woman turned quickly to the clerk. "Forget that cake," she said. "I'll take that lemon meringue pie—and don't wrap it."
>
> She laid down the money, picked up the pie, hit the other woman squarely in the face with it, and stalked from the shop.

Was this what America and the people back home were like? I wondered after reading that newspaper story. Were we expected to toss away our lives so that someone could pay off his mortgage? (I was bitterly aware of the unpaid mortgage on my own home, of the hundred dollars a month that was my wife's sole income, and of my legal liability to pay up my accrued debts within six months after I should arrive home and be discharged.) Maybe I had no right to feel so violently bitter.

I hadn't risked *my* life yet, and I was conscious of the mock heroics in my attitude. But the fact remained that my life *was* on a note-of-demand and I was likely to be called on to pay up. Others had already paid up—so that another mortgage back home could be written off?

Since that time I have had occasion to wonder if someone might not raise the question of the *suitability* of that kind of news item reaching the men on the fighting front. I know damn well that there must be thousands of people, well-meaning and sincere, who would argue that such unsavory revelations should have been kept from our tender sensibilities: it would be "bad for our morale." Well, it *was* bad for our morale. Whose fault was that?

My argument and the argument of every man I talked to was that we had a right to know about things like that if they were happening back home. No one had a better right; not a soul back in that fat country of ours had a better right to know that there were some who were gaining weight on a diet of blood. Maybe our knowing was a knowledge that would pay off ill in the end; maybe it is partially responsible for the inevitable postwar bitterness that many veterans carry like a live grenade in their pockets. (What the hell am I talking about—"*maybe* it's responsible"!) But I never heard of a soldier who deserted or refused to fight because of it, I never encountered any men who refused to risk their own lives for the preservation of civilians who were busy paying off mortgages. Whatever bad effect it had on our morale, it wasn't our fighting morale that was affected: the disfiguring results are being displayed *now* in the peace world, the postwar world that has no homes for us, no patience with our pleas for tolerance and understanding, no charity in its tawdry schemes to chisel us for clothing, food, jobs, cars, and homes.

I sound more bitter, more maladjusted than I am. My own personal complaints are small: I have a job that is stimulating and good, and I came home *to* a home. I was lucky. But I know many veterans who have neither home nor job, who are hurt and bewildered and will eventually be angry because the world hurries coldly by and offers them not even the crust of understanding. How come?

What I want most to know is this: How *many* mortgages were paid off? How *many* people should have been hit in the face with lemon meringue pies? I cannot and will not believe there were many. But sometimes I wonder . . . every now and then I wonder.

As for the news item, I firmly defend our right to read it, whether we happened to be overseas or not. In spite of the daily bitching about "4F bastards" and "draft dodgers" and the story about the jerk with the wealthy old man (always with a wealthy old man) who hastily found an "essential" job in a war plant when the draft breathed down his neck—despite the savagery of our griping, we never really decried the importance of the stateside jobs. We had a grudging respect for the factory worker, the shipyard worker, and the farmer; we felt a kind of pity for the white collar worker even though we admitted that *somebody* had to do it. But we knew the value of what we were doing, too, and we thought the term "heroism" rather ill-used when applied to home-front labors. I think our balance was healthy, in general. And we hated the guts of the mortgage payers and thought the woman who threw the pie ought to get the Bronze Star, and we bitched a little and felt a little sick at heart. And went out and took the next town on schedule.

Sunday, December 3.

The Red Cross Clubmobile is due here this afternoon and we are excited at the prospect of seeing some women, American women. The coffee-and is incidental: the girls are the big attraction. [The Clubmobile, for unexplained reasons, failed to show up.]

We were told that the woods between us and the plains of Cologne had been taken. The armored moved up toward the front several days ago, and yesterday the artillery moved up and began shelling the small towns that still blocked the path to Cologne. Once those towns were softened up, we'd move forward.

For lack of anything more interesting, I went to church today. Protestant services, held in the open air and about thirty feet from the two dead Germans who have not yet been buried. I went because I felt like singing. Unfortunately, I'd just finished rereading Stephen Crane's "The Open Boat," and with that stern negation of morality still chilling my blood, the mewling of "Safe in the Arms of Jesus" was an intolerable mawkishness. I watched the faces of the thirty-odd men who made up the congregation, looked for the visitation of peace on the tired, strained faces. It didn't come.

After the service I roughed out a short story. It wasn't good and it will never be finished, but I quote it here because it's the easiest way to describe what happened.

They straggled from the dead factory. Some of them opened ruined doors and stepped out gravely and with dignity, as though from their own homes; many walked casually through the raw shell holes in the sides of the building. Picking their way over rough heaps of brick and mortar, balancing across crazily tilted steel girders, they came in their several manners—diffident, earnest, half ashamed. They formed a ragged half circle where the little chaplain waited. A late straggler stepped swiftly across the courtyard, his movements curiously blurred, as though lacking the last fine edge of coordination. In the shadow of the tilted helmet, his eyes were very tired.

When they had come to where the chaplain stood, they kicked aside the broken tiles, the discarded clothing, the German burp gun, and the shrapnel-torn lengths of gutter pipe. Forming a meek line (this was army training and instinctive and no command was necessary), they accepted the thin red hymnals with the docility of well-trained dogs accepting the largesse of biscuits. Then they squatted soberly, sitting on their upturned steel helmets, and waited for the grace of God. No one looked at the two dead Ger-

mans who sprawled in the shadow of the building, their
faces covered with the skirts of their own overcoats, their
muddy feet turned out and strangely flat against the
ground.

He wasn't really a *little* chaplain. Actually, he was a big
man with broad cheekbones, a wide mouth, and the singularly sweet and vacant smile of a Swede. His uniform was
well-fitting, but again, it didn't seem to fit at all; somehow it
gave the impression of hanging on him uncertainly. The
man who had been late in arriving sat well to the back of the
ragged semicircle and looked curiously at the chaplain. *I bet
. . . he thought. I bet . . .*

The chaplain's voice was high and uncertain, his manner
tentative. Everything about him was faltering, and the man
thought, *He's been overseas too long. He's had it! In this
place and before us, with those two dead Jerries lying over
there . . . it's no dice . . . no dice.*

They sang first, the chaplain setting the pitch and starting
them off because there was no field organ. "Sweet Is the
Hour of Prayer," all three verses and pitched too high, the
male voices straining to reach the high notes and cracking.
After a moment the man on the outer edge of the circle
started singing. There was a perverse satisfaction in bel-
lowing the banal and uninspired harmony as loudly as possible and he sang it strongly. But why was the harmony part
always a monotonous third below the melody in these
dreary hymns?

Responsive reading followed, and the bleating voice
drained all the magnificence from the words, changing the
sonorous phrases into something arid and barren. The men
chanted the responses vigorously, rolling the language on
their tongues, feeling the beat of it like a jazz rhythm. Star-
tlingly, between the phrases of their full chorus rose the thin
voice of the chaplain, clutching at protest and fighting for
command.

Another song, "Onward, Christian Soldiers." Even the
most devout in that unshaven group were pricked by the
incongruity, the familiar words suddenly as bitter as aloes:

> Onward, Christian soldiers,
> Onward as to war!
> With the cross of Jesus
> Going on before . . .

There were embarrassed smiles, furtive glances in the direction of the two dead Germans, the belts around the dead waists that were fastened by huge buckles. The dull sunlight caught the buckles, and those sitting nearest could see the uncompromising boast of shining letters, set in bold relief against a background of dull metal. GOTT MIT UNS!

They swung into the next verse:

> Brothers, we are treading
> Where the saints have trod;
> We are not divided,
> All one body we,
> One in hope, in doctrine,
> One in charity . . .

The chaplain felt the rising amusement, and his eyes flickered timidly over the lustily singing men. As they reached the end of the chorus, he held up his hand for silence. He did not explain why only three verses had been sung instead of the four originally announced.

The sermon followed, mercifully brief because legs were going to sleep from the sharp pressure of helmet edges against thighs and buttocks. He faced the restless men defiantly and read the text in a high, nervous voice. It was from the 46th Psalm: "Come, behold the works of the Lord, what desolations he hath made in the earth. He maketh wars to cease unto the end of the earth; he breaketh the bow, and cutteth the spear in sunder; he burneth the chariot in the fire."

He was soon lost. The men closed themselves against the turgid rhetoric and withdrew, and sensing their retreat, he pursued them in wild metaphysical leaps, fumbled despairingly for words. "The trembling of the mountains and the desolations in the earth stand for the turmoil in the world today, and that turmoil is because man has broken God's laws. God created the turmoil because we broke His laws, and God will put an end to it and will stop all wars when men in their innermost consciousness receive God into their souls!"

The circle drew tighter together, and now the chaplain was a long ways away from them, a tiny leaping figure on a far distant stage. *Poor guy,* they thought. *He's had it!* They felt an embarrassed pity because they were strong, and out of pity they endured the empty divinity school phrases the defeated man was reciting in a last spurt of despair.

At last it was over. They repeated a prayer, sang "Jesus Is Calling Me," and rose to receive the benediction, furtively pulling at their crotches to loosen tight underwear. They returned the little red hymnals, and after a momentary hesitation drifted off, disappearing into the shadows of the factory as they sought their beds. For a moment the chaplain looked after them and his face was tired. It seemed to be coming apart, like something that had been mended with poor glue. Wearily, he packed the hymnals in a small trunk, climbed into the jeep with the large white cross painted on the hood and SWEET CHARIOT painted gaily on the windshield, and gave the driver an order in a low voice. They bounced away, and only the straggler watched them go. Then he turned to hunt his own bed, and as he fumbled with the blankets on the dirty straw he was dimly aware that something significant had just happened, a signal had been flashed. There was something in this he meant to think out sometime, but not now. He fell asleep quickly and did not dream.

That's it. It's no story, but it is reasonably accurate in its measure of the church's failure to provide real consolation or encouragement to men at war.

Perhaps I'm too hasty. I think there must have been many

men who found a measure of comfort in what the chaplains
gave them; I think there must have been some perceptive and
intelligent chaplains. I know there were some gallant ones,
and gallantry helped, but it wasn't enough. Let it go at this: I
found a momentary peace in the ministrations of the Church
only twice during the war, and though I am not a Catholic,
they were Catholic services that gave me a measure of serenity. The first time it was a GI service; the second occasion
was after the war, and I walked into a cathedral and found
myself in the middle of a civilian service and could not understand a word that was said.

Most of the chaplains I met had slipped into one or the other
of a pair of pitfalls, the first of which was an attempt to reconcile the naked contradiction between the theory of Christ and
the fact of war. Their earnest and stubborn strategy was frequently the old line "God's on our side because we're the right
side and so anything you do to help the right side win is okay,
even if you violate the teachings of Christ." Devious, and
hardly convincing. Sometimes they attempted an elephantine
maneuver, top-heavy with rhetoric and symbolism, to prove
that it was the sickness of our own souls that had created the
present chaos and we must "face the Light of Truth in ourselves first" and so forth and so forth. This was weary and
indigestible fare for men who were sick of the whole damn
mess and hated the things they had to do, and whose thoughts
were fixed on symbols less airy—a woman's arms, and small
faces peeping through a white picket fence.

The second pitfall, encountered through well-meant blundering, was "being one of the boys," and working too hard at
it. The rough camaraderie of male companionship, bawdy,
lusty, and vigorous, is denied them. And their endeavors to
break down the walls that set them apart from other men are
always fumbling, gauche, and pathetic. I think it's swell for a
minister to unbend sufficiently to take a drink with the boys.
But his presence inevitably sets the tone of the conversation,
and if he is wise, he will not stay long. He will be more highly
regarded if he has his drink, tells his quiet joke, and departs.

He goes down in the esteem of other men when he attempts to level the walls entirely and tells progressively off-color stories, relating (even though as case histories) some of the startling sexual aberrations he has encountered in his official capacity. The circumstance of war makes a difference, too: an off-color story that would provide a wicked relish if related by a minister in civilian life comes as an additional shock when everything around you is mean and ugly and twisted, and only the word of God and its chosen vessels retain even the dim hope of serenity.

December 4.

Two German planes came over and strafed us today. No one was hit, and our ack-ack batteries in the field knocked down one of the attackers. It plunged to the ground about two miles away, trailing behind it a comet path of flames and dark smoke. We watched silently and did not rejoice until it had slipped behind an intervening hill and we could no longer see it.

The doughnut wagon did not come, and there was no mail today.

December 6.

We left our comfortable cement factory on December 5. Every place we leave always seems, in retrospect, to have been a veritable boudoir of luxury, even though we bitched about its discomforts and inconveniences all the time we'd been there. It always seems to be a steady progression from worse to worse.

In open trucks we rode for three hours in circles—at least we got back into Belgium somehow and passed through Eupen—and ended up in Germany once more, on the fringe of the Hurtgen Forest. This is the front, and we're on it. The German lines are on the edge of the woods two miles from us. The 12th SS is in position there, we are told. It's to be a waiting game we play here: we're holding against the danger of counterattack, and they're poised for further attacks from us. We may be here two weeks or a month.

It's a quiet sector. Only an occasional plane, and the artillery fire is sporadic on both sides. It makes for a strange day. Hours and hours of quiet are broken only by the moaning of the wind and the sound of the church clock in the little village behind us, telling the hours in a hoarsely sweet voice. At intervals one of our big guns snarls a few rounds over our heads, and we see them burst in the woods in vivid exclamations of orange fire. Then the German guns answer. Yesterday my squad was in the stable of a German farmhouse, getting warm before going out for our stint on the line, when several German 88s opened up and lobbed a few dozen shells over. Some of them landed close enough to scar the walls of the building across the road with shrapnel. We played a form of Russian roulette during the shelling: one of the windows in the stable, lacking glass, was covered with a square of cardboard. The concussion of every nearby shell sucked the cardboard from the window, and then one of us dashed into the road to pick it up and replace it in the window before the next shell came in.

We live in the mud. When we arrived here, it was midafternoon. We waited in the muddy road until dark, hugging the hedgerows and trying to be inconspicuous. We were relieving another company, and strategy demands that shifts in the disposition of units be performed as secretly as possible.

Just got word that one of the men with whom I bivouacked in the Bastogne woods was killed this week. He was assigned to an outfit at the same time the rest of us were, less than a month ago. Poor Gilman . . . three weeks . . .

At dark we moved into our positions, a line of dugouts that hugged a hedgerow along the edge of a field. The field was a pond of mud, with here and there a drowned clump of harsh grass forlornly protesting emptiness. The dugout in which Shorty Fennell and I lived was a good one, as dugouts went. There was straw on the bottom—wet, of course—and a wood roof that didn't leak in more than a dozen places. No central heating.

Shorty's nickname is well arrived at—he's hardly more

than five feet tall. His mother is Polish, his father Irish, and when his parents separated, Shorty and his brothers and sisters were reared in an orphanage. I love the guy and trust him even with the secret of my private fears.

I'm a little humble to realize what a long way I've come, what a long way I *had* to come since April 4, 1944, the day I was inducted. I discovered early in my army life that a Phi Beta key had never taught me how to mix unobtrusively, without protest and condescension, in the all-male melting pot that was the army. I didn't know how to talk to men who couldn't speak my special language, and I couldn't speak theirs. I didn't know where to look for a common meeting ground with them. Inwardly, of course, I was very superior about it all, and I bedded down with annoyed smugness each Sunday afternoon when the first strains of the symphony on the barracks radio brought a howl of protest from all sides: "Fer Chrissake, get somethin' decent, will ya?"

I had a rough time of it for a while in basic training. Not that I was ridden unmercifully or made the butt of crude humor. On the contrary—there were walls of ice around me. I learned that a four-syllable word, impeccably enunciated, was a better weapon and a better defense than a pair of brass knuckles. I was left alone. And that was the hardest thing of all to bear: the sense of being shut out from some warm and mysterious camaraderie that, it seemed to me, was the only thing that could make army life tolerable. It took a painful while before I learned how to melt the ice barrier, how to get through it and into the magic circle. I was a mighty proud joker when I saw the suspicion fade and knew that my education and my accent were no longer held against me.

Attitudes of suspicion and hostility in varying degrees of rigidity are encountered throughout the army, of course, as in any arbitrarily created group where traditional barriers of background and training are summarily leveled. The astonishing thing is that in spite of regional differences, social differences, religious, political, and economic differences, men learn to work together and live together.

I was lucky. From men like Shorty I learned that education, like other so-called "differences," was only a fortuitous accident, a thin gloss carelessly applied, and under it walked the fundamental man, naked and unashamed. I was doubly fortunate in learning this before I was commissioned. The officers most hated by enlisted men, the officers responsible for the mud rightly flung at the army "caste system," are officers who never learned it, or forgot it too soon.

Returning to Shorty: Between us there was no awkwardness or strain. As a combine, we clicked from the beginning, and from it we each gained the additional strength of a united front.

The first night in our new positions near Eupen was not happy. Both Shorty and I pulled guard duty, but he was blessed among men: he had overshoes. I lacked even the much publicized "combat boots," and still wore the familiar ankle-high clodhoppers. Our field was a sticky pool of snow and mud, dotted with deep puddles of icy water. The mud ranged in depth from six to twelve inches, and I had not yet figured out how to stand in twelve-inch mud and keep it from oozing over the tops of five-inch shoes.

Early the following morning I walked to the C.P. to fill our canteens. Finding no water there, I trudged through the mud to the nearest farmhouse, from the doorway of which a young woman, baby on hip, had smiled and waved to us on our arrival the day before.

My timid knock was answered at once by the same smiling woman, and she invited me in. I demurred; my feet were encased in dripping blocks of mud, and her kitchen was spotless. But she insisted, I weakened, and for half an hour I sat in the anteroom to paradise. A soft chair by a glowing stove, two cups of warm milk, and gentle kindliness from the young woman and her husband. (He had a twisted foot, which explained his civilian status.) We grieved with each other on the evil of war—he had five brothers in the Wehrmacht, and all were dead or missing—and he said to me, "All any man wants is to be able to work and to come home at the end of the day to his wife and children." Oh, and it's true, it's true!

In spite of their hospitality, I was careful to reveal nothing that could be called "information." They seemed good people, kindly people, but how could I be sure? Already I was bewildered by the seeming contradiction that lay between what these people represented as a *group*, and what, as simple human beings, they seemed to *be*. General Eisenhower had issued orders prohibiting all intercourse between soldiers and German civilians, and I could have been punished for exchanging a simple *Guten Tag* with that farm family. Yet our officers and ranking NCOs were billeted in German homes, sharing them with German families, and only the lonely doggie shivered forlornly in the mud and cold. Or so I argued to myself, working up a fine case to justify my behavior. I salved my conscience further by trying hard to believe that these people, living only a few steps from the Belgian border, may have escaped a really thorough Nazi indoctrination. But I was aware of the weakness of such argument. Does a disease recognize the black boundary lines drawn on a map? Does it stop short where the map says, "This is where Germany ends and this is where Belgium begins"? So I kept my mouth shut on topics related to the war, and our conversation was innocent.

Another night of guard duty in shoes still wet from the night before. We were under the most stern orders not to remove our shoes at any time, even during the daylight hours, when we did nothing but huddle in our blankets. The threat of counterattack was ever present, and feet newly released from wet shoes puffed up grossly, so that it was impossible to get the wet boots on again in a hurry.

I played a grim game with myself on guard duty that night. I found two boards to stand on and tried to guess how soon they would sink and the mud creep above my shoe tops. There was a cold wind blowing, and sleet and snow in the air. No lights except the noiseless flashes of distant shells, and on the horizon a sporadic flickering, like heat lightning. I counted the minutes—minutes, hell! I counted the seconds! I shifted my weight from one foot to the other, allowing two deliberate, painful seconds per foot. It's a long, long two hours when you count to sixty slowly, 120 times.

December 7.

Three years today . . .

We spent the day in our blankets. We were forbidden to move about in the daytime except to satisfy the most insistent demands of nature. We were under constant enemy observation.

Our exposed position made for very unsatisfactory chow. We went to breakfast in the dark, one group at a time, and ate hurriedly, racing back to our holes so the next group could go up. Always, the food was cold, and there was never enough. Lunch was cold C rations, eaten in our holes. Supper was like breakfast: up the road to the C.P. in the dark, eat, rush back. Then another long night.

Tonight, however, our customary gloom changed abruptly to joy: another squad came to relieve us on the line for twenty-four hours, and *we* were going to spend the night and the following day in a hayloft. We stumbled up the road in the dark, joyous even through the mud. It was worth joy and much gratitude—our beds were sweet-smelling heaps of dry hay in the stone barn behind the platoon C.P. It wasn't warm in the barn, but the hay, the dryness, were real luxuries. I had a special break and was assigned as a telephone guard in the C.P. for the night, in the dining room of the house. An easy chair, a hot stove, an electric light! I hugged the fire until I felt the sweat trickling down my body inside my woolen underwear. I took off my shoes, propped them against the side of the stove, and watched the steam curling from the toes. I hung my socks over the hot stovepipe, turning them frequently to prevent their scorching. I slept on the floor near the stove, except for my period of duty on the phones, receiving reports from our outposts and calling them in to the company C.P. It was altogether a beautiful night.

One day in three we were to be relieved on the line and permitted to rest in the barn. The three rifle squads of the platoon would take turns on the line so there would always be one squad in reserve, resting.

The civilians in the farmhouse were women and children: three of the women old and sweet-faced, two younger women, a little girl of three, and a baby. The women did all the farm work and the chores. One of them, discovering that I spoke a little German, chattered at me in great delight. She showed me a letter, which I couldn't read, from a twenty-four-year-old nephew who had been in a New York State prison camp for two years. He'd been with Rommel in Africa.

Outpost duty last night. Three of us spent the night there, a bitter cold night with a raw wind blowing and the hail and rain rattling down the back of our necks in spite of our most complicated tricks with a blanket. I discovered that it's a very difficult operation to wrap yourself snugly in a blanket and at the same time keep your M-1 in your hand, ready for instant use. It was a long night.

This waiting business is tough as hell. I don't know that it's really worse than being in action, but sometimes it seems so. I thought of dead Gilman, alive a short week ago, and wondered which of us was next. We spend so *much* time doing nothing—lying in our blankets, talking idly and without interest, or thinking in silence. Too much time to talk, too much time to think.

Last night Shorty and I were in bed at six P.M. Our trick at the outpost was to start at midnight, and I should have slept for six hours. But I didn't sleep, it was impossible to sleep. I twisted and turned inside the blankets, and my bones screamed at the long hours and my brain screamed at the long waiting . . . for something, *something*!

The Jerries were shelling us again, fumbling for our positions with terrible fingers. We watched the shells landing in the field around us, peeping with frightened eyes through the cracks in our "shelter" and in feeble bravado making small bets on the next hit.

I spent most of the long hours making plans for my homecoming. Each small detail was carefully polished to the last shining perfection. I debated seriously on small things. Which would be the perfect hour to come home? Early morning, late night, during a meal? Would I like the kids up and awake when I came in the door, or would the final drop of sweetness lie in arriving after dark, going up the stairs to the nursery, and opening the door softly . . . to see them warm in sleep, tousled and sweet-smelling?

It was an endless and intoxicating game, but under the monotonous drip-drip of these days and nights, the magic of it palled a little and the old refrain started bleating in my brain again. *When* will it be over? I stood the long hours of guard, looked up at a malevolent and secretive sky, and my face twisted and writhed—not with sorrow, but with the madness of the prisoner, the sense of being trapped and bound—and the prayer wheel in my brain spun around and around: "When? *When?*"

The army newspaper, *Stars and Stripes*, is singularly uncommunicative. There's been no word of peace lately. News of any sort is rare, and it appears I'll lose my eighteen-franc bet that the European war will be over by Christmas. We're getting very edgy. In spite of the shells whistling overhead, this sector is quiet, too quiet. We ask each other questions that no one can answer: *Why* is it quiet? Is another push brewing? Why is the entire northern sector dormant and all attention focused on Patton's reported breakthrough in the south? What's happened to the Russian drive in East Prussia? Why doesn't it end, *when* will it end?

This way lies madness, I know. Something has to happen soon or we'll all be at each other's throats. Already there's bad feeling between men who were friends only two weeks ago, and there have been several vicious fights. We go about too silently those days. And still the snow comes down—a foot and a half deep now—and in sick wonder we ask ourselves, "How can you fight when it's like this?"

December 11.

We'd just been told that tomorrow or the day after we were moving back into Belgium. And we'd be billeted in *houses*!

We were hysterical with joy, in spite of the rumor that the purpose of this vacation was to train us for river-crossing operations. That meant the Rhine. But we could not be sobered by that consideration: we'll cross the Rhine when we come to it, but for Pete's sake, let's get warm and dry first!

I was a little ashamed of my happiness at the prospect of civilization again; we'd been out there so short a time. But I found it didn't take long to get pretty damn sick of mud and cold and snow and constant wetness. Judging from our sick-call book, many men reacted to those conditions more violently than I did. Each day saw new cases of grippe, trench foot, bad colds, and even pneumonia. Several cases of jaundice, too. Why jaundice, I wonder?

That night I was in the farmhouse again, on phone guard. I was very grateful for the warm room because I'd had the GIs for two days. I was weak and groggy and aching all over.

Notwithstanding my physical state, it was an unforgettable evening. Sitting meek and unnoticed in a corner, I'd been listening to the conversation of our platoon sergeant and some of his friends.

The sergeant's name is Misa, shortened by everyone to "Meese." We have no platoon officer, and Meese is the real boss of the first platoon. He was with the 1st Army through Africa, Sicily, and the Normandy landing and St. Lo breakthrough. Tonight he and his buddies were reminiscing, and I listened, spellbound, unwilling to turn away and go to sleep. The stories I heard, the gaudy, bawdy, gallant stories ... I made surreptitious notes, fearful of forgetting tales like:

The day the company was trapped in a little town by an overwhelming counterattack. A task force of tanks was sent to the rescue and rumbled in, guns blazing, to form an iron screen while the company retreated across the river. Four wounded were forgotten, however, in the turmoil of the retreat, and Meese and a medic went back for them that night, returning to the battered town over the one bridge still standing. They located the four men, three of whom were able to walk, and led those three over the bridge to the safety of our lines. Then Meese went back for the fourth man, who was badly wounded. Half carrying, half dragging him, he got the man to the water's edge, but it was so near dawn that he dared not risk another bridge crossing, a perfect silhouette against the lightening sky for an early-rising sniper. While Meese pondered the problem and sweated, the wounded man kept groaning, "I'm gonna die . . . leave me here, Meese! Take my wallet and leave me! There's a hundred bucks in my wallet, Meese. It's for you . . . take it! G'wan, take it and leave me here . . . I'm gonna die!"

At this point in the story, Meese paused and said meditatively, "That's just what I shoulda done—taken the dough and left him! Two months later the bastard writes me from a hospital in England and says 'Thanks.' Why the hell didn't he send the hundred bucks?"

In the reeds at the water's edge, Meese found a boat—it lacked oars—and lifted the wounded man into it. The river seemed shallow, and he prepared to wade across, pushing the boat before him. He shoved off hard, and as the boat lunged forward, pulling him momentarily off balance, he felt his feet leave bottom. Shallow, hell—this was deep! In another moment the current caught the boat and it swung downstream, heading toward the German lines. Towing the boat with one hand and swimming with the other, he fought the water and at last reached the far shore, not far from our lines. And delivered the wounded man to the waiting medics.

Then there was the time, in the same hotly contested town, when a Jerry and a GI left the safety of their respective positions simultaneously and started sprinting toward the same doorway. Instantly dropping from active participation in the war, Meese and his companions made hot bets of fantastic proportion on the outcome of the race, and then, with the dispassionate intensity of gamblers, settled back to watch. The GI won, and the German, acknowledging defeat with a cool shrug, turned and started for another refuge. Only then did the interested gamblers recall that sport was sport but there was a war on and this guy was an enemy. So they shot him. And after solemnly settling their wagers, resumed the serious business of taking the town.

And the time a shell smashed a building, and a flying splinter of rock hit a nearby Joe in the rear. He dropped his rifle in the panic of approaching death and collapsed on his face, weeping bitterly, "I'm wounded, I'm fatally wounded! Get me a medic, quick! Help, I'm dying!" An unsympathetic buddy heaved another rock at his floundering shape and yelled, "Get up, ya stupid sonofabitch, and *look* at your ass! That was only a rock that hit you!" The "dying" man peered anxiously over his shoulder at his unblemished rear, said "Oh!" in a chastened tone, picked up his rifle, and started fighting again.

Another time, in the blazing afternoon of an Italian town, another Joe felt the sudden violent impact of something hitting *his* rear, and a moment later a warm flood running down his leg. Dropping his rifle, he began to run in circles, waving his arms and screaming, "I'm hit, I'm bleeding to death! Help me . . . somebody help me! I'm hit!" Finally someone took pity on him and in obscenely blunt terms told him to stop his goddamn yelling and look at his goddamn canteen. A bullet had punctured it, and its contents, red Italian wine that had been heated to blood temperature by the sun, had drained out, soaking his pants and running down his leg.

He spoke, too, of the time a certain general—sorry, no names unless the reference is complimentary!—visited the front and inflicted a needless half hour of concentrated shelling on the battalion because he refused to accept the counsel of combatwise men, of lesser rank, naturally. The general insisted on climbing to the crest of a certain ridge, below which the troops were emplaced, well-concealed and invisible to the enemy. So he stood there, looking intrepidly toward the German positions and fussing with his maps and field glasses. Sharp eyes in the German lines caught the glint of sunlight on his glasses, German brains made hasty but accurate computations, German guns found the range, and the pounding started. Men died horribly on that ridge in the next half hour, but the general received a slight scratch from shrapnel and was hastily carried away in a stretcher. Later the home papers screamed in headlines, GENERAL BLANK WOUNDED IN FRONT LINES, and sang loud paeans of praise for his devotion to duty and what a wonderful guy he was to risk his important life just to bring the comfort of his presence to the men on the front lines.

Those are some of the stories I heard. To go along with them, here are some hasty sketches of a few of the men in this outfit:

Ketron (I'm not sure of the spelling): Two and a half years with the outfit and thus truly an old-timer. Hails from the deep South, twenty-six years old, unmarried. Blond, personable, a face that is easily merry. He is gentle with the new replacements, kind and patient. His favorite word, employed in ways new to me, is "harassing"—"That was downright harassing ... the most harassing thing I ever did see ... they'd harass the ——— out of us with that damn burp gun!" His next-favorite word is "harmless." (As a matter of fact, that's a favorite word with the entire outfit.) It, too, has strange uses and applications. Sometimes it means literally "harmless"; often it means the exact reverse, "harmful"; sometimes it means "useless, ineffectual," especially when used in reference to persons—"the most harmless guy you ever met."

Wiggy: No one can spell or pronounce his real name. Hungarian mother and a German father who died when Wiggy was a baby. He's nineteen now and fuzzy-faced. His accent is an unbelievable and hilarious blend of heavy Slavic, Harvard Yard, and slum. His favorite sayings: "Dere's jist me ma an' me, dat's all! ... Chee, I miss me ma! ... Me ma is da swellest cook ... Four letters, dat's all I had from me ma in four munts!" Poor kid ... his ma speaks English very badly and writes it not at all. Her infrequent letters to Wiggy are written by a neighbor at her dictation.

Wiggy sings himself to sleep every night. I like the kid, but his singing is execrable! Not only does he sing out of key and out of rhythm, but he has the maddening and unmusical habit of never *finishing* a song, never making the full circle of the cadence, never arriving at the final resolution. He will repeat a phrase over and over again, and each time he approaches the middle of the chorus, I make the mental prayer, "For God's sake, go on, *go on*! Finish it!" But he never does—he just starts from the beginning again.

That particular failing of the unmusical drives me to the point where I want to beat my head against the wall and howl! I remember a wistful harmonica player on the bleak train ride from Fort Dix to Camp Wheeler who made one night a screaming hell for me by playing, over and over and over, the first sixteen bars of "Over There." He never finished the song, never played the complete chorus all night long, but he played the unresolved half chorus until I shuddered like a frayed violin string.

Wiggy's choice of music is oddly touching. His favorite songs are "K-K-K-Katy," the "Notre Dame Victory March," and—Christmas carols! When we stayed in the cement factory near Eschweiler, he slept next to me on the floor, and every night when the room was quiet, soft over the heavy breathing of the sleeping men I'd hear Wiggy singing . . . a faint murmur of sound, barely recognizable as a song. Straining my ears, I'd hear, "Noel, Noel . . . Noel, Noel . . . Born is duh ki-i-ing of I-I-Israel."

That day, Wiggy went to the hospital. Trench foot. [Note: I never saw him again. He had it bad, and after a long hospitalization, was transferred to another outfit. I wonder if he got back to his "ma."]

Dillon: Irish, black Irish out of Chicago. A friend of Shorty's. Bill's a little moody at times, a little unpredictable, but a helluva good Joe. Married, but no children. He has a beautiful, rich voice and he loves to sing. He knows hundreds of old songs, including many I have never heard, and he will sing for hours with little urging, or, lacking an audience, will sit quietly in a corner, singing to himself. One night in the cement factory the talk died away as the men settled down for

the night, and those who continued to talk dropped their
voices to a murmur. The night was quiet, the sound of guns
only a distant mutter, and homesickness hung in the room like
a heavy mist. Bill had been singing quietly in the corner all
night, and one by one the talkers hushed to listen. Old songs,
songs that everyone knew, the songs that people sing when
everything's right and the world is good. He finished "Love's
Old Sweet Song." There was a moment's hush, and then he
started "Home on the Range," so low, so soft, you could
hardly hear him, the big voice like a muted cello.

> Oh, give me a home where the buffalo roam,
> Where the deer and the antelope play;
> Where seldom is heard a discouraging word,
> And the skies—

The song was never finished. A lonely Texan raised his
head from the blankets and said savagely, his voice shaking,
"For Chrissake, shut up, will ya?" The room was quiet after
that. But I woke during the night and heard a man crying.

Dillon went to the hospital that day, too. The medic didn't
know what was wrong with him, but it was bad. [Note: Bill
was very ill. Can't remember exactly what it was, but I believe
it was jaundice. At any rate, he was shipped to England and
spent the duration of the war in the hospital there, rejoining the
company in Bamberg some weeks after the war ended.]

December 13. Minerie, Belgium.

Following the customary hours of waiting, the familiar hike
through mud and snow, the usual frigid ride in an open truck,
we were neatly tucked away in this little mining town, not far
from Verviers. As per promise, we were billeted in houses.
There are nine of us in *this* house—which has been labeled
"Number 152" by the army—and all of us are wedged into a
single small bedroom. Never mind, we're in a house! With a
stove, even. And cots to sleep on, nine cots so tightly jammed
together that a sneeze from the man in number one will shake
the bed of number nine. Still, it seems like luxury to us.

We'll be here for an indefinite period, we were told, anywhere from two weeks to a month. At any rate, we're assured
of spending Christmas here. We're under no illusions, having
been informed with brutal directness that we are resting before
going into something rugged. But the important thing is,
we're *here*, and miraculously free—we don't even have to
carry arms when we go out! Blackout regulations have been
relaxed and we smoke on the streets after dark without challenge. There will be overnight and weekend passes to Verviers, Liege, and Paris, baths, movies, clean clothes, USO
shows, light duties . . . ah, don't wake me up! To cap it all, I
already found three pianos in passable condition and have
been joyously pounding all afternoon in happy disregard of
the pain of my frostbitten fingers.

I write this while sitting only a foot away from the cherry-
hot stove in our room. The heat is making me very sleepy, but
there are a few things I must record for you before I forget
them entirely. Most of them are quite small, hardly worth
relating. (Yet, do you remember? "Words must have been
made by man for telling about quite small delights only. . . ."
Very well, these are small delights.)

The army would be a treasure trove for the scholar interested in speech differences, for the poet who seeks the flavor
of rare and authentic idiom. I have been listening carefully to
the speech of a Texan and a southerner, pondering a judgment,
and decided that I prefer the Texan. It is simple speech, so
honest and unswerving that the softer syllables of the South
proper are mincing in comparison.

My nomination for "Worst Citizen-Soldier of the Year"
is a guy named B. He has the sharp features of a weasel and
something of the weasel's shrewdness, but no real intelligence. He talks ceaselessly, but without purpose, relevancy,
or coherence. His nose drips. Thirty-three years old and
convinced that his advanced age should excuse him from
the rigors of army life, he mutters darkly about the draft
board that "railroaded me because the chairman of the board
had a nephew who wanted my job." B. is certain that "an

old scar on my lungs" has freshened, and each night pre-
dicts, with snivels, that he'll be coughing blood by morning.
He has a standing offer of one thousand dollars—on cold
days he raises it to two or three—to anyone who can get him
out of the army. He is invariably the source of the latest rumor, and always he has a better ending to the story someone
else has just finished telling. He is stuffed to overflowing
with misinformation, which he presses shrilly upon anyone
unwary enough to be maneuvered into a corner. He bitches
without cease but is essentially a rabbit, cringing and back-
ing down without shame when told to "put up or shut up."
He is late for everything, and at the end of every line, then
complains bitterly because he *is* at the end. He is invariably
the last man in the outfit to read our rare copies of *Stars and
Stripes*, but when the well-thumbed paper reaches him at
last, he immediately reads every item aloud in the "Hey
fellas listen to this" manner of one revealing information
new and startling. All the bets are that he will prove completely craven when we go back up, but there's a growing
belief that he'll get a bullet hole in the back of his head
before we go back up.

I started to tell you about the women in the German
household we just left. They were gracious in manner and
never once hinted that we were unwelcome guests in their
home. They were gentle and sad and kind. The small baby,
incidentally, was named Sylvia, a curiously English name to
be attached to so unmistakably German a baby. Sylvia's
mother did all the heavy chores on the farm, and was silent
and unsmiling at all times. She hadn't had word of her husband in five months and did not know whether he was a prisoner or dead.

One night I talked at length with the old ladies and was
startled and amused by the naïveté of their questions about
America. We are still the land of golden mystery, heavy with
rich promise, to the average European, it seems. It is assumed
that Americans are spared even the minor unpleasantness of
bad weather, and the old ladies were dumbfounded to learn

that it snows in New York State. They had believed that oranges and lemons grew in profusion throughout America, and snow was found only in Canada.

I edged them toward comment on Hitler and Goebbels and Germany in the war. I think I believed them when they said the German people never wanted war and wished desperately for it to be over. (When they said "German people," they meant people like themselves—peasants, small landowners, villagers—not city people. In Germany, as in America, there exists a gap of distrust and suspicion between the people of the land and the people of the city.) And I acknowledged the sincerity of the fear and loathing on their faces when reference was made to the SS and the Gestapo. But when they said, "Hitler! *Pfui!*" I wasn't quite convinced. I think the authenticity of Hitler's godhead is not yet seriously questioned by the average German. I wonder if it will be questioned even when we have won the war and brought him to trial and punishment?

The validity of their contempt was questionable on further grounds: although they appeared to be sincere in their distaste for the end results, the *now* results that Hitler's dreams had visited upon them, the *intermediate* results—the results up till then—must have been highly gratifying to them, and I have no doubt they licked them up like a cat turned loose in a creamery. Having crucified their own Cassandras in the purge of intellectuals, liberals, and dissenters, they were now second guessers themselves—and getting quite good at it. Emotionally, I sympathize with second guessers—are we not all guilty? And these little people are pathetic creatures. They mounted a horse that promised (and proved) he could run fast, and by the time they realized they had passed their destination and could not now dismount, the horse had become a tiger. With which elaborate metaphor I gracefully withdraw from this discussion.

By peasant standards their home was luxurious. The furnishings were comfortable, and included some very handsome modern furniture. And everything was spotlessly clean. Even the cows' tails were laundered daily!

By way of contrast, the Belgian home in which we had our quarters afterward was noticeably poorer, though neat and clean. But not *quite* so clean. It was a very old house, by the way: the date carved in the stone over the door was 1758.

We couldn't desire more hospitality than greeted us there. The family that occupies the house had moved into one room to make room for us. All of them—the old couple, the son and daughter-in-law, and the three grandchildren! When we arrived in the morning, cold and wet and hungry, the old lady insisted on making a pot of coffee, apologizing meanwhile for its poor quality. It wasn't very good, but the sensation of being an honored guest was.

One last thing I must report before hitting the sack tonight. While we were up on line, shivering in our mud holes and standing guard in puddles of ice water, word got around that I spoke a little German. One day a runner came in search of me: a certain officer billeted in a farmhouse wanted me to report to him. I trotted up the road on the double, for the moment forgetting my water-soaked shoes, my cold and aching body. My brain whirled with dizzy excitement. What did he want of me? To interrogate prisoners? A soft desk job? Maybe I was going to be a spy! (My blood ran cold, not entirely with the thrill of anticipation.)

I knocked at his door, removed my helmet, scraped five or six pounds of mud from my shoes, and entered on the command. Saluting, I stated my name and reported according to the Book. Stretched in lazy indolence on a couch, his shoes off, he didn't bother to sit up. A pot of coffee was simmering on the stove, and the pervasive warmth of the room made sweat spring out on my face. Food on the table, soft quilts, pillows, easy chairs, a radio, a couch! Want to know why he sent for me? I was ordered to summon the aged frau who owned this house (and spoke no English) and tell her to provide a better radio and an easy chair with an adjustable back! My small knowledge of German deserted me utterly when I learned how I was expected to use it . . . and maybe I didn't try very hard, anyway. I did what I had to do, he dismissed me impatiently, and I returned to my mud hole, blind for once to the puddles on the road.

Not all officers were like that. And it wasn't that I blamed him for living comfortably or felt that he ought to be living as we were. It was the cruelty of having my nose rubbed in the evidence of that contrast; it was his careless indifference to our lot; it was his arrogance in summoning me from a mud hole and ordering me to use my knowledge of German for his personal comfort—then sending me back to my dirt without saying, "Thanks, soldier," or offering me the small grace of a cup of hot coffee.

I hated that officer ever afterward, with a fierce and abiding hatred. Fortunately, he was transferred to another outfit before many weeks passed.

December 15, Minerie.

Ten days to Christmas. That's how I mark off the days.

We've started a training program here. Honest! Close order drill, calisthenics, inspections . . . war is hell!

The weather remains crisp and clear and the sun is faintly warm all day. Today I saw buttercups in the fields and a rose blooming in a garden. June in December.

Speaking of blossoms, my wildflower soul has been shocked near to swooning by the spectacle of young Belgian children smoking cigarettes. And I mean children, even as young as seven years, and I mean really smoking, not the strutting mischief of an American kid aping his elders. Kids of both sexes stroll the streets, unconcernedly puffing cigarettes and inhaling with Mephistophelian savoir faire. There is something pale and wizened and almost evil about these children . . . the guttersnipe greed with which they race for the smoking butt just discarded by a passing soldier, the viciousness of their fighting over it, the cocky and snarling triumph of the victor. And it makes me "come queer all over" to see a barefooted, dirty-faced little girl, dressed in a single thin garment and lacking even the hint of a budding breast, yet puffing a cigarette with the hardened, calculating grace of a pool parlor pickup. Incongruity—something much worse than incongruity—meets me on every street corner and jolts me like a slap in the face. And they look so wise, so weary and jaded with the evil knowledge of flesh, that I feel bucktoothed and virginal beside them, a gauche and fumbling beginner in a school whereof they hold master's degrees.

I wonder what the war news is. We have had no direct news, but an English-speaking resident of the village—a charming Irishwoman who married a Belgian many years ago—told us that the radio reported a big German counterattack and all fronts were static at the moment, holding only.

I learned that the reason we were relieved from our line position in Germany was that three other divisions had pushed up almost as we'd pulled out, and attacked the German positions on the ridge we'd been watching so grimly. I should have guessed: guns and ammunition had been moving up to our sector all the preceding week, and even as we pulled out that dark morning, the "Long Toms" in the field near our kitchen were blazing away in earthquakes of white fire. That must have been the softening up before the push.

Today we saw hundreds of B-26s and P-38s overhead. And for the past several days the Jerries have been sending dozens of buzz bombs through the sky, day long, night long. More than I've ever seen before. I've seen as many as five in flight at the same time. I wonder what's brewing? One story going around is that a probing arm of our attacking forces is getting so dangerously close to one of the places from which the buzz bombs are launched that the Germans are using them up as fast as possible to save them from capture. Somehow that story doesn't ring quite true.

One more thing I forgot to tell you about: the last night I had outpost duty was memorable for one thing. About two o'clock in the morning our ack-ack batteries fired some practice rounds to clear their guns. The spectacle was so breathtaking that I woke the other men to see it. (Was it Benito Mussolini who chanted so rhapsodically of the "beauties of war"?) It was a soundless display, the guns so far distant and the wind so strong that the report of the shells could not be heard. And it was a display almost theatrically vivid: the night was black and starless and the rounds a brilliant, glowing crimson. In an enchanted silence the shells formed a magical coruscation in midair, floating up and out in long, slow curves of scarlet, a chain of red Christmas-tree lights flung against the black sky. And as each fireball reached the predestined point in its curved flight, it exploded briefly in a small, blinding flash of white fire. The entire scene—although too restrained in decor, perhaps—was suggestive of a backdrop for an Ice Follies, and you half expected a spotlight, a blare of trumpets, and Sonja Henie gliding forth in one of her usual appropriate costumes—a Hawaiian grass skirt or an Indian chief's war bonnet.

Today we had a dress formation for the purpose of awarding some decorations. The townspeople contributed to the festive air by hanging flags and banners from their windows and then assembling in admiring awe in the square by the old cathedral, taking photographs and applauding warmly and vigorously as the men to be honored stepped forth. The delight and approval of the civilians made us stick our chests out still farther, and the ceremony was truly impressive.

December 15. From a letter:

Today, in an old issue of *Time*, I read about the Morgenthau plan for Germany after it has been conquered. I was sickened by it and its implications, and began to understand why Germany so desperately continues to fight a war that has long since been lost. The men with whom I talked about the article hate Morgenthau violently, not only because they believe his proposal blind and evil—though they hate the Germans, too, you understand!—but because it was so ill-timed. They believe, and I half agree with them, that the war would end sooner and with less pain and bloodshed if the politicians at home would keep their big mouths shut and lay off the fire-breathing talk of vengeance. If there's any fire-breathing to be done, let it come later, and let it come from the people who have most cause to talk of vengeance.

I am enclosing a clipping I took from that same issue of *Time*. I send it to you for two reasons: one, that it was written by that favorite person of mine, C. E. Montague; and two, though it was written in the time of World War I, it is strongly relevant to what I have written regarding the old ladies in the German farmhouse and the young couple who gave me hot milk. Here it is:

> How can you hate the small boy who stands at the farm door visibly torn between dread of the invader and deep delight in all soldiers as soldiers? . . . It is hopelessly bad for your Byronic hates if you sit through whole winter evenings in the abhorred foe's kitchen and the abhorred foe grants you the uncovenanted mercy of hot coffee and discusses without rancor the relative daily yields of the British and German milch cow. . . .
>
> When all the great and wise were making peace, as somebody said, with a vengeance, our command on the Rhone had to send a wire to say that unless something was done to feed the starving Germans, it could not answer for discipline in its army: the men were giving their rations away and no orders would stop them.

There is little I can add to Montague's statement. However, I believe the problem was simpler for the soldiers of World War I. The enemy was whoever wore a German uniform, and it was as simple as that. And notwithstanding the extravagant propaganda stories of "Belgian Nuns Ravished" and posters of children whose arms ended in bloody, mutilated stumps; in spite of the fighting hate that such propaganda may have inspired in the Allied heart, there was no basic conflict of ideology between the Allies and Germany. It is that which makes our problem so difficult: for them the enemy was an emperor, an army, a military aristocracy. We, too, fight an enemy, but our enemy is a people and not alone an opposing army. The people entire are our enemy because we fight an abhorred ideology which we believe has infected a nation, is blood and bone of that nation. And so, although our impulse is to accept unquestioningly the "uncovenanted mercy of hot coffee"—because we are not naturally a suspicious and reluctant people—and to discuss innocent topics "without rancor," we are torn by the everfresh need to decide how much of this "uncovenanted mercy" is just that and how much is sly and deliberate expediency. Where does the human being leave off and the National Socialist begin?

This is the thorn that tears our sides. And sometimes, in sick alarm, we wish that we could be more ruthless, perform this dirty business without also lacerating our own sensibilities, and having done, get us to our homes and forget what we have done.

I wonder if—when I'm civilian again—I will ever be able (or have the desire) to recapture for brief moments the peculiar kind of despairing homesickness that frequently overcomes each of us here. I think not. There is sometimes a lecherous delight in wounding the spirit with old memories, but a recapitulation of old misery, a return in entirety to past pain, is impossible except to the spiritually unhealthy. A faint whiff of it, perhaps—I think there will be moments of partial evocation. And you will glance at me in sudden alarm, until I look up and see you there and pull my world snug about my ears once again. So should it be, with all fortunate men.

You ask a lot of questions in your recent letters. I'll answer the possible ones, in the order asked.

Food: The food situation is enormously improved of late. We eat well. For breakfast this morning I had a huge scoop of oatmeal, three flapjacks drenched in apricot syrup, bacon, and coffee. It seemed adequate. There are still occasional meals of C rations, but that hasn't happened recently.

Bread: You ask about the bread I mentioned buying while we were in the Bastogne woods, and you want to know if bread was included in our meals in camp. Yes, it was: our army meals included bread, white bread, tasteless bread, bread of bleached sawdust. But the bread we bought in town or from the peasants who walked out to our camp to peddle it was a sour rye bread with an intoxicating smell and a crisp, crunchy crust. It was a rare luxury, and it tasted wonderful going down, but I found that once down, it lay in my stomach like a lump of lead. But it was good to eat.

Clothes: The wooden sabots I mentioned are worn by all peasants, regardless of sex or age. Entering a house, they leave the wooden shoes at the door and go about indoors in the black felt slippers that are worn inside the sabots. Sabots are always worn for farm or garden labor; for social occasions, church, or shopping, the citizenry don ordinary leather shoes, a little dowdy by our standards and very worn and tired. Clothes in general are like those at home—alas, no peasant costumes!—but neither as fashionable, as well-tailored, nor of such good quality. Years of war plus a native frugality explain that.

I've seen only a few of the "Victory" turbans you describe the smart Parisiennes as wearing. (My social observations are necessarily a little rural.) They are truly enormous and gaily colored and successfully worn only by a woman with a flair for style.

As for men's clothing, due largely to the prevalence of the bicycle as a means of locomotion, most of the very few men to be seen wear either plus fours (shades of my dashing youth!) or motorcycle breeches and black leather puttees.

Geoff and Sukey will be interested to learn that little boys in Belgium and France wear skirts. And even after they have graduated from skirts per se, they continue to wear skirted smocks of black or dark blue to school. (I can fairly hear Geoff's howls of outraged masculinity if you tried that on him!)

Buildings: There are no wooden buildings here. Everything

is of brick or ancient fieldstone, and many of the buildings are whitewashed. Often a mosaic in colored tiles is worked into the face of the house, and there is usually a niche over the front entrance that holds an image of the Virgin, or the Holy Family. Some of the figures are very lovely—I saw one today, very old and dim in outline but still graceful and gentle. It was carefully dressed in a new coat of paint: the Virgin in a robe the color of the sky, touched with gold, and the Babe in a scarlet smock.

December 16, Minerie.

Christmas Eve is a week from tomorrow. I can't lift my spirits over that homely fact and I find myself getting very bitter about the whole thing in a melodramatic sort of way. As if the birth of a Jewish sage and poet-prophet nearly two thousand years ago is of any avail to us today! We pray to God, and our chaplains invoke the blessing of that deity and his anthropomorphic son upon us. Then, heartened by the certain knowledge that God is on our side, we gird up our khaki-clad and itching loins and go out to hunt Germans, who in turn bear emblazoned on their belt buckles the quaintly incongruous legend *Gott Mit Uns!* It's a wonderful world. If I possessed a little more ruthlessness or a little less conscience, I'd be a gangster or a politician when I get home and a staunch pillar of the Episcopal Church on the side.

The buzz bombs continue. There is rarely a moment of the day or night when the heavy rumble-rattle cannot be heard overhead. We have become so accustomed to their constant presence that we no longer lift our heads at the familiar sound. The principal targets seem to be Liege and Verviers. When they land in the latter city, fifteen or sixteen kilometers from us, the heavy explosions rattle the windows here and shake loose plaster from the walls.

In the air the buzz bombs seem grotesque denials of the laws of aerodynamics. They are clumsy and misshapen, and notwithstanding their speed of flight, oddly lumbering in movement, the noses dipped slightly toward the ground with the tremendous weight of the explosive-heavy heads. At night they are blazing comets that move mysteriously across the sky, casting a rosy and ambulant nimbus behind the clouds.

We cannot understand why there have been so many in recent weeks. Is it the last all-out gesture of Hitler? That's our latest hope, based on encouraging late news of 1st Army successes this week.

Monday we start a formal training schedule. I've been selected (probably because of my classic brow!) to become the "tommy gun" expert of the squad. So on Monday I will report to the supply room, pick up a "tommy gun," and trot off to "Tommy Gun School."

This afternoon the entire battalion marched to Thimister, the next town, to say farewell to General Huebner, who is being transferred. The general decorated Colonel Grant, our battalion commander, with the Bronze Star and the Silver Star, and in a brief speech referred to the record of G Company as one "that no outfit could surpass." Is it being shamefully adolescent to admit that I cast scornful and superior eyes on the men of E and F companies?

Apropos of not very much, I guess, our current C.O.—Captain Shelby has gone home to the States on seventy-two days' leave—has issued an order forbidding us to wear either scarves or wool-knit caps in any formation. We cursed him under our breaths because a helmet is a cold and cheerless weight lacking a warm cushion of wool on these early-winter days. But we complied, naturally. And today, at the ceremonies for the general, not a man in the company wore either a scarf or a wool-knit cap. We marched the five miles to Thimister briskly, getting well-heated with the exercise, then stood ankle-deep in a marshy field for an hour and a half, waiting for the general to arrive. The sweat on our bodies turned to ice, our clothing was damp and clammy, and our teeth began to chatter. Our miserable state was not made more tolerable by the sight of our C.O.—and every other officer on the field—with beautiful, thick wool scarves snug about their respective necks. But the last crushing indignity came when General Huebner removed his helmet to wave it in cheery salute to the assembled men—and revealed a wool-knit cap on his head!

Oh, I've said it before and I'll say it again—the army's a wonderful place!

CHAPTER FOUR

"We didn't know this was the Battle of the Bulge until several days later."

December 20, morning.

I am sitting on the roof of a dugout somewhere in Belgium, or perhaps Germany—I'm a little confused—with a blanket wrapped around my shoulders. I believe I am in full view of German observation on the hill across the valley, but I'm beyond the range of small arms and I can always dive into my hole if they start lobbing shells over.

The past three days have been rough, unpleasant, and bewildering. I've had perhaps twelve hours' sleep in that period, and I'm numb from the lack of it so I'm not sure these comments will make any sense.

To go back to Sunday, December 17 . . .

After being assured by our officers of a long rest in our warm Belgian billets, a runner woke us at five-thirty A.M. to tell us we were ordered to an indefinite "alert." The Germans were dropping paratroopers in our vicinity, and the order from HQ was for at least one man to be awake and on guard in every house where troops were billeted. I don't need to tell you that none of us went back to sleep.

At ten A.M. the runner returned. "Get your stuff packed!" he said. "You're on a four-hour alert!" Sadly, silently, with no kidding, no boasting of prowess soon to be displayed, we packed. Merry Christmas!

We all hurried to write one last letter, that last and

most important letter. Then the word came: "No more letters will be submitted for censorship and mailing. Pack away or tear up those you have written." Things were popping fast and no officer had time to read our letters. We went to chow.

While we stood in the chow line, the order came to report to the company C.P. at three-thirty, packed and ready to leave. With our usual chow, we were given two thick sandwiches and told to save them until we got an order to eat. Our next meal was in the uncertain future, and those sandwiches might have to last a long time.

At three-thirty we said *"Au 'voir"* to our Belgian friends. They gathered at the windows and doors of their homes and gave us brave but uncertain farewells. They kissed us, shook our hands, and there was fright on their faces. We marched to the C.P. silently but for the sound of heavy feet on the cobbled streets and the faint tinkling and creaking of our arms and equipment. The town crept to the side of the road to see us go, a thin line of women and old men and children standing in frozen attitudes, gripped by old fears. Only the children tried to smile. As we passed, we saw the women, one after another, throw their aprons over their heads to hide their tears. It was a strange and somber farewell, and its pace was cortegelike.

It was six P.M. before we left the village, jammed in army trucks, cold, wet, and hungry. And scared. It was a long ride. All we knew was that we were heading for the front and our road was being strafed by Jerry planes. We were warned to be ready on an instant's notice to get the hell off the trucks and into the ditches. Fortunately, Jerry didn't come over—I don't know how we would have been able to abandon ship in a hurry when men and weapons and packs were wedged so tightly, so inextricably, together that to tense a leg muscle meant discommoding at least eight other men.

The traffic congestion on the road was made to order for enemy planes: tanks, jeeps, trucks, and "meat wagons" traveling both ways and with only the dimmest lights showing.

We would drive fifty or seventy-five yards and stop. A wait.
Another twenty yards and stop. Another wait. Then half a
mile and stop. A wait. The total distance we traveled that
night was not more than twenty miles, but it took us six
hours.

We passed through Verviers, a large city. It was in total
blackout, but as we passed the Civil Affairs Building, an
incautious civilian opened a door briefly and I caught one tran-
sient, poignant glimpse of a Christmas tree in the foyer, brilliant with shining gold tinsel and crimson lights. I felt sorry for
myself for a long time afterward.

At midnight we detrucked. We were in the middle of a pine
forest, the ground heavy with snow and slush. Not a building
in sight. Our squad was deployed along a road that branched
from the main highway and cut through the woods. We were
to dig in immediately on both sides of the road. I think I was
not alone in my sense of shock: others who were equally green
were suddenly realizing that this was, in truth, war! And the
enemy was near, so near that we were cautioned about noise,
cautioned to challenge every unfamiliar figure, cautioned to
keep eyes and ears alert, cautioned to be wary of danger from
the rear as well as from the dim black and white mysteries of
the forest that faced us. When we completed the digging of
our two-man shelters, we stood guard for the rest of the night,
one man resting while the other guarded.

Shorty and I removed our packs and dug a hole nearly a
foot and a half deep before we realized it was filling with
water as fast as we were digging. We weren't aware of it earlier because we couldn't *see* what we were doing, and
although we stood in the hole while digging, we were already
so cold and wet that a little more ice water made no impression at all. We held a brief, despairing consultation and decided
to dig another hole. I ate one of my sandwiches and enjoyed a
gloomy satisfaction in thus defying authority.

The new hole proved to be as sievelike as the first one. We
were only six inches above the water table. At three A.M. we
decided the hell with it: we'd finish in the morning, when
we could see, and take our chances on Jerry artillery until then.

Knowing I would not sleep—physical discomfort always has me wambling in throes of self-commiseration—I told Shorty to sleep if he was able and I'd stay on guard for the night. After we piled a thick matting of pine branches in the hole, Shorty went to sleep. I wrapped a blanket around my shoulders and over my head and tried to forget how cold and miserable I was and how my neck ached from the weight of my steel helmet. I counted the night away with cigarettes, cupping them in my hands to conceal their glow, and decided with sick and romantic abandon that there was small choice between death by pneumonia or a sniper's bullet. Pneumonia just took longer. Long before morning I left off starting nervously every time a tree in the forest behind me creaked with protest under its weight of snow. I began to imagine, almost with longing, several score of king-size enemy soldiers creeping up behind me with knives in their teeth.

Dawn came at last. I ate my second sandwich and made hot chocolate from a D-bar and water from the nearby, and doubtless unsanitary, stream.

All day we waited for something to happen, playing at sentry duty in growing carelessness. Rumors were thick: "The Twenty-sixth has been wiped out" . . . "The Germans have retaken Eupen" . . . "Paratroopers have landed all over Belgium" . . . "The Allies are retreating throughout the entire northern sector." We didn't know this was the Battle of the Bulge until several days later. I guess it was a good thing we didn't know how grave the situation was.

Gloomily, we saw the extension of the war into a far distant future. And only a few hours ago the end had seemed so rosily near!

Nobody really *knew* anything—where we were, when we would move out, or where we'd go from here. Some of our officers and noncoms told us it was possible that we might not be needed. Perhaps this was a false alarm and maybe we'd return to Minerie and pick up our vacation where we'd dropped it. Shifting our tired weight from one frozen foot to the other, we thought long thoughts of warmth and food and waited.

We stayed another night. The eighteenth of December, the week before Christmas. Between guard tricks I lay on a bed of soggy pine branches at the foot of a pine tree that dripped and whimpered all through the night. I tried to sleep and could not. There was some small comfort to be found in doubling up our guard tricks with the men from the next hole to ours. It meant standing guard for two hours instead of one, but we could talk in low whispers, we were not alone in the night.

On December 19 we were fed. With the chow truck came our bedrolls, an assurance that we would be staying for an indefinite period. We trudged up the slimy road to the place where the bedrolls had been dropped—in the mud, naturally—and carried them painfully back to our holes, tottering under the weight. Within two hours we were ordered to take them back up the road and prepare to move out.

No one seemed to know where we were going, but the whisper, "Minerie?" rustled faintly through the waiting ranks of tired, dirty men. I abandoned hope when the top-kick handed me two flares for my grenade launcher, plus careful instructions on when they were to be used. At the company C.P. we stripped to a basic combat load, dropping our overcoats in a pile by the side of the road and making another pile of our extra blankets. We kept one blanket apiece. At last the trucks rolled up; we clambered aboard and were off.

A few minutes before we left I peered over someone's shoulder to read a recent "poop sheet"—a mimeographed news sheet, issued daily, but rarely seen in our outfit. In it was the official news that Von Runstedt had launched a counteroffensive on a seventy-mile front, and that German paratroopers had been dropped over a wide area. It didn't look good.

We rode about fifteen miles, passing road signs pointing to towns like Malmédy and Stavelot, which the poop sheet had informed us were threatened by the German thrust. Finally the trucks halted. We climbed off and continued on foot, a column on each side of the road and twenty yards of safety between men. Approaching a village, we saw American tanks, tank destroyers, machine guns, and antiaircraft batteries bristling at every conceivable point throughout and around the village.

December 21.

Tonight is the longest night of the year. But every night is that when you're on guard duty.

I'll go on from where I left off yesterday when my cold hands dropped the pen and refused to pick it up again.

We moved swiftly through the village, but just as G Company started down the main street, we heard planes. All hell broke loose on the instant, with ack-ack and machine guns chattering like my teeth on the dog watch. We spread like frightened quail, diving into the muddy ditches that bordered the road. Shorty hit the ditch, which had a sizable stream in it, flat on his stomach. That seemed unnecessarily uncomfortable, so I hugged the bank and tried to look as humble and inoffensive as possible. (Not that humility has any noticeable effect on the dispassionate judgment of machine-gun bullets, but humility comes unbidden when the danger is close.) A moment later three Nazi planes, bombers, roared over our heads, seemingly so near that we swore later we could feel the heat of their engines. Why they failed to strafe us I cannot tell; we were visible enough, certainly, and they couldn't have missed knocking some of us off. It was a blood-quickening and mercifully brief experience; not without comic relief, I thought, as I watched Shorty climb from the ditch, his face a muddy mask and his clothes oozing water with every step.

We waited briefly on the chance that the planes might return. They did not, and we continued through the village. On the far outskirts we were assigned positions and ordered to dig in. Our platoon was on the point; that is, we were the most forward element of our group, and between us and the enemy there was nothing but scenery. I wished for something more solid. We huddled on the southern slope of the most beautiful little valley, but whether this was Belgium or Germany, I could not tell. I did know we were only a few miles from Malmédy, and near us was a village called Waimes.

Shorty and I dug a two-man hole where a hedgerow and a fence met. Seventy feet behind us, at the top of the hill, lay the road. Our nearest neighbors, a bazooka team, were on the other side of the road, and Shorty and I felt naked and forgotten in our lonely spot.

That first night, December 19, Shorty and I alternated on guard, two hours on, two off. It was bitter cold and we missed our overcoats. For outer garments we wore only thin sweaters and cotton field jackets. No gloves. Exercise had kept us warm during the march, but the long, motionless hours of guard in a damp hole were something else again. In my off-duty hours I tried to sleep and could not. Even though I rolled myself up in our two blankets, the chill of the ground crept through and held sleep away.

All that night the artillery roared, and continues still. If this was a battle, they were more disorderly affairs than I'd imagined, because the guns, *our* guns, seemed to be firing from all directions—as did the Germans—completely boxing the compass, with us in the middle. Even our squad leader didn't know exactly where our lines were. Our mission was to hold against possible attack from two areas. But it was precisely from those areas that most of our artillery seemed to be firing, throwing their shells into the German lines—against which we had apparently set our backs! Hopelessly confused, we appealed to the squad leader for clarification, but he said helplessly that his orders were to put us where we were and he could explain no more. We were very unhappy about our position. Our skin prickled with the sure knowledge of Jerries moving upon us from our rear while we, all innocent, kept careful watch in the direction of our own forces.

The buzz bombs kept coming. They threaded the sky in a bewildering haphazard of objectives, although most of them appeared to originate from the area where we believed the German lines to be. We observed one that behaved very oddly: after zigging where it should have zagged and vice versa, it seemed to catch fire. I could see the bomb clearly—it was about two A.M. and a clear night—and when the heavy sound of its muttering abruptly ceased, I held my breath and waited for the crash. It kept to its course, however, and the flame from its exhaust grew larger and brighter as it drew away, finally passing from sight beyond the horizon. There was much talk of it today, and many of us thought it might be a new secret weapon. It lighted enormous stretches of open sky and glowed in vast rosiness when it slipped behind the scattered clouds.

The artillery and machine-gun fire never stops, day or night. Lying down, you feel the concussion of the big shells in your stomach and, curiously, in your throat.

Shorty and I spent most of December 20 working on our dugout. (The old soldiers were right: you never get through working on a dugout. First you work for safety, and you work fast. Then, if a lull comes and you're still around, you work for comfort. And you are still improving, adding last touches, when the order comes to move on and you start from scratch again at the next stop.)

We enlarged our original hole, laid planks in the bottom, and covered them with a foot of straw. Both planks and straw were filched from the nearby farmhouse. Then a roof of heavy boards—we raided the farm woodpile for those— gunnysacks over the boards—we raided the granary, too— more straw over the gunnysacks—another foray on the barn—and finally two feet of earth over the straw. This was a palatial dugout, warm and sweet-smelling. We were very proud.

Again on the night of the twentieth we stood all night, two hours on, two off. But I slept warmly in the off hours and rose the next day feeling nearly human. Only once during the night did anything noteworthy occur. During one of my guard tricks a shell from our artillery struck a building in the nearby German-held town, setting a fire that burned fiercely for most of the night.

One of the more shocking incongruities in this latest phase of the war is the presence of civilians. The morning is thunderous with artillery, peppered with the crackling of small-arms fire, and then, in one of the small silences that fall occasionally like a lull in drawing-room conversation, we hear the mooing of cows, the sound of roosters crowing, and hens shrilly proclaiming motherhood. We watched a small boy and his dog romping together in the yard of a farmhouse in the valley below, the valley we have named "No-Man's-Land" and regard with suspicion and fear.

Today a seven-man daylight patrol went out on reconnaissance. We watched from our holes, saw them slip over the shoulder of the hill and through the woods at the head of the valley, moving cautiously and with rifles ready, rushing across open spaces that could not be avoided or circled, employing all the subtle, life-cautious tricks we'd been taught in basic training, tension speaking in every line of their straining bodies. And lo! Even as they progressed at their stealthiest, around the corner of the path came three civilians, a man and two little girls. They bowed deeply to the staggered and obviously outraged men of the patrol, the man removed his hat, and the three of them politely stepped from the path to allow the patrol through. A few yards farther along the path came another pair of civilians, a man and a woman, equally nonchalant, equally expressive of polite wonder at the curious antics of these men in uniform. A little disconcerting for the patrol, I thought. But even as I leaned against the dirt wall of my dugout, gasping with laughter, I was angry with a boiling rage. Because of the civilians, this serious death game in which we were engaged was made to seem like a neighborhood frolic of Cops and Robbers, and we were grown men discovered playing boys' games when we should have been doing the work of men. We felt, obscurely, that the civilians weren't playing fair; they were out of character. Or maybe we were. Anyway, Hollywood was never like this!

December 22.

It's a fatal mistake to make a dugout too comfortable; you always move out the next day. So we moved yesterday. Not the entire platoon—only our squad and a machine-gun section. We moved into the hills to the junction of a cart road and a footpath. The machine gun was mounted at this intersection, and Shorty and I, as rifle protection for the gun, were sent down the road to guard the left flank. Our bazooka team was assigned to the right flank, and in addition a hasty minefield was laid across the road on the right flank. The reason for the minefield, and its haste, was all too apparent: the fresh tread marks of a Mark IV tank were very evident on the road.

Shorty and I dug separate holes in a row of pine trees, parted from each other's comfort by fifty feet. Ahead of us was an empty, snow-covered field, and beyond it the German lines. However, with the exception of roving patrols, we felt relatively safe from German infantry. The tanks were the threat.

Six of us were to take turns standing guard through the night, from seven to seven. The two machine gunners comprised one shift, Shorty and I another, the bazooka man—Leo Allen, from Watertown, New York—and his partner made the third team.

I ended that long winter's night with a deep and lingering suspicion of all weapons platoon men. The machine gunners, a selfish and cowardly pair, screwed us royally on the guard business. Neither Shorty nor I had a watch, and the machine gunners knew it. With devious trickery and much manipulating of the hands on *their* watch, they succeeded in so befuddling us that when dawn came and we compared notes with the bazooka team, we discovered that Shorty and I had stood guard for over six hours, Leo and his pal for more than four hours—and those canny bastards, the machine gunners, had spent the night snug in their beds except for one small, under-nourished guard trick! Roll me over!

I could not sleep because of the cold. Our overcoats were returned to us yesterday, but an overcoat and a blanket don't provide enough warmth when my bed is the winter ground. Snow began to fall at ten P.M., a damp and clinging snow, and it fell throughout the night. My dugout was too short—I stuck out at one end—too narrow (I was forced to lie on my side), and only partially roofed. So today my fingers are cracked and swollen, a most subtle agony because fine woolen filaments from my clothing catch in the cracks and are drawn searingly across the raw flesh beneath.

Do I dwell on these physical miseries too much, these body aches from cold and wet and chap, and not enough sleep and not enough to eat? It would be more manly, more in the Spartan tradition, to gloss over such complaints, I know. But these are the things that gnawed at men fully as much as the threat of bullets and the fear of death; these are the things that whittled men to puny, whimpering smallness. These are war, too.

Shorty and I finished our last guard trick at four A.M., then sat together and talked until dawn, listening to the artillery and wincing at the howling of concussion-maddened dogs in the village.

We'd been ordered to be packed and ready to move at five A.M., because we were chowing at five-thirty and pulling out immediately thereafter. Five A.M. came, and five-thirty, and six, and we were wet and cold and the snow continued to fall and it was still dark. At six-thirty a messenger found us and told one of us to come for breakfast. (The chow system in the front lines is for one man of a team to go to the chow truck, eat, and take his buddy's food back in his mess gear. The waiting man gets cold food, of course, so they alternate in the business—one man getting breakfast, the other getting the next meal, and so on. Sometimes the system is altered slightly. The man who goes back gets two portions of every-thing in his mess gear, takes the food back to the hole, and both men eat together from the same gear. Then they *both* get cold food. The latter system was the one employed this morning, December 22.) I brought back a slopping mess gear of cold, unsugared oatmeal, cold flapjacks, and a dripping canteen cup of cold coffee. We ate with gusto. Then we stood around and waited until ten A.M. Finally the order came to pack up.

Wearily we returned to the C.P. and to the place where I write this—a stable, the foulest, most stinking stable I've ever seen. Our gear is in another of the farm buildings, but we're huddled in the stable with the cows because the heat of their bodies makes for a little warmth. Or so we tell ourselves. Poor beasts, they are very restless and complain ceaselessly in low moos. Small wonder—every damn one of them has a cold, wet, GI overcoat spread over her back! The theory is, the heat of the cow's body will eventually dry the coat, and truly, there *is* a little steam arising from the sodden coats. I don't think the cows are enjoying it much.

I don't know what comes next. When we reached the stable we were told we'd remain overnight. An hour later we were told we'd move out in half an hour and dig in in another field. We're sick with thinking about it because the snow is falling in fat, wet flakes, and the air is raw, and altogether it's as cold as the hinges of hell. But we're still here. Either we'll spend the night here or we'll move out after dark.

I don't have a helluva lot of spirit or pride at the moment. There is only a kind of determined tenacity, a stubborn "damn it all, I *will* hang on, and without whimpering . . . except to myself."

Saturday, December 23.

Christmas Eve tomorrow night. Is there a fat red candle in the window at home, as usual? And will it be a *big* tree?

We stayed in the stable the night of December 22. At six P.M. we were told that we'd each pull an hour's guard duty during the night, and shortly after that we were called out to unload several truckloads of barbed wire. At seven-fifteen the order came to get dressed and fall out, carrying all our ammo and arms. We were to act as guards while engineers laid several hundred mines and strung barbed wire in a sector half a mile away, where attack was expected.

It was one of those rare and perfect winter nights. It had turned much colder. The snow was crunchy underfoot—a helluva thing from the strategic point of view, but a familiar and lovely sound for all that—and the ground was hard and frozen, a delight to walk on after months of mud. There was a blinding half-moon, the stars were bright, and the evening star hung low in the sky and blazed like a snared buzz bomb. But it was *cold*. We stood guard in pairs, an hour on, an hour off. In our relief periods we retreated to a nearby farmhouse and sat in a cold, dark room, trying to warm frigid hands and feet over the flickering heat of a pocket-size heating unit. (These come in chocolate-bar size, and a fifth of a bar is supposed to heat a canteen cup of soup if you have soup, or coffee if you have coffee, or anything else if you have anything else. There are no directions on the box for warming feet.) We expected the job to last all night, but we'd finished by one-thirty.

In spite of the terrible cold, it was a memorable night. A few buzz bombs came over, the artillery was heavy—we watched the angry splashes of scarlet and gold all around the horizon—several German planes swept overhead, pursued by our ack-ack, and we saw one burst into bright flame and spin, Icarus-like, to the indifferent earth. I looked at the evening star, the Christmas star, and the old Christmas songs sang in my heart: "The Holly and the Ivy" . . . "In Dulci Jubilo" . . . "We Three Kings" . . . "O Little Town of Bethlehem" . . . and I remembered our Christmases and our shared joys and all the small things of Christmas—the wrapping paper and the seals, red ribbons and bayberry candles, greens in the window, trimming the tree and the mounting glory of it, the smell of Christmas spices and baking Christmas cookies. There's a lot I'll have to catch up on when I come home.

Back to our stable at two A.M. and to bed. Up at five-thirty for breakfast. I think I was still asleep while I ate.

A good mail haul today. Old letters—the most recent dated November 18—but it's mail. So far I've received no Christmas boxes, although some of the men have been getting them. [Note: My first Christmas box arrived several weeks after Christmas; my last on Easter Sunday. I mean this as no criticism of the mail service, which performed miracles. It was just one of those things.]

My most nagging worry these days is that I cannot write you. I know that soon you will receive the letter that told you I was back in Belgium, and the date of writing on that letter will just barely predate this big German counteroffensive which we know is being played up mightily by the papers at home. After that, there will be a long blank period, a time of silence. And I know all that you will be imagining, dreaming, and I can do nothing to spare you that needless torment, nothing I can do to prevent it. The officers will not censor letters for us when we are on line, a condition that may continue for weeks. Or months.

Don't know what's to happen tonight. We may stay here; we may move up; we may go out to string wire again. Last night one of our officers told us that two Jerries captured yesterday morning had admitted that a big attack was scheduled for today. We expected it at dawn (which explains the wire-and-mine detail of last night), but it is now late afternoon and nothing has happened. We're ready to move at a moment's notice—just in case we get it after all.

The same officer assured us that when this counteroffensive is broken and the Germans pushed back once more, it will be "the end of the war." When statements like that issue from the lips of authority, we are obliged to fight to maintain our precarious and tough-minded balance. It's always a losing battle, so far as I'm concerned: before I've finished counting to ten I find myself making plans, estimating the number of days it would take to get to Syracuse, New York, from here.

And according to this day's *Stars and Stripes*, the stock markets are soaring to new and crazy heights, drunk with the news of German successes and the hopeful prospect of the war continuing indefinitely. Christ, what a crazy world—where one half fattens on the other! I remember young Gilman, dead before he knew why he was here, what he was fighting for, and—okay, skip it.

December 24.

Afternoon, and bitter cold. And bitter thought, nor any comfort anywhere. No mail, no packages today.

A little excitement last night. Assigned to wire detail again, but this time *we* strung the wire. A slow and painful job, made doubly difficult by the burden of weapons and ammo that encumbered us. Imagine, if you are able: a night of zero temperature and the scene a snowy hillside. To protect your hands against the wire, you wear voluminous canvas gauntlets, the utility mitts worn by expert wire stringers. But your fingers soon grow numb from the cold, and the gauntlets are clumsy, fumbling things and you pull them off disgustedly, preferring to work in bare hands, ripping and tearing your flesh on the icy barbs and too cold to feel the pain until some minutes later. At last the stiff fingers refuse to bend at all and awkwardly you slide them inside your shirt, coaxing them back to throbbing life against the offended flesh of your belly—the only part of your body that is yet warm. You start to work again, and as you bend over, the rifle slung on your back swings forward, whacking you soundly on the noggin while the sling begins to twist and strangle you. In the meantime your ammo-weighted belt drags painfully at your hips and the hand grenades clipped to the edges of your jacket begin to weigh about eight pounds apiece. Finally, just as you are about to perform the last delicate adjustment on a strand of wire, that goddamn gas mask swings around and dangles in front of you, directly in the way of your once-more-frozen hands. Great sport, the whole business.

It was another wonderful winter night. But I was busier than I'd been the night before, and there wasn't time to brood lovingly over the memory of Christmases past. About eleven P.M., after we'd been working for four hours, the enemy started to throw mortar shells at us. There had been a bustle of Jerry activity for some time previous—flares, observation planes, and the like—and we were painfully aware of our silhouettes against the snow, picked out in stark relief by a glaring moon.

The first shell landed a safe distance away, but the second came in only 150 yards from where two engineers, the platoon sergeant, another noncom, and myself were working. We hit the ground. There were no dugouts at hand—not even a hollow in the ground—and we feared the shells would fall in a "ladder" pattern: an artillery design in which the successive shells "search out" the target as though moving up the rungs of a ladder. After a tense moment of waiting, the sergeant took off in search of the rest of the squad. (Our work had tended to split us into separate small groups, working independently. Our immediate group was alone on the hill, with the rest of the detail scattered in the woods behind us.) A moment after the departure of the sergeant, the remaining noncom took off for the nearest outpost, shouting something over his shoulder about "calling the C.P. for orders." (He was an excitable twenty-year-old and something of a little bastard—not that there's any connection.) The two engineers and I alone remained, and they agreed as one man that they were "engineers, not infantry," and took off. For a moment I hesitated, then decided the hell with this hero's death business. And I took off, too.

I met the excitable young noncom on the road. He was even more excited than usual, waving his arms and yelling incoherent orders to get back to the C.P. because "beaucoup Jerry tanks and infantry were heading our way." Hastily assembling, we raced for home on the double and counted noses when we got there. Three men were missing. One of them was Shorty.

We sat in the stable for a while, talking in low tones, listening nervously for the artillery barrage that would signify a real attack. But nothing happened. After a bit, in spite of alarms and worries, we drifted off to our respective beds.

Just as I crawled into bed, sick at heart with wondering about Shorty, he appeared and slid in beside me. His story was

simple: he'd been working near our first line of dugouts and
dove into the nearest foxhole when the shelling started, sharing it with the occupying doggie until the danger seemed to be
over. The other missing men were safe, also. One of them had
come in with Shorty, and the third had been discovered at the
C.P. When the first shell landed, he went to pieces, weeping
hysterically and cowering in a dugout until a soldier led him to
the haven of the C.P. This might sound like cowardice, but it
wasn't: the man was one of the old veterans of the outfit, with
a good record in Africa and Sicily. But he'd been wounded
three times—he returned from the hospital only a few days
ago—and had reached the saturation point. He couldn't take it
anymore, that's all, and no one blamed him.

In the morning, the attack having not yet come, we learned
that the "beaucoup tanks and infantry" were the vision of an
excitable sentry who saw a Jerry patrol and permitted his
fancy to mushroom it into a large-scale attack. And at four
A.M. a Jerry patrol fired on one of our outposts and wounded
two men.

According to rumor, our officers, and the newspapers, it
might well have been the end of the war if this big German
offensive was stopped. That bright hope was our sole topic of
conversation. I tried not to consider it; I tried to shut from my
consciousness everything but the immediate job, however
painful, small, or dirty. Because if I allowed myself to think,
my thoughts would be of Ree, and how it was for her at that
moment—the sudden full stop in the flow of my letters, the
ominous news broadcasts, the scare headlines in the newspapers. And always, pounding in her brain, taken from my last
letter, "somewhere in Belgium" ... somewhere squarely in
the path of the Von Runstedt juggernaut. To contemplate what
her days and nights must be like ... and there was nothing I
could do about it.

It is still December 24.

I am writing this in a foxhole, from which I have just witnessed a sight particularly thrilling to the earthbound infantry-

man—a mass bombing attack by our planes, thousands (count 'em!) of our planes. Wave after wave of bombers and fighters sweeping serenely across the sky, long silver bodies glistening, thin plumes of smoke like bridal veils trailing, and above them, below them, around them, the dark blossoms of bursting ack-ack. I say "sweeping serenely." That's a misstatement: not all of the enemy ack-ack missed, and I saw several planes explode in the air or dive in long, graceful swoops to the ground.

To us in our foxholes, cold, miserable, and disheartened by inactivity, the spectacle was alcoholic in its effect. I saw men with tears on their cheeks, and I know my own eyes were blurred. We strained our faces to the sky and yelled vulgar, heart-warm encouragement: "Give it to the bastards, you beautiful big-assed birds! . . . Pound the living ———— out of 'em!" And so forth.

It was the size of the attack, the number of planes involved, that was the real miracle. I gave up trying to count them after I'd tallied six hundred in twenty minutes and saw them still coming from the west. And now, good night. I feel happier, cheered by what I cannot help but believe was a good omen. Maybe it'll be a good Christmas after all.

December 25, and a Merry Christmas to you.

Last night after chow we relieved a squad that had been on line for several days. So I spent Christmas Eve and will spend Christmas Day in a dugout facing the German lines. Ah there, Adolf! *Fröhliche Weinachten!*

It was a beautiful and grim Christmas Eve. Shorty and I spelled each other on guard throughout the bitter cold night. The cold I could endure, but an additional misery landed on me in the middle of the night. I got the GIs! That's *always* a tragedy, of course—although in normal life, with the luxury of a civilized bathroom at hand, it would seem only an embarrassing annoyance—but this time the tragedy was of major proportions. You see, our dugout is on the crest of a hill, smack in the middle of an open field and with never a bush or tree to provide cover. It's not modesty that bothers us, you understand: it's snipers. We peer anxiously in the direction of the German lines, unbutton our pants in the dugout, hold them up with one hand while we clamber out, and get the business over in a hurry. We wipe on the run—our naked and chilled buttocks quivering in anticipation of a bullet—and button up again when we're once more safe in the dugout. A half-naked man crouching on a hilltop is a defenseless creature, unnerved by the constant sense of his nakedness framed in the sights of an enemy rifle. I winced and shook each time I dropped my pants, expecting every moment to be caponized by a German sniper who combined marksmanship with a macabre sense of humor.

The artillery fire was heavy until midnight. Then it died away, became sporadic. (Because it was Christmas Eve? I wonder.) In the strange silence, the war seemed remote, and I was several thousand miles from Belgium for a few moments. All night long I discounted the time difference between us and tried to see what you were doing. . . . Now she's telling the kids for the hundredth time that yes, *yes*, *YES*, they'll see Santa Claus tonight . . . now she's getting them into their snow suits—it must be just about time to start for Mother and Dad's and the usual Christmas Eve festivities. . . . Now everyone is there, and the house is bulging with noise and joy. . . .

And thus, until six o'clock this morning . . . Now she's home and in bed . . . sleeping . . . crying, maybe? . . . Wonder if the fat red candle is burning in the window for me, burning all night for me? It was, I knew it was . . . I could see it in the Belgian sky and in the German lines, and it was inside our dugout, making a pine-scented, rosy warmth where a moment ago there had been hoarfrost and frozen mud.

We got no breakfast this morning, Christmas morning. Our squad leader forgot to send a messenger to tell us to come to chow. We waited and hoped and peered anxiously for sight of the runner until there was no longer any point in hoping. Except that it was Christmas morning, I didn't mind the missed meal: my interior was worn out from my late tussle with the GIs. Later in the morning I opened a can of C rations, made a little coffee, and ate two dog biscuits. Shorty opened a can of hash and ate it cold. Christmas breakfast! We munched in unhappy silence, and I brooded over the memory of our customary Christmas *stollen* (how ironically German!), so richly stuffed with raisins and nuts and citron.

A beautiful Christmas Day, clear and not too cold. Many planes overhead . . . many shot down and plummeting earthward. God rest you, merry gentlemen!

The artillery was vigorous. I watched the shells bursting on the hillside and thought incredulously, It's not . . . it can't be Christmas Day! This couldn't happen on Christmas!

The lack of mail, especially Christmas mail, is a blessing. Lacking tangible evidence to the contrary, I could regard the day almost calmly and say, "See? It isn't really Christmas after all!" (Who did I think I was fooling? I wonder.)

We had a real Christmas dinner, although it was cold when we got it. Turkey, dressing, potatoes, giblet gravy, corn, coffee, cake, and a fistful of hard candy. A feast.

Must stop writing now. My legs are going to sleep from the cold, and my fingers are so cracked with chap that I cannot hold a pen with comfort. A Merry Christmas, darling! And a merrier one next year.

December 26.

Still in my dugout on the hill. I am sitting on the rim of it, ignoring the possibility of snipers and determinedly relishing the warmth of the sun on my back. This is an admirable feat of concentration because the sun warms only the thin surface of my hide, and my legs, dangling in the hole, remain stubbornly numb. Within, I am stiff with cold, a core of ice encased in faintly warm skin. Dirty skin.

Heavy shelling throughout the night and all day thus far. Our artillery is really laying the wood on the little town in the valley below us. Some of the buildings are but a few hundred yards away, and we watch the movements of the German troops with something more than curious interest. There seem to be quite a lot of them.

Last night a small and daring task force of our engineers crept close to the town and mined a road on its outskirts. An hour or two later a German light tank innocently rumbled down that road. The sound of the explosion when it hit a mine and blew up brought a smile of satisfaction to the face of every doggie on the line. Shortly afterward, one of our tank destroyers scored a direct hit on a German tank or half-track. It burned most of the night.

My morale hit a new low last night. I wallowed in black despair, near to the frenzy that must often afflict a man imprisoned in solitary confinement. During the day it was my memories of other Christmases . . . but at night it was the bitter cold . . . the absence of everything I love—music, books, conversation, Geoff and Sukey, you—they all piled up, making a load of misery before which even Ella Wheeler Wilcox would turn away defeated.

Must stop. The Jerries are sending us holiday greetings. More later.

December 27, and back in the stable again.

We were relieved last night after chow and came back here to spend the night.

Do you recall the man I told you about, who went to pieces when the Germans started shelling us, the night we were out on a wire detail? He's no longer with us. Here's what happened:

All the following day, the twenty-fourth, he sat morosely alone in a dark corner of the stable. Learning he was from Syracuse, I rushed over to him, ready to call him "Friend! Pal! Brother citizen!" He responded to my joyous questions with grunts, unfriendly monosyllables that indicated a complete disinterest in hometown reminiscences. Complete disinterest, period. Colorless face heavy with a black stubble of beard, he huddled deep in his overcoat and stared before him, seeing things that none of us could see. He spoke to no one. The old men looked at him, talked among themselves quietly and turned away, helpless. We were uncomfortable and uneasy, infected in spite of ourselves by his tension.

At dusk we wearily prepared to return to the line. We started off, single file, and the forepart of our column had just rounded the corner of the barn when we heard a shot from the rear. There was a startled yell from the assistant squad leader, "Hey, Sarge, c'mere! Joe B. just shot himself!" The sergeant raced to the rear and we sat down in the snow to wait.

It was true, the poor devil *had* shot himself—but only in the hand. A bullet through his palm. He said it happened while he was "loading his rifle." We said nothing among ourselves, although every one of us knew that it's impossible to shoot yourself through the hand while loading a rifle. Today we heard that he's to be court-martialed, and we're in a fine rage.

It's a particularly maddening example of "the army way." Everyone here—noncom, old vet, new replacement—has known for days that the man was teetering on the verge of collapse. His nerve was gone, and it was no secret. His officer should have been aware of that, too; it's his business to know such things, and to take the proper measures. Here in the front lines a man in that condition not only is unable to guard his own life, but is a threat to the lives of the men around him. Lives hinge on each other here, and no man survives by himself alone. That being so, why not send a man in his condition to the rear, ship him to England for a few months of real rest? Why use him, or any man already so pitiably used?

And now they will court-martial him. If real justice were done, his court-martial would be conducted not by officers and before officers, but by doggies and before doggies like himself; by men and before men who have known the same small agonies of sleepless nights and weary days, the cold, the wet, the mud, the long marches, the full loads on aching backs (there are no jeeps to carry the gear of enlisted men) ... by men and before men who have lived the slow terror of always the unknown, the score rarely revealed and the odds always against them. Officers, no matter how worthy, cannot fully comprehend the cumulative weight of the small miseries. But small miseries will break a man quite as thoroughly as a surfeit of battles, guns in the head.

[Note: The passage above was quoted from my journal as I wrote it at the time. That's the way I felt, and I was an enlisted man. It's the way we all felt, and as such it can stand. A footnote is necessary, however, because in the months that followed, I acquired a different slant on the subject.

[The original statement is correct in the main, and I reaffirm the salient points: (1) the man should not have been sent out again; (2) his commanding officer should have been aware of his condition; (3) his trial should have been conducted by enlisted men, not officers; (4) officers do not fully appreciate the small miseries that wear on enlisted men. The stoutness of my belief in these four points is not shaken. However, point 2 deserves the justice of this addendum: his commanding officer may have been aware of his condition and yet been helpless to do anything about it. Long before I was commissioned, while I was still a buck sergeant—but commanding a rifle platoon—I made bitter acquaintance with that tragic circumstance. There were long weeks when the platoon was so short of men, so skeletonized, that every man physically capable of carrying a weapon and moving on his own two feet had to be used. There was no choice. Had I listened to my conscience and refused to put into the lines men who should have been in rear area rest centers, I'd have doubled the work, doubled the danger, and risked the life of every other man in the platoon. Too many times the assigned job was too big, the sector too large, the objective too loaded with danger, and I had to use every man available, including even the recognizable borderline cases. I'd have used even the lame, the halt, and the blind. And I'd pray and cross my fingers, hoping they wouldn't break, that they'd be stiffened to one more effort by the knowledge of our need for them. I'm humble with pride to remember how few of them did break. They were great guys.

[I don't know where the fault lay, but it was somewhere in the rear. Remembering how long we rotted with inaction in the Bastogne woods, waiting to be used, while at the same time the men of the 16th Infantry fought and died in the Hurtgen Forest and waited for replacements, I am led to believe that most of the time there were large pools of replacements in the rear, stagnating in snarls of red tape. They just never reached the front fast enough, and I never commanded or was part of a full-strength platoon at any time during the war. Our full complement of personnel, our full T.O., was not attained until long after the war was over.

[A further footnote: The outcome for the man who shot himself was a little happier than seemed likely at the time. In view of his previous good record, the court-martial charges against him were dropped. Several months later I saw him once more. He was working with our kitchen crew, a member of our mess sergeant's staff. He was never returned to line duty.]

To get back to December 27.

As I said, we returned to the stables last night. Three days ago Leo Allen and I, on private reconnaissance, had discovered a vacant top floor in one of the farm buildings. Now we moved in, ignoring the outraged squawks of the chickens who roosted in the room below and thus regarded our intrusion as an invasion of their privacy. From a discarded benzine can we constructed a stove, attached a length of stovepipe—we patched the shrapnel holes with flattened tin cans, tied on with wire—and voilà, we had an apartment! Five of us slept on mounds of hay we filched from the barn, but it was not a night of uninterrupted domestic bliss. We had just gone to bed and I was snug and warm in my new sleeping bag when the call came, "Get it on! We're stringing wire tonight!"

It was another clear, still night with a nearly full moon. Our task took us well within small-arms range of the German lines, and we were not happy. A couple of burp guns could have wiped us out. But there was no sound, not even the occasional remarking of rifles.

It was a grim and tense business for all that. The shelling of the village had continued into the night and several buildings were blazing. The silent flames so near us, the still night, the engineers, ghostly in white snow garments and laying mines in silent haste, and we ourselves, laboring wordlessly and freezing to immobility each time the stubborn wire uttered a protesting "twang"—all the ingredients for a fine dramatic tension were present. But like all dramatic moments too finely attenuated, too long unresolved, the magic in the scenery and the props began to wear off and the whole affair became pedestrian and tiresome as the night progressed. We were conscious of being very weary, and after a while we were careless about keeping our voices at whisper level, and hell, those dumb Jerries couldn't see us, and for Pete's sake, how long have we gotta work anyway?

And then the villain of the piece made his entrance—out of the clear night a German plane suddenly dove toward us and zoomed only a few hundred yards above our heads, the roar of its motors shaking the ground and tearing at our ears. He was upon us so quickly that we could do nothing but freeze where we were, hoping pathetically that he would mistake our motionless figures for misshapen tree stumps in that snowy field. In a moment he'd passed over us ... he was gone! Instantly we were hot-footed into action, racing for the frail shelter of a small, tin-roofed outbuilding nearby. There we waited for fifteen minutes, but the plane did not return and we went back to work.

Twenty minutes passed and suddenly he was upon us again, so low that we could see the black bat shape clear and evil against the milky sky. This time we stayed in the field after he had gone because we were so nearly finished with our job. We worked frenziedly, the hasty sweat chilling our bodies like a needle spray. Once more he zoomed overhead, and our hearts stopped as we waited for the burst of his machine guns. Still he did not strafe. We were bordering on hysteria when we finished what was probably the lousiest wire-stringing job in the ETO and raced from the field, slowing our flight only when we were safe in the shadowy lanes between the hedge-rows. It was midnight when we reached home. And we slept like angels, warm for the first time since leaving Minerie.

A strange and terrible thing happened yesterday as we were being relieved on the line. I had come in before Shorty—he stayed out there until the relief arrived to take over our dug-out—and when he joined me at the C.P., he was still excited and sputtering with rage at what he'd just seen.

Our artillery had been shelling the small village in the valley for hours. Although many of the buildings had been wrecked by fire and shell, a scattering of civilians still lin-gered, clinging with desperate hope to their homes. Yester-day afternoon the Germans evicted them and headed them toward our lines. There were twenty women and children and three old men, and some of them were wounded. Wav-ing white flags, they approached our lines slowly, fearfully. They were fifty yards short of our positions and clearly visible against the unbroken white of the open field when the Jerries in the town behind them started lobbing mortar shells.

Shorty said it was a bad ten minutes up there—the wretched civilians lying on the ground, clawing at the frozen snow with desperate, bleeding fingers, and over the sound of their cries the flat, vicious explosion of bursting mortar shells and the dangerous humming of shrapnel. Some of our men, ignoring the bursting shells, ran out and dragged or carried the fainting civilians to the nearest holes. There were some wounds from the affair, but happily, no deaths.

Ho Hum Department: Tonight we go out on wire detail again. Last night's order stated, specifically, "a single-apron barbed wire entanglement." A moment ago came the order to return to the same place and make it a *double* apron!

December 28.

Four hours on wire detail last night, and I looked forward to a warm bed when we finished. Six men were required for

a reconnaissance patrol, however, and I was one of the unlucky ones.

I was scared. We rested in the kitchen of a farmhouse until
twelve-thirty (I didn't sleep), and then dressed ourselves in
makeshift snowsuits that had been fashioned from sheets.
We were in combat dress—no overcoats, no galoshes—and
the snowsuits hooded our helmets and covered our bodies
to the knee. The sleeves were crudely mandarin, huge and
entangling.

At one A.M. we set out, our mission to go as deep as possible into German territory and discover what we could about
the German force opposing us—its size, disposition, equipment, outposts, and so on. We were to try to take a prisoner or
two, but a firefight was to be avoided unless thrust upon us.
Until five A.M. our artillery would take an intermission. We
had to be back by then or run the risk of being under the fire of
our own guns when they opened up.

I think I have never been so cold, so wretched, so frightened. I decided that a patrol was the worst of all war assignments, particularly in winter. (Nothing I experienced in later
months changed my mind—patrolling remained the job I
hated and dreaded beyond any other.)

It is the slow piling up of fear that is so intolerable. Fear
moves swiftly in battle, strikes hard with each shell, each new
danger, and as long as there's action, you don't have time to
be frightened. But this is a slow fear, heavy and stomach-
filling. Slow, slow . . . all your movements are careful and
slow, and pain is slow and fear is slow and the beat of your
heart is the only rapid rhythm of the night . . . a muttering
drum easily punctured and stilled.

You wait for zero hour at the point of departure. Huddled
in a shadow, you listen to the last low-voiced instructions, get
the final checkup: "Joe, tighten the stacking swivel on your
rifle—I heard it rattling . . . Mac, leave your wristwatch here
or put it in your pocket. It shines like a headlight! . . . Gantter,
your shirt shows. Pull your sheet closer around your neck . . .
Now listen, you guys! We go out in this order: first Joe, then

me . . . then Mac, Parks, and Gantter . . . Bryan on the end. Keep plenty of distance crossing the open fields, close up when we hit the hedgerows or the trees. If you see anything, freeze! Don't get trigger-happy—that ain't your job tonight! If we hit the ground, stay there until the guy ahead of you starts to move, or until you hear me tap with my fingernails on the stock of my rifle . . . twice I'll tap, like this!" In the un-breathing stillness the faint tapping of his nails on the smooth wood is like the clattering of castanets.

"Okay . . . here we go! And for Chrissake, *be quiet!*" While he was talking, your eyes slipped past him and to the white fields ahead, to the dark patches of trees, the shadowy smears that were hedgerows.

Now you're ready. While you were busy with last-minute preparations, the men in the nearest hole made a gap in the barbed wire. Wrenching several of the iron supporting stakes from the frozen ground, they have flattened the sagging wire by lying on it, and now you can cross. One by one you go over the wire, lifting the skirts of your snowsuits high to keep them from catching on the barbs. A wire twangs as someone steps clumsily, and you freeze for thirty seconds. Then on again. Once free of the wire, you move swiftly, your flick-ering eyes returning anxiously and always to the comforting shape of the man ahead. The crunch of snow is alarmingly noisy, and you experiment briefly with techniques of walk-ing, trying to minimize the dangerous creaking. Knees high, feet coming down flat? No . . . it slows your pace and you begin to fall behind. There is an agonizing moment when you cannot see Parks, the man ahead, and you leap forward fren-ziedly, snow-walking techniques forgotten in the impulse of your panic. The snow is deep, over your knees, and already you're tiring.

Now you're in the middle of the field, moving steadily toward a hedgerow that debouches like a dark artery from the distant huddle of trees. The hedgerow looks safe, inviting, and you wonder why your leader continues to move forward on the naked breast of the field when the shadows of the hedgerow promise such haven. You turn your head for one swift look behind, in the direction of our lines. There is nothing there, you can see nothing. Not a man, not a dugout, not a suggestion of the wire entanglement through which you passed not five minutes ago. The six of you are alone, midway between worlds.

A fierce whisper from someone ahead: "Down!" You collapse noiselessly in the snow, falling flat but remembering to keep your rifle upright so the muzzle will not be clogged with snow. You're quivering with excitement and fear, and your helmet has slid over your eyes, so you cannot see. Cursing silently, you struggle to right it, feeling a bubble of hysterical laughter in your throat. What a Sad Sack! Fifty million helmets in the army and you can't get one that fits!

A few convulsive movements and at last you can see. You lift your head a cautious three inches and peer ahead. Nothing! Not even the white-clad bodies of the other men. There, in the trees! A shadow that moved? *Did* it move . . . was it (you finger your rifle, fumbling for the safety catch) . . . no, only a branch in the wind. A faint sound—there on your right, in the hedgerow! No, it comes from the left, from *that* hedgerow! Now every bush holds menace, every shadow. In what covert lies the patient sniper, pale eyes watching? Behind which tree the machine gun, the burp gun? If they see us, why do they wait? Until we're on our feet again, a slow line of easy targets, and then—one short traverse of the machine gun?

So you lie and wait and count the seconds and quiver at the many small voices of the frozen night. You begin to be conscious of cold—biting, searing cold—and with a sense of shock you realize that the warmth of your body has melted the snow under you and you're lying in a pool of ice water. Your genitals flinch and withdraw and you feel them tightening, drawing up . . . up . . . inside your belly, retreating to the dimly remembered fetal warmth. The raw humor of hysteria shakes you, and you recognize it as hysteria but for a moment you cannot control it, you do not want to control it. (S'posin' . . . s'posin' they really did pull up . . . s'posin' they got stuck there, didn't come down again? . . . I knew a guy, what'd he call it? . . . Testicular descension or declension or something . . . what would I say when Geoff asked me? . . . "Well, son, they weren't exactly *shot* off, but I did sorta *lose* 'em in the war!")

The cold deepens in your bones and blood, and your teeth begin to dance. With shaking fingers you fumble in your pockets for a stick of gum. You chew it, jerkily, and wedge the softened wad between your teeth. It muffles the sound of chattering, though the jaws continue to jig.

Still you lie there . . . colder . . . colder . . . colder. Fear is forgotten now and only the cold remains. At last a faint blur of movement ahead, a faint whisper—"Come on!"—the faint suggestion of a white arm sweeping in the "Let's go" signal you learned in rifle squad training at Camp Wheeler. Slowly, stiffly, you arise. Then forward. Before you've taken ten steps your dripping snowsuit has frozen and become a widely flaring kite, a crackling mockery of camouflage. Without slowing your pace, you try to crush the stiffness between your hands, soften it with rubbing so that it will not rattle. At last the hedgerow, the clump of trees. A stealthy searching of the little grove. All clear! And you relax a little, breathe deeply for a moment. The first leg is over.

A brief consultation and you start off again, still moving toward the German lines. Now it is routine: the open fields, the stealth, the whispered order—"Down!"—the slow paralysis of waiting, the advance, the relief of the next hedgerow. With every small advance your tension grows: the whispering of your garments is an alarum tremendous and shattering; the creaking of a frozen branch is heavy with danger. Those trees ahead—there's a Jerry listening post there; that hedgerow must be the first line of enemy positions—it's *got* to be, don't you see, because that's the logical place *for* a defense line!

There was more than two hours of it. At last we stood on the rim of a sunken lane frequently traveled by the enemy, to judge from the trampled snow. We lay in ambush for an hour, waiting for the German who would be the prize of our expedition. But we were unlucky—none passed.

Cautiously, we crept to the farmhouse, which was being used by the Germans as a C.P. In the yard were light tanks and armored cars, ample indication of the enemy's armor and equipment. Once, an eight-man patrol passed nearby, not close enough for us to latch on to a possible straggler. Me, I was just as glad. The hell with this prisoner business, this patrol business! I was cold and I wanted to go home.

At four-thirty we turned back, racing across the field with reckless abandon as we neared our lines, our frozen snow garments grotesquely extended and crackling like frozen sails. We turned in our report and hit the sack. Got up at six-thirty long enough to have breakfast, and went back to bed immediately after. Tonight we go back to the lines.

In response to my fervent pleas, my wife's letters were now extra thick, extra fat, requiring double postage. However, the letters contained therein were brief notes only: the extra thickness was a padding of toilet paper, the most precious gift I could receive during those winter months. Far from conventional bathroom facilities, and afflicted almost constantly with the GIs, we came to regard toilet paper as one of the supreme achievements of civilization. [Even the exquisite Marlene Dietrich, bless her, can testify to the misery of the GIs, having herself been a sufferer during her ETO tour. One tribulation I am confident the lovely Marlene was spared: I'm sure that someone, possibly a major with nothing else to do, saw to it that she was supplied with paper!]

I'm no stranger to certain rural customs: I've heard about corncobs, and I know how the hairy-chested will sneer at my whimpering, but they don't grow much corn in Europe and I have it on good authority that a handful of pine needles is no substitute. You can use a lot of paper with a touch of the GIs, and a dozen trips a day is only a *mild* case. Figure that in terms of paper consumption! Fortunately, many of us carried one or two books in our packs, gifts of the Council on Books in Wartime, an organization I cannot praise enough. Even after having been read, those books continued to minister to our comfort. I knew one guy whose sole remaining treasure in life was a pocket-size Shakespeare. Alas, poor Yorick! First he worked his way through the comedies, starting with the ones he liked least, but at last he was compelled to begin on the tragedies. He'd reached the third act of *Antony and Cleopatra* when at last a truck arrived, loaded with supplies and sundries.

I was luckier than he in my period of woe—my book was a historical novel of no great significance, and the manner of its destruction gave my conscience no qualms. On the contrary, it gave me an obscure satisfaction, and I never tore out a page without recalling other historical novels of similar quality that I would have enjoyed so using.

Passage from a letter, written December 28, 1944:

Last night, huddled around the stove in our chicken-roost bedroom, we fell to talking about the abnormality of our life up here. We discovered, to our mutual surprise, that none of us have had any compelling sex urge for months. It puzzled and even disturbed us that it should be so because, aside from one nineteen-year-old, we are all mature married men, well-accustomed to a normal sex life. We batted the subject around for a while and finally came up with an answer that should allay any worries you might have—at least so long as we're in combat! We decided that we are incapable of normal human feelings in a world that is violently abnormal, alien to all our habitual patterns. Existence itself has a dreamlike quality and normal appetites hint of the grotesque. I suspect that abnormal desires, perverse tastes, vices of a spectacular and violent nature would frequently seem more authentic, more in character than the normal. If we were stationed in or near a town, our hunger would be as insistent as though we were civilians; if we were anyplace where the life around us approached the normal, the urge for satisfaction would be irrepressible. But this, this life that is no life, this eating, breathing, sleeping, defecating—this is a cardboard imitation and we no longer recognize our own flesh.

And if you prefer a less esoteric explanation—we're just too damn cold to think about sex!

December 29, 1944.

Something new has been added to my winter costume. Taking an O.D. bath towel, I drape it carefully over my head, on top of my wool-knit cap. Held in place by the weight of my helmet, the towel falls over my shoulders and back, a combination hood, snood, and wimple. It helps to keep the icy winds from fingering my spine. In spite of taunts from Shorty, I am convinced that it gives my unmistakably Nordic features a soulful Arabic cast.

I wish the smug people at home could see this "best-equipped army in the world," particularly in our present dress. We read about us in rare magazines and hometown papers, and we look at ourselves in stark amazement. No matter what the papers say, we *look* like Czech guerrilla forces. Shorty has constructed a fancy headgear from an extra scarf he skonavished. Since it was of double thickness, he opened one end of it, making it into a kind of sock. With his jackknife he then cut a hole in one side of the "foot," a hole just large enough to encircle his eyes, nose, and mouth. Pulling the thing over his head, he flips the loose ends about his neck, claps his "steel" on his head, and voilà! A balaclava helmet, homemade!

Another GI, Schiaparelli, boldly removed the wool liner from a sleeping bag, slashed off the bottom at knee length, cut two armholes with a jackknife, and *he* had an overcoat that was the envy of the entire company.

I've invented a new game to while away the guard hours. Lacking a watch, Shorty and I must guess when our two-hour tricks are up, and my invention serves as both game and clock. Here's how it works:

The average "popular" song contains 32 bars or measures. Allowing four beats to the measure (since a fox-trot is in 4/4 time), there are thus 128 beats to the chorus of a song. Two songs, or two choruses, would then contain 256 beats.

Establishing a mental beat and drawing on my repertoire of

"pop" songs, I progress through the alphabet: "As Time Goes By"..."At Last"..."Am I Blue"..."At Sundown"..."Begin the Beguine"..."Blue Skies," and so on. Not singing or whistling—I *think* each song through, following the convolutions of melody and chord in my brain, and when I have thus "sung" two songs, I know that five minutes have passed. (To compensate for the 44-second difference between my 256 beats and the 300 seconds in five minutes, I set a rhythm that's a shade slower than one beat per second.)

Part of the game, from night to night, is to avoid repetition and use only songs I have not "sung" on previous nights. Another self-imposed challenge is the avoidance of tunes I dislike—"Dinah," "Blueberry Hill," "I Love You Truly"— even when I've exhausted my stock of titles for that letter of the alphabet. For tough letters like X and Z I substitute "I" titles because there are so many of them.

It's a good game because it's semiautomatic: the top half of my brain remains alert and clear and on guard. And it helps to shut out the dreary refrain that forever tries to sneak in the back door of my consciousness: "When will it end?"

A sorry business, isn't it? Such are the pitiful subterfuges to which we resort—anything that will bridge, even for a moment, the pit of misery over which we're suspended.

The winter of 1944–45 was the real beginning of the long debate at home on the fascinating question "Will He Be Changed?" It was, by all accounts, a field day for the feature writers, particularly those prominent in the female magazines. One of the few *sane* articles was written by Dorothy Parker, but most of them were pretty bad. Ree was interested, naturally, and sent me a boiled-down version of the typical article, inviting my comment. I was happy to oblige:

First of all, my comments are mine only, although I believe that most married men, *happily* married men, would submit the same answers. For single men the problem is different and infinitely more complex. Anyway, here are my comments, point by point:

(1) No, I won't be homesick for this life. I'll not be homesick for "packs and field kitchens." [Sic! Honest, that's what the article said!] Nor for dugouts and C rations and army shoes, and the weight of several hundred rounds of ammo dragging at my shoulders. Nor for mud and snow and cold, and a week's stubble of beard on my face and a month's dirt on my body. Nor will I be homesick for danger, lie awake nights pining for the familiar sweetness of German 88s crooning over my head. I *will* miss some of the men I have known, but the friends I've made will be friends still when we are civilians again. As for being homesick for guys with whom I can talk, knowing they understand—ah, if you only knew how good it would be to come home to people who speak my language!

[I was wrong here. I learned when I reached home that, without discarding my old civilian language, I had learned a new tongue in the army, a special language born of an experience foreign to the civilian. I *was* homesick for that language; I am still, sometimes. Perhaps I sound like a "barroom veteran," a sentimental drunk who slobbers fond army memories over his third beer. That isn't so, but I think every veteran has known what I have experienced, bitter times since I came home. You're talking to a civilian (maybe he used to be one of your best friends) and suddenly there is discomfort present, a nausea that hits you abruptly because you realize that you're bouncing your words against a stone wall of incomprehension. More than that and worse than that, it is a disinclination for the mere effort of comprehension. Somewhere back in the war months the route of common experience had split, becoming two roads where there had been only one. It was the unique friendship that could conquer, thus divided.]

It assumes that this war experience will be the greatest thing in a man's life. That seems to me an exaggerated judgment. My active participation in this war is a circumstance that has obtruded on the life I had planned. I don't discount its importance, nor can I predict its particular effects on my life in the future. But as I see it now, the circumstance of my soldierhood doesn't stack up with the importance of being a husband and a father, doesn't stack up with the importance of accomplishing something in my chosen career.

(2) It *will* be difficult in some respects to take up once more the responsibilities of a civilian, "after depending largely on the decisions of others in my life." But I'm a rebel at heart and resentful of having my life directed and molded by the decisions of others. The prerogative of making my own decisions again will be zestful rather than otherwise.

(3) On the futility of making anyone at home "understand things"—that will be a tough problem for the inarticulate. Being naturally a gabby sort of person, I expect less difficulty. It's a frustration I won't encounter too often.

[I was wrong about this, as I indicated above. But I am convinced that the gap could have been bridged, however tenuously, if the people at home had tried to understand, had wanted to understand. Most of them didn't: in part because they were tired of hearing about the war, in part because they were more concerned with the recounting of what *they* had endured and accomplished, and partly because they had been persuaded by feature writers and such that we didn't want to talk about our war experiences and it was bad for us to be urged.]

(4) Yes, I have built a "dream house, a dream life, a dream family." But I don't think the reality will seem meager and unsatisfying. It will be different, it won't be the dream come to life—that I know!—but I think it will be the reality and not the dream that has the extra richness. [Lacking a few small details, I was right on this.]

There will be other problems a little more complex, a little more difficult to define. Certainly there will be a readjustment, which will vary in intensity with the individual. But it *needn't* be painful! Remember, the adjustment from civilian to soldier was tough, too, but mostly because it was unwelcome. It was rape, not seduction, and we resisted. Our roots clung valiantly to home soil. We're ready and

eager for *this* readjustment, for the change-back from soldier to civilian, and most of the sins and blunders committed will come from overanxiety.

And I repeat, the whole business will be much more
complex and painful for the single man. The married man
coming home to the very private haven of married love has
a security, a starting stake that cannot be matched by even
the most devoted and understanding parental love. Children
will help enormously, too.

[Everything I have observed since coming home bears
me out on this point. I think a survey of veteran troubles and
veteran unhappiness would indicate that an overwhelming
majority of the cases involve either single men or men who
married hastily, in a romantically patriotic mist, shortly
before shipping overseas.]

December 31, and the end of this lousy year.

Yesterday we had a little barrage of 88s from Jerry. We
huddled in our hole, bracing ourselves against concussion,
the dirt from our roof cascading on our heads with each
shell, tensing ourselves against the One. It didn't come,
although a close one landed not thirty yards from our hole. I
was greatly comforted that my current siege of GIs was in a
"lull" stage. It would have been a helluva time to *have* to
leave the dugout.

Notwithstanding the daily testimony of shells, this has not
been an active sector. We are holding and the Germans are
holding and that's about all that can be said. A little patrolling
every night, a little small-arms fire occasionally; the remainder is desultory artillery fire. No deaths in the past week,
although several men have been wounded. Yet our forces
dwindle daily, a sick list composed of men suffering from
frostbite, trench foot, the "bloody GIs," and similar line dis-
eases. Several cases of pneumonia. It is a slow, whittling-
down process, an exquisitely long-drawn attenuation of our
numbers and our morale. A war of attrition. And no replacements arrive.

About three more months of wretched weather to live

through. Last night we were permitted to stay in all night: no patrol, no wire-stringing, no guard duty. We kept the stove red-hot all night and slept close to it.

Every now and then I am engulfed by a wave of unreality and I feel like a sleepwalker, moving with outstretched hands and shuttered eyes through a room that is strange and filled with alien terrors. There is always the bitter shock of awakening, the realization that I am here and this *is* my life and all I have to live.

January 1, 1945.

Happy New Year! When would you like me to arrive home? My fingers are crossed for (a) the end of the war by February 1; (b) home by Easter. Wonder how wild I am in my guesses. [Note: Haw!]

No New Year's Eve noisemakers last night, but we had our own special brand of New Year's excitement. Here's what happened. Our kitchen being several miles to the rear, chow is brought up at mealtime in a jeep and trailer. The kettles are set out in the courtyard of the farmhouse and thus screened from enemy observation. Last night we formed for chow when the Jerries opened up with some of their six-barreled mortars, and their apparent target was the courtyard. We scrambled for the shelter of the house and barn—built in 1781 of massive gray stone—and in a moment the steaming kettles were deserted. We bided in safety until the danger appeared to be over, but no sooner had the line re-formed than the shells started to drop again. I filled my plate with "seconds," so I fared rather well. But the Jerries were obviously zeroed in on the courtyard, and many of the men—the sensible as well as the timid—scurried to the cellars, eschewing food for the moment. Tempted though I was to follow their wise lead, my stomach won an easy victory over common sense. Dessert was raisin pudding, and I like raisin pudding. I had the courtyard, the chow line, and the raisin pudding to myself, and the mess sergeant was hiding in the cellar. So I had thirds. And then—well, damn it, I *like* raisin pudding!—I had fourths and fifths!

No casualties from the shelling, but most of the remaining

windows were shattered by concussion, and a direct hit started a fire in the hayloft. We formed a bucket brigade and worked for an hour and a half before the last spark gave up.

Another uninterrupted night of sleep and warmth. I can face the next forty-eight hours on the line with equanimity now. We go out after chow tonight.

Today a German plane was shot down, crash-landing just in front of our lines. The pilot was unhurt, and he was marched to the C.P. for questioning. He swaggered in, wearing an insolent grin and a beautiful fur-lined flying jacket. Half an hour later he emerged from the C.P., minus both grin and jacket. At chow tonight Lieutenant Jim Krucas was resplendent: *he* was wearing the jacket . . . and the grin! *C'est la guerre, c'est les brass!*

From a letter:

You say you want to know more about the minutiae of this life because the Hollywood version doesn't ring quite true? Bravo, me love, you're a wise and discerning female!

You ask what I'm wearing to keep warm. Here's the list, from the bottom up: overshoes (at last!), shoes, double-sole woolen socks, woolen drawers and undershirt, wool shirt and trousers, sweater, another wool shirt over the sweater, scarf, field jacket, overcoat, gloves, wool-knit cap, the towel snood I described to you, helmet liner and steel helmet. Sounds like enough insulation, doesn't it? Perhaps too much. But it's betwixt and between: it doesn't keep the chill out during the motionless hours of guard duty in zero weather, and it's too heavy and sweat-provoking for any kind of action.

Our dugouts are much more solidly constructed than they were in Bastogne. We make them deep and roomy, and roof them solidly with wood (any kind of wood—old fence posts, doors, beds, etc.) and pile several feet of earth on top.

No, I haven't seen any USO shows. Some weeks ago while we were in Germany, Marlene Dietrich came through with a unit, and a few of the guys were selected to go. But our quota was small and my luck was bad.

A minor footnote that you will like as I do: recent prisoners have informed us that the Germans have a special name, a most felicitous name for our big artillery pieces, the 240s. They refer to them as the "Whispering Death." On the other hand, the American doggie, a tough-minded, sardonic realist—and how sharply this points out the difference between the German mind and the American!—calls the German six-barreled mortar "Leo the Lion"!

January 4, 1945.

No change in our routine here: forty-eight hours on line, forty-eight hours' rest in the farmhouse. Nothing else, save the patrols. We shell the enemy sporadically; they return the compliment in a weary tit-for-tat fashion, neither side trying very hard.

The days go by so slowly. I mark them off on a homemade calendar, and each canceled day is a minor and bitter triumph. I've reached the point where I hate to see the rare copies of *Stars and Stripes*; Allied gains are minute and the reports are tepid.

This morning, as we bull-sessioned in our chicken roost, the talk took a diverting and horrible turn and we exchanged stories about men whose sex organs have been maimed or destroyed. The talk of lonely men is curious. Each one of us—there are eight now sharing this room—soberly admitted that he didn't want to go home, he *won't* go home if he's hit like that.

January 5, 1945.

Out on another recon patrol last night, from midnight until five A.M. It was pretty bad. We went deep into Jerry territory, so close we could hear them talking and coughing, but we failed to get a prisoner. Again we laid an ambush by a well-worn trail and stretched on our stomachs in the snow for a solid hour and a half. I use the term "solid" advisedly: that's how our blood felt when we gave up at last and creaked our way homeward. No point in describing the patrol in greater detail—it was like the other. I still hate and fear patrols worse than anything else.

Shorty promised that if anything happens to me, he'd see to it that my writing case, these notes, and all my personals were delivered home to you.

We go back to the holes tonight.

January 8, 1945.

Tonight I'm really low, hitting rock bottom. Too much snow and ice and mud, too many long nights and too little sleep, too few letters—the total of my woes up and hit me over the head and I am thoroughly cowed and miserable.

Three nights ago a runner appeared at our hole. It was ten-thirty, and he said we were to pack up, we were being moved to another position on the line. See? Like I told you, it's always that way—Shorty and I had completed our hole that very day. After long and painful scraping, we had at last made it long enough and wide enough and had just hung "tapestries" on the walls to keep out the damp—gunnysacks cushioned with straw and pinned to the dirt walls with twigs. So now we had to move, and in an evil temper, we packed up, staggered after the guide, and finally arrived at our new position. We regarded the unbroken snow with bitter resignation. We had to dig a new hole, starting right then. This would be our "night" home, and each night we would stand guard here. Our "day" hole, which we'd been told had already been dug, was in a hedgerow a hundred yards to our rear. Two positions were necessary because the night hole was nakedly exposed to enemy observation and we'd be unable to leave it in the daytime.

We started digging. After removing two feet of snow and ice from the site, we discovered that our entrenching tools would not dent the iron-hard ground. I borrowed an ax from the nearest farmhouse and we chopped the top layer of frozen earth into manageable lumps. A thin snow that froze as it fell added an additional soupçon of misery to our woe. We worked all night, and shortly before dawn I went to chow, bringing Shorty's breakfast back with me. Then we picked up our gear and moved wearily to the "day" hole we'd been told about. We hurried as we approached the spot, anticipating something like the comfortable two-man hole from which we'd been hauled the night before. Already we remembered that old dugout of ours with the sentimental warmth of home.

At first sight of our new home we dropped our gear and looked at each other in stupid disbelief. Sure enough, there was a hole, but it was for one man only, and he a midget. Shorty, five feet two, was unable to squeeze in.

Tearing off the wooden roof—it had to be chopped loose— we started digging again. The ground was frozen and very rocky, and we worked in dull anger, saying little. We labored throughout the day and barely finished replacing the roof when it was again time for us to return to the night hole for another twelve hours of guard duty. About that time a very small German, armed with spitballs or a bean blower, could have whipped me to a standstill. I'd had no sleep in three days and I reeled when I walked.

Painfully, we resumed work on the night hole, and another rifle team appeared and began to dig a hundred yards from us. We worked without pause until midnight, stopping when a runner hurried up to tell us that a German patrol had been reported moving through the woods, heading our way. We passed the word to our neighbors and they left their digging to join forces with us. (Their hole was but a scratch in the frozen ground, offering no protection in the event of a scrap, while ours—after two nights of digging—had progressed to a depth of two feet!)

The four of us huddled in the hole, peering over our low barricade of sandbags, straining to see movement in the misty gray of the open field, suspicious of every quiver of sound in the whispering hedgerows. Shoulder-to-shoulder, we sat on sandbags in the bottom of the hole, our knees touching our chins. Our legs cramped and we felt the bitter cold crawling up our bodies, inch by tortured inch. One of the visiting team had brought two blankets, and we draped one over our eight legs. The other we tried to stretch to cover four backs.

It was a long wait and nothing happened. At three-thirty the squad leader of the other two men came along and told them to take off, back to their daytime hole for some sleep. (They took the blankets with them, the dogs!) Our squad leader didn't show, and Shorty and I hung on until dawn before returning to our own daytime hole. Got a little sleep, but spent most of the day working on the hole, trying to make it livable.

From now on we'll get only twenty-four hours' rest after each forty-eight-hour trick on the line. The system is: two squads on line, one resting in the rear. Tonight we go back up again, this time relieving a squad in still another section of the line.

I learned that Shorty and I were moved because the Jerries took three of our men in a raid on one of our outposts and their capture left a gap in our line.

It snowed all night, and is still snowing, and I'm a little sick inside at the prospect of going back out tonight. My muscles and bones ache with fatigue, all my joints (particularly my fingers) are badly swollen, and my nose drips like a . . . well, like an old drip. How am I going to get through the next forty-eight hours out there?

In spite of the cold and the misery and the long dreariness of the hours on guard, there was often a piercing sweetness to the winter nights. At times it was possible to forget the circumstance of war; sometimes the guns would be silent or become a far-off murmur, like summer thunder. Then the earth had the black-and-white vigor of a woodcut, and the blaze of the stars was intimate and searching. I invented new mental games and tormented myself with visions of home. One night I heard music. In my head was the golden bell voice of Flagstad, singing the "Liebestod." I could hear the dark shifting patterns of the horns, the long sweetness of strings, and over all rose that magic voice, spiraling slowly upward in the last affirmation of grief and triumph . . . so real that the old poignancy caught me unprepared—"Tristan is dead!"—and I was undone by it. I stood in the brittle starlight, to all appearances a sentry on duty, but with eyes so blurred I could not have seen an enemy patrol fifteen paces from me. The tears froze on my cheeks and I didn't know and it didn't matter . . . "Tristan is dead!". . . Loki had slain the sun god and all the world was winter.

January 31, 1945.

There's a long gap between this and my last entry because things happened fast after January 8 and I was too busy to write. Now I'm having a helluva sweet time trying to sort out the sequence of events.

We returned to the lines on the night of January 8—that much I remember clearly. And I had a tour of duty at the "listening post," an assignment I didn't like. The listening post was, simply, a standing place in a little grove of trees, 150 yards forward of the nearest dugout and on the uncomfortable side of our barbed wire. You took a field telephone with you when you went on duty and reported frequently to the C.P. If too long an interval elapsed between calls from the post, the C.P. assumed that the man out there had been killed or captured. The assumption was usually correct.

After the listening post, there was a day's rest in the chicken house, and then back on the line again, an emergency call to fill in a squad that was shorthanded. It was necessary to supply four men from our squad, and we drew cards for the assignment. My gambling luck was at its usual low level, and I groaned as I reached for the rifle I'd just placed in the corner. The lucky ones—and a more unfeeling bunch of stinkers I never saw—curled themselves comfortably around the glowing stove and made sleepy and unkind remarks.

Shorty, having drawn a high card, was not going out. My partner for the night was to be the man I described a few pages back as the "Worst Citizen-Soldier of the Year," whom I've called B. A night in his company was not a happy prospect.

The squad leader to whom we were being loaned indicated that our post was to be the night hole where Shorty and I had labored so many hours. Already the night was off to a lousy start, but the real wallop came later, when we arrived at the hole. Only a few days before, Shorty and I had been jerked from our snug dugout and sent to this desolate spot to plug a "vital gap" in our line. So the shallow night trench we'd scratched in the frozen ground was still unfinished, and now filled with new snow. It was evident that no one had occupied the position since we'd been there. Now it was a gap, now it wasn't, now it was—were the Germans also dancing about in their positions as erratically, or was someone in the C.P. playing games?

Well, we were there, and unless B. and I were to spend the night digging, we would have to stand guard in the open, an easy target for a passing patrol. I decided to stand: I'd spent enough hours working on that damned hole. B., already whimpering, flatly refused to have anything at all to do with a place so inhospitable. Rolling himself tightly in his blanket, he lay in the snow and felt sorry for himself. During the next eight hours he groaned without cease, wept bitterly, and offered me five thousand dollars—a new high for him—if I could help him get out of the army. I'd have done it for free. He could not sleep because of the cold, but he refused to get up and share the guard duty. Two hours before dawn my patience wore out, so I kicked his ass until he arose, then I told him to get the hell out. Weeping, he trailed off to the barn, and I settled my chin in my blanket, feeling almost at peace with the world.

That night was a long ten hours. I spent most of the time perched painfully on the low branch of a tree, grimly regarding the desolate expanse of frozen field and wondering if any Germans were stupid enough to leave a warm fire and come out in this weather. No one came to relieve me, and at dawn I gave up and started for the barn. . . .

Again the days blur. I recall Shorty and I being separated and sent to different positions on the line for a brief period. It was while we were out there that Miller, a grinning, freckle-faced guy, was killed out on patrol. It happened at four-fifteen one morning, fifty feet from the "point" dugout where I was on guard duty.

Miller, an old man in the outfit, had been second in command of an eight-man patrol that had gone out at midnight, led by Lieutenant C., our new platoon leader. The lieutenant was a recent transfer from a stateside ack-ack outfit, and he didn't know from first base about infantry. Perhaps he was a nice guy, personally, but he was no infantryman. The platoon always felt that he was directly responsible for Miller's death, and I guess he was. He lasted only a couple of weeks. Shortly after Miller's death, he was hospitalized with the flu and never returned.

By three-thirty A.M. the eight-man patrol had completed its mission and was on its way back. I counted heads as it neared my position. One . . . two . . . three . . . four . . . five . . . six . . . seven . . . eight! No casualties, no prisoners. They broke even.

Suddenly the eight figures collapsed noiselessly in the snow, flat on their stomachs. I couldn't figure it out. I learned later that the lieutenant believed a German patrol was trailing them, and, being strictly the eager-beaver type, he wanted to get it. (No one ever tried to explain why he chose to set an ambush fifty feet in front of his own lines, directly in the path of the supporting fire he might require from us! But that's what he did, and he was in command: his decisions were the law.) For forty minutes they lay there while Miller, an old hand at this game, repeatedly urged him to bring the patrol inside our wire and there await the enemy patrol. The lieutenant refused. I could hear the faint murmur of their voices and see the dim blur of movement every time Miller left his own place in the snow and crossed to the lieutenant, trying once more to persuade him.

At four-fifteen our artillery opened up. That was someone's mistake, because the artillery had been ordered to remain silent until six A.M., the deadline hour for the return of the patrol. Only three rounds were fired, two of them screaming harmlessly overhead as they sped toward the German positions. The third round, an airburst, was short, and it caught Miller. He alone of the eight men lying in a close semicircle was hit. He said simply, "I'm hit . . . help me . . . help me . . . !" and died.

As the first shell whined over, I dove for the bottom of my hole. When the short round exploded, I cowered under a rain of frozen earth from the roof of my dugout. A few seconds later there was a hubbub of hysterical sobbing as the remaining men of the patrol fought and tore their way through the wire. Two of them plunged headlong into my hole and the rest took trembling shelter beside it, huddling against the side and talking in frenzied gasps. They said Miller had been hit and they thought he was dead. The lieutenant raced for the squad leader's dugout, slid in on his stomach in one movement, and frantically called the C.P. He excused himself from going back to help with Miller: he "had to report."

I stretched myself on the sagging wire, holding it down with the weight of my body while two of the men in the patrol went after Miller and carried him in. After a while the medics arrived, but there was nothing they could do, we knew that before they got there. Gently, we laid his body beside my hole and straightened his arms and legs before they stiffened. We sat close together in the hole and tried to talk, but were conscious of the body outside . . . how cold the air was . . . the brightness of blood against the snow . . . how gaily he had played with the children in the farmhouse the night before. It was several hours before bearers came and carried his body away.

Blunders are not as infrequent as they ought to be. Men are killed or wounded daily by the miscalculations of our own artillery, our own planes, our own faulty weapons and imperfect ammunition. Some of it's inevitable, I know, but it's the last tragic irony so to die. I hope there's no last-second realization for those who die that way, no final, biting awareness of blunder and waste.

Most of our casualties-by-accident are the fault of fumble-fingered gun crews and defective shells. Short rounds are the major cause, and the principal sufferers are the men in the most forward and exposed positions. Last week one of our men had his jaw blown off.

* * *

A few nights ago the Germans captured one of our outposts. Three men. When the telephone reports from the outpost abruptly ceased, a search party was sent out. The men had vanished, and so had the telephone, and there was only the mute evidence of a GI helmet in the snow.

Afterward, there was much discussion on the fate of the captured men. One of the men was a Jew, and although he undoubtedly threw away his dog tags in order to conceal his name and his religion, it was believed likely he was shot anyway, on the double assumption of his markedly Hebraic features and his circumcised state. (It's commonly believed, whether true or not, that Jewish soldiers captured by the Germans are summarily executed, and that a man who is circumcised, whether Jewish or not, is regarded as such by the Germans.) Today our gloomy suspicions were confirmed: several recent Jerry prisoners, quizzed individually about the raid on the outpost, admitted that the three men had been "executed."

[Note: This story has a strange and happy ending. One afternoon, several months after the end of the war, I was reminiscing with Leon Loeb, the company mail clerk, and we recalled the capture of the outpost. The day's incoming mail was delivered as we talked, and Loeb began to sort it. Suddenly he exclaimed in blasphemous wonder and held out two cards for my inspection. I looked at them, at him, and we exchanged foolish, happy grins. The cards were Change of Address forms, requesting that mail be forwarded to a certain military hospital in the States. And the names on the cards were those of two of the men who'd been captured on that long-ago night. They had sweated out the war in a German P.W. camp, were released at the end of the war, and were shipped home. We marveled at the happy circumstance and spoke sadly of the fate of the third man, the Jew. Two weeks later *his* Change of Address card appeared in the mail!]

We were relieved about January 10 for a brief rest. That night we walked to the nearby village of Waimes. Our lieutenant blundered and led us in bleating circles for two hours while he tried to locate the houses in which we were to bed down for the night.

In the morning all was indecision. No one knew whether we were staying in Waimes, going back, or going forward. Shorty and I amused ourselves exploring.

Our house had been the property of a lady pharmacist named Otti Riegel. Her shop on the ground floor was a shambles of broken glass, oozing syrups, pills, and ointments, but the living quarters on the second floor were still livable. We prowled in the attic and deduced, from the litter of correspondence and photographs, that she was a Belgian Nazi, or a German Nazi residing in Belgium. We also found some pencil drawings of remarkably faithful, or hopeful, details of male anatomy, which indicated that Otti was a right lusty wench.

The schoolhouse next door was our second field of exploration. Before the Von Runstedt breakthrough, it had been used as an American field hospital. Hastily abandoned by our troops in the December retreat, it was a veritable treasure house of medical supplies and equipment. In the attic, however, was only schoolhouse junk: desks, blackboards, books, primers, chalk, exercise books. Other junk, too: furniture and dishes from private homes. (The Belgians were no dopes: they knew that American planes and artillery spared schools and churches as much as possible, and all through Europe such buildings were jammed with the larger valuables of civilians.)

Rummaging through the dishes, chairs, sewing machines, and tables, I picked up a small wooden cylinder—a miniature rolling pin carved with curious figures—and a pang of homesickness swept me. It was a cookie press, employed in the making of spicy Christmas cookies called *springerle*, and exactly like one my grandmother had used when I was a small boy.

We skonavished two cans of ether and returned with them to Otti's house. Shorty said ether would burn, and we needed a light. It did burn, fine, with a delicate blue flame, but we couldn't figure out a way to stop it from exploding. In the end our neighbors complained so bitterly about the smell that we had to throw the cans away.

Figuring we'd be leaving soon, we hesitated to install a stove in our room. But night came and we were still there, and all night we shivered on the cold floor while our wiser neighbors in the adjacent rooms lolled comfortably near warm stoves. In the morning we said, "The hell with exploring, let's get warm!" and rigged up a stove. We should have known better. Getting comfortable in the army is like waiting for a telephone call that doesn't come and doesn't come and *doesn't* come and finally you decide to take a bath and just as you get wet all over, the phone rings. Our stove was just beginning to burn well when the order came to pack up.

We saw twenty-four German prisoners brought in just before we left. They were searched and questioned in the alley between our house and the school. Everyone went over to take a look at the supermen, and I went, too. But I couldn't take it: I felt sick within five minutes and returned to the house.

I'm a sucker for words, I'm the dewy-eyed answer to a demagogue's prayer, and I guess I'd been snowed under. I'd thought we stood for something a little better, a little higher, than the Nazi brutality we professed to abhor. Hell, I even thought we were fighting to put a stop to that brutality! I had believed we were sincere when we called the Fascist and Gestapo practices a denial of our civilization and our humanity. I really believed we *did* believe in the dignity of man. And the scene in the alley sickened me because it was wrong and I knew it was wrong and there was nothing I could do about it.

Killing is clean. An enemy is an enemy is an enemy, and as long as you can believe that, you can kill . . . you shoot to kill. But torture is dirty, torture is ugly, foul, twisted, debasing both the victim *and* the wielder of the whip.

The twenty-four Germans in the schoolhouse alley had been killing Americans, or attempting to. They were doing what they'd been disciplined to do and ordered to do, just as we did what *we* had been trained to do and ordered to do.

There was no immediate evidence to connect these twenty-four Germans with specific acts of brutality against Americans or against American allies. And even with such evidence, I would still protest the deliberate viciousness of their treatment that afternoon. I'd protest for reasons of pride if every other argument were shot to pieces under me: pride in our own highly touted American principle of justice, pride in the much more fundamental principle of humanity.

Some of the prisoners were found to have American cigarettes in their pockets; some of them wore small articles of American equipment. These were singled out for special treatment beyond the slapping and mauling that all were getting. They were regarded as cold-blooded murderers of innocent American soldiers, and they were beaten, slugged by hard American fists, kicked in the testicles by vicious GI boots, knocked to the ground and trampled upon. Most of them were young—seventeen, eighteen, nineteen years old—and some were crying, helplessly, like children. And their "crime"? The American cigarettes in their pockets, the small items of GI equipment they wore? The odds were, they had picked up these things, as we'd picked up the German loot *we* were carrying about. And I mean we *really* carried it! Nine out of ten of us wore or carried some article of German issue—as I was then wearing a German Luftwaffe belt—which we'd picked up somewhere. These prisoners were part of a victorious German army that had swept through an area lately held by Americans. It was natural that they would have in their possession bits of the vast litter that a retreating army leaves on the field.

When at last they were led away, I watched from my window. They were forced to run down the street, even the lame and the wounded, with their hands clasped awkwardly on top of their heads. Beside them ran one of our officers—gentleman by act of Congress!—screaming obscenities at them in an incoherence of rage. As he ran he jabbed their rumps with his bared trench knife, and the gray-clad buttocks grew dark with blood. His reason? Justification? Excuse? His brother was wounded the night before by a German shell fragment. The fact that these were German *infantrymen* did not prevent him from paying off his grief and resentment on their helpless bodies.

Maybe I'm soft; maybe I shouldn't be wearing a uniform. But brutality, however sweetened by the hot justice of the moment, is brutality still, and it doesn't matter whether its agent is a German, a Jap, an American, or the deacon of a church.

There are many who will shrug helplessly and say: "But it's war! What can you expect of men in war?"

My answer to that is unprintably vulgar, so I'll say, simply: War is not always insanity, constant and unrelieved. There are moments, yes—there are moments when the precarious framework of our morality goes under, drowned in a black, atavistic surge. But they are moments only: the flood retreats and the old structure still stands, even though damaged a little. The danger is this: there is a heady intoxication in the giving over of one's self to that black torrent, a blind and animal exultation that sings dangerously in the blood. It is the death wish made manifest, and I have seen men bow to it, seen them voluntarily and eagerly forswear the responsibility of their morality to wallow, dazed and raptured, in that bloody bath. The Germans in the Battle of Hurtgen Forest who advanced singing, their arms outstretched, were drunk with more than wine; the Americans who baited the hapless German prisoners in Waimes were intoxicated with more than victory.

If there is a theme to this sermon I sing, it is an old and worn one, simply this: we are kin to both the apes and the angels. We have a propensity for labeling our more admirable qualities and calling them "American virtues." Our consciences thus drugged, we're free to relish the cruelties and barbarisms of the enemy; we bounce in orgasms of horrid pleasure and chant at the top of our lungs, "*Americans* were never thus, never thus, never thus!" Crap! When you read your newspaper's account of the Malmédy massacre, the 140

Americans who were shot down in cold blood by their
German captors, don't get your b——s in an uproar. I can
match that story with accounts of German prisoners who
were shot down in blood equally cold by some of our own
"gallant boys." And it doesn't matter that in my stories only
two, or five, or eight German prisoners were shot, whereas
140 Americans were murdered at Malmédy. Because the
number doesn't qualify the crime, does it? Murder is not a
matter of quantity—one victim or one hundred, it is still
murder, bestial and foul, an act in denial of all law and all
humanity. I hope the Malmédy murderers are caught and
executed, but believing in that justice, I must also believe in
the justice of executing those Americans guilty of the deliberate murder of unarmed and unresisting prisoners of war. I
believe that.

We left Waimes about January 12 and moved up, passing
through ruined Faymonville. In that village we lingered until
dark, seeking refuge from a sudden German barrage in the
wrecked houses.

I had forgotten Christmas was so freshly past. Now I
remembered, was obliged to remember. The half-ruined house
in which we huddled had been hastily abandoned by its inhabitants while they were in the midst of their Christmas preparations. Flung on the bed in one room was a partially trimmed
Christmas tree, some of its ornaments still unbroken ...
shining gold, silver, and crimson. A Star of Bethlehem glittered on the tip, and fastened to several of the branches were
glass birds with flowing silken tails. My German grandmother
had had such ornaments for her Christmas tree.

It would have been lighted with candles, the softly shim-
mering light I remembered in magic years past. The clamp
candle holders were already fastened to the dry and withering
branches, and boxes of ornaments stood nearby. The men
amused themselves with tossing the unbroken ornaments
against the wall, and the unheated air chimed with the muted,
silvery tinkle of that small destruction.

There were dirty dishes in the kitchen, and the remains of

an interrupted meal. And there was a Christmas decoration on the table, a centerpiece someone had been arranging. That, too, was unfinished, incomplete. Red candles and sprays of evergreen, and one space empty. The missing branch lay beside the white bowl, dropped in haste and not picked up again.

The people will come back, some of them will come back. And I think there will be a special agony when they come home, when they return to this dead house and find, ironically preserved, the symbols and promises of everlasting life, peace on earth, goodwill to men.

The front room lacked most of one wall. In the corner, exposed now to the incurious daylight, was a broken rocking chair. It stood by a wall cabinet filled with sewing gear—buttons, darning cotton, pins, thread. On the floor by the rocker was a pair of steel-rimmed spectacles, old and very worn. They had been broken, smashed neatly at the bridge.

The barn smelled of dead cow, and calves wandered forlornly in the silent, empty yard. The countryside is filled with bawling, homeless calves, untended and unfed.

In the stable I saw eyes shining from a dark hole in the floor, and bending down, discovered a cat. Hidden and safe, it cowered and would not come out, but its eyes followed me, unblinking, until I grew uncomfortable and went away.

We moved out as it grew dark. The bodies of German and American soldiers lay in the roads and ditches and in front of the houses. One doggie, shot in the head, had fallen upon a fence. His body hung on the pickets, limp and shapeless as a scarecrow thrown carelessly from an upper window, a thing of rags and straw. Under his dangling head three daffodils, miraculous in the snow, were speckled with blood.

We had nearly reached the battered farmhouse that was to be our company C.P. when the German artillery zeroed in. One shell landed very near, and I hit the ground as it exploded, pelted with lumps of frozen earth and pain stabbing my back. For a single terrible moment I had a bright vision of my torn flesh, but a little self-exploration revealed that I was still unpunctured. My "wound" was a sharp-edged buckle on my pack, gouging me in a tender spot.

We started to dig in. Shorty and I had nearly finished our hole in the hedgerow when we were assigned to outpost duty. Floundering waist-deep through a field of untrodden snow, we reached the point designated as the outpost and again started digging. Three attempts convinced us we'd hit water no matter where we dug, so we gave up in disgust. Scraping a shallow trench, we sat on our packs in the soggy pit and felt sorry for ourselves. We wrapped blankets around our shoulders, but our feet dangled in eight inches of ice water. At dawn we returned to our dugout.

After a cold breakfast we looked for straw for the dugout. Under a manger in the barn, carefully concealed, I found a locked suitcase. Immediately I had visions of fabulous loot— Leica cameras, pistols, the German crown jewels. Furtively, we carried the case back to our hole and broke it open. For a moment of shamed silence we were unable to meet each other's eyes. No pistols, no jewels . . . nothing but three well-mended white tablecloths, a woman's slip, and seven pairs of boys' socks. The socks had been darned many times at toe and heel.

I wasn't very proud of myself. Then, resolutely tough about it, I appropriated one of the tablecloths for a snow-camouflage garment, forced one on Shorty for the same purpose, and the third we draped over our leaky roof to prevent the snow from drifting through the chinks. The slip and the socks we replaced in the suitcase, which we set carefully against the rear wall of our hole. Some spring, maybe . . . when the fields are sprouting green and the farmer and his sons are filling in the holes the *verdammte Amerikanische* dug . . .

We stayed two days. At three-thirty on the third morning we were awakened. "Get it on! We're moving up!"

We struck our shelters in a howling blizzard and packed. Tiny pellets of snow lashed our faces with the stinging force of buckshot. Cold, cold, cold, and a fierce wind.

This was attack, and we knew it. We stripped down to basic

combat equipment, surrendering our packs to the supply sergeant. We made separate bundles of our personals and turned them over to Supply, also. We carried only weapons and ammo when we started. No extraneous gear, no luxuries. No overcoats. I was happy to pare down because my load was a heavy one: as grenadier, I carried a full sack of heavy rifle grenades, but being assistant to the BAR man, I carried a full complement of that weighty ammunition as well. In addition, I was burdened with the normal load of a rifleman—a full rifle belt, two bandoliers, five hand grenades.

Our objective was a forest, five miles away, and we had to break trail the entire distance through knee-high, waist-high snow. It was a dull, teeth-gritting monotony of hard work. It's difficult now to describe it—the intense cold, the feather-bed thickness of snow that made every step a reluctant persuasion, the darkness that was hard and real, pressing against your eyeballs . . . and always the fear of getting lost, of drifting away from the line of moving men that you could neither see nor hear in the blackness of the noisy night.

When we reached our assembly point, the edge of a little wood, we started to dig in. Two digging hours later, three medium tanks rumbled up and we prepared for the push, heading for the dark forest ahead, which was believed to be empty of German troops. There were several open fields intervening, marked off by wire fences that would have to be climbed, cut, or crawled under. The entire operation was company in scope—no other units involved—and the third platoon was assigned to ride the tanks, coming in our left flank, while the first and second platoons made a frontal assault.

So we started. As we moved from the shelter of the trees, the wind hit us from the right with the wallop of a fist. (Official reports put the wind velocity that day at very near fifty miles per hour.) It scooped up the snow on the open fields, puffing it into a cloud so thick that we couldn't see the forest ahead of us.

We moved out in a huge wave, each man breaking his own trail and no man directly behind another. It was no gallant dash, this—not like the movies. This was slow, laborious . . .

floundering. Men fell and could not struggle to their feet again for minutes. One heavily laden bazooka man went down and could not rise because of the hammering of the wind, until someone freed him of his burden of ammunition. A few yards of progress and we paused for a moment, crouching on our knees and sucking great mouthfuls of snow-whirling air into our tortured lungs. The forest was a blurred mass, appearing dreamlike through the storm of white for a brief moment and then dissolving once more.

As we struggled forward, the tanks moved out from our left flank, a thin arm that curved ahead to clutch at the nearest line of trees. Suddenly, a rattle of machine-gun fire burst from the woods and we saw the men of the third platoon tumbling from the tanks, falling into the deep snow. We raced for the shelter of a nearby copse, and safely there, peered from behind slim trees to spot the German positions. We could see nothing, but fired in the general direction of the sound anyway, hoping to draw enemy fire away from the men of the third platoon, who were pinned down in the open field.

For two hours the tanks fought it out with an unseen enemy while we waited, unable to help, but safe. That's a misstatement: only some of us waited and only some of us remained safe. The grove that sheltered us was a small island in a sea of white: the clouds of whirling snow had settled as the wind died, and to strike out from the shelter of the trees in any direction was to step directly in view of the Germans. Frequent bursts through the branches over our heads informed us that our presence was known and they were waiting. Behind us, only a field away, was a low hill, crested with trees. If we could reach that ridge, we could move unseen and safe and flank the enemy. The consideration that gave us pause was how suicidal it would be to attempt to cross the field. Only our valor-hungry lieutenant was not convinced: he gave an order and four men took off, running for the trees on the hill. They were chopped down by a German burp gun before they'd gone thirty yards. Three of them were seriously wounded, and the fourth—Rose, the platoon runner—was killed. Undaunted still, the lieutenant proposed to lead the rest of the platoon over the same route. Our noncoms saved a lot of lives that day: they flatly refused to obey his orders, and he gave way before their fierce insubordination. We stayed in the grove until dark, and at last it seemed that our tanks had cleaned out the machine-gun nests.

The wind, the snow, and our rebellious noncoms kept us alive that day. But not all of us: the company suffered forty casualties.

I cannot forget one of them, an Italian boy I hadn't remembered seeing before. He was still sitting upright in the foxhole he'd been digging when a slug caught him squarely between the eyes. His helmet was lying carelessly beside him, as though he'd taken it off to cool his head, sweaty from digging. Leaning against the dirt wall of his foxhole, he was smiling gently, his eyes half closed, his head tilted back, and the bullet hole very small, very neat . . . not messy. The snow was very white, his hair very black, and only a delicate thread of scarlet to mar the ivory of his face.

Forty casualties. Ginto, the medic of the third platoon, was killed. He was a company favorite and one of the few "old" guys remaining. When the burial party went out several days later, the wolves had been at him. Others, too. There were no reports available on the number of men who perished of quite small wounds, died because they fell in deep snow and were not found in time, died of shock, of cold, of bleeding to death and no one to see.

After two days of pushing, the company now consisted of forty-seven men. Three rifle platoons and a weapons platoon—total, forty-seven men. There were twenty-nine men in the three rifle platoons. Not all of our losses were from enemy action, however: there were many casualties from illness, particularly trench foot and frostbite.

We dug holes and stayed in the forest that night. And somewhere in this chaos of events is the confused memory of a foxhole where six of us slept one night, piled and tumbled together.

The days are a rapid blur: pushing, digging in, outpost duty, patrols, pushing, digging in. . . . Then Shorty went to the hospital with frozen feet, and now Greg Luecke and I alone remained of the group of replacements assigned to the first platoon back in the Hurtgen Forest. The rest of our "classmates" were gone.

Greg and I shared a foxhole after Shorty left. Greg was BAR man and I was his assistant. For greater firepower, we carried the BAR when we stood guard, but there were many dawns that found us wearily prepared to defend our little section of line with a weapon that was frozen thick with hoarfrost, useless and impotent. (I'm not complaining about the BAR: it's a magnificent weapon. But it's also a delicate and complex mechanism, and in below-zero weather the moving parts frequently became sealed tight with ice. After some experimenting, we stopped oiling the weapon because we discovered that the oil itself froze. Dry, it was more nearly workable.)

Our squad now consisted of four men. We stood guard in three-hour shifts, all day long, all night long, and the cold was a never-ending agony. There was no way to get warm.

Chow was scanty and uncertain. We were far out on the point, so far from the chow line that the kettles were nearly empty by the time Greg or I got there. Frequently the food was entirely gone, and then we ate cold C rations . . . if we could get the C rations. Sometimes there was nothing at all, and we just pulled our belts tighter and hoped.

Replacements began to arrive, and rumors sprang up that we were going to be pulled back for reorganization and a brief rest.

Our line stretched along the crest of a ridge, with the enemy on the hill opposite and a deep valley as the No-Man's-Land between us. Greg and I guarded a position in the middle of the line, but we had neighbors. Four hundred yards to our left the woods curved out before us like the horn of a crescent moon, and we knew that another platoon had several guard posts in the curve of the horn.

One day a couple of new replacements joined us, and I helped them dig their foxhole, instructing them with self-conscious and weary patience. Glancing up for a moment, I saw four figures in snow-camouflage garments emerge from the valley and start to climb the hill. Instinctively, I stepped behind the nearest tree and hissed a warning to the green replacements to get the hell out of sight. Then tardy logic shamed me: this had to be one of our own patrols returning from a mission—nothing else would explain the bold, open manner of their approach. Besides, there had been no challenge from the guard posts in the woods. Still . . .

When the four were still several hundred yards away, their actions became puzzling. Leaving the edge of the woods, they moved horizontally across the breast of the hill until they seemed to be directly in front of me. There they paused, knelt in the snow, and began setting up what could only be a light machine gun. It was pointing toward us.

I had already sent a messenger after Meese, and at that moment he raced up and I pointed out the strange sight. Instantly he declared, "They're doggies . . . looks like one of our patrols!" but he lifted his binoculars and studied them. Abruptly he was hopping up and down and swearing with rage: "The sunsabitches are Jerries! Gimme a carbine, someone!" We opened fire but the range was too great: the four Germans hightailed it for the valley and we failed to wing even one.

As for the men in the platoon on our left and why hadn't they seen the four Germans: they were probably sleeping in their holes. It was difficult to remain tensed for danger all the time.

Remembering now, I am aware that it must seem a very dull kind of war to anyone who wasn't there. Where is the violent action, the bloody combat, the whistling shells and the hand-to-hand derring-do? Where are the pitched battles, the Hollywood extravaganzas of mud and blood, the Gettysburg and Argonne spectacles?

All I can say is, the moments of high drama were just that—moments. There were battles and bloody assaults. But for every minute of dramatic encounter with the enemy, there were long dreary hours of waiting, watching, stalking, patrolling, digging in, guarding, more waiting, tense but uneventful miles of pushing, then more digging in and more waiting. To people who long for tales of single-handed heroism, it must seem anticlimactic to be told of the "gallant boys"—man, whoever dreamed up that phrase ought to get a Good Conduct Medal, pinned right through his hide!—who went to the rear with trench foot, frostbite, and similar unromantic ailments. But that's the way it was.

That vast numbers of people still have a phony idea of war even in this enlightened and jaundiced day can be blamed in part on the Richard Harding Davis school of journalism. Since returning home I've talked to many civilians whose vision of modern warfare is a little askew. The Homeric phrases of the correspondents frequently conjured up a phony. Examine, for instance, that iron phrase "a tank battle." To many civilians, led astray by a magnificently written but puffed-up account, a "tank battle" meant hundreds of tanks rushing madly around the countryside, bumping each other like Dodgem Juniors in an amusement park. A battle of tanks was truly a grim affair, and bloody and dramatic enough—I have no wish to minimize it. And there *were* panoramic tank battles, magnificent as tapestries, especially during the African campaign. But for Pete's sake, a tank is a costly weapon, hard to replace and worth preserving. It's also a death trap for the luckless crew that gets rash—and gets caught. There was no dearth of heroics in tank outfits, but those guys didn't go out looking for valor, slavering over the smoky fields of Europe in search of an excuse to be picturesquely reckless. It took a lot of war bonds at $18.75 per to pay for a tank; it took a lot of time to train a crew to handle it, and the men in that crew were plenty cautious, as it was their business to be. More tank battles were won by shrewdness, speed, and outguessing than by fender-bumping. (And just for the record, some of the tankers I knew were *too* damn cautious! But that's another story and I'll come to it.)

As for the jokers who thirst for heroism in large doses, they'll have to look for it in the movies and the comic magazines.

Meese came back from the C.P. one morning and told us to pack up: we were moving back to Faymonville for a rest. No relief outfit came to take our place: the front had shifted and we were no longer needed in that sector.

A final irony: the day before we moved back to Faymonville we were at last issued the winter equipment about which you'd been reading for months back in the States: knee-high shoes (called Snow-Paks) and heavy wool socks, scarfs, elbow-length gauntlets of leather and waterproof poplin. Late though they were, we welcomed them.

The company started for Faymonville, leaving me behind as a one-man guard over the piles of equipment that would be picked up by half-tracks and "weasels." To pass the time, I policed our late area, picking up forgotten ammunition and equipment.

Let no one ever grumble that the occasional frontline shortages were due to the derelictions of American industry and failures on the home front. In that snow-choked pine woods was enough equipment—clothing, blankets, ammunition, and food—to make a Czech or Chinese guerrilla army weep for joy. Only weapons were lacking: apparently no man was bold enough to throw away or abandon a firearm. Knives, axes, bayonets, and entrenching tools—yes. But no rifles, machine guns, or BARs.

Painstakingly, I searched the area, gleaning hand grenades, clips and full bandoliers of M-1 ammunition, rifle grenades, bazooka rockets, belts of machine-gun ammo. When an officer appeared, making a last inspection tour, I waved proudly toward my pile of salvage. He glanced at it and said carelessly, "Oh, don't bother with the ammunition! Leave it here! There's plenty in the rear, and we can't be bothered with taking all this crap back!"

We left it. The only things we took—because I threw them on the jeep trailer when he wasn't looking—were two full boxes of hand grenades and a dozen bandoliers of M-1 ammo. And as we drove to Faymonville, we dribbled bits of equipment at every sharp turn in the road.

CHAPTER FIVE

"There is snow on the altar . . ."

January 1945. Faymonville, Belgium.

The first few days here were given over to the unfamiliar delights of baths, shaves, haircuts, and clean clothes. And sleep. Then the new replacements began to arrive. Some were two weeks out from the States and very green indeed. And very young. With their assignment to platoons, reorganization was begun.

We have a new squad leader, an Oklahoma Indian known, naturally, as "Chief." He is one of the old men of the outfit, recently returned from the hospital following wounds received some months ago. Reputedly the best sniper and the best one-man patrol in the company, he is also, in some important respects, a sonofabitch. He has the sneak's habit of helping himself to the property of others and the bully's habit of blustering mightily when discovered. He is moody and given to bursts of wild temper. The company grapevine has warned us to beware when he's been drinking: three sniffs of a cork and he runs amok, taking with him a tommy gun for comfort. He is unpredictable and erratic at all times. Anyway, he's the new leader of the first squad, and I'm his assistant, although my rating remains at the same moldy state—private.

We've taken over what's left of the houses in this battered town. I think there cannot be an undamaged building in the entire area. Dead cattle and horses litter the fields and streets. Already they swell and stink. There's a dead horse near our chow line, and at every mealtime we must hurdle its grossly swollen belly, the rigid legs pointing in the air like dried branches.

Faymonville was in the path of the "Bulge" offensive. Long ago, during the fall of Belgium, German troops were quartered here. Last year our advancing armies pushed them out. Came the Bulge, our forces retreated and the town was reoccupied by the Germans. When the Bulge was deflated and the Germans again withdrew, we returned once more. With such a seesawing of armies, it's surprising that Faymonville exists at all.

Our house is in the quarter of the town that took the worst beating. Not a room is whole. Most of the roof is gone, and the second floor is a windswept shambles. The ceiling of our room drips constantly, and daylight peers through the sieved walls. There are no windows, of course. We nailed blankets and comforters over the empty window frames, and we live in perpetual dusk, lit dimly by candlelight.

Scattered like confetti in the mud around the house are the homely, small things that once marked this as a home. Pictures, well-scoured pots and pans, old letters and colored postcards, the scraps of bright embroidery that bespeak the good hausfrau, broken dishes, shattered furniture, toys—the empty and mournful things that say simply, "A family lived here."

The house has been fiercely fought over, several times. The exterior walls are pocked with the scars of many bullets, and around it lie shell cases and clips of ammunition, German and American.

The cows in the barn have been dead a long time.

The civilians are returning to Faymonville. Every day we see them—old men and young women, children. All wear several layers of clothing, all carry backbreaking loads of house gear, push baby carriages, carts, and wheelbarrows that bulge with feather ticks, luggage, treasured bits of furniture. They move wearily, their heads inclined to the ground, their shoulders curved under the freight they carry. When they reach home—the place where home used to be—they stand and look long at the crumbled walls, the bare girders of ancient roofs, the shards of broken roof slate, the dead animals, the rubble of dismembered furniture scattered like old bones in the street. Sometimes they weep, the weak tears of the aged. But they are never surprised—these were old anticipations in the blood, now come to bitter fruit.

Today an old man and his daughter returned to their home, the building just across the road. She was very pregnant. I'd been watching them for an hour. She bent painfully over a mound of rubbish, sorting the fragments of roof slate—the large pieces here, the middle-sized ones here, the splinters . . . Already the old man was on the roof, patching the gaping holes. Just now she brought an armful of wet linen from the house and carefully hung it on the branches of a ruined apple tree in the front yard. From the filthy mud of the street, she'd salvaged her tablecloths, doilies, pillow slips, and towels, rinsed them in cold and soapless water, and now they flap in the cold wind. Why should there be tears in my eyes?

A rest camp has been set up in nearby Herve, and already I have had an overnight pass. Had a hot shower, saw a movie, and stuffed myself with fabulously expensive Belgian pastries. But I returned to the outfit with a curious sense of coming home.

Listening to the poker table conversation in the next room, I arrived at the conclusion that the GI would be virtually speechless if a certain four-letter word beginning with F were lifted from his vocabulary. I kept a tally: thirty-four times . . . in two minutes!

I don't object to the word: it's the dreary monotony of hearing it over and over again, a repetition that would be equally wearing if the word were innocuous—"consarned" or "blasted." It's the paucity of expression, fraying the nerves like the dripping of a faucet in the night.

I'll have to watch my own language when I get home. I'm brought up sharply now and then by the realization that my vocabulary is increasingly narrowed to the elementary one-syllables, some of them not designed for mixed company or the eager ears of little children.

Christ, this is no life . . . this suspension between worlds!

Most of the time I manage to get by, filling the hours with the fundamentals of eating, sleeping, and the particular job of soldiering at hand. But when there's a lull in the monotonous rhythm of this dull laboring for survival, when I permit myself the luxury of thinking, feeling, remembering, a sense of unreality washes over me in huge waves, and I am submerged. It is as though all vital processes except the beating of my heart have stopped, stopped because there was no purpose in continuing.

I went to church today. Protestant and Catholic services were being conducted in the village cathedral by army chaplains. I chose the Catholic service because I wanted the solace of form, ritual—I didn't *want* to understand what was said. The chaplain foxed me: he preached a short sermon in English.

Drawn by the tolling bell, some of the townspeople attended services, too. They entered timidly, not sure they would be permitted, and we smiled at them to let them know it was all right. Although they could not understand the sermon, the ritual was familiar to them, and the Latin chanting, and they crossed themselves and genuflected with a trembling ardor unmatched by any of the GIs present. Three *very* old women entered and took the pew in front of me. Their faces were secret with the closed-in sightlessness of the ancient, and they tottered as they walked, leaning heavily on crooked canes. They wept silently throughout the service.

There are many old graves under the shell-scarred lawn of the cathedral. And five new graves, guarded by very new wooden crosses. Hanging on each cross is a German helmet.

The rose window behind the high altar must have been beautiful once. Now it is a twisted agony of melted lead that sags and bulges grotesquely. Shells and bombs, including incendiaries, struck the church several times, and the magnificent windows were shattered and burned. Scattered on the floor are jewellike gleamings of scarlet, deep blue, emerald green, and amber. Directly behind the baroque wreckage of the high altar is a gaping hole in the blackened stone. There is snow on the altar and on the floor behind it.

In the chancel of the church there is an evil mess where some soldier, German or American, demonstrated the staunchness of his warrior heart by defecating on the ancient stone floor.

Today the Red Cross Clubmobile arrived, carrying hot coffee, doughnuts, free cigarettes, gum, and two American girls. We splashed eagerly through the rain, more interested in the girls than in the customary handout of coffee-and. The front is a homely girl's idea of heaven—scores of unattached males, and all of them anxious to exchange at least *one* word, all loath to leave after receiving their coffee and their allotted smile. The girls were attractive, gracious, and skilled in handling masses of woman-starved GIs. We returned to quarters convinced that the American girl has something her European sisters lack. I don't know *why* the sight of two American girls in slacks should be more exciting than the sight of equally attractive Belgian, French, or German girls in more feminine costume, but that's the way it was. Maybe it was the lipstick, which seems uniquely American and an undreamed-of luxury in these war-ravaged areas.

There's a hardware store in our sector, shelled and ruined and open to the weather. Apparently it serviced all the nearby countryside, and the owner was a canny buyer, because there are attached vast sheds and barns, crammed with goods, most of it damaged. Stoves, dishes, glassware, pots and pans, pails, thermos bottles, mops, brooms, scythes, stovepipe—a veritable treasure house to the GI, who must make his home from whatever he can find, beg, or skonavish. The raids on this stockpile have been constant and thorough: all of us required stovepipe for the stoves in our billets, and we prefer to eat from china whenever possible. Of late our chow line has been a miraculous thing to behold: instead of the customary tinware, you see everything from hand-painted fruit bowls to fine-cut glass.

Yesterday the owner of the hardware store returned to town, arriving on the scene just in time to see a Joe emerging from the store with his arms loaded. The old man danced in his rage like Rumpelstiltskin, snatching the stuff from the arms of the astonished soldier and screaming, "Mine, mine! Not for you! . . . No steal!" The racket attracted a helluva lot of attention, including that of the C.O., and the old man made a violent squawk to him about the sacredness of his property. The store and all its attached sheds and barns are now *off limits*.

I am a little staggered by the implications of this episode. Faymonville was ruined and desolated by war; our guns and planes, and the guns and planes of the Germans, made rubble of it. And now it's been liberated, it's a free town again, free of the hated German conquerors. However, to that old man—as to hundreds of others in similar towns—the better fate would have been to continue living in the semislavery imposed by the Nazis rather than to have their homes and their property destroyed in the name of a vigorous freedom. We "liberated" these people (I guess!); we restored to them the freedoms their statesmen and poets, their own best minds, so passionately desired, but the cost when reckoned in the sacrifice of material things is difficult for them to accept. Confronted with wreckage and desolation, many have a hard time clinging to the reality of those larger freedoms. Most men want only to be let live, and the hardware man would have preferred to trickle out his life under Nazi rule—tax-ridden, despised, disenfranchised—but living a life *nearly* normal and conducting business *nearly* as usual. His outraged screams indicate that he would have preferred that to finding his home full of holes, his cattle dead, his dishes broken, and his stoves being carried off (although only to the house next door) by his "liberators." His point of view is short, and average, and to be expected. There *are* people here who face the wreckage courageously, willing to accept it for the precious sake of the larger intangibles.

* * *

A strange day today. Although heavy snow still blankets the fields, the weather has been unseasonably warm, and this morning we got up to find the village wrapped in a heavy mist. Stepping outdoors was like being caught in the first reel of a Hitchcock movie. Stretching gauntly from the house as far as the eye could see were the stripped, broken apple trees, gesturing crazily against the blackened skeletons of houses seen through mist. Curiously, for a long time the morning was silent—no guns, no planes, not even the rumble of army trucks. Only the far-off cawing of rooks. With every moment anticipation grew that someone . . . some One moving in mystery and tragic intensity, would come through the mist and the broken orchard. But no one did . . . all setting and no plot!

February 5.

We have been alerted for the past two days. We don't know where we're going, and the long-drawn uncertainty is making us edgy. No matter how bad it may be, it would be so much better to *know*!

We left on February 6. A truck ride to another woods, a wait until dark, then a walk in the night rain and the mud. Six and a half hours later we ended up on the banks of the Roer River. It hadn't been a pleasant walk, and floundering through the slimy muck, cursing the darkness, I remembered the pleasure I had found in night walks at home. The midnight stroll with the dogs each night . . . the dark shadows under the maple trees, the infrequent streetlights that sifted a soft radiance through the leaves, making gently dappled pools for wading. Rarer walks on country roads, and the white glimmer underfoot . . . lifting your eyes to marvel at stars you had never seen in a city sky. Far away now . . . the distance of centuries from this German mud, this pure Aryan night.

We walked in single file, close together so no one would get lost. Chief had gone with the advance party, which preceded us by several hours, so I had the squad. The forced march was a rough introduction to soldiering for some of the new men, and I cajoled, swore, threatened, and persuaded, trying by all means to keep them moving. All along the line of march men were falling from exhaustion, collapsing in the mud or staggering grimly to the side of the road before passing out. One of my new men fainted, and I had to use the last few precious drops of water in my canteen to revive him. Over his protests, we split up his load, and he struggled to his feet and doggedly kept going. I rode his tail like Simon Legree until we reached the Roer, not liking my role very much. But he made it.

The Roer lies in the valley below us, and we're dug in on the side of a steep hill. Across the river, on hills that sheer abruptly from the water's edge, are the Germans. As I would later discover, we were not in Belgium anymore but in Germany. Our holes, lately inhabited by another outfit, are halfway down the hill, and it took us an hour to descend the tortuous hillside trail in the dark. Chief and I and a new man named Frank Eifler share the same hole. As dugouts go, it's not bad, but it leaks.

February 10.

We've been here four days now, expecting to move out at any moment. We get two meals a day—breakfast and supper—both of which are served up in darkness and at the top of the hill. The first time we tried to find our way to the chow line we were forced to resort to a military braille: we traced the phone wire from the platoon C.P. near us to the company C.P. at the top of the hill, passing the thin wire delicately through our fingers and moving blindly through the night-black woods. The trip took us an hour and a half, although in daylight it would be but a ten-minute walk. The following day the engineers marked a path with white tape, tying the tape from tree to tree. Thirty minutes was par for the course after that. Playing in the rough was forbidden: before departing for the far side of the Roer, the Germans had heavily mined our hill, and it had not yet been cleared.

The squad on our right flank is in houses, the lucky stinkers.

Shorty is with that squad. He rejoined us at Faymonville but was assigned to another squad in order to keep a balance between old men and replacements.

Far out on our left flank is an old castle. A neighboring platoon is stationed there. They have a long trek to chow, and the Jerries have our mealtimes so well figured that every morning at breakfast time and every night at suppertime the enemy mortars and machine guns open up, just as those poor buggers from the castle start for chow. So far no one has been hit because they've learned to anticipate the gambit, but it's demoralizing nonetheless.

We can see the Roer clearly. It is swift and swollen, flooding most of the valley. We've heard that the Germans blew the dams above us to halt our advance, to slow us down. Every time I look at the grim hill across from us, the sheer slopes that we may be required to assault, I am well content to have my advance slowed down. Even stopped for a while.

We left the holes on February tenth, or maybe the eleventh. I don't know whether we went forward, backward, or sideways—I'm sure only that we moved, that we walked a long time through the mud (and a blizzard) and ended our journey in another pine woods. The Roer is not far away, although we cannot see it. We're to wait until the river goes down.

We waited until February 25.

We were confident in that period that the European war was nearly over. No longer a matter of months, but of weeks. Even days. I guess that was the feeling at home, too, although the Bulge had sobered some of the premature rejoicers. I thought a lot about what it would be like when the end of the war came, how the "Cease Firing" would affect us. In a letter to Ree I conjectured: "There'll be a few tears, I think, and some devout prayers of thanks, and a nervous, high-strung gaiety bordering on hysteria. But maybe I'm wrong. Maybe there will be only a quiet weariness and a great relief, as though something heavy had tumbled from our shoulders."

[One of those guesses was right. I learned which one it

was somewhere in Czechoslovakia, on the last day of the ETO war.]

Eifler and I set up housekeeping together in the woods. Through a series of swapping deals far too complicated to remember, we acquired four shelter halves and constructed an elaborate but unorthodox tent at the edge of the woods, bordering on a field. We collected pine boughs for a bed, ruthlessly slashing off live branches. A far cry from the Bastogne woods, where we'd been forbidden to cut a single pine tree because Belgium billed the USA for every tree felled or damaged by American troops, or so we'd been told.

Every afternoon Frank and I built a small fire that we maintained to the last moment of dusk, the hour of curfew. Having no guard duty, we spent long, luxurious hours in bed. It was a good war at that moment.

Last night I had a dream that haunted me all day. I dreamed that a cow with a gaping wound in its head leaned its starved body against a snowbank and looked at me with empty eyes for a long moment. Then, laying its ruined head against the snow, it died—quietly, without sound of crying—and the body sank and swiftly dissolved into a shapeless huddle against the earth, as I have seen the bodies of animals long dead. Why should one who is not a farmer be so oppressed by memories of starved and frightened beasts? Often I recall them more vividly than the dead men I have seen. The animals, the broken spectacles of an old woman, forsaken toys discovered in ruined houses . . . the testaments of innocence.

For weeks Frank's been waiting for word from home that his baby was born. His first child, it was due some weeks ago and he's pretty confident that the big event is over. Frank's a quiet, likable youngster and a very earnest guy. He brought a box of cigars with him when he came overseas so he would have the proper tokens of new parenthood to distribute when the time came. Since we expect to shove off at any time, he broke down today and passed out the cigars, gravely assuring everyone that although he didn't know whether it was a boy or a girl, he was sure it *was*! Although he doesn't smoke, he saved one cigar for himself and lit it last night when we went to bed. He felt he *ought* to smoke one for his firstborn—it was his first responsibility as a parent. The first tentative puff brought on such a paroxysm of coughing and thrashing about that he nearly pulled the tent down around our ears. He persisted valiantly for a few minutes but at last decided that the gesture did not require entire consumption of the cigar. Soberly, I concurred, and with great dignity he dropped it in the ditch behind the tent.

Our fireside talk is not devoted exclusively to home, food, and sex. Lately we've been discussing a news item from a recent *Stars and Stripes* that recounted the details of a meeting between De Gaulle and Giraud in Metz. De Gaulle is credited with two statements that alarm the pants off me: "We will make the Rhine a French stream from one end to the other," and, "It is a curious peace that is being prepared for us."

Those statements have an ominous ring. Most of us don't like France in the role of the fourth policeman of Germany. Some share in German control, yes, but not on a parity with the Big Three. For twenty-five years France has kept a slovenly house, and there is small evidence that the more noxious closets have been cleaned out. De Gaulle as a housekeeper is yet unproven, and he may be a good one. His inferior statesmanship, however, is already revealed.

His pronouncement on the guardianship of the Rhine indicates that France will be as avaricious after this war as she was in 1918. As for his second statement, heavy with grievance, it hints that France will be the same screaming termagant at this peace table that she was at Versailles—greedy, vindictive, and jealous, ready to sabotage larger interests out of pique, avarice, and the desire for revenge.

Making the Rhine a French river would be tantamount to making Germany a dependent vassal of France. The Rhine a

free river under the jurisdiction of the Big Three is the way we
see it here. But this is the woods of the Roer, and we're young
and trusting, believing still in words that start with capital letters. So we say, hotly, "A free river, yes, but not French! Germany would be destroyed and impotent—and a good thing,
too!—but France would be too powerful, too dominant."

With a France that is still rotten inside—and we think she
is—a French Rhine would be a disaster for Western Europe
and the world. We are soured by the memory of French chi-
canery, French "diplomacy" during the past twenty years; we
remember the "impregnable Maginot line," the "phony war,"
the newsreel pictures of French soldiers bicycling home for
supper each night in the early days of the war. We feel that
France—like England, like us—is not entirely innocent of war
guilt.

From a letter to Ree, dated February 14:

You ask if there are compensatory human relations in war
to make up for some of the misery. That's a difficult question.
They are not truly compensatory, because they are incomplete. They are half relations only, sometimes comforting and
close, but arising primarily from the need of the body to reassure itself with the warmth and security of another person at
hand. That sounds cold and snobbish, and I guess it is. That
self-accusation runs me right into the ground every now and
then. I'd like to be able to deny the charge; I'd like to say that
I don't judge and grade and label another man's taste in
music and books; I'd like to say that I don't measure his likes
against my own and find mine superior. But I *can't* say that,
damn it! The other night the twilight conversation moved
softly and we felt warm and close and easy, and somehow we
got started on books and poetry. Because that is always suc-
culent bait to me, I began quoting what shreds and fragments
of poetry I could remember. No sequence, no plan to my rambling. I had just finished "When I have fears that I may cease
to be," and the silence was deep and embracing. Then, out of
the darkness and the silence came the question, honest and

sincere and interested: "Didja ever hear Edgar Guest read his poetry?" So all right, goddamn it, I winced! I made my reply as sincere as I could because the question had been deeply, honestly meant, and the talk went on from there. But do you see what I mean? The magic had gone from the evening for me. Later that night the realization came to me that I should have been happy and proud. Had they not been moved by Keats's lines, they would never have had the courage to bring out their own treasures. That was the important thing, and I was overwhelmed with belated shame.

I like these guys. Some of them I'll never forget, like Shorty. In my own defense all I can say is that I have been self-consciously longhair for so many years that I am frequently disconcerted to find myself with a crew cut—and liking it. I am learning humility, but slowly.

From a letter to Ree, written February 15:

Complaining that there is much you don't know about war, you refer to my silence on things like "going into combat" and ask for explanations. That phrase, "going into combat," makes me wince. It smacks of the heroic, a mixture of ancient history and ham, battles that were prearranged and orderly affairs (if they ever were!) in the days when knighthood was in flower.

I don't know how much knowledge you have picked up from books and movies, so I'll make my explanation very elementary. Remember, too, that personal experience is my only source, and everything I say may be belied by the reports of others.

An outfit is (a) in the rear, thus out of danger and the likelihood of immediate action; (b) moving up to the line; (c) in defensive positions on the line; (d) making a push, which may mean house-to-house stuff in a village; (e) waiting in an assembly area for the strategic moment at which to embark on a push. A push may mean trouble, may mean "going into combat," but it ain't necessarily so. And being on line may mean that you're getting the living bejesus shelled out of you, but again, it ain't necessarily so. No two situations are identical, and you don't know beforehand what you may encounter two hours from now. The thing is this: "going into combat" can out-Hollywood Hollywood—and sometimes does. Or it may be as innocuous as a tug-of-war at an Epworth League picnic. Don't, for heaven's sake, picture this life as one bloody battle sequence after another. It's an ugly, dirty, miserable, frequently dangerous business, but it is not a constant slugging it out in hand-to-hand combat with the Jerries. I wish the rules of censorship would permit me to be more specific in my letters so that I could ease the dark tension under which you live. But I can only plead with you, "Don't imagine the worst when my letters are infrequent or noncommittal!"

From the same letter:

Thanks for sending the quotations from the new Leland Stowe book *[They Shall Not Sleep]*. The guy's apparently been around in this war. So far as my own small knowledge goes, he is entirely correct in saying that "our men in uniform . . . are ill-informed about current events and major developments between the Allied governments." And it *is* our Orientation Program that's partially at fault. The trouble starts further back, of course—it starts with the men themselves. In justice to *Stars and Stripes* and *Yank*, I must admit that current events are reported, however cursory or slanted the manner. The basic fault lies in the men, in the "not thinking about politics or economics or sociology" backgrounds from which we've sprung. And the most evil footnote to a statement of that condition is that nonthinking is condoned and even subtly encouraged by the army. I've watched the men here read *Stars and Stripes*, and waited for comments about the Greek situation, or Poland, or Italy. Baiting them with questions, I've discovered that they haven't read *that* news because they weren't interested in it. The direct progress of the war, yes! But aside from developments of a purely military nature, their interest lies in news of home. They will have none of the world picture, thanks just the same.

That's the basic fault: the soft unreality in which we Americans are cushioned from birth, a way of life in which who's pitching for the Yankees this year is more important than who's running for the presidency of the United States. That disinterest in real problems, that absorption in the romantic and the trivial, is peculiarly American and doesn't exist in any other country in the world to such a degree. Obviously, the army cannot be held responsible for this basic condition, but the Orientation Program of the army was designed (in theory, at least) to meet the problems of disinterest and ignorance. And the job is not being done.

It is not only that there is little or no effort to educate the politically ignorant; worse than that, we are frequently misinformed, informed in sketchy fashion, and bluntly advised to shut up when we want to exercise the rights of free men. Under the masthead of *Stars and Stripes* is the newspaper's credo, a statement credited to George Washington: "When we assumed the role of soldier, we did not lay aside the role of citizen." Army administration tends to scorn that admonition, understandably, perhaps. The commanding officers of armies, the makers of policy and decision, are professional soldiers for whom the prosecution of wars is a career and a business. They are right in arguing that winning the war is the first consideration, and I would not have their efficiency hamstrung by the well-meant blundering of congressmen, politicians, and presidential advisers. But someone ought to remind these professional soldiers that *we* are batting in this league, too, and we have entered this profession reluctantly. There are fifteen million of us who were civilians first, soldiers second, and someday we will be civilians again, preparing to pick up civilian tasks and responsibilities for which our months and years in the army have ill prepared us.

What Stowe says is deeply troubling. The one bright thing I see on the credit side of the ledger is the evidence of the letters that appear every now and then in the "B-Bag" column of *Stars and Stripes*. There *are* men, here and in the Pacific, whose brains have not yet fallen victim to army sleeping sickness, men who will be prepared to battle the peace when they come home, if they have to.

This noon I saw the first miracle of spring, a promise so bright that I am warmed yet by the memory of it. A small thing only—a butterfly dancing incongruously above the muddy road—but men called in wonder and pointed it out to each other with more joy than if it had been Dorothy Lamour, sans sarong, strolling along the road.

As if to remind us that there was a war on, we had winter and death and desolation a few hours later.

Four days ago a big tent was erected in the field near my tent, and the word soon spread that we were going to have movies every day. (Formerly a hospital tent, the red crosses have been smeared over with paint so the Germans will not be able to accuse us of cravenly seeking the immunity of the red cross.)

There are two showings nightly: at six and at eight. I went to the early performance tonight, and while we waited for the tent to fill so the movie could start, some enemy planes came over. (The Germans are aware that a push is brewing, and daily they send out reconnaissance planes to scout our strength.) Their appearance was greeted with the customary signs of recognition from our ack-ack batteries. It was noisy and exciting, and most of the men crowded out of the tent to watch the fun. A few of us, having choice seats, stayed inside to retain them. We were a little blasé about the fun outside—we'd seen all this so many times before, and stuff. You know. Perched uncomfortably on an empty gas can, I was talking to a neighbor when a man sitting a few feet in front of me grunted or coughed and gently, slowly, toppled forward on his face. There was a puzzled hush for a moment, and then, uncertainly, the laughing and talking in the tent resumed. Then someone bent over the fallen man and shouted, "Get a medic!" and our paralysis was broken. We turned him over. His hand and arm were covered with blood and his face was a red mask. Before we could carry him from the tent, he was dead. For a long time we could not guess how he'd been hit, until someone discovered a two-inch slit in the canvas roof, directly above the box where he was sitting. A piece of falling shrapnel from our own ack-ack had knifed through the canvas and pierced his back as he leaned forward, elbows on knees.

We carried his body outside and the medics took it away. The tent filled, and we were soon absorbed in watching the enchanting Miss Bergman storm beguilingly through *Saratoga Trunk*. Not until I was in bed, some hours later, did the memory of his face return and drive away sleep. It was the eye I could not forget, the half-open eye drowning in blood. All through the night the darkness of my tent was lit by the faint gleam of that half-open eye, rolled back in the bloody head . . . and how it blinked rapidly for a terrible moment, trying to wipe away the blinding blood in a last, automatic obedience.

You used to hear a lot of bitter comment about "rear echelon heroes." Or maybe *you* didn't—maybe it was strictly army talk and the civilian never heard it, never guessed the gap between line troops and rear echelon. But the gap was there, and I guess it was inevitable. In our rational moments we appreciated the work done by rear echelon units, and we recognized our own dependency on that work. But when the going was rough, when the chow was late or nonexistent, when the weather was below zero and there'd been no mail and the mud was up to our asses, we'd bitch and grouse about "those bastards all safe and warm in the rear." None of the bitching was serious: we didn't really mean it, but it lent a bitter savor to our own misery. I mention it now only because at times there was serious misunderstanding, real rancor. Once, I came nearly to blows, via correspondence, with one of my best friends, who was with an Engineer's outfit back in Normandy. I had just received a letter from him, which I read in my foxhole on the hilltop near Waimes. It was during the most bitter period of the Bulge, with deep snow and below-zero temperatures. It was a good letter, but there were a couple of things in it that made me forget my chilblains and start a scorching reply on the spot. He asked, "What kind of quarters do you have?" and he went on to comment, "I understand frontline troops are being billeted for the winter." And then he told me of the suite of rooms he shared with another noncom in a Normandy hotel.

It took me a while to realize that he was honestly interested in my life—he wasn't just rubbing it in! And my anger was not truly directed against him, nor did it spring from a study of the contrast in our lots. He was lucky and I envied him, sure! But something was wrong because he didn't *know* how it was for us; we weren't in the same war. And it seemed a hopeless task to try to explain to him what this war was like from my point of view, and it seemed a little unfair that the misery couldn't be distributed more evenly. We sure as hell had more than our share, we thought.

There were other sharp reminders of the distance between frontline and rear echelon troops. One of them was a letter from another friend in the rear, received in February while we waited in the woods for the floodwaters of the Roer to subside. He told me his outfit, snug in Brussels, was putting on a play: *Arsenic and Old Lace*. Aw hell, what's the use?

From a letter written February 18:

Have I told you about our "lighting" arrangements? As you know, fires are not permitted after sunset, but lights under cover are okay so long as no ray can be seen outside. Our usual light is a crude gasoline flare, a bottle or can filled with gasoline and a bit of rag as a taper. When nothing better is available, heating units are used, but they last only a few minutes.

Our present light is a German canteen filled with gasoline. We punched a hole in the aluminum cap and inserted a length of tent rope for a wick. The lamp burns fine, but it throws off a black, sticky smoke. All the next day we spit black sputum and blow our noses black.

* * *

A few days ago we passed through a town that had been almost completely destroyed. The church—imposing even in the tiniest village—was in ruins, and only a fragment of tower and a broken wall remained. Once, the high altar had been framed in a high Romanesque arch upon which bloomed cherubim and angels, a heavenly host that hovered over the altar. All was gone now—the wall of the apse, the stained-glass windows, the high altar, the arch. Actually, half of the arch remained, hanging jagged and crumbling from a fragment of wall, and painted on that scrap in blue and coral was the figure of a kneeling cherub—just the single bright shape, exposed to raw daylight and the winter eyes of strangers. The revelation was indecent, somehow, compelling the curious to lower their gaze and hurry by.

The failure of the army Orientation Program continued to bother me, and I wrote frequently about it to Ree. In one of her answering letters she quoted a statement made by Helen Kirkpatrick of the *Chicago Daily News*, as reported by Leland Stowe in *They Shall Not Sleep*. Miss Kirkpatrick, discussing the American army's poor record in the field of soldier education as compared to the British, said that in her belief American soldiers were deeply concerned with serious issues, controversial subjects. To prove her thesis she claimed, "A vote taken among two units—one the Air Force and the other ground troops—showed that the majority would prefer serious discussions to floor shows." And hotly she declaims, "Yet they are provided with floor shows of fifth-rate quality."

The implications are seriously misleading. A vote polled in an Air Force unit would be a useless measuring stick to estimate the percentage of thinking men throughout the armed services. It must be remembered that the Air Corps was largely handpicked, and numbered the greatest percentage of college men of any branch of general service. As for the ground force troops that were polled, I'd like to know what unit it was!

No, the implications are false even if the bare statement is accurate. With the exception of selected groups like the Air Corps—which would be comparable to a college-level group —most branches of general service would show a range of intellectual virility no whit different from one revealed by a civilian poll that embraced all levels of education, income, religion, place of residence, type of work, and family status. The only common denominators in any army poll are: (1) age group; (2) present occupation; (3) sex. And like any heterogeneous assemblage of civilian males, an army unit would present the usual ratio of dolts and dunces, business brains and Babbitts, artists and asses, thinkers and chest thumpers.

I cannot resist a parting shot: I'd be more inclined to agree with Miss Kirkpatrick if her final sentence had read "*Because* they are provided with floor shows of fifth-rate quality." But that's throwing a dirty punch at the USO. Many of the USO shows stunk on ice; many of the entertainers weren't good enough to win, place, or show in a grange hall amateur contest. But some of them *were* good, and all worked gallantly under conditions that tested the heart of any trouper. Whether good, bad, or indifferent, it was the kind of entertainment we liked.

Most of the men I knew sought recreation in the following order: a woman, a bottle, a crap game, a show, a book. Funny thing . . . can't remember ever hearing a Joe say, "Y'know what I'd like most of all right now? A good, hot political discussion!"

February 20, 1945.

Today was Christmas for me. I got two of the Christmas boxes that were mailed last October from home. The cookies were still crisp.

I did something hasty that shames me now. In one box were some toys for small children, gay, inexpensive trinkets from Geoff and Sukey that I was commanded to give to "some little Belgian kids." I held the toys helplessly in my hands, an incongruous note of color in the gloomy forest. Give them to some Belgian kids? Sure, but where? When?

We'd be moving out soon and my pack was crowded, and I felt oddly shy about carrying the toys until some future time of gift-giving. Finally, aching inside, I walked to the edge of the forest and scooped a shallow hole at the base of a big tree. There I placed the small packages, wrapping them carefully in a scrap of canvas. I covered them over, mounding the soft earth and pine needles high, and soberly returned to my tent.

Last night I attended the early movie again. To bed immediately after, to lie awake listening to the music and dialogue of the second showing. Over and under the silly words and the brittle chattering of Lana Turner and Robert Young, I heard the mutter and rumble of distant artillery. (Add screen credits: "Sound Effects, courtesy of Adolf Hitler.")

It comes as something of a shock, but for the first time in my life I find myself the eldest of a group of young men . . . the old man. The man nearest my advanced years is a child of twenty-seven. It's a new responsibility for me, and I wonder if I exhibit the mature judgment the youngsters have a right to expect of me. Four men in the squad are husbands and fathers, but I'm the only one with two children—that is, if I count only the "Union members" of the squad and disqualify the southern boy, who has, in addition to a legal child in North Carolina, an extracurricular offspring somewhere in England.

We're a pretty good representation of the army melting pot: two men from Oklahoma, one from Michigan, one from North Carolina, one from Indiana, one from Missouri, one from Pennsylvania, and one from New York. One college graduate, one who never finished grammar school—all the rest high school graduates. A good bunch, but I miss Shorty and Greg Luecke and Leo Allen.

A few days ago I was summoned to the company C.P. and ordered to lay out a sand table—in this instance, a mud table—of the town we are to assault when we leave here. Working from maps and aerial photographs, I laid out a relief map eight feet by twelve of the town and environs, complete with buildings and streets. Then the C.O. gave us a briefing on our forthcoming assignment. I think he understated the difficulties, and deliberately, but it was good to be told explicitly what our task would be. I wish *more* preliminary briefings were given. The NCOs usually get one, but the rest of us go out blind.

It's February 23 now. It has been an indolent interlude here in the woods, but tomorrow night we push off. The Big Push. We're a little frightened, and our spirits veer wildly from wisecracking to sudden silence and back again. We spent the day cleaning weapons, replenishing our ammo, getting our gear ready. I've been transferred to the second squad, as an assistant squad leader. "Acting," of course! Wonder if I'll ever get out of the "acting gadget" class. Ketron is squad leader of the second and a helluva good guy. Overseas two years and not wounded yet. Wow!

CHAPTER SIX

". . . the quiet figure lying in the stubble, the blue overcoat like wings beside him . . ."

February 25.

We left the woods in the morning, crossed the Roer, and entered newly captured Düren, which was still burning. Düren was a ghost city, and many of the ghosts were very new. The dead littered the streets like empty orange skins. This was a rich city of many beautiful homes, tumbled marble now and scorched mahogany.

No bridges into the city remained, but engineers were busily constructing temporary ones of heavy timbers. There was a large sign over the one on which we crossed: YOU ARE NOW ENTERING DÜREN, THROUGH THE COURTESY OF THE 8TH DIVISION.

The next town was Niederau, and there we left the trucks and took shelter against sporadic shelling. The town had been captured only a few hours before. Between shells we strolled in the ruined formal garden behind the house in which we'd taken refuge. Crocuses bloomed there, and from the dark shadow of yews an indifferent marble Eros simpered at the chickens that scratched for grubs at his feet.

There was a piano in the house, a good piano, with a volume of Mozart sonatas open on the music rack. I thirsted for the astringent coolness of Mozart, but the men wanted "Stardust" and "Deep Purple." They were right: what have larks and nightingales to do with a burning city?

In the few hours that we lingered there I witnessed again the strange fever of destruction that attacks soldiers. I watched in silence while windows were smashed by deliberate rifle butts, while lace curtains were shredded and fine furniture scarred by bayonets. I protested weakly when two men, finding nothing of value in a handsome sideboard, gave vent to their disappointment by tearing the magnificent carved doors from their hinges. My protest accomplished nothing. They looked at me suspiciously, regarding my pleas as a mark of weakness. They were diverted from further meaningless destruction by the discovery of a secret cupboard under the stairs. Torn open, it revealed neat stores of linen and damask, blankets, satin comforters, also three watches, two cameras, and a cigarette lighter. I shrugged and gave up. Okay, so this was war. Wrapping myself in a comforter of green satin, I dozed on a sofa.

In the afternoon we took off for Kreuzau. E and F companies had the dirty work of assault, while G Company was in reserve, to be called upon only if needed. We made fast time from Niederau to Kreuzau because the road was under harassing enemy fire. En route we met files of prisoners being escorted back to Niederau. It was a cheering sight: things seemed to be going well up ahead. Most of the prisoners we encountered were pathetic denials of the super-race fable. They were dirty (as we were), frightened (as we were), bewildered (as we were), but despairing, as we were not. Whipped in spirit, they were relieved to be prisoners and done with it. They regarded us sullenly; a few smiled in timid greeting.

As company-in-reserve, we waited in the portion of the town that had fallen under the first assault wave. Fighting continued ahead of us, and we could see flickers of movement among the buildings, the darting figures obscured momentarily by clouds of smoke and dust. It was cold waiting, but the house next door to us was afire, its cellar a red-hot pit of burning coal. At frequent intervals I ran over to warm myself, standing as near as possible and half strangling on coal gas.

The owner of our house had obviously been a man with literary tastes. His library on the second floor held not less than five thousand volumes, including the collected works of James

Oliver Curwood, in German—an evidence of that romantic German interest in the America of cowboys and Indians. Other shelves bore witness that not all Germans were good Nazis: I found several Thomas Mann books, as well as a copy of *The Good Soldier Schweik*.

Kreuzau had been the original objective of the day, but it developed that G Company was to push on and take the next village, Drove. We were to be accompanied by two light tanks.

We left Kreuzau at dusk. On the outskirts we paused near a burning mansion for half an hour, waiting for full darkness. We watched the flames lick the interior walls of the house, stood on tiptoe and looked through empty window frames to see the beautiful formal staircase sink smoothly under this bright flood. The dining room was yet undamaged, and we watched intently as the room dimmed with smoke. A dark patch appeared on one wall and spread until the entire wall was black and blacker still, and a small hole appeared in the center of that blackness and a tongue of flame licked inward greedily, grew larger . . . then violently the wall was engulfed and the flames sang with the arrogant voice of trumpets.

At last we started, moving in a skirmish line across an open field, the first platoon leading and keeping pace with the two tanks, which moved forward on the road beside us. We knew that the field was thickly seeded with antipersonnel mines and we were jittery. It was dark and there were humps in the ground that you couldn't see until you stumbled over them and were chilled with sudden fear. The tanks encountered a roadblock, and we halted for a moment. Stupidly, the tanks did the obvious things. They attempted to go around the roadblock, and one of them ran over an antitank mine, subtly planted by the Germans to check that gambit. The ensuing blast shook our nerves considerably, and then we had one tank. We shook a little harder a few minutes later when a sudden sharp explosion told us that someone had stepped on an antipersonnel mine.

At length we reached the outskirts of Drove. The first building was an apartment house, a huge barracks of a building, and we left the field to surround it and search it.

I cannot tell how it feels to enter a strange and hostile building in the dark. There's fear, of course, and tension, and even a kind of exhilaration. Enmity is there like a solid presence, and shadows crouching in doorways and windows are evil. The creaking of timbers, the clattering of loose tin in the wind, are cold hands that stretch toward you in the darkness. Someone is waiting for you . . . at the head of the stairs, machine gun leveled at the landing . . . perhaps around the corner of that half-open door. So you drive yourself, whip yourself into movement, trying to remember what you were taught in Basic Training about the proper way to search a house, and you challenge *"Komme sie raus!"* in a loud voice because you're afraid to show fear. And the squad is mostly green men and you have to put up a front to prove that the job isn't so bad. So you bellow loudly, fire a few rounds through the ceilings of the rooms, heave a couple of grenades into the cellar, and there is complete and dead silence presently, and a moment of pure panic because where the hell has the rest of the squad gone? You find them outside, huddled under a window and afraid to move, and Ketron chews their asses for bunching up in front of a building. You all feel better then, and you move on.

The second and third platoons had passed us while we searched the apartment house. (Clearing a town is a leapfrog business: while you clear one group of houses, the platoon behind you pushes through and works on the next buildings. When you've finished, you bypass them and so on.) We caught up with the other two platoons, passed them, and continued through the dark and blasted streets, hugging the buildings and stepping over the dead. Our assignment was to move through the town to the "point," clear the houses there, and take up positions against possible counterattack.

When we reached the far end of town, Misa pointed out the house the second squad was to occupy. We moved upon it silently, approaching it from the rear through an orchard honeycombed with German foxholes. Ketron and I each took half of the squad and we circled the house, meeting at the main door. We consulted in whispers for a moment, then stepped into the hall. In my boldest voice I challenged, *"Komme sie raus!"* and from the basement came the faint reply, in English, "I surrender!" Stuttering with surprise, I yelled, *"Komme sie raus!"* and paused a moment before adding, weakly, *"Immediatement!"* (Damned if I could think of the German for "Make it snappy!" Wonderful to be a linguist!) We heard footsteps on the cellar stairs and saw the faint glimmer of an approaching light. Finally he appeared, a German soldier in breeches and sleeveless sweater. He carried a carbide lamp, and he complied agreeably when I ordered him to put it out. In his thirties, he was completely self-possessed and unafraid. The situation had its element of humor. He was so much more in command of the situation than we who trembled there with nervous suspicion. He was willing, even eager, to surrender, but there was no servility in his manner. He indicated clearly that this was an affair of honor, arranged between gentlemen. He vowed there was no one else in the house. They had all gone away and he'd been alone there for *"eine stunde."* He wanted to return to the cellar for his coat before being marched off to prison camp, and I nodded permission. The nights were cold, and his coolness of spirit had surely earned him a warm body. I accompanied him while the rest of the squad waited in the hall, alert for trouble.

The cellar was a surprise. There was a glowing kitchen stove, a table covered with dishes, a white-painted bed in the corner, several mattresses on the floor ... even a tapestry hanging on the whitewashed wall to dress the place up a bit.

The man's calm aplomb was a constant amazement to me. All day he'd been expecting our arrival and passed the hours preparing for it: washing and shaving, packing his personal belongings. He talked freely as he busied himself assembling his gear, making disparaging remarks about the Nazis, comments like *"Deutschland ist alles kaput!"* and even an intimation that the Gestapo was responsible for his presence in the German army. When he was ready, I ushered him upstairs and sent him to the company C.P. under guard.

Then we looked around. Our situation was peculiar. The house itself was on the very point of the town, the last house on the road. The rub lay in its construction. All the windows were in the north and south walls, the narrow ends of the house. The west side, beyond which were our nearest neighbors, was a blank wall, innocent of door or window openings. The east side, facing an orchard, a field, a hill, and the enemy, had but two openings: the "front door" and a small window on the landing of the stairway to the second floor. A helluva setup for defensive positions. In the event of counterattack we'd *have* to stay and slug it out—we couldn't get out of the place without passing under the noses of the Germans.

We set guards at the windows, arranging the guard tricks so two men at a time could get a little sleep in the warm cellar. At two-thirty A.M. Leo Allen, now our platoon runner, brought orders from the company C.P. that all men were to remain awake: counterattack was expected at any moment. I made numerous pots of coffee from the jar of ersatz coffee we found in the cellar—and lousy stuff it was, too!—and fried the cold boiled potatoes I found in a kettle behind the stove. One at a time the men came down to get warm and have a bite to eat. We hadn't eaten since six the previous morning.

During the night, German soldiers who had been hiding in cellars and lofts tried to slip out of town. One of our scouts—Bob Berthot of Niagara Falls—saw a moving shadow in the street and challenged it. The shadow whirled and fired at the window where Bob stood. Bob returned the fire and missed, but the noise woke the men in nearby houses and rifles began cracking throughout our area. The total bag was seven prisoners, two of them wounded.

At four-thirty I woke Ketron, who had been asleep for two hours, and took his place on the bed. Half an hour later he rushed in and called to me: "The Jerries are counterattacking!"

We could see them in the half dawn, coming down the sides of the high hill to the east, slipping through the field and working their way to the ridge beyond the orchard. That ridge was only a hundred yards from the house, and safe from our fire. But they had to cross a stretch of open ground to get there, and we opened up. They weren't expecting it, and they hightailed for cover.

We weren't happy. Not only were we trapped in the house, unable to leave it while the Jerries were out there, but we had no means of communication with the C.P. Or with anyone. The 26th Regiment had pushed through Drove during the night to attack the town on our right flank, and our phone wires had been ripped out by passing tanks. We had no way to report our plight, no way to ask for ammo or reinforcements, no way to contact medics if we needed them. We felt uncomfortably deserted, as though we eight were alone against the numberless Germans moving so ominously through the field.

The next seven hours were a ride on a runaway merry-go-round. We were dizzied and blurred by speed and excitement. We watched so intently that our eyeballs ached, firing whenever we glimpsed a scrap of blue-gray uniform or caught a hint of movement. Once, a blue-clad rump appeared squarely between the sights of my rifle, and when I squeezed the trigger, it leaped convulsively, as though it had been caressed with a hot iron. We crowed with vulgar delight.

The Germans succeeded in working their way to the ridge, and from there opened up on us with rifles, machine guns, and burp guns. Since our one firing position was the window on the landing, we crowded around it, and even the men guarding the other windows left their posts and flocked to the landing, only to be chased back to their assigned positions.

Ketron and I circulated nervously from post to post. We were uncomfortably aware that the south side of the house was our soft spot: the orchard offered a convenient avenue of approach to the very windows of the house, and the enemy could be upon us in a moment.

I climbed the stairs to the attic. It wasn't a smart place to go; half of the roof—the half facing the enemy—had been blown away, and I was in a helluva spot if mortars were brought up against us. It would be a good position until that moment, however, because I could look over the top of the ridge and beyond it, and see enemy soldiers who were concealed from the men on the floor below me. So I lay in the plaster dust on the bare floor, open sky and broken rafters above me, the tangled clutter of anyone's attic around me—trunks, old books, clothes, broken furniture, and discarded toys.

It's hard to write this next part, because this is where I killed a man. The first one. The first one I was sure of. It ought to be told simply, because it's important that you should understand what it's like—how you feel when you have trapped a small, running creature between the cold sights of a deliberate gun and pulled the trigger, and suddenly the creature has stopped running and is lying there, and now it's a man and his body is naked and soft and crumpled. It ought to be told without hint of boast, and yet so that you would see there's something of the bragging boy in the sense of achievement; it ought to be told without sentiment, and yet so you would see what a big thing it is.

I saw a German soldier rise from behind the protective shoulder of the ridge and start to run to the rear, sprinting across the open field toward the hills. Perhaps he was a runner, a messenger—I cannot remember that he carried a weapon. It occurred to me later that he must have been young and very green, because he ran in a straight line, an easy course to follow with the sights of a rifle. He had unbuttoned his overcoat for greater freedom in running, and the skirts flapped like huge blue wings around his legs. He was a moving dot of blue, a clumsy blue object to be stalked deliberately ... now, impaled within the sights, the blue coat was enormous, presenting itself to my squinted eye like a cloud, like a house, like a target painted solid blue on the firing range at Camp Wheeler. I squeezed the trigger and he fell. He did not move again, and the skirts of the blue overcoat made a patch of unnatural color in the field where he lay.

For a moment I was triumphant and my eyes lingered on my prize, confirming it. There he was! ... He was there, still lying there, and it wasn't a game any longer. He hadn't risen to his feet, dusted himself off, and thumbed his nose at me gaily before starting to run again. He lay there, quiet now, and he hadn't moved, and I laid my rifle on the floor of the attic—carefully, because of the plaster dust—and put my head in my hands. I wanted to be sick, but there wasn't time to be sick.

And I thought, Poor bastard . . . he was hungry and cold, too
. . . scared and homesick and missing his people and tired of
war. And I was sick and ashamed because I never hated him,
never him specifically, and I never wanted to kill him. And it
was an evil and an ugly thing that this man, this particular
Hans or Ludwig or Emil, should lie dead on a field because I
had willed it; it was an evil and an ugly thing that this particular man should never again hear music or feel the hands of
his children upon his face.

Then I picked up my rifle and went back to my job.

The fight lasted throughout the day, and other men in
blue-gray went down, not to move again, but their falling did
not hit me as a personal thing. They were moving targets,
that was all. But again and again my eyes turned back to the
figure lying quiet in the stubble, the blue overcoat like wings
beside him.

A new danger developed while I was in the attic. Two
German tanks, painted white, appeared on the crest of the hill.
They were easy to see against the dark background of pine.
One was a light tank, a child's toy beside the grim hulk of the
other, which we recognized as one of the dreaded Tigers.
Between our house and the tanks was only the field, a bare and
empty space. I didn't see how they could miss us.

As the tanks opened up, the Germans behind the ridge
started a mortar barrage. I scurried down the stairs to Ketron
and we conferred hastily. We figured the Jerries would throw
a lot of lead and then rush the house from the ridge. We
sweated it out, fearing the one solid hit from the Tiger that
would surely come.

The tanks had been observed by our tank destroyers in the
center of town, and the resulting fire was hot enough to force
the Tiger from its position on the hill. It lumbered away toward the lower end of town, and we heaved king-size gasps of
relief. I started for the attic once more, and Ketron turned to go
to the cellar. I'd just reached the attic when a breath-walloping
explosion rocked the house and plaster dust billowed up in a
choking, blinding cloud. Coughing and strangling, I crawled

to the stairway on hands and knees and yelled down, "Everybody all right? Anybody hurt down there?"

There was a hubbub of sound and I heard Ketron's voice: "Help me . . . help me!"

Feeling my way down the stairs, I bumped into someone who identified himself as Joe Hornung. Believing that Ketron was with me, Joe had been on his way to the attic. I sent Joe toward the cellar to care for Ketron, and I got to work, hurrying the nerve-shattered men back to their posts to prepare for an enemy rush. Fifteen minutes later the rush hadn't materialized, there was a lull on our front, and I went downstairs to see about Ketron.

The front door had been blown clear from its hinges. It leaned in the archway opening on the parlor. Broken laths protruded from the battered walls, and plaster dust was inches thick on the floor. A tank shell had scored a direct hit on the door. The gaping doorway exposed to enemy observation a stretch of floor that had to be crossed in order to reach the cellar. I bounded over it like a frightened rabbit and went down to Ketron.

There was blood in the hall, blood on the stairs, blood on the cellar floor. Ket was stretched on the floor and Joe was bandaging his leg. "How bad?" I asked, and Joe replied, "I think his leg's smashed above the knee. And there's a bad shrapnel wound in the inner side of his thigh." I looked. Another two inches and Ket could have forgotten that girl back home—he'd have been a bachelor for the rest of his life.

When Joe reached him, Ket had been doggedly crawling down the cellar stairs, dragging his useless leg. He was losing a lot of blood. There was nothing I could do for him, and my responsibility now was the squad. I left him in Joe's care and went upstairs.

The day wheeled slowly by, and after a while the tension lessened. The Germans showed no inclination to storm the house, and the whole business became a dreary guard detail, a matter of watching as intently as our tired eyes would permit, firing at each furtive glimpse of blue-gray uniform. Ketron needed medical aid, but we couldn't get it because our phone connection with the C.P. was gone. During a lull, I leaned from the south window and yelled loudly to attract the attention of our nearest neighbors, a hundred yards away. They heard me and waved, but a solo voice wasn't strong enough to be understood. Collaring two men, I formed a trio, and through our concerted vocal effort we got our message across. A medic appeared within half an hour and without haste, without fear, walked the length of the house in full view of the Germans on the ridge, entered by the ruined doorway where Ketron had been hit, and asked where the wounded man was. I was breathless with admiration of his cool daring.

It took nerve to be a medic. Geneva Convention notwithstanding, medics were fired on sometimes. Often it was accidental, but sometimes it was not, and many men swore bitterly that the Jerries always tried to get our medics. (I don't believe that. That afternoon I saw an example of what *can* happen, the mistake that is so easily snowballed into legend.)

The medic who came to care for Ketron walked—(walked, not ran!)—the length of the house in full view of the Jerry lines. Finding that a stretcher would be necessary, he went back for it, and appeared a little later accompanied by four bearers who carried a folded stretcher. As they entered the door a shot came from the German lines. Only one shot. Leaving the house with Ketron on the stretcher, their progress was slow as they maneuvered through the doorway, and again a single shot came from the German lines. They continued with their ticklish job without looking around, but the men in the house were raging, convinced that the Germans were deliberately trying to kill our medics. They vowed vengeance and swore that they'd fire on the next German medic they saw. I argued and pleaded with them to no avail, and finally said bluntly that I'd shoot the first man who fired on a German medic. My argument was that some eager beaver in the German lines had failed to note the folded stretcher, the dim red crosses on helmets and armbands, and thought simply that we were getting reinforcements. Seeing the medics leaving, a similar eager beaver, or perhaps the same one, had assumed that *we* were running out. Proof of my theory lay in the fact that on each occasion only a single shot had been fired, and had the intent been truly evil, there was ample time and opportunity to pick off every one of the medics as they walked the length of the house. It seemed evident to me that the shots were mistakes, fired in haste, and the fire halted as soon as the mistake had been realized.

The risks our medics took shocked me because their immunity was so scantily guaranteed. There was little in their dress to indicate their calling. Lacking only weapons, they wore the usual GI uniform, and their sole distinctive markings were red crosses on a white ground, painted on the four sides of their helmets, and white armbands, also marked with a red cross. A helmet and an armband, that was all. But helmets got dirty, scratched, chipped; armbands became grimy rags, twisted, narrow bands that were indistinguishable on dark sleeves. I'm surprised that *more* medics weren't killed. And I was filled with admiring envy of the way the Germans protected their medics, as demonstrated that day.

Casualties in the German ranks had been high, and the field was dotted with motionless splotches of blue-gray. The German medics appeared during a lull. From a clump of trees on the hill a large white flag was raised, bearing an enormous red cross. The man carrying the flag remained hidden in the trees for several minutes, waving the flag back and forth slowly, calling our attention to it. Then he stepped out and stood motionless a moment longer, still waving the flag. He walked down the hill to a wounded man and stood by his side, the flag held high. After a moment four stretcher bearers and a medic came from the clump behind him, to where he stood. Swiftly they did their work, and the bearers took the loaded stretcher back up the hill while the medic and the flag waver moved to the next casualty. Soon the bearers appeared again, emerging from the same clump of trees and carrying the empty stretcher. They carried it open, a man at each pole. That was important, I thought, because the grouping of four men on a stretcher is distinctive and not likely to be confused with four infantry replacements coming to reinforce a threatened position.

Slowly, they cleared the field of their wounded, and I watched intently, hoping a little. There was a figure in the middle of the field, his blue overcoat spread wide. At last they walked over there and the medic kneeled for a moment. Only for a moment. Then he rose and walked away without a backward look, walked across the field to another blue-clad form, and the bearers followed him, their stretcher hanging loose and empty.

Around noon the Germans started to withdraw, slipping through the tall grass, darting across open ground, working their way back to the hill and the shelter of the trees. They suffered many casualties en route, because they took foolish chances in their eagerness to get away.

About one o'clock we saw someone walking along the road that led from the ridge into town. He was staggering, reeling from side to side, and we could see it was a German soldier. I ordered him in when he reached the house. In his hand he carried a safe-conduct. (Our planes showered German lines with official safe-conducts that promised fair treatment to German soldiers who surrendered honorably. They were signed by Eisenhower.) When we'd examined our prisoner, we looked at each other in silence, respect and admiration battling the sense of triumph that is the rightful mood of the prisoner taker. He had walked in—no one knew how far—carrying all of his equipment except his weapons, and he had seven wounds in his body. One thigh was horribly torn by shrapnel, the raw meat squeezing out in ugly red and white bulges. Below this was another, smaller wound. A gaping wound in the calf of the other leg. A bullet hole in his shoulder, a bullet hole in his neck, a bullet hole in the middle of his back from which dark, rich blood pulsed sullenly, and another shrapnel wound at the base of his spine. He was a lot of man. He didn't whimper when we dressed his wounds, although we were clumsy. Having done what we could, we laid him gently on a sofa and spread a torn quilt over him. He had to lie on his face, one leg on the sofa and the other propped on a chair next to it.

He was in his mid-twenties, seemed well-educated, and

spoke English. His uniform was of the Luftwaffe, but he told us that this had been his first day in the infantry. (An indication of how desperately the Germans needed men. And gasoline. There was no shortage of planes and pilots in the Reich, he said, but there was no gas. As a result, many men had recently been transferred from the Luftwaffe to the infantry.)

Our phone line was repaired during the afternoon, and I immediately called the C.P. to report our prisoner. I asked for a medic and an ambulance. The answer I received made us sick with helpless rage. The C.P. refused to send a medic: the officious noncom on the phone, who refused to let me speak to an officer, said that since we'd already bandaged the man's wounds, there was nothing more a medic could do. There was, of course; our repair work had been crude and inexpert, and we had no morphine, something he needed desperately. At first he'd been stoically silent, but then we began to hear small moans, quickly stifled, but moans. The C.P. also told me that we had no ambulance: we'd have to care for him as best we could until we were relieved, and then we could turn him over to the relieving outfit. He'd be their baby.

Twice more I called the C.P. and pleaded for medical aid. The man's courage reproached us all. Now the moans were more frequent, forced from him, inched out over an iron determination that faltered only momentarily. He became delirious and we bathed his head with water, feeling sick and helpless, ashamed of our own uniforms and unable to look at the table where we'd placed the safe-conduct he had carried in his hand. The safe-conduct promised him "medical attention as required," and that he would be "removed from the danger zone as soon as possible." Even if the C.P. chose to disregard Eisenhower's orders, over and above those orders were the basic humanities that, theoretically, we were fighting to preserve.

We were relieved at dusk, and the wounded German was still in the house when we left. I think he was unconscious—he didn't answer when I bent over him to promise once more, however feebly, that he would be cared for soon. The outfit relieving us promised to take good care of him. I hope they did. I'd like to think that he lived.

After reporting at the C.P., we had our first hot meal in two days. Then we found a barn and rested in the hay for an hour, exchanging stories—most of them exaggerated—with the other squads and platoons. Our casualties for the day had been surprisingly light: half a dozen dead and a dozen and a half wounded. Among the dead was Boyd Smith, leader of the first squad, who had returned from the hospital only two days before. He'd been given the Purple Heart while in the hospital, and mailed it to his mother immediately. After comparing what we knew of mail service versus the speed of official notices, we decided that his mother would receive the medal and his accompanying letter almost simultaneously with the official report of his death.

Heard an ugly story from Chief as we lay in the barn. He claimed he'd seen a woman with the Jerries on the hill. She had started to run across the field, her blond hair streaming. She wore a green dress. He played with her for a while, teasing her with bullets that landed directly before her flying feet. At each shot, each deadly puff of dust, she would throw herself on the ground and lie there for a moment. Then she'd get up and start to run again. Tiring of the game at last, he ended it, and when she went down the next time, she stayed down, the green dress flung vulgarly above her naked hips.

We were sickened by the story, but didn't know whether to believe it. You never could tell with Chief's stories, and this one might have been true. It's common knowledge that the Germans are frequently attended by camp followers. We've captured some. (They always claim to be nurses, but questioning usually reveals that their talents, though possibly equally hygienic, were employed in more robust activities— surcease for the healthy and whole, rather than the wounded. "Horizontal refreshment," we called it.) At any rate, sometimes there *were* women with the Jerries. And Chief's ability as a sharpshooter was well-known, so his story may have been true. True or not, we weren't amused.

We rested in the hay for an hour, and the fever of action drained from us slowly. The hammering in our heads lessened and we curled up, ready for sleep. Then the order came: "On your feet!" We were to push during the night and take the next town, Soller. The men reeled with weariness as they fell into line, and we moved out along a mine-flanked road, under enemy fire.

Soller was not far, and the nervous shells that dropped along our route kept us moving briskly. Half the town had already been cleared, and we were to finish the job. It was the night we cleared Drove all over again—sweating, tension, and terror; darkened houses and shadows that moved.

A certain episode of that night is still an unexplained mystery. One of the men, hearing a suspicious noise, immediately hailed, *"Komme sie raus!"* There was instant silence. He called again, and again there was no answer. Alarmed, he yelled for the platoon leader: "Hey, Misa!" And a strange, unhuman voice echoed him, "Misa!" Again he called, "Misa!" and the mysterious voice repeated, "Misa!" Only the single word. They sent for me, and I arrived just as Misa hurried up. Standing in the darkest shadow I could find, I hurled orders and threats in bad German at the dark house. And the mocking reply came back, "Mee-ee-sa!" Nothing more. The voice had a cavernous, echoing quality, seeming to come from the cellar. Cautiously, we crept to the cellar door, opened it, and yelled down. There was no reply; the voice was silent. We fired a few shots down the stairs and through the floor and finally tossed a grenade into the dark hole. Still no sound. Mystified and more than a little shaken by the experience, we finished clearing the village. An hour later Misa returned to the house, determined to ferret out the mystery. He found nothing. It remains a mystery, and the most reasonable explanation we were able to invent was that it was a parrot, left behind by its owners. A parrot, an exotic tropical bird in an almost medieval German hamlet of half a hundred houses? Well, *you* suggest a better answer!

The first platoon was, as usual, on the point of the town. We spread out in a fan-shaped line in a garden, in the middle of which was a German-constructed dugout. It was well made: long enough to hold ten men, buttressed and braced with heavy timbers, and deep. The earth floor was thick with the blankets and quilts left behind by the fleeing Germans. Misa suggested it as a central C.P. for all the squad leaders since the entire platoon was emplaced in the garden, and we moved in gratefully. (I was acting squad leader, now that Ketron was gone.) I spent most of the night helping one of the greener replacements dig his foxhole, and tottered off to bed at four A.M.

The hours that passed while we dug had a strange beauty. The night was very black, no moon or stars, but out in the field a hayrick blazed, set afire by a stray shell. Clouds of heavy white smoke billowed into the air, and we were choked with the acrid taste of burning hay.

Before we'd finished our digging, someone in authority decided that the half-dozen hayricks still standing offered too kindly a cover to the enemy, providing them with a convenient route to come almost within spittin' distance of us. The order came, "Burn the hay!" White phosphorus grenades were fired at the hayricks, and within five minutes all of them were ablaze. The nearby buildings were thrown in startling relief against the encircling night, and we were nervously aware of how nakedly we ourselves were revealed in that glare of light. After a while the flames subsided, but another danger arose: the heavy smoke hugged the ground, and a blanket of haze cut our visibility to less than fifty feet. Tears streaming from our aching eyes, we peered into the smoke, halting our digging in tense alarm at every small sound. The fire disturbed a nearby owl and he hooted fretfully throughout the night. A macabre touch that was hardly necessary, I thought.

February 28.

A dim and misty day. With hungry eyes I noted the magnificent brussels sprouts in the garden, wondering if there was time to cook a mess of them. There wasn't. At ten-thirty A.M. the familiar word came: "Get ready to move!"

After an uncomfortable passage along a mined road under enemy artillery, we reached Vettweiss. We halted there, and the platoon wearily collapsed in the elegant home of a wealthy apothecary. An imposing library filled one room of the mansion and I browsed happily. It was an astonishing collection. Several shelves were given over entirely to Nazi-approved histories of Germany—glorious Germany, valiant Germany, warrior Germany, virile and clean-jawed Germany, endlessly depicted in hand-to-hand combat with hordes of evil-looking wretches with slanted foreheads and greasy mouths. (I only know what I saw in the pictures.)

Food arrived at three and we hurried to the chow truck, stepping carelessly over the dead bodies that dotted the streets. Then more waiting, and our tension mounted with each passing moment because they didn't tell us and they *didn't* tell us when we'd be leaving. At last the official word came: after dark, about nine o'clock. Meanwhile, we'd better rest.

The cellar of the mansion was crowded, every man trying to find stretching space. I discovered a curious cement "room" in the very middle of the cellar. It was an indoor air raid shelter, and the only entrance to it was a small opening close to the floor. I wriggled in on my belly and was delighted to find it furnished with mattresses and quilts. Another man, Guyette, crawled in with me and we made ourselves comfortable. I didn't know Guyette well. He was a new replacement, but he seemed a nice youngster—dark, quiet, clean-looking. He bubbled now with a shy excitement, because only a couple of days ago word had come from home that his first baby had been born. He was proud and happy, and his new delight in his manhood was a gentle thing to see. His joy made me feel old and tired and a little soiled. We talked for a while, then fell silent. And slept finally.

At dusk we were awakened and briefed. Our immediate objective was the town of Gladbach, and the first platoon's job was to set up some roadblocks on the far end of town and latch ourselves firmly to the three roads that converged there. We were advised that we might have to throw a bridge across the creek on the edge of Gladbach in order to reach the pinpoint on the map that was our assigned position.

We moved out, again over a mine-studded road. In Gladbach we paused for an hour before pushing on. We'd been hoping that the 26th, which had taken the town, managed to bridge the creek: we were like cats in our loathing of water and we knew that the stream would be swollen and icy. The 26th *had* managed to build a bridge, but it was knocked out by delicately accurate German artillery. They'd tried again, and the second bridge had been blown to bits.

Cautiously, we crept out of Gladbach. Arriving at the creek, we found it deeper and swifter than we had expected, and that it was actually *two* streams. Down a slippery clay bank, we waded the first stream—one man fell flat, weapons and all—crossed a thin spit of land, waded the second stream, and clambered up the steep bank on the far side. Wet, cold, and disgusted, I crawled up the bank, my fingers reaching for the weeds at the top, when *wham!* Blinding white light burned my eyes and I threw myself back down the bank, stars jigging under my closed and aching eyelids. I listened to the thin and evil hissing of the shrapnel and tensed myself. The first squad was just ahead of me and I could hear someone groaning. I waited a long five minutes, then lunged over the rim of the bank and across the road to the dark shelter of the trees. As the men joined me, we moved out hurriedly, passing a dark and motionless shape on the road. (Next day we learned that two men had been wounded by that shell and one killed. The dead man was Guyette. For a time they hadn't been able to identify him because they couldn't find his head. It was lying in the ditch on the other side of the road.)

With ragged nerves to prick us on, we moved along briskly, but soon we had another bad five minutes. With no preliminary whine of warning, a shell hit the road a few yards ahead of us. I had never seen a shell explode with such dazzling white light, but Misa—wise old man!—recognized it instantly as an American bazooka rocket and realized that we were being fired on by our own troops. There followed a screaming and obscene dialogue between Misa and some unmistakably American voices in the woods. Most of the exchange consisted of Misa describing in violent detail precisely what he was going to do to the "goddamn ——s who were firing those sunsabitchin' ——s at his —— men."

At last we reached the fork in the road. Ahead of us,

crouched on a low hill, was the woods in which we were to place an outpost. Our Intelligence had reported that they "didn't *think* there were any Jerries in the woods, but they weren't sure." Weak assurance in the middle of the night.

Chief and I led our squads up the right fork—his squad on the left side of the road, mine on the right. In the black silence we failed to notice that our road split and became two, parted first by a thick hedge of thorn apple and then, as the distance between us increased, by the width of a field. I became suddenly aware of this when we reached the end of the hedge, and on my left, instead of the road I expected to see, an open field appeared. Now the sky was filled with low, scudding clouds and the moon began to peer out fitfully. On the far side of the field I could dimly see Chief and his men. The moonlight also kindly revealed the barbed wire fences that divided the field.

I told the scouts to cut a path through the barbed wire so we might join Chief on the main road. We started crawling across the field—the scouts first, then me. Reaching the first fence, the lead scout cut the bottom strand and the wire twanged loudly. We froze and waited. When nothing happened, he pushed through and moved on. The second scout was just passing through the opening when the hysterical rattle of a burp gun burst from the woods ahead. We hugged the ground, feeling with desperate fingers for a hollow, a depression in the arched breast of the field that would offer cover. There was a moment of blind panic and then we realized with a surge of warm relief that the enemy gunner was shooting at Chief's squad, which had incautiously silhouetted itself against the night sky for a moment. Somebody else was getting it, but we were safe for the moment—that's all that mattered to us. Kind of a callous way of looking at things? Yeah, ain't it?

Raising my nose from the mud a few inches, I looked for the scouts. They were gone, vanished . . . lost in the dim grayness. I couldn't call aloud, but I whispered their names and the thin sound seemed a scream. There was no answer; they were dead . . . or perhaps they had gained the upper road and joined Chief's squad. At any rate, the open field was a lousy place for brooding: the sky had miraculously cleared and the moon was brilliant. I wriggled backward across the field to the bank and found Misa waiting there with the word that the C.O. wanted the squad to work along the bank and reach the woods. He wanted us to "wipe out those Jerries," they were "holding us up!" O gallant phrases . . .

Leaving the BAR team with Misa, I started off with the three remaining men of the squad, crawling on our guts in the ditch. It was a slow, painful progress and I looked back frequently, needing the visual assurance of the three men following. They were there, all right, but I felt alone and damn well scared. My pack interfered with crawling and I sloughed it off, and then my gas mask. The three-quarter moon hung steady, glittered on my glasses like sequins and I winced, imagining the sniper's bullet pierce my eye and the bright crystal slivers drive deep into my brain.

The mud in the ditch was foul-smelling and slimy, and I hated the feel of it and myself for being squeamish at such a moment. Nettles whipped my face, and my hands and knees flinched from the knife edges of unseen stones. Ahead of us the woods were black, but we could hear movement in the trees—they were there, all right . . . they were there . . . wonder if my ass is low enough? . . . why oh goddamn it why doesn't that bitchin' moon go away, and goddamn 'em anyway!

I stopped. The protecting bank on my left had dwindled away and ahead of me was an open space, fifty feet wide and flooded with moonlight. On its far edge were the brooding woods and the patient guns, the eyes watching for the black shape that would attempt to swim that white pool. I wiped my sweaty hands on my pants, nervously clasped and unclasped my rifle. Glancing backward, I saw the quiet figure of the man behind me . . . waiting for me to make up my mind.

Maybe I'd have made the woods . . . I don't know. But while I hesitated, trying to whip up my courage, I heard my name whispered. Word had been passed up from the rear that we were to withdraw, not attempt it. Shaky with relief, I crawled back to where Misa huddled against the bank. He said the old man had decided it was too risky: we'd try something else. We retreated to the fork in the road and were joined there by the other squads. I worried about my missing scouts, but they drifted in shortly. They had been with Chief's squad.

During the night the Jerries withdrew, with the exception of a few stragglers who surrendered in the morning. One neither surrendered nor fled. He was lying dead of a bullet wound in the throat when we went up to take a look at the enemy positions.

The hill was a honeycomb of trenches, passages, and cross passages. German equipment and arms were scattered throughout the woods: blankets, mess gear, canteens, rifles, burp guns, machine guns, hand grenades, bazookas, and ammunition. Who said the German army was feeling the pinch of shortages?

[That rumor of "shortages" circulated persistently, and perhaps an examination of the whole picture would prove it true. But not according to our experience. Everywhere we went we captured vast supplies of German arms and equipment, and we saw no evidence of shortages until the very end of the war, except for gasoline and medical supplies. German tanks and planes needed gas, and there was progressively less; wounded men needed drugs, and there were literally none. In Bamberg after the war I saw hundreds of amputees, Germans whose arms or legs had been amputated at shoulder or hip, often for quite minor wounds. There had been no drugs to halt gangrene, and the German surgeons had been ruthless.]

As the night sky started to lighten I noted a glimmer of startling white in the black shadows of the roadside. With the coming of true dawn, the black and white patchwork was identified as a cow, a young and pretty beast, vivid as the lithograph on a dairy calendar. She did not rise when daylight had come, so I went down to investigate. As I drew near, I saw the blood on her right flank, but she struggled to her feet and stood motionless, regarding me steadily. Her leg hung limp, and I saw it was broken in several places and cruelly torn by shrapnel. She made no complaint but looked at me with bewildered, pain-filled eyes. They asked nothing, and that was the thing I could not bear. I climbed back up the hill and asked the men if one of them would volunteer to shoot her. Quickly, through the head. One volunteered, and I forced myself to watch him. She died quietly, making no sound, and the heavy body sank unstruggling at the side of the road. It was curiously comforting to see that the suffering head rested on a soft patch of grass, shaded by the trees overhead.

Shortly after daylight the kitchen jeep arrived with hot coffee and C rations. Then we moved up the road several hundred yards, passing the woods we had besieged in the night. At the edge of a wide field we dug in once more. And so we spent the day, and I tried to forget the spitting rain, the cold winds, my wet and aching feet, my sleep-heavy body. It was March 1, the winter was over, there was an occasional flash of sunshine, and the war was dying. I lifted a German blanket from the abandoned equipment in the woods, curled up in my hole—which was a kind of cave, dug into the steep side of a sandbank—and slept for an hour. Then we were told we'd be relieved, and pulled back to some town for a rest.

CHAPTER SEVEN

"There was a moment of silence when the morning stood waiting, not breathing. . . ."

March 3.

We're in the town of Gladbach, to which we retired two days ago. Since then we've done nothing but sleep, wake to eat, and return again to sleep. There's a stove in our room, and we cannot get enough of this blessed warmth. A final miracle: the windows are unbroken. We keep the doors tightly closed and drowse contentedly in the heat.

I dine from china these days. It is apparently a German custom of long standing in these parts to honor a child on his First Communion by presenting him with a porcelain cup, designed for the occasion. I've been drinking my coffee from such a cup, presented to one Friedrich in 1887, and have grown quite fond of it and of the fat cherubim who simper so pinkly from its sides. My fancy has been caught by another ceremonial cup, however, which is lumpy with full-blown, life-size gilt roses. Having shaved this morning, I do feel elegant and airily rococo with such a cup in my hand. It's my last opportunity for such elaborate refinements—we're alerted for a move before dawn tomorrow. Ho hum.

I've been officially "put in" for a buck sergeancy. I have to wait until confirmation filters down through channels, and then—an "acting gadget" no longer! One privilege to which I look forward hungrily is our next rest period in a room alone.

List among other army complaints: "Always a private and never alone."

In spite of early Hitlerian efforts to revive the ancient Teuton mythology, Germany today offers denial to the feeble Allied propaganda that whimpered of empty churches and a dying Christianity. If one could accept the evidence at face value, Germany is as ardently religious as France and Belgium. The average home in these small towns is a rat's nest of holy pictures, plaster images, relics, crucifixes, testaments, and rosaries. Enshrined in a niche over the main entrance of most houses is a statue of the Virgin Mother or the Holy Family, and it is the rare room that lacks a crucifix, a lithograph of the Bleeding Heart, and a wall receptacle for holy water. Catholic Germany . . . and what an ironic paradox that a people so seemingly devoted to One who preached "Love thy neighbor" should be the most intolerant, the most rapacious and warlike nation of our time.

March 4.

Early in the morning we left Gladbach and rode in the rain to a town whose name I do not know. We detrucked there and waited for darkness, took shelter from the rain in an empty house and "explored."

I'm the world's lousiest looter. While the canny soldier busies himself searching for jewelry, pistols, cameras, and liquor (usually in that order), I am deep in somebody's fruit cellar, gorging myself on canned fruits. This house was notable for the preserved strawberries I discovered, cold and sweet, as large as plums and floating in thick syrup. I ate a quart, then started on a can of plums.

My remarks about looting would doubtless offend a lot of people. Well, perhaps George really did win that Leica in a crap game, and maybe it's true that Johnny swapped a Luger for that string of pearls. There were men who didn't loot, and their relatives can be proud of them. But I'll hazard a guess and say that eighty percent of the men looted, whenever and wherever possible. I make a distinction between confiscation and looting. All weapons, for instance, however outmoded or rusty, were legitimate prizes according to the rules of warfare, as were cameras. But there were strict orders prohibiting the seizure of jewelry, silverware, personal belongings, clothing, food, and so on. Sometimes a special order was issued, putting a specific *Verboten* on leather goods, furs, etc.

The officer or noncom bestrode a delicate fence on the question of looting. By superior command he was constrained to repress pillage, but the officer who followed every command to the letter soon found himself no longer in rapport with his men. I could not agree with the rule of thumb frequently quoted by field grade officers that "it isn't necessary for an officer to be liked; the important thing is that he be respected." That's double-talk to me—in the intimacy of frontline army life, respect and liking are too closely bound to permit a clean line of demarcation to be drawn between them. It may be good barracks discipline, but it isn't for the front line.

Most of the officers I knew best agreed with me that the liking of the men was a necessary element of real discipline and morale—not spit-and-polish discipline, but the kind that held when all the chips were down.

All of which is a roundabout way of saying that sometimes I deliberately shut my eyes to the acquisition of items the army regarded as loot. There were also occasions when it became necessary to step in and say flatly, "No! This you will not take!"

Looting was base and I do not seek to justify it, but it rarely distressed me, as did deliberate, purposeless destruction. I winced at the havoc we visited upon German homes—the furniture smashed, silks and laces ripped for the fun of hearing them tear, delicate embroideries and fine linens used as toilet paper, books and pictures defaced, fragile porcelain thrown against a wall, noble crystal shattered in a tinkle of outraged chimes. It was the bullyboy aspect of war that sickened me.

A final word on looting: in writing this I have employed the reference "the men," and it will be interpreted as meaning "enlisted men." Let me set that straight. Notwithstanding the many fine and upright officers who did not loot, the most ruthless, avaricious looters of all were officers. The explanation is simple. It's not that the cupidity of officers was greater, but that—by virtue of their bars, their leaves, their eagles, or their stars—they had greater opportunities. True, they could only rarely indulge in the furtive searching of bureau drawers, but they could loot on a grand scale quite beyond the humble GI. When we moved into a town, the most handsome houses were set aside for officers' quarters. Looting in mansions was always good, and many an officer's home in the States is now enriched by objets d'art he did not purchase. Further, the enlisted man's domain of command was never more than a house or two at best, while officers frequently had control over large areas of conquered enemy country and over items in quantity. There were jeeps and trailers to transport the belongings of officers—belongings that included both regular army equipment and those "little things" picked up en route—fine hunting rifles and shotguns, chests of sterling silver, rugs, oil paintings, fur coats, all the cumbersome things the overladen doggie was forced to pass up because he was physically unable to carry them on his back. If I seem particularly bitter, I have reason: once, I acquired a magnificent double-barreled shotgun, a weapon fashioned with loving care by the hands of a craftsman. For all of one weary day I carried it; then, bleeding inwardly with self-pity and rage, I surrendered it to the officer who had several times offered to "take it off my hands." I could carry its added weight no more. I saw it the next day in his jeep, swaddled tenderly in a shelter half to protect it from being marred. He hadn't offered to carry it *for* me—he just wanted to help me out by "taking it off my hands"!

Lastly, an officer could send home loot of a sort that the GI did not dare submit for mailing, knowing it would be censored or confiscated. Further, we believed firmly that postal inspectors in the States would open the packages of an enlisted man with more alacrity than those mailed by a major or a colonel. And so officers could—and *did*—send home fur coats, sets of fine china, boxes of silverware, lace curtains, Oriental rugs and the like, and the doggie did not, because the doggie would have had his ass chewed and been asked to explain his "outrageous looting."

At dark we moved to the edge of the no-name town and relieved Easy Company. I had to split my squad: half in one house, half in another. My C.P. was in a cellar already occupied by two women, two children, and an eighty-nine-year-old man. They'd been there for some days and furnished it with a bed, several chairs, and a stove, plus a rocking chair for the old man. It was cold and the kids were fretful and would not sleep, a circumstance not surprising, considering the way kids, women, blankets, and quilts were tumbled together on the crowded bed. The old man dozed restlessly, stretched between two chairs, a quilt around his shoulders. He did not speak to us or notice our existence by so much as a glance. We sat near the stove and talked in low voices, feeling our lack of welcome but too tired to care.

Next door the men shared their cellar with a doggie who'd been killed by a freak shell that afternoon. The shell had come clean and sharp through the cellar window without touching the frame and killed him where he stood. Of the other three men in the cellar, one was slightly wounded.

The night was long and uneventful. The squad being far below normal strength, every man was overworked with guard duty, so I waived my prerogatives and stood guard for two tricks, sustained by a comfortable sense of virtue.

Early the next morning we pulled out for the town of Weilerswist. Arriving there, we spent most of the afternoon in a factory near the railroad tracks, waiting for darkness to cover our next move. An adjacent warehouse was filled with boxes and crates, labeled and ready to be loaded on a train that would never come. Curious, we kicked the slat from some of the crates and discovered plate glass, car fenders, blowtorches, flatirons, and washing machines. A reassuring display: as long as the world continues to manufacture flatirons and washing machines, the final debacle is not yet at hand. An ingenious doggie decided to take along a blowtorch "to heat his next foxhole," and the idea spread. Within an hour a blowtorch dangled from the pack of every man in the battalion, and jeeps from units behind us were racing up in dusty frenzy to drive away with springs groaning under a load of blowtorches. The American doggie is a wonderful guy.

We moved out at dusk, and the next twenty-four hours were just like the twenty-four preceding: into another town (Metterich?), go out to the point (yes *sir*!), dig in, stand guard. I pulled guard with the men again, and it was a raw, rainy night. I felt low, and wanted desperately to sleep. Finally I did, for two hours, the first in forty-eight. I fried some potatoes when I got up, and after eating felt much better.

The pattern was the same on the next day, March 6. This time the town was Brenig (I think!). The name may be wrong—many times we never knew where we were, and town succeeded town so rapidly that all blurred together. Ernie Pyle said it: "Eventually it all works itself into an emotional tapestry of one dull, dead pattern—yesterday is tomorrow and Troina is Randazzo and when will we ever stop and God, I'm so tired." No one ever said it better.

At Brenig the third platoon ran into trouble and we were held up. We halted at a prosperous farm and waited for the firefight on the other side of the town to sputter out.

As we carve deeper and deeper into Germany, we find that most of the villages are unscratched, or scratched very lightly. These tiny agricultural hamlets, most of them without any military significance, have been bypassed by our bombers. This farmhouse, for example, was unscarred by war save for a few small cracks in its smooth plaster walls, the result of a bomb that had been jettisoned in a nearby field by a wounded American bomber. For the farmer and his family, that "bombing" was the high spot of the war. They told me the story in highly excited German, pantomiming their remembered fright with dramatic clutching at their bosoms and much rolling of eyes.

Civilians become more and more of a problem as we advance. They get in the way, and they require of our emotions a softness we're loath to give—the giving is painful, and it makes for inefficiency. Civilians absent, we could be tough and ruthless and a helluva lot more comfortable. But now . . . ! We limp past houses that are draped in white, every window fluttering hysterically with sheets, pillowcases, tablecloths— mute pleas for mercy. The people huddle together, well out of our path, and only barely concealed behind the frightened faces are the ingratiating smiles, tugging at the leash of fear and wanting only a nod of tolerance, the flicker of a grin from an American face to warm them into full beaming. Most of the faces are ready to beam—a few diehards glower and look contempt upon us.

Back to the prosperous farm. I posted the men and they dug in. I retired to the kitchen and called the men in, one at a time, for the benison of half an hour near the stove. (One of the most unpleasant features of these pushes is that we move at such a clip that we're drenched with sweat before we've gone a mile. We're warm while we're moving, sometimes too warm, but once we stop, the March air chews the marrow from our bones in the space of minutes and the wet wool of our garments hangs clammy on our shivering flesh.)

So I sat in the kitchen, drank hot, but vile, ersatz coffee, and talked with the farmer's family. They moaned a plaint that has become very familiar of late: *"Deutschland ist alles kaput!"* I wondered if they knew *how* "kaput"? But they were pleasant and tried hard to be agreeable, even the shrewish-looking hausfrau, the obvious boss of the household, squeezing out an occasional tight smile. She was busy with supper, a meal apparently composed of fried potatoes and canned fruit. The potatoes smelled like steak to my starved nose, but I refused their not-very-pressing invitation to share their meal. They loaded the food on platters and disappeared down the stairs to the cellar, their present living quarters. I watched the steaming platters out of sight and then cursed myself for being weak and spineless. Why the hell didn't I commandeer the food for myself and my men? After all, *we* were hungry and *we* were the conquerors! No, it wouldn't do . . . I couldn't sustain an arrogance like that.

The men had just finished their holes when the expected order came: "Okay, get it on!" With groans, curses, and whimpers, we started off again. I was breaking in a new pair of shoes, and this final move seemed the last indignity my tortured feet could endure.

Those shoes . . . I have them yet: size $9\frac{1}{2}$ A and curled upward at the toe like Turkish slippers; $9\frac{1}{2}$ A, and my correct size is 8 or $8\frac{1}{2}$. The story is this: I arrived overseas with two pairs of shoes, which fitted me properly and felt good. But a soldier's life is a muddy one, and after endless soakings and dryings, the shoes shrank and shrank until walking became an agony. In one vagrant encounter with our supply tent I asked for other shoes, but the supply sergeant brushed me off. However, while we were in Gladbach, Supply caught up to us. Loeb, a buddy who worked in Supply, tipped me off one afternoon that the cognac was flowing and the supply sergeant mellowing into carelessness, sprawled in the kitchen of the farmhouse where he'd set up his stand. Sneaking around corners and down alleys, I crept up to the house from the rear. As I slipped into the shed where the shoes had been dumped, I could hear the drunken singing of the sergeant and his cronies. There were the shoes, a great pile of them—some new, but some of them secondhand turn-ins. Before entering the shed, I'd loosened the laces of my own shoes and now I shucked them off. I had to move fast now . . . get out of there before someone came. There's a pair of new ones, I thought, combat boots, too. Try 'em on! Mmmm . . . a little large . . . $9\frac{1}{2}$ A. Wow! A full size larger than my others! Well . . .

But I wanted combat boots, and the new blond leather looked beautiful, and I assured myself that the extra length would be an advantage—think of the extra warmth in wearing two pairs of woolen socks! I made the swap, burying my old shoes in the middle of the pile, and raced away with laces dangling and buckles flopping.

So now I was on the road out of Brenig, my new blond shoes like red-hot cases of lead on my aching feet.

No, not quite. Before starting out for Brenig, we'd been

given a hot meal at the C.P., and after chow most of us crowded into a stable for a last smoke. There was no light save from our glowing cigarettes, and no room to sit down. So we stood, jostling each other, and, being tired and thus easily given to horseplay, trading evil for accident with brutish humor. An awkward GI heel treading on your toes merited a swift kick in the shins, and it didn't matter if you kicked the wrong guy. A jaw nearly dislocated by the swinging combat pack of someone who only wanted to turn around was quickly repaid by a swift butt stroke from the M-1 hanging on your own shoulder. Heaven help the guy behind you who might get slapped silly by the muzzle, as well as the luckless victim who got the butt in his ribs. All good clean fun, and the night was not filled with music. But it lightened our spirits. The humor went out of the sport for me, however, when my bazooka man, an amiable but blundering sheepdog, turned suddenly in the dark, the bazooka hanging from his shoulder striking me in the mouth and putting an unmistakable finis to the wobbly peg tooth I'd been carefully guarding for months. Henceforth and until the end of the war I was known, off and on, as "the Tooth." The tooth itself I saved and wore for state occasions, like the first drink of the evening on the evenings when we had something to drink. I'd set it carefully in place and hold it with my lip for a brief, one-sided smile. After the third drink it ceased to be important, and I'd remove it and store it in my watch pocket again.

Then, finally, I was on the road out of Brenig, aching feet, toothless jaw and all. This time I thought I'd make it beyond the village limits.

The town we took that night has no name in this muddy odyssey. We'd only been told that it was believed to be crawling with Jerries. As usual, my squad was assigned the point on the far end of town, and we experienced the customary eerie tension as we passed through the darkened streets. The town was spilling over with the dregs left by a whipped and fleeing army—tanks, trucks, artillery pieces, ambulances ... dead men.

Our objective was a road junction with a house on one corner, a water tower on another, and a helluva lot of open ground beyond. When we arrived at the house, I pounded on the door with the butt of my rifle and yelled, *"Komme sie raus!"* Ten seconds later a faraway voice quavered the information that only civilians were within, all old people, and they were in the cellar. I shouted in reply, *"Komme sie raus anyway!"* and almost immediately the door opened and a white-haired man stepped out. I asked if there were any German soldiers about. (This is not quite so naive as it sounds. Many times we were spared a fight and the possible loss of some lives by permitting German soldiers to surrender through the medium of civilians. If we stormed their hiding places, they would fight back, selling themselves dearly out of fear and desperation.) The old man answered that there were no soldiers in the house but only civilians—five women and three old men, like himself, and all had been asleep in the cellar. I said I'd have to see for myself and made a move to enter the building, but as I stepped forward a voice from behind the old man said calmly, "I surrender." I backed up hastily and ordered the voice to show himself. It turned out to be a young man in the uniform of a Luftwaffe pilot. Furious at the elderly civilian (and part of my anger was fear, of course—I knew that), I ordered them into the dark house and pushed them toward the door that was sewn against the inner gloom by a thread of light. Kicking open the door, we saw five women and three men, just as the old man had said. But not asleep in the cellar, not even rubbing their eyes with sudden waking. Fully dressed, they were gathered around a dining table on which were the remains of a recent meal. The coffee cups were still full and steaming.

Stuttering with sudden rage, I looked at the old man and exploded in bastard German. *"Du hat gesagen 'nicht Deutsche soldaten hier,' hein? Was ist das hier?"* and I pointed to the Luftwaffe pilot. At once the German soldier hastened to say that they hadn't known he'd been in the house; he'd been hiding there without their knowledge. Eagerly, the old man

chimed agreement, and the trembling diners swore the same.
And I knew damn well that all of them were lying. The truth
was pathetically evident: the guilty fear on the faces, the
tightly sealed house, the bald lie about everyone being asleep
in the cellar when on the table the coffee cups still steamed.
And for the final clincher, the bed of quilts under the piano in
the corner of the room and the German field pack that lay near
it. But I felt pity for them. I could see them sitting around the
table—not as they were now, old and frightened, but as they'd
been before I pounded on the door—listening with greedy ears
to the apple-cheeked hero, the warrior, the defender of the
Fatherland against the barbarous invaders.

   We sent them back to the cellar and swiftly searched the
house. No more prisoners. After posting the men, John
Sturgos, my then second in command, and I started to dig our
foxhole.

   There was sporadic fighting in the town as the lurking
enemy soldiers were rooted out. Our sector remained quiet
until about four A.M., when I heard someone coming down
the road, approaching the town. There was no attempt to
walk quietly. The footsteps were frankly noisy and firm, and
I guessed that this was the friendly patrol I'd been warned
might come through our position during the night. At any
rate, whoever was approaching would have to pass the three
men I'd posted along the road. I listened, expecting to hear a
challenge, "Who goes there!" but there was not a sound. I
began to sweat a little. Were they asleep, all three of them?
Or . . . dead, lying quietly with their throats cut?

   The footsteps drew nearer, became a form . . . a single man,
but it was too dark to pick out uniform details. I challenged.
"Halt!" The figure kept coming, and again I yelled, "Halt!"
Still coming, and without a moment's hesitation. But why the
hell didn't he stop? Who was he? Closer now . . . I could see
him more clearly, swinging his arms—swinging his arms?
Where were his weapons? Where was the rest of the patrol?
Why didn't he halt? Who the hell was he, anyway? *What* the
hell was he? I yelled again and my voice was a scream, and he

kept coming. Twenty feet away . . . fifteen . . . ten . . . *he was a Jerry!* And Sturgos fired. Then at last he halted. He was un-hurt: Sturgos had fired over his head. (I never asked John if his aim had been deliberate.)

While John escorted our prisoner to the C.P., I started off to find out what tragic fate had overtaken the three men along the road. I had a cold presentiment of what I'd find—three bodies twisted and quiet in their muddy holes. I was wrong. They were twisted all right, but only because they had jammed together in one hole in order to converse more easily.

After I'd recovered from the first shock of speechlessness, I asked mildly if they had seen "that joker who just went down the road." Yes, they had. Had they challenged him? Yes, they had. Did he know the password? Well, they didn't really know because he hadn't answered their challenge. Had he halted upon their challenge? No, he'd just kept right on going. At that point I blew my stack! I chewed ass until I could almost taste the blood; I threatened them with one-man patrols and other fearsome penalties. I swore that I'd have their b——s hanging from the rooftree of the highest house in town. I put on a *helluva* fine show. And their answer? "Well, Sarge, we knew you and Sturgos were right there by the house, and when he didn't stop, we figured you'd stop him and find out who he was!" How the hell did we win this war, anyway?

There were other prisoners that night, but none that we had to persuade with bullets or go out and get. They just sort of fil-tered in. Seventy was the total company bag, and the company that relieved us took another sixty the following day. It was like scaring mice out of the straw.

At five A.M. we were relieved and fed. We'd been hoping for a rest, but had to clear the town of Bornheim and put out roadblocks. The town was partially captured, but fighting was still going on.

Just after dawn on a cold, misty morning, we reached Bornheim. Skirting the edge of the town, we hastened to our assigned sectors. The platoon was split up, each of the three squads being given a separate road to clear. Mine was the road leading to the point, and my orders were to keep going until we reached a crossroads. According to our photo maps, there was a house at the crossroads, and in it I was to station an outpost.

In cautious single file we started down the road, and as we drew near the first house, I saw three figures approaching us. The morning fog and the mist of rain on my glasses made vision doubly difficult, but I noted that the leading figure wore riding breeches and boots, a not unfamiliar civilian garb. We were not alarmed: we'd been encountering civilians all morning. But when this "civilian" suddenly whipped a burp gun from behind his back and opened fire on us, I realized I'd made a slight error in judgment. We hit the ground as one man and returned fire. There were no casualties. The three hightailed it for cover, and a flurry of movement on the road behind them indicated there were others. In a flash the road was empty and the morning was hushed and still. We hugged the bank and I removed my glasses and wiped them dry so that I could see.

Now, and for the first time, I felt a personal anger toward the enemy. In the wounding of Ketron and the death of Boyd Smith, there had been no impulse to anger. I accepted them as a part of the whole dirty business, inevitables to which a soldier gives a grudging nod and a shrug. My anger at the old civilian in the last town was the anger of a player at a spectator who tries to get into the game, the drunk who reels out on the field and intercepts a pass on the three-yard line, ruining the play. But *this* anger on the road out of Bornheim was a new emotion, a hot and blinding desire to punish opponents who would thus violate the rules of the game.

All of the houses were still, too still. No morning smoke rising from the chimneys, no sound of life anywhere. The buildings looked peaceful enough—simply farmhouses that had not yet awakened. But I knew now that their sleepiness was a cheat, that within them was wakefulness and tense whispering and eyes watching—men with guns who wore civilian clothes and walked softly, smilers with knives. And my anger

mounted. When Misa called to me from the window of a
house behind us and said he'd send up a couple of tanks, I
yelled back, "Hurry 'em up!"

Soon the two tanks rumbled up, and the men hugging the
bank fell in behind the first one as it passed. Crouched behind
its protecting bulk, we moved slowly along the road until we
were less than two hundred yards from the first house. In the
field to our right a wounded German lay among the cabbages.
We had nailed him in that first spit of fire. He waved and
called and we ignored him, but he persisted, sniveling that he
was *gewunden* until I told him to shut up, he'd be cared for by
our medics very shortly. He at least was in his country's uniform—it was the bugger in the civilian clothes whom we
wanted to get.

At last the tank groaned to a halt, as if to catch its breath.
Then it lurched forward a few more yards, paused again,
moved a little farther, and stopped once more. There was a
moment of silence when the morning stood waiting, not
breathing. Even the wounded man in the field ceased his
moaning and was silent. A long moment . . . then the cold
snarl of machinery from the deep bowels of the tank and the
grating of steel on steel. Smoothly, ominously, the long barrel
of the 75 swung around, steadied, came to rest, pointed
directly at the house. Another moment of silence while we
peeped cautiously around the rear of the tank. Then the morning exploded and the tank reared up in the air a little and
rocked back upon us, and we were frightened by the sudden
swift life in this monstrous thing. When we looked again at the
house, there was a gaping hole in its creamy plaster and dust
rising in thick clouds, and there was the hoarse sound of wood
tearing and the thumping of things falling on nearby roofs.
The tank fired again, and a third time, and new holes appeared
in flowers of dust. In the moment of silence between shells we
could hear the hysterical squawking of chickens and the
bawling of cattle. There were no human sounds . . . or none
that were recognizable as human.

Six times the tank fired, and between rounds sprayed the

house, the outbuildings, and the woods across the road with machine-gun bullets. The machine-gun fire flushed a single German soldier from the hill. He came toward us running, his hands strained so high above his head that he could barely keep his balance. He was young, not more than seventeen, and in uniform. A new uniform—the perfect picture of the Wehrmacht warrior, from shining helmet to form-fitting overcoat. The only unwarriorlike thing about him was the color of his face. A pasty green, it was shaking with fear, like a pudding being jiggled before it was set. Against the green skin the blond fuzz of his young beard and the adolescent pimples were pitiful and revolting. He could not control his trembling, and his body jerked violently with each roar of the 75. I sent him to the rear, and we moved forward with the tank for another seventy-five yards. The tank sprayed the house once more, and then we rushed.

Kicking open the side door, I yelled the usual *"Komme sie raus!"* There was an answering wail (female) from the cellar and the hurried response (male), *"Ja! Ich komme!"* Colorless with fear, a middle-aged man climbed from the cellar and tremblingly approached. Stuttering incoherently, he swore that there were no German soldiers in the house, but I brushed past him and started down the cellar stairs, still angry and feeling very tough. My anger and my phony toughness vanished when I reached the cellar and saw the four women there, one of them holding a baby in her arms. Three of them were hysterical, and they huddled close to the old lady who stood erect and faced me. The unquestioned matriarch, she stood while the others whimpered against her skirts. In her upheld hands she held a crucifix, and by it and the Virgin Mother and Jesus Christ she swore there were no soldiers in the house. I believed her.

This was total war, though not as total as had been visited upon Warsaw and Rotterdam and Stalingrad, and they had never expected it for themselves. And we pitied them and tried to despise them so that we wouldn't hate ourselves too much.

There were no Jerries in the next house, but we took one

prisoner in the third. Now we could see the house at the cross-roads, five hundred yards away. Five hundred yards of open ground—we'd have to run for it. We did.

The house was empty. Behind it and curving to the left was a quarry, rimmed by a sand cliff two hundred feet high. At the quarry entrance, just behind the house, a small brick building snuggled against the base of the cliff. It seemed to be only a toolhouse or guard's cottage, but we put a few bullets through the windows just for luck. Although there was no return fire, Sturgos and Berthot wanted to search it, and I told them to go ahead.

As I walked toward the main house I heard the shattering flatness of exploding grenades behind me and swung about hastily. For a moment I stared, pop-eyed. A small group of German soldiers were plainly visible on the cliff top, leaning over the edge and dropping potato mashers on Sturgos and Berthot directly below, opening their hands and dropping the grenades casually. I heard Sturgos yell, "I'm hit!" and he came running toward me, his face streaked with blood. Behind him came Berthot. I sent Sturgos to the rear—he wasn't badly hurt, fortunately—and asked for a tank to be sent up.

Soon two light tanks approached, and I asked the gunner in the leading tank to dust the top of the cliff with .50 caliber machine-gun bullets. Far to the left a German soldier appeared on the rim of the quarry, his hands high above his head. He started in our direction, vanished in the depths of the quarry, and appeared again a few minutes later, still heading toward us. I screamed, *"Schnell, schnell!"* and he began to run faster. In a moment he had joined us behind the shelter of the tank, another green-faced adolescent warrior.

Barely had he and the accompanying guard loped off to the rear when I heard a flat, evil explosion that seemed familiar. I turned toward the sound in time to see another shell explode not fifty yards away. In the air, a third mortar shell curved lazily downward, and from the look of it, our names and serial numbers were written on the nose. I yelled to the men and we raced for the cellar. As we reached safety there were two explosions, sharp and close together, and I knew that one of them was not a mortar shell. Then silence. I waited a moment, then crawled to the corner of the house for a look. Far down the road I could see the rear end of the second tank as it streaked toward town. And in the middle of the cross-roads was the first tank, silent now, black smoke billowing from it, moving slowly and without direction toward the potato field across the road. It had received a direct hit from a German bazooka.

Someone was calling. "Hey! Hey, soldier!" It was one of the tankers, crouching in a ditch fifty yards away. He yelled again, "Hey, go out and stop that tank!"

With what I've always thought was rare wit, I bellowed back, "How do you expect me to stop the goddamn thing? With my foot?" What the hell did a rifleman know about the mysterious workings of a tank? And why the hell should I run across an open courtyard and risk my neck for his lousy tank when he could get to it himself and in safety by crawling up the ditch?

The tank rolled relentlessly forward until it nudged into the soft earth of the plowed field. It stopped then, and slowly the smoke drifted away and all was quiet again. A few minutes later the tanker made a rush for it, frantically clambered inside, and seconds later it was roaring back to town, buckety-buckety. (It carried two dead men back—the gunner and the tank commander.)

Now we were alone, my squad of three and myself, alone in a deserted farmhouse with the enemy on two sides, possibly three . . . thick as crumbs at a lap supper. On our right lay a broad field and an orchard, and beyond it the section of town that was still in the hands of the Germans. Three of the four roads at our crossing led into enemy territory and were logical avenues of approach for an armored counterattack. There wasn't any way out for us. The road to safety, the road back to town, was now exposed to the raking fire of the Germans on the cliff. And we hadn't received any orders to pull out; we'd been told to "hold it."

That sounds like a bid for a tin medal. It isn't. If I'd had any sense I would have pulled out, order or no order. I stayed because I was so fuzzy-brained with weariness that I couldn't think beyond the exigencies of the moment. My head was a squirrel cage rattling to the mechanical echo of the order I'd been given at a fresher time by someone else: "Set up a strong point in the house at the crossroads . . . the house at the crossroads . . . the house at the crossroads." Okay, I stayed—not because I was filled with a holy fervor to go down valiant under many spears. I stayed because it didn't occur to me that it was possible to leave.

Anyway, there we were—four riflemen. Not even a bazooka or a BAR, just four rifles. Two of the men were my scouts, Bill Bowerman and Bob Berthot, both of Niagara Falls. About twenty years old and fine youngsters, but a little green. They'd been with the company only since February. The third man was older, but he'd been with us only four days. Fresh out of Jersey City, he had sailed from the States on February 10 and been whipped into a frontline outfit so fast that he was still dizzy. This was his first action, and he was unable to talk above a whisper, so shaky that he could not hold a match steady enough to light a cigarette.

I scouted the house for defense positions and found one. One! Like the house in Drove, there were too few windows and one side of the house was a blank wall. No second-floor windows were usable. I posted a man at the one strategic window, put another at a window that faced our lines and cautioned him fiercely to watch for signs of activity in the town, some indication that help was on the way. I ordered the third man to rest for a while so that he could spell one of the other two later. I wandered restlessly from place to place, stoutly muttering words of encouragement though I knew damn well that my own tail was carving a deep groove in the ground behind me as I walked.

I don't know why a counterattack never came. We could have been set upon from three sides and we would have been helpless. But nothing happened, even though our continued rifle fire must have informed the enemy of our presence. Perhaps they presumed a much larger force than four men: certainly we threw a helluva lot of lead in their direction to convince 'em of that. After a while we observed furtive movements *away* from the cliff, men running from secure positions, scampering over the skyline and away. One German behaved very strangely. I watched him descending the face of the cliff, apparently trying to get to the little brick house. When I nailed him, he did a flopping swan dive into a pile of brush behind the brick house and we saw him no more.

The tension wore off after a while, to be replaced by a kind of drunken excitement, the secret bubbling of inner gaiety that makes some drunks happy drunks. The livestock in the barn looked hungry, so I fed them and it became a game of delicious nonsense. The rabbits were first: outside their hutch was a basket heaped high with superb brussels sprouts. It seemed an extravagant diet, but the great Belgian hares lit into the tender sprouts with the aplomb of long familiarity, and I went away well pleased. The horses and the goats were something else again: I knew goats and horses ate either straw or hay, but I was damned if I knew which. One they ate and one they slept on, but which was which? To return to the house and ask for help would be an embarrassing confession of ignorance, and since the only route was via belly through a courtyard sprinkled with chicken droppings, I asked myself, Is this trip necessary? I decided that horses ate hay, and was stymied a moment later by the realization that I couldn't tell the difference between straw and hay. I grabbed an armful at random, dropped it before the horse, and stood back to observe his reactions. He sniffed at it disdainfully and turned a solemn eye on me. Hastily apologizing, I backed from his stall and made good on my error. Then I fed the goats, gave water to all the animals, threw some grain in the yard for the chickens, and returned to the house.

In the kitchen cupboard I found a loaf of rye bread, two jars of jam, and a bowl of delicious cottage cheese. So I ate. My next discovery was a pail of still-fresh milk, and I made some hot chocolate from an old D-bar I dug from a pocket. I carried a cup of the hot drink to Jersey City, who was still trembling.

A rickety board fence connected the outbuildings to the house. A door in the fence opened on the quarry, and by hooking my toe under the door to hold it from swinging wide, I could open it cautiously for several inches and peer toward the enemy lines. Observation was good, and I registered a 5— well, maybe a 3 anyway!—on the first target to show himself.

So the day passed and the exchange of fire died to an occasional sputter. When another hour had gone by and there had been no further shots and no sight of the enemy, I sent the two kids upstairs for a nap while I stood guard at the window. The unbroken quiet was more nerve-racking than the previous noisy hours had been, and I wondered if a counterattack was brewing. Another hour of quiet passed and I decided the Germans had really fled. In a second reconnaissance through the house I found an egg and selfishly ate it all.

It seemed safe now, and I decided to send a man back to the C.P. to ask for further orders. I was on my way to wake the sleepers upstairs when I saw two German-helmeted heads bobbing along the courtyard wall. I whispered for Jersey City to come to my side, and we waited. When the wearers of the helmets reached the gate I yelled, "Halt!" and their hands shot up. The startled bewilderment on their faces was real and they were quick to say that they had come in to surrender. One was limping from a slight leg wound, and they were very tired, very dirty, and very sick of war.

Jersey City woke the two boys while I guarded the prisoners, and I told Bowerman to take our haul to the C.P. and ask for orders. He took off down the road, prodding them along on the double while we watched the cliff anxiously, rifles ready. In thirty minutes he was back: Misa wanted us to pack up and come home.

As we passed through the town, familiar faces smiled at us from the windows of the houses and men poured out to

surround us. We were astounded to learn that we were the
heroes of the moment. We shrugged deprecatingly at this
earthy-tongued praise but were puffed by it nonetheless.
That moment was ours, and not for a million bucks would
we have admitted that what seemed like a heroic stand from
the vantage of the town had been only a rather dull guard
routine for us. We were heroes, goddamn it, and we ate it
with spoons!

The sweetness lingered for days: my hungry searching for
food while we were "pinned down out there" *[sic!]* was interpreted as a supreme nonchalance in the face of danger, and I
blossomed like a rose under the awed regard of my companions. Football heroes and such are at liberty to scoff at the
naïveté of this confession, but any man who looks back on
a boyhood in which he never won a fight will appreciate how
I felt.

At any rate, it seemed like V-E Day to us. When I entered
the C.P., Misa said, "Whaddya tryin' to do, win the goddamn
war all by yerself?" Ahh . . . comfort me with apples—the hell
with apples! Comfort me with big fat syllables!

We gulped furtively and exchanged secret looks when we
learned why we were thus crowned with laurel: observers in
town had counted several hundred Germans on the cliff above
us. We'd been given up as dead or captured many hours ago.

The German with the burp gun who had started the day's
activity had been captured. (He was in uniform, incidentally,
but it was of an unusual type.) He claimed that he'd been
forced to fire on us: a German officer with a pistol leveled at
his back had been standing behind him. He also insisted that
he had fired at the ground so that he wouldn't hit us!

He'd been captured near the house that our tank had
shelled, and the old woman with the rosary, emerging from
the cellar, had flown into a rage when she saw him. Seizing a
handy chunk of stove wood, she started to beat the bejesus out
of him, cursing him for not being "a *real* German soldier." In
her eyes he was personally responsible for the destruction of
her home.

After eating, we curled up for some sleep, woke up for supper and back to bed once more. At five A.M. we were roused and told to pack up, we were going after some snipers who were harassing the supply lines of the 3rd Battalion.

It was a wet, gloomy morning, my feet hurt, and I wasn't happy. About nine o'clock we saw our objective—a scattering of buildings by a railroad track. My squad was ordered to clear the signalman's shack, the house at the crossing, and the trenches in the field beyond. There was no sound from within the house as we crept up to it. The rear door stood a little ajar and I kicked it wide, then leaped backward hastily. The three German soldiers who stared, bug-eyed, from their seats at the kitchen table were as startled as I was.

The kitchen was a small arsenal—rifles, burp guns, grenades, machine guns, and piles of ammunition. Food, too—rye bread, jam, fruit, and a supply of the canned meat rationed to German troops. (Delicious meat, incidentally: it made our tasteless and monotonous C and K rations nauseating in comparison.)

The bunkers in the field were well-constructed. There was a luxurious subterranean six-man bunkhouse, containing a stove, and the trench system that radiated elaborately from the bunkhouse embraced nearly seven thousand square feet. Apparently, the three Germans we captured in the house were the only troops manning this strong point. Piled near the trenches as though in preparation for placement were more than sixty mines, some of them antitank Teller mines and some the terrible S mine, nicknamed "Bouncing Betty."

The day passed quickly, the men standing guard duty in the rain and sleeping between tricks. Hot chow was brought up at dusk, and we prayed silently that we wouldn't have to move out before morning. It was a cold, wet bitch of a night, and we were warm and comfortable and very tired. At seven P.M. Misa sent for me and drearily I trudged to the C.P., knowing damn well what to expect. It was worse than I'd imagined: we were going to attack Bonn during the night.

Misa briefed the squad leaders carefully, and I liked the

assignment less and less. Soberly, I walked back to my bunkhouse and called the men together for the bad news. The tired faces grew still as I talked, and I sensed the flicker of expression behind the noncommittal eyes. It's a dirty assignment. No one knows what lies ahead in Bonn or what kind of trouble awaits us. All that is certain is there *will* be trouble. The platoon's objective is a triangular chunk of the city, a triangle of apartment houses and business buildings bounded by three broad streets. We take the triangle and hold it—that's what Misa said. We'll set up four strong points, two of which are my responsibility because I now have the largest squad. (There are eight men in my squad; six in the other squads.)

It's dark now, a black night, and we're waiting for the kickoff. There has been no talking in the bunkhouse for several hours. We hug the fire, and eat, and say nothing. Some of the men started to write letters, brief and labored and broken by many long pauses. Finally they stopped and put them away unfinished, or crumpled them up and threw them in the fire. What is there to say now?

CHAPTER EIGHT

"I'm beginning to hanker for a world less exclusively masculine."

I think this is March 9.

I *know* we are in Bonn, and I know, too, that in a short time I'm going to be very drunk. Even now I feel no pain.

Last night we crept through thin, raining blackness and entered a ghost city. Guns thundered on the other side of Bonn, and we could see the glare of shells and houses burning crimson against the dark sky. But where we passed was only stale destruction and silence and the smell of old death. And the skin crawled cold on our backs because we knew there were snipers hidden in the gutted buildings, watching us, waiting. . . .

We parted from the rest of the platoon at the apex of the triangle and set out to establish our two strong points. Ruins and rubble choked the streets, and twice we lost our way, mistaking the raw gap where a building had once stood for the street turning we sought.

Bonn was our first city, the first time we'd tackled the job of clearing buildings five and six stories high, the first time we'd seen at close hand what war could do to a large city. There didn't seem to be much left of it, although most of the damage had been done a while ago. Many of the buildings showed evidence of recent care—shell holes boarded up, shattered windows replaced by cardboard, rubble piled neatly by the curb.

Our progress was not silent. In the darkness we bumped into things, stumbled over each other, and cursed and clattered loud enough to wake all Bonn. I capped this burlesque of "carefully on tiptoe stealing" by falling into a bomb crater in the middle of the street and requiring the aid of two men to pull me out. I hadn't realized the damn things were so hard to climb out of. Then, climbing through a window of the building on the corner, I failed to see the table piled high with household equipment and fell ass over teakettle in a clatter of tinware and glass.

Leaving four men in the corner building, the rest of us moved to an apartment house a block away, smashed an entrance through a boarded-up window, and set up our second post. For the balance of the night we waited and watched. It was cold, a quiet, penetrating cold, and we hung the stiff folds of the living-room rug over our shoulders and huddled together for warmth. There was no furniture in the apartment except a davenport and a dollhouse. In the kitchen was a stove, which we regarded wistfully but dared not light.

Every two hours—at two, four, and six A.M.—I was required to send a contact patrol to our other strong point and thence to the strong point beyond, which was held by another squad. On the uneven hours—one, three, and five A.M.—the neighboring squad sent a contact patrol out to us.

Bill Bowerman and I did the patrols, and on one of them we had a fright that turned our bones to Jell-O. As we left our building we heard tanks nearby and wondered uneasily if they were ours or German. We'd reached the middle of the block when, with a shattering roar, the tanks turned the corner and came charging down the street. Our eyes raced helplessly for somewhere to hide, but there wasn't a damn place we could reach in a hurry. A high concrete wall guarded the nearest building, and there was no visible opening in it. We flattened ourselves against it, hoping foolishly that we would be inconspicuous against its creamy whiteness. The tanks were nearly upon us now, and we tensed ourselves. . . . Were they ours or German? The question arched in our throats and it was hard to breathe. One tank thundered by . . . then another. We hung against the wall, impaled by fear. The third tank approached and we strained to see . . . Christ, to see just a little bit! But in the misty dark there was nothing to see, only the blurred shape of a darker darkness hurtling by . . . and from it a fragment of voice and a fragment of phrase, "Friggin' sonofabitch . . ." We slumped in exquisite relief, appreciating as never before the incomparable savor of Shakespeare's tongue.

I'm sure that tank crews felt a sense of easy familiarity with the tools of their trade, but many infantrymen were secretly awed and a little terrified by them: by their forbidding size, their sound, their grim and evil appearance. Even our own tanks affected us this way. We'd grin with silly pride when they lumbered past, and we'd preen foolishly on the rare occasions when we were lucky enough to hitch a ride, but we weren't at ease on them.

The night ended at last. Rummaging for loot, I found a large swastika flag that had been discreetly hidden away in the attic. I stowed it in my pack: "Souvenir of Bonn, 1945." We built a tiny fire in the kitchen stove and I made some feeble soup from a dehydrated preparation I found in the cupboard.

The civilians appeared as soon as it was light, emerging from seemingly nowhere like black beetles from an old log when the ax strikes. Most of them came from the "bunkers" —vast subterranean air raid shelters—to which they retreated every night, emerging in the day only to procure food and to inspect the latest bomb damage to their homes. They queued up at the door of the bakery across the street, and we sat in the window and watched them—women, children, and old men, each with a purse in one hand, ration stamps convenient in the other. At seven o'clock the line started to move forward, and within half an hour the bread supply for the day had been sold and the latecomers were turning sadly away.

Our presence in the window was noted, and we were accorded a recognition that varied in quality and degree. We had an amiable conversation with a fourteen-year-old boy who sat on his bicycle and grinned up at us. He said everyone in Bonn was hungry. There was no meat in the city, no butter, no eggs, no milk. The diet was bread; bread and potatoes. I wondered what was on the menu in the Warsaw ghetto the year before last.

When the last customer had gone, the baker stepped out for a stretch and a breath of air. He glanced at our window, appeared to hesitate, and reentered his shop. In a moment he was out again and coming toward us, a paper-wrapped package in his hand. He smiled ingratiatingly and held up the package for our inspection. He wanted to make a deal: a half-pound wedge of marzipan for a pack of cigarettes. I shut my ears to the squeals of outraged conscience and made the swap. We were hungry for something sweet, and I was lousy with extra cigarettes. So both of us were guilty of "giving aid and comfort to the enemy."

At noon the city was in our hands, completely ours except for mopping-up operations. Our part in the victory had hardly been glorious, but we felt like conquerors nonetheless. We were led to another section of the city, ushered into a vast apartment house and told to make ourselves at home. At once we started the scramble for quilts, mattresses, candles, and drinking stuff, the necessaries of GI housekeeping.

Now I'm going to leave the kitchen where I've been writing this. Shorty is waiting for me in his squad's suite of rooms on the floor below. There's a piano there, and we have ample supplies of beer and wine. All this day we were pursued by civilians and by displaced persons, most of them drunk, all of them eager to embrace the nearest American. We were not surprised by the ardor of the erstwhile slave laborers, but it was startling to receive moist and fervent kisses from the bearded lips of elderly gentlemen who were unmistakably German. However, since such a display of emotion is always accompanied by the invitation to "have a drink," we accept the excesses of affection as nonchalantly as possible. And take the drink.

The next day.

We just heard the sobering news that we're leaving Bonn and moving to a little village, a disciplinary move occasioned by our "unsoldierly and shameful behavior." Not *our* behavior: The charge was leveled against the whole regiment. As a matter of fact, G Company—according to the HQ grapevine—was absolved of any blame, a circumstance that puffed us with self-conscious and surprised virtue. But innocent or guilty, we were exiled with the rest of the regiment.

It was a wild night. Or so I'm told. The last thing I remember was my frenzied search for a bathroom somewhere around midnight. I reeled through the lightless hallways, jousting with walls and sudden corners, my need driving me on in whimpers of self-pity. Finally, with a last sob of maudlin despair, I stumbled downstairs to the street, dimly located the gutter in front of the house, and unbuttoned in time to save my dignity. But the curbstone—surely a treacherous German device!—rose relentlessly under my feet, tilted . . . more . . . more . . . and unbuttoned and unfinished, I staggered irresistibly backward across the sidewalk until my head connected smartly with the brick wall of the building and I sat down very gently. It's a little dim from there on, but I got to bed somehow.

The celebration in other parts of Bonn was a little more vigorous, involving the pursuit of frauleins and fraus, both the willing and the unwilling, as well as some more serious offenses. One avid Joe hit upon the bright idea of halting passing civilians with a threatening wave of his M-1 and relieving them of their jewelry and watches. The last and sobering offense was committed by a drunken soldier who commandeered a civilian car, ran amok in it through the city, and ended his ride by driving it over the curb and up on the sidewalk, killing a small girl.

While the night was still young, a soldier from one of the units downstairs had come in search of me. With a Cheshire cat smirk on his face, he asked if I "wanted some." I considered gravely for a moment, slowly plodding through the obliquity of this invitation, and finally decided no, I didn't. My attitude toward sex was not what you'd call lofty, but I couldn't get interested in some countertossed girl when I'd just discovered a good piano. Further, the piano was handsomely crowned with a full complement of bottles, and Shorty and I had just invented some new and breathtaking harmony for "I Want a Girl."

The invitation was extended to the other men in the room, but only one man was interested. The others, sprawled comfortably on the floor near the piano, decided in favor of the less frenetic delights of music and liquor.

Early the following morning the same soldier from downstairs shook me awake and agitatedly begged me to come down and talk to the girl. She'd been there all night and now was sputtering German at them and they couldn't understand what she was saying. Bleary-eyed and unhappy, I pulled on my pants and we went down. The four anxious-faced men who were talking in low, worried tones looked up gratefully as we entered, but the frowns of anxiety returned as I walked to the closed bedroom door. Already they winced in anticipation: the girl would demand to see an officer . . . she'd charge "Rape!" . . . she'd get 'em all, the fifteen or twenty men who had called on her during the night, some of them more than one time. Even if she turned out to be a reasonable kind of whore, the least they could expect was a bill of staggering proportions, marked "For Services Rendered."

I opened the bedroom door and tried not to look at the rumpled bed as I queried. *"Bitte, was willst du, fraulein?"* She was a moderately attractive blonde, clothed at the moment and wearing a white blouse, gray slacks, and a blue coat. She sat wearily on the edge of the bed, her face sagging with fatigue, her skin the color of old putty. She spoke rapidly for a moment and I listened attentively. Then I turned to the anxious men standing behind me, grinned, and said, "She wants to know if she can go home now. And would you like her to come back tonight and bring a girlfriend with her?"

And we laughed like idiots, the bewildered girl looking at us suspiciously and saying, *"Was? Was?"* Between bursts of uncontrollable laughter I told her yes, of course she could go home, and yes, come back tonight with a girlfriend. She went off, walking unsteadily but almost straight—I don't know how the hell she could walk at all—and I asked B. how much money they'd given her. He answered in puzzled astonishment, "Not a goddamn cent! She never said a word about any money!" And we roared with laughter again.

Several hours later came the evil news that we were moving to a little village, beyond the reach of city temptations. I wonder if she came back with her girlfriend.

Waldorf is a small town only a few kilometers from Bonn. Signs of spring are everywhere: daffodils, crocuses, and rain. I am now officially a buck sergeant and inflated out of all proportion to the three modest stripes. But Loeb, my HQ friend who gets all the inside dope, told me something that has tormented me all day, and I look at the teeming rain and it's a right day for my misery.

Loeb says I am well regarded at HQ for my zeal (the word is his) in the affair at the crossroads, but the warm words are tempered by the cautious qualification that I "overextended" myself. It is said that I was supposed to have stopped at the group of houses the tanks blasted. In a very tentative fashion the buck is being passed so that it would appear that I failed to understand my orders or rashly exceeded them. My conscience is square with myself: I know what my orders were, and I know that I did not misunderstand them. But it doesn't matter where the blame should lie, or whose was the original fault of misunderstanding: the sickness that turns within me has for source the relentless fact that I *did* go up there and I *did* draw a tank up after me. Unwitting or not, I was the instrument by which two men died needlessly, and I do not even know their names. And I cannot forget the strange and whispering silence after the shells had landed and I peered from the corner of the house to watch the dead tank, smoke-wreathed, roll sluggishly and without direction into the field.

Still in Waldorf.

I'm comfortable and warm, sitting here in the living room of a German farmhouse. Tonight I sleep in a bed. I can even take my clothes off.

We share this house with women and children. There are no men in the village, not even old men. Most of the villagers were tearfully happy to see us once they realized we intended no harm to them. They embraced us and sobbed that we "freed them from the Nazis." Maybe they even thought they meant that. But we know that the real reason for these grateful tears is that our arrival meant there will be no further bombing and shelling of Waldorf. Whatever the reason, we shrugged and accepted the gestures of friendship. And the nonfraternization order was ignored to the complete satisfaction of everyone, GI and villager alike.

March 12.

Still here in Waldorf, still faithfully finger-crossing every hour on the hour, praying that our luck will hold a little longer.

I've been sitting in the kitchen, talking with the women. They are openmouthed with envy of everything American, and their questions about that golden land are many and eager. They are truly astounded—and a little disgruntled, secretly—to learn that America was never bombed, in spite of what the Nazi propagandists assured them. They try to remember the time when they, too, accepted safety as a matter of course, but the days of terror and the nights spent in the cellar are still fresh.

When I casually mentioned that my wife and children receive a hundred dollars a month from our government, they were momentarily speechless. The German government gives *them* nothing, they said. Then they asked wistfully about clothing, women's clothing. Could it still be bought in America? "Yes," I replied, and they sighed in unison. Even stockings? I considered hastily—I'd heard about the nylon lines—and then said firmly, "Yes, even stockings. *Silk* stockings!" That finished them, and I didn't have the heart to continue. They arose heavily and with somber faces began to prepare the thin soup of cabbage and turnips that was their evening meal.

It's a bleak and comfortless world these women have known since they signed over to their blasted führer. Perhaps the large cities—Berlin, Hamburg, Munich—still throng with gowned and groomed women (I recall the photographs of Frau Goering, lumpily elegant in white satin and sable), but these women in the kitchens of Waldorf and Drove and Soller were the ones whose destiny was decided in the pronouncement of the three K's for German women. *Kinder, kuche, und kirche:* children, cooking, and church. From this barren today, those who can remember the Empire, or even the Weimar Republic, lean backward in a golden nostalgia.

Now that I've had a little sleep I'm beginning to hanker for a world less exclusively masculine. I don't mean that I'm having trouble keeping my pants buttoned—or maybe I do mean that—but I hunger for the feminine attributes of the normal world. Our existence is so goddamn male—male voices, male shapes, male smells. I'd like to smell perfume again and see a woman walk across a room ... feel silk between my hands. I'd like to hear women laughing. The peasants in this house have thick bodies and their clothes are shapeless. Their faces are scrubbed and shiny and unexciting; they stride like men, and their voices are admirable instruments for the calling of pigs and cows. At this moment, if a woman strolled by ... just strolled by, the scent of Chanel No. 5 an insolent veil over her shoulder, I think ... yes, I think I could be led by my nose.

March 13, Waldorf.

We started a training program today. Manual of arms, saluting, and close order drill. It's a tough war. But we're comforted with news of movies soon, and showers and clean clothes. And the Red Cross doughnut wagon is due.

From a letter to Ree:

I think your loneliness is even more poignant than mine. You follow old routines, familiar patterns, and because you must do alone the things we used to do together, my ghost haunts you at every turn. Here there are no evocative symbols; there is nothing that says to me, "This is where she walked . . . this is where we used to meet . . . here she sat in the evening, where I could see her when I looked up from my book." I am spared these small reminders, and grateful for that mercy. I have learned, too, that rest periods are bad for my peace of mind. When I am busy, when there is action, movement, danger, I forget you entirely, and return to you only when there is time for remembering. Sometimes I cannot find you at all, cannot bring you near. You remain just beyond my fingertips, misty and not real. Curious how strangerlike you are to me then . . . and I to myself.

In my mail today was a letter from the Lion's Club in Syracuse, a reminder to attend the weekly luncheon meeting at the Hotel Syracuse on Friday, February 8. Sent to Camp Wheeler, it trailed me to Fort Meade, then to Camp Shanks, across the Atlantic, through Belgium, across the Roer, and finally to Waldorf, Germany. Reserve a place for me, O Brother Lions!

Shorty and I are having a small feast tonight. He owns a can of sardines, and I have cheese and assorted tidbits from the Christmas boxes I've just begun to receive.

Of the replacements who joined the first platoon in the Hurtgen Forest, only four remain: Shorty, Greg Luecke, Leo Allen, and myself. Greg and Shorty received their buck stripes when I did and are leaders of the first and third squads, respectively. Leo is the platoon runner now. Our rapid advance is not so much a tribute to our abilities as a commentary on the number of casualties the platoon has suffered since November.

Helmuth, Josef, Maria, Johann, and Margarita are engaged in a screaming game of tag, centered around the table where four of us are trying to write. We know, and the kids know that we know, that a handful of candy will buy peace and quiet for a while. A daily gambit. Wonder if my kids are such artful creatures. Wonder what my kids are like.

Daily we encounter more and more slave laborers. On their clothing they wear labels, stitched or painted, that identify them according to nationality and pronounce their serfdom. Like a tag on a dog: "This is Rex, Property of ——." The labels on the Russian and Polish slaves are very large and conspicuous. We are told that Russian or Polish slaves who ran away were not captured alive. Pursuit of a Russian or a Pole was considered an inefficient expenditure of German energy: the order was to shoot on sight. The labels made identification easy, you see, and there were so *many* Russians and Poles. . . .

We tell the slaves that they're free and will soon be back in their own countries. They're happy, but bewildered and uncertain. Many have had no word from home in several years, and they're afraid of what they may find when they return. Some have no destination: they saw the firing squads and the gallows, the torches, the evacuation vans for women and children, and they know that nothing remains of their native villages.

March 15.

Spring, boring from within, has taken possession of Waldorf. The day is unashamed blue and gold, crocuses blow cool flames across the tender green grass, and butterflies waltz in loving pairs through the orchard. Today I watched the unfolding of yellow and purple pansies. Summer is icumen in.

In many ways "resting" is worse than combat. When you're on line or pushing, you know you have a job to do, it's likely to be unpleasant, and you settle down and face it. But here every day is more poignant than the one preceding because you know it may be your last, because this can't last forever and why the hell don't they alert us and get it over?

Tonight the regimental orchestra played an open air concert in the street. It was good to hear American jazz again. The civilians came to listen, too, keeping a respectful distance away. I watched the German faces as they registered the impact of this strange American music ... faces that showed delight, bewilderment, distaste, contempt, and even a kind of fear. American jazz is rough, vigorous stuff for ears accustomed to the sugary banalities of German popular music.

One child caught my eye and I returned to her again and again, studying her covertly. A fairy-tale child ... eight years old, silvery blond and pigtailed, superbly Nordic. She listened gravely and her face had a purity, a delicacy of modeling, that set her apart from the lumpy, wriggling kids around her. But though she'll grow up and be lovely still, the odds are against her in this racked and unhappy country, and embittered, race-conscious sons will be bred on her warm silver body by an embittered, race-conscious German male. And—maybe because it was spring—the fun went out of the music for me, and I walked soberly back to the house.

March 16, Waldorf.

Another spring day, lucent and pale gold. Margarita gave me a bunch of violets and the scent fills the room.

There shouldn't be a war on. . . . I can't believe there's a war on. Outside the kids are yelling, fevered with mysterious games. Some of the men are playing catch in the cobbled street, and American voices are calling the same happy vulgarities Americans always call when they have a baseball and a couple of gloves.

I'm getting into a bitch of a mood with this interminable waiting, this expectancy that's never resolved.

In some forgotten town I picked up a pocket-size English-German dictionary. It is an astonishing volume. Compiled by a German and published in Leipzig, it purports to be a scholarly work, and perhaps it is. But I'd like to know where and in what fashion the guy acquired his knowledge of English. On every page are scattered words that sound like double-talk to me: "bewet ... cavesson ... civism ... diluviate ... edacity ... fulgurate ... ogganition." These are solemnly avowed to be in good English usage—"part of every cultured Englishman's vocabulary," says the preface—but good English usage where? In what high circles?

The personnel of my squad having changed many times over, I'll call the roll again:

Bill Bowerman, the assistant squad leader, from Niagara Falls. Originally one of the scouts. I've mentioned him before. Not quite twenty, a helluva nice kid with an ingenuous grin. Bill is levelheaded and mature, betraying his age only occasionally with adolescent horseplay and unexpectedly youthful guffaws. He's all right.

Bob Berthot, first scout. Bill's pal—same age, same hometown. Bill and Bob met for the first time when they were drafted, and they've been inseparable ever since training camp. Bob's a good kid, but he's a little given to puffing himself and assuming what he believes to be the "combat soldier manner" when he meets a replacement greener than himself. He does the dangerous work of a scout without demur, but his imagination needs throttling down on occasion.

"Red" Hull, BAR man. From Missouri, I believe, though he's not unknown on Chicago's Clark Street. More than six feet tall, deceptively lazy in his movements, given to the spinning of tall yarns that delight everyone and fool no one. His rich, booming bass voice is unforgettable once you have heard it. A former truck driver, it's easy to picture him in the cab of a truck, disarmingly insolent, grinning, and completely sure of himself. Redheaded, of course.

Ellis Herrington, Red's assistant on the BAR. A Tennessee farmer with a refreshing twang to his voice. Black hair, black eyes, quiet, serious, likable. The quality of his silence endows him with a striking virility.

Joe Hornung, bazooka. A house painter from Peoria, Illinois. Joe is the man who rushed to Ketron's aid when the Jerries counterattacked in Drove. Joe is always late, always slow, always forgetting something. Warmhearted and friendly, but given to rare, nervy bursts of temper. He tenses up too much for his own safety when things get rough.

Frank H., a discard from Shorty's squad. Frank has now made the rounds of the squads, being transferred from each one just in time to save him from a violent and unheroic end. He's on the last go-round now and will be shipped out of the company if, after fair trial, I find him too hard to handle. He is insolent, lazy, disobedient, and slovenly, and there are low murmurs among the men of a wide saffron streak. The captain is trying to give him every possible break, but I think the gesture is wasted. He has been in the army for three years, but landed overseas less than a month ago, having been escorted across the Atlantic under guard and regarded as a prisoner until his assignment to us. (Assignment to a combat outfit was frequently the justice served on chronic f———ups.) Frank boasts of his many sentences in the stockade back in the States. In the short time he's been with us, it's been noted that his equipment gets "too heavy" for him when we're on a forced march, and he throws it away, piece by piece, arriving at our objective nearly empty-handed. I've made him Joe's assistant on the bazooka. If he can't get along with slow, easygoing Joe, it's a damn sure thing he won't be able to get along with anyone else in the squad.

John Basile, rifleman and grenadier. Twenty-nine years old and from New Jersey. A former buck sergeant in antiaircraft, he's been in the army for more than two years but was transferred to the infantry only a short time ago. He doesn't think much of it. Arrived overseas three weeks ago. I think he'll be okay, but at the moment he's being dramatic about a blister on the bottom of his foot. He limps pathetically and heaves agonized sighs at every rest halt, but I've seen a lot of blisters, and histrionics don't move me. My feet hurt, too. He forgets that blisters are hardly the novelty to an infantry outfit that they might be to an ack-ack crew. But I sympathize with him secretly: it *is* a whopper of a blister and perhaps his feet are too soft to take this punishment.

John Albert, our newest member, eighteen years old and fresh from the States two weeks ago. I've tentatively assigned him as second scout. He's a good kid and he'll be all right, although at the moment he's a little nervy at the contemplation of combat.

So there they are, a typical rifle squad. Young and not so young, single and married, bold and timid, the sober and the simple. Men in uniform.

March 17, Waldorf.

And a chilly and unjoyous St. Patrick's Day it is. I've been sitting close to the kitchen stove and talking to Maria. She's a modestly attractive young woman nearing thirty. (I'm guessing at her age because she gets kittenish when we ask her how old she is. The colonel's lady and Judy O'Grady . . .)

Maria and her mother share this house with two other families. Most of the work falls on Maria's narrow shoulders—the housework, the gardening, the care of the chickens and rabbits. Not any more work, surely, than our farm women perform at home, but Maria's equipment is unbelievably primitive. Her "washing machine," for instance, is simply a huge iron vat mounted on legs. A fire of briquets on the grate under it heats the water and a scrubbing board completes the "machine." There is no soap.

The house is wired for electricity, but there's been no electricity for many months. Even with that lack supplied, there are no household gadgets: no electric vacuum cleaner, no electric iron, no electric percolator, toaster, sewing machine, Mixmaster.

But her lack of modern housekeeping conveniences would not be enough in itself to stir my pity: it is the desperation in her eyes when I see her talking to the men billeted in this house, the fear and panic in the twisting of her hands. This is a village of women, and most of the young men who left this place have long since been reported dead or missing or taken prisoner. Few of them will ever return. At night when Maria's work is done and she sits in the kitchen with a candle and a book she's read many times before (there are no new books), her face is locked and tight and she accepts despair. Often she does not see the words on the page, and I know that before her eyes are the years ahead, starved and dry and acrid.

More and more the war is dreamlike. There is even the dream knowledge of suspension, of swinging dangerously over black and bottomless space. And you wonder when will it break, this thin and fraying rope. . . .

CHAPTER NINE

"... hot water ... and nine fried eggs for breakfast ..."

March 20, and Waldorf is already remote.

This is *uber Rhine*, east of the Rhine, and the great river is behind us. I sit in what was the courtyard of what was a German farmhouse. Here in the sun, with fat geese grumbling from a muddy ditch and hens exclaiming excitedly over the new crop of bugs this spring, it's momentarily possible to disdain the broken roof slates under my feet and the bullet-riddled tin washtub that is my easy chair.

We left Waldorf on March 18, heading east. It was spring, and the earth stoutly refused to admit that we were About to Cross the Rhine. War and the passing of armies had preceded us. We took a route well-marked by a web of communications wire strung along the roadside by our Signal Corps. A tree, a telegraph pole, a chimney or a weather vane—any projection where wire could be hung bore the tangled skein. I suspect one linesman of delicate irony, an eye for subtle cruelties. The anguished Christ on a roadside crucifix seemed oddly distorted, out of proportion, and I stared closely as we drew near. Around His middle, in addition to the customary clout, He wore a corset of black communication wire, wound thickly and with careful precision from armpits to loins. A sardonic comment, a deliberate juxtaposition of protagonist and antagonist.

We detrucked in an elegant little Rhine town, with many beautiful villas. The cobbled streets seemed oddly familiar, and then I remembered that eleven years ago I had ridden down these same streets on a bicycle, a hot-eyed, eager young tourist.

We crossed the Rhine on a pontoon bridge two miles above the now famous Remagen span. A smoke screen concealed our crossing and we could not see the other side, but we knew the river was wide from the time it took to cross it. The smoke was white and thick but odorless and nonirritating, barring a faint chemical taste.

The Rhine behind us, we walked to the village of Rheintal-breitbach. (I think that was its name.) My bunch moved into the home of a widow whose only son was missing in action. Several of the men, including company headache, Frank H., laid claim to the old lady's bedroom, and tremblingly she came to plead with me, fearful that we might evict her entirely. I assured her that she was safe and that I'd get the men out of her room, and she embarrassed the hell out of me by grabbing my hand and kissing it frantically.

We didn't stay overnight after all. An hour after our arrival, orders came to pack up again. We climbed aboard tanks and tank destroyers and raced into the town of Aegidienburg.

My C.P. was in a large house, with twelve civilians living in the cellar: two men, an old woman, four younger women, two babies, a pair of six-year-old girl twins named Krista and Kristal, and a Russian slave girl. The owner of the house had owned a tool factory on the Rhine. He spoke enough English and I enough German so that we conversed easily. He was very ingratiating, very contemptuous of the Nazis, and completely a phony. He stated that he had once spent eight months in a concentration camp, but the facts he let slip didn't jibe with the anti-Nazi feelings he professed. To begin with, he was wealthy. (There were three cars in the barn, and he owned a town house in Bonn and a villa on the Rhine, in addition to this farm.) Further, he was a prominent industrialist, and opponents of National Socialism were not likely to remain the possessors of factories, particularly those that manufactured war matériel. (He boasted, incidentally, that his factory had been in full production throughout the war, until

Allied bombing raids knocked it out for the third and final time only a few months ago.)

He mentioned carelessly that most of the labor in his factory had been supplied by foreign slaves. Wealthy, an industrialist, an employer of slave labor, and *not* a Nazi? If I needed further proof, I found it in the way he spoke of the Russian house slave, the familiar and contemptuous manner in which these people always speak of servants and animals: "... stupid, of course, but a good worker." A dependable animal.

After the civilians had retired for the night, I talked with the Russian girl. She spoke of her "owner" with bitterness and anger and pointed contemptuously with her thumb to the cellar door.

She is from the Ukraine, near Voroshilovograd, and she wants to go home. She does not know whether her parents are alive: when her town was taken by the Germans, the healthy and the strong were put in one group, the aged and unfit in another. The town was looted and burned to the ground, and she doesn't know what happened to the old people. That is, she cannot be sure. But she wants to go back, and she speaks ardently of the time ahead when she will work for herself and be no longer a slave.

Shortly before the crossing of the Rhine, the Gestapo came to this village and rounded up the foreign slaves, transporting them eastward. Her owner concealed her in the cellar, a neighboring farmer did the same with his young Russian male slave, and then these two good Germans solemnly assured the Gestapo that they had no Russian workers.

When the factory owner relates this story, he offers it as proof of his high regard for the girl: he "saved her from the Gestapo." She agrees with the facts but gives them a different interpretation: the women of this household are lazy and slovenly. They needed a servant and she was convenient. (Incidentally, she told us that the civilians drank champagne every night during the last week in order to get rid of it before the Americans came. The bastards.)

The dead in the village are beginning to smell. One German soldier lies in a ditch nearby, and in the cellar of a house down the road are two more, very ripe. Yesterday a civilian sought me out and led me to his house, where a young German soldier lay dead upon a bed. He had been wounded the day before, and the civilians had tried to patch him up. I arranged for the disposition of his body and then engaged in a flirtatious conversation with the farmer's sister, a refugee from Bonn. She was a sophisticated and provocative blonde, wearing well-fitting slacks and a thin blouse open down to here! She spoke French, used her eyes and hands with effect, and wiggled her plump rear as she talked. When she leaned forward and the blouse gaped and I smelled her perfume—oh brother! I steamed with hayloft visions and ogled her like a Victorian dandy (ogled is the word!), clicking my heels and bowing over her hand as I said *"Au 'voir."* As I walked back to my C.P. I mentally arranged guard tricks for the night that would suit my convenience. But alas for the best laid plans of mice and men—only the mice got laid that night. Orders from HQ kept me busy long past the witching hour, and I slept alone (when I slept) on a red plush sofa in the living room of the tool manufacturer's house. The following day we were transferred to another section of the town. And the sun beats warmly on me here, and the geese grumble contentedly. I've decided geese have more character than chickens.

The past several days are a blur of color and movement.

Three days ago I sat on a washtub by a ruined farmhouse and wrote letters, the sun warm and the war far away. That afternoon we climbed into trucks and moved out for a town whose name I do not know. En route we crossed the Reich-autobahn, the famous superhighway of Germany. Shell holes pockmarked it as far as the eye could reach, and grass grew rankly through wide cracks in the concrete. Route 20 in New York State was never like this.

There was the customary confusion when we reached our

destination and detrucked. Harried officers and noncoms debated our disposition for the night while we stretched on the muddy grass along the road and chain-smoked and bitched. Night fell, the discussion continued, and the grass was cold. Finally we were led to an imposing mansion and instructed to settle ourselves for the night.

The front door of the building was locked, and we climbed in through a broken rear window, cursing over the furniture that barked our shins in the dark hallways. Suddenly a woman's voice, old but as faintly sweet as the ringing of an old bell, called, "What is it?" The voice came from the cellar and the words were English.

I hesitated, then replied, "Do not be afraid! We are American soldiers and we are going to spend the night here."

There was a pause, and then I saw the moving glimmer of a light in the dark hole of the cellar stairway. The light moved upward, grew larger, became a candle flame. Then the same voice, nearer now and remarkably beautiful, said gently, "You are welcome, of course. But this is a hospital, and we have sick ones downstairs."

Now I could see the speaker, a nun, white-coiffed, and the aging, patient face. Abashed, I told the men to settle themselves quietly and with a minimum of breakage. We talked for a moment longer, she standing on the top step of the cellar stairs, her face innocent in the candlelight. I was miserably aware of my unshaven cheeks, my dirty hands, the foul smell of my clothing. She assured me that the sick in the cellar included no German soldiers, only the civilians of the town—women and children and old men whose bodies had been shattered by bombing and privation. Finally she said good night, and wished me a pleasant sleep under the protection of Our Lady. I watched her go downstairs. When she had gone and the last faint flicker of light disappeared, the night was a lot blacker than the absence of one small candle would explain. She to her job, and I in the morning to mine. But mine was to destroy, to maim, and hers to minister to those we hurt. Where was the right and where the wrong in this? Where did the black leave off and the white begin? I slammed and locked a door against the painful probing of these questions and set off to find the men. They were already settled, and soon I was, too. I slept on an operating table.

We moved out at dawn. In the dim half-light the handsome old mansion was clearly identified as a Catholic hospital. Commemorative plaques, holy pictures and plaster saints, a large sign over the front gate, and a Red Cross flag on a pole in the garden. One wing of the hospital had been devastated by a bomb that had sliced smoothly through three floors, shearing away the outer wall. We assembled in the road and I watched the door, half hoping. But no one appeared. And so we started on the road to Soven. It was March 21.

We made one stop en route; not really a village because it was only a single building. But it was a *big* building, a giant square of masonry with an open courtyard in its heart. Two sides of the square constituted living quarters, three and four stories tall, and the remaining sections were a labyrinth of barns, stables, sheds, granaries, and storerooms. There were a lot of civilians wandering about. Feudal estate or communal farm, it was a self-sustaining unit, reminiscent of Brook Farm and similar nineteenth-century utopias.

We were ordered to hold up there for further orders, and I stationed the men in an apple orchard on the crest of a hill. On the far side of the valley the red roofs of a tiny town appeared dimly through a thick haze of smoke: Soven, perched on the summit of a hill. Fighting was going on in the valley below us, and every now and then a batch of prisoners trailed up the hill, escorted by a few grinning doggies.

Early in the afternoon we saw a heartwarming sight: a long column of prisoners, 161 of them, and striding at their head a German colonel, complete with swagger stick and monocle à la Erich von Stroheim. He stepped along disdainfully, refusing to acknowledge by the flicker of an eyelash the cameras that started clicking the moment he came in sight.

A couple of men from the company that earlier in the day had taken the courtyard village, which seemed to be a communal farm, told us there was something in the stable we should see. We looked. The "something" was a dead Jerry lying in the hay, the back of his head a gaping ruin, the flies thick on the still-wet blood and brains. For some reason he was wearing a GI uniform. Shoes, trousers, shirt, sweater, overcoat—all unmistakably American. Maybe he wasn't a spy, maybe he'd had another answer—but if so, no one had bothered to hear it. Apparently, five minutes after he was brought in, he'd been led into the stable, a carbine placed behind his ear, and his brains blown out. I wish I knew his story. He was sprawled on the hay ... slender, bespectacled, intelligent-looking. His lips, half open, were finely cut and sensitive.

Shorty and I discovered a storeroom and raided the canned fruit. Delicious cherries and prunes, very cold and sweet.

There was a kind of caravan parked in the courtyard, great covered wagons like old-time circus vans. They were padlocked, but we peered through the tiny windows. The wagons were filled with the belongings of refugees, probably from one of the Rhine towns, who had retreated to this place for safety.

Finally, we moved on toward Soven, hurrying into the valley on the double because the road was under fire. We paused briefly in a village that had just been taken and took refuge against a fierce burst of enemy shells. In one house we found a slab of bacon, potatoes, and onions, which we fried in a savory mess. It tasted fine.

There was a Russian slave girl in the house, tanned, stocky, and strong. Her teeth, both uppers and lowers, were of polished steel, and when she stood in the sun and smiled—oh, brother! But she was merry and friendly and cooperative. *How* cooperative I cannot say: several of our lustier men tried to get a little hayloft cooperation, and I suspect that our alliance with Russia became a little more solidly established on a popular level. It was a tough war.

We were briefed on the plan for taking Soven: first, an artillery barrage to soften it up, then an assault by two platoons of infantry, of which we were one.

We set out, moving up a deep draw that knifed the smooth

side of the hill. Moss was gentle under our weary feet, and the task awaiting us at the top of the hill seemed unreal and impossible: this small world in the heart of the hill contradicted violence and flame. Violets and snowdrops lipped the banks of a tumbling little brook, and primroses and daisies spilled jubilantly down the slopes on either side. At one place the brook formed a small pool, and seven fat white geese paddled contendedly there, unperturbed by the shells whistling overhead. I am more and more convinced that geese have character.

We rushed the village, a desolate place of blazing ruins, smoking timbers, and dead cattle. Many buildings were still burning, and a heavy pall of smoke hung low. For ten minutes it was an accelerated version of our customary assault procedure: clear one building, rush another, clear and rush, clear and rush. I don't know when I first became aware of the planes—I'd seen them and heard them, but their presence hadn't quite registered. Suddenly they were there, low in the sky and heavy over us. At that moment a tower of smoke and debris rose into the air like a dark geyser fifty yards away, and simultaneously something knocked me to the ground. Then I was being pounded by fragments of brick and wood, and someone was screaming. But these were *our* planes—I could see the markings on the wings plainly, they were our planes and this couldn't be happening to us, God wouldn't let this happen to us!

I don't think I was really scared at first—that came a few seconds later. First it was incredulity, bewilderment. But fear moved in fast and nightmare followed. We rushed for the nearest building—one man scratched at the ground in nerveless hysteria while we belabored his ass with our boots to get him to his feet and moving—and into the safety of the cellar, which was jammed with screaming women. I hugged the corner of the building, yelled to stragglers, and watched the village blossom hugely in puffs of orange flames and black smoke. I could see some of our men only a short distance away, lying on their stomachs among the cabbages in a garden.

Someone threw a yellow smoke grenade—yellow means "We are friendly troops"—in a desperate attempt to halt this attack by our own planes. But the wind whipped away the first puffs of smoke, and the next bomb, falling near, smothered the grenade with dust and debris. Meanwhile, the planes began to strafe, the heavy *cr-rump* of the bombs punctuated by the screams of the diving planes.

Suddenly it all ceased, and there was a silence so intense that the crackling of the burning houses seemed very loud and the droning of the planes like the intimate presence of bumble-bees. I learned later that my friend Loeb had managed to spread a yellow "panel" where the planes could see it and realize their mistake. (Wonder how those bombardiers felt when they saw that yellow strip?) "Panels" were made of a kind of oilcloth and came in various colors, each color conveying a specific message. They were peculiarly brilliant in tone, almost luminous, and could be seen for miles.

When the planes were gone, we picked up where we'd left off, working our way through the village, clearing and rushing, clearing and rushing. As we neared the road that was our primary objective, I heard the rumble of nearby tanks. Knowing damn well that there were no armed units with us, I reflected that this was turning into a bitch of a day. We concealed ourselves and waited. The rumble grew louder, and a moment later the evil snout of a German tank appeared on the road. In the open turret the tank commander stood erect, a bold and careless figure. That was a good sign: obviously the Jerries didn't know that a handful of *verdammte Amerikanische* were within spittin' distance. The situation was one of rare perfection—the tank only fifty yards away, traveling broadside to us, and moving slowly. Even in basic training you never got such a perfect bazooka shot.

A few yards to my rear the bazooka man crouched behind a shed. In a loud whisper I told him to hold his fire until the tank was directly in front of us, and then I turned my eyes again to the road, watching tensely as the tank approached the designated spot. Almost there . . . now! Fire now! But nothing happened; the tank rolled along and nothing happened; it drew ever nearer the safety of the next group of houses and nothing happened. Forgetting caution, I called back to the bazooka man and ordered him to fire, and again nothing happened, the tank passing beyond the shoulder of the next house and then gone. It had hardly disappeared when the nose of another tank appeared, following the first. Again I commanded and begged and pleaded; my voice broke and I think I was crying, and still he didn't fire. And the second tank passed, unhurt.

When it was gone, I ran back to find out what had gone wrong with the bazooka, what had happened to the man carrying it. The poor bastard told me that he hadn't been *able* to fire because his assistant wasn't there to pull the safety pin from the rocket! That's what he'd learned in basic training—that the assistant pulls the safety pin—and so (his tone said) if his assistant didn't happen to be around, how could he be expected to fire the weapon? I told him to pull the goddamn pin himself (I could hear another tank approaching), and at that moment the lost assistant, Frank H., appeared. I asked where he'd been, and he said he was looking for his bag of bazooka ammunition. What the hell did he mean, "looking for it"? I roared. Well, he'd put it down for a minute outside some house and then he'd gone on and forgotten it. When he remembered and went back for it, he couldn't find the house. His carelessness meant that we now had but one rocket.

There wasn't time to properly ream him out. I gave hasty orders and prepared to return to my forward vantage point. Before leaving, I told a grenadier to move to a position where he, too, could get a shot at the approaching tank. And *that* poor bastard had tears in his eyes as he showed me his grenade launcher, packed solid with mud. He'd dropped his rifle in a ditch during the bombing attack.

This whole episode makes us look pretty slipshod and blundering, but it demonstrates that the war wasn't always heroics and cool efficiency in our army. True, not all bazooka teams were compounded of slow wits and carelessness. But when you were short of men (and you were always short of men), you used what you had, even when you knew beforehand that they'd probably bungle their particular job. There wasn't any choice.

The third tank appeared, and just as in the first one, the tank commander stood in the open turret, carelessly exposed. And at last our bazooka team went into action. The result was what you might expect: it was the only rocket we had and it was too low, damaging the tank only slightly and failing to halt it. Bob Berthot saved the day: hunched behind a steaming mound of manure, he picked off the tank commander with a rifle bullet.

Leaving the squad, I began to work toward the end of the village, following the direction taken by the tanks. I kept to the rear of the burning houses, out of sight of the road. There was a sweating, retching moment in a turnip patch when I stumbled over something pink and naked and newly dead. For a few palsied seconds I thought it was the body of a newborn baby, and then I realized it was a baby pig, so young that the skin was still moist and raw.

Darting through ruined gardens and dancing like a cat over the hot and tumbled bricks of houses still smoldering, I reached the crossroads at the end of the village. The tanks were there, catty-corner from the house where I crouched. They had drawn under the sheet-iron roof of a vast hay shed, a skeleton structure of heavy poles and open sides. There they rested, the muzzles of their guns facing us. The tank crews were covering them with hay, and I could catch stray fragments of their conversation, hear the sound of their feet as they climbed around. I slipped to the courtyard at the rear of the house, preparing to go back and collect some men with anti-tank weapons. A second house stood on the far side of the courtyard, fronting upon the side road that led to the intersection. As I darted across the open yard I saw something moving in the field and altered my course slightly, heading for the house. It was very quiet now; there was no sound but the crackling of flames and the low moaning of cattle.

Fragments of food and scattered articles of German

equipment in the kitchen of the little house indicated the recent presence of the enemy. In the bedroom on the second floor I found a window that offered observation of the field, and screening myself cautiously behind the cheap lace curtains, I peered out. Stretched across the field in a long defense line were several dozen German soldiers, hurriedly digging foxholes. A hundred yards beyond them stood an ornate house, and in the shadow of the porte cochere was the darker shape of a German tank, large size. In the neighboring field two self-propelled guns had drawn into position, facing the village. It was an impressive setup, and I recalled with pain our own lack of armored protection.

I raced downstairs and out the back door, heading for home. As I stepped from the house I heard the rumble of a tank and froze against the back wall. I caught sight of Bob Berthot then. He was on the opposite side of the courtyard, crouched beside a crumbled wall, and from his strained position I knew that he, too, had heard the tank. I considered the width of the yard between us and wondered if I could get across before the tank pulled up. The twenty-five yards between me and safety stretched wider and wider, and I teetered in an agony of indecision while the noise of the tank grew steadily louder. Then it was too late, the tank was in sight, moving up the road toward me, less than twenty feet from where I stood, rigid and unbreathing. I shook under the slow grinding of its advance and prayed that it would keep going, not stop. . . . Please don't let it stop here! It stopped as it reached the courtyard, stopped and swiveled to face the village. I could hear the talk and laughter of the tank crew; I could see the black hulk of the tank when I inched to the corner of the house and strained my vision around it. I could have reached out and touched the blunt nose of the 88.

I couldn't see Berthot now, but I whispered his name. He didn't hear, and I tried again. Then again and again. On the sixth try he appeared, directly across from me but concealed from the tank by the wall at his side. The tank having shut off its motors, he assumed it had gone and started to his feet. Frantically I waved him down again, and then, across the courtyard that separated us like a wall, I loud-whispered my instructions and sent him back to report. In a few seconds his twisting, dodging figure was out of sight—and it was a lonely day then. If I were going to be killed or captured, I wished I wasn't alone, I wished that someone was there with me.

With the shoulder of the house screening me from the tank, I crept to a chicken house and crawled in. Watched by gravely curious hens, I searched for an exit to the field beyond. There was a window, but it was blocked by a bicycle and a clutter of discarded furniture. With trembling, feather-tipped hands I cleared the window and crawled through. My rifle clattered against the window frame and sweat sprang out on my palms, but I was out in the field, I was moving. I might yet die, but not like an animal, not trapped and cowering.

I crept along the base of a low wall, the prickling skin of my body reminding me that a sharp-eyed sniper in the German C.P. could easily pick me off. Then the wall came to an end and an eight-foot gap stretched between me and the buildings toward which I yearned. Only eight feet to safety, but under the nose of the German tank.

They saw me when I streaked across, and the 88 let go with an angry *whoosh!* The shell exploded a short distance away and I was pelted with twigs and bits of brick.

Home again, I reported to Sergeant Torrey, who had become our platoon leader when Sergeant Misa went home on furlough. Somebody, whether Torrey or one of the officers, flubbed his dub in the hours that followed, because nothing was done about knocking out those damned tanks, not a blasted thing. After a tormenting period of indecision, Shorty and his squad were ordered to the house from which I'd seen the tanks, their mission "to keep watch on the hay shed." When Shorty reached the house, he found that the tank that had scared the pants off me was gone, and only the two in the hay shed remained.

Sometime during the period in which we were stalemated

by indecision, I went back to a building I'd passed en route to the crossroads. It was a fine brick stable and there were animals inside, suffering. The stable itself was undamaged, but the bricks were hot to the touch, and smoldering wood and hay from the burning buildings on either side had made a choking torment of the air. Entering the stable, I discovered that the beasts were chained to their stalls, safeguarded by their cautious owner before he himself took off for safety. I winced from the sight of the swollen tongues, the bloodshot eyes, the poor heads that strained at the stanchions. The lock of one stanchion was broken, and I freed the animal that had been imprisoned by it. She looked at me with dumb eyes, and I could not force or persuade her from the stable and into the open air. Unable to break the mesh of chains and locks securing the other animals, I carried water in my helmet from the nearest well and poured it into the feeding troughs. I'd thought they would lap it greedily, but they sniffed at it and would not touch it, looking back at me with frightened eyes. Whatever it was they asked of me, I could not understand and could not grant, and I left quickly.

I collected my squad and we scooted across the road, dodging the bursts of machine-gun fire from the tanks at the crossroads. Our assigned position was another "courtyard village," a house and attached outbuildings enclosing a great square courtyard. The house proper was gutted by fire, but tottering walls and smoking rafters testified to the original size of the building. It was still burning.

There were civilians in the cellar, living there while the house burned down over their heads. They came out when they heard us and ran to us, weeping and hysterical. One man was crying bitterly, brokenly, and he wanted to embrace us. I dodged him—I was suddenly unbearably tired and oppressed by all that remained to be done, by all that had been done. He disappeared in the cellar, returning a moment later with a bottle of schnapps, but I told him we had work to do and could not drink until later. I watched him to make sure that he took it back to the house. Then we started to dig in. It was dark now, but the burning village crimsoned the sky, threw our shadows in giant, flickering relief against red clouds. Smoke from burning hay writhed heavily over the ground.

On a bed in the cellar lay the patriarch of the house, wounded in the afternoon's bombing. Our medic dressed his wounds, but we could not satisfy his pleading daughter, who begged us to get an ambulance and take him to a hospital.

Bales of hay smoldered on the lawn before the house. Originally they had guarded the cellar windows against shrapnel, but catching fire from the burning house, they had poured smoke into the cellar until pulled away from the windows. They burned a long time.

Directly across the road was a fine modern house of stucco. With the houses on both sides burning fiercely, it was only a matter of time until it, too, started to burn. We watched the progress of the fire as it swept from room to room, licking the creamy walls, laughing triumphantly from conquered windows. The old fascination of fire was irresistible, and in our transfixed pleasure there was little trace of the horror that would temper our relish of a fire in our own hometowns. This was spectacle; this was circus; this was Rome blazing, and Tyre and Nineveh, and no personal stake of kinship involved us.

The house belonged to one of the women in the cellar. There was no surprise on her face when she saw her home burning—only a numbed acceptance, an emotionless misery more painful to observe than hysterics. She could not stay away from the sight. She would go to the cellar, but within half an hour she would be at my side once more, looking steadily at the blazing ruin across the road. She said nothing to me, and I heard only a few low moans, but she stared until her eyes filled and the tears rolled soundlessly down her face. She covered her head with her apron for a moment, and her body rocked in the silent impotence of grief, the ancient rocking grief of women.

Most of the civilians were in a large cellar room bulging with beds, chairs, dishes, and luggage. Torrey set up his C.P.

in a storeroom, sharing the space with a vast bin of potatoes. The room smelled beautifully of apples. In an adjoining storeroom there was a luxurious bed of inlaid wood and a refugee from Bonn, a wearily attractive woman of thirty. She was dressed in a dark blue shirt and slacks. Haggard with fear and exhaustion, she looked curiously like the "gray girl of Bonn." Her husband was a Luftwaffe officer, and there had been no word from him for many months. She smoked an incredible number of my cigarettes and talked nervously in a dull monotone. At the faintest whisper of sound from a distant plane, she would run to me and wrap her arms tightly about my waist, burying her head on my chest. I could feel the violent quivering of her body, and I would pat her shoulder gently and murmur meaningless comfort. When the planes were gone, she'd straighten up, toss her hair back, and ask for another cigarette.

The house burning over our heads kept the cellar pleasantly warm. Only two outside walls remained now, and the flames were playing with them, teasing them with light, flirting tongues. From the road it appeared that the adjoining buildings were also burned to the ground, but the courtyard behind them was sunken, and a layer of rooms below the road level stood unharmed. The irony of their survival was that they were workrooms: a laundry, several grain bins, a pump room, a root cellar. No living quarters remained. The same irony of destruction had fingered the buildings across the courtyard where the farm laborers had lived: the living quarters were gone, and only the living quarters. The front wall of one building had been sheared away, exposing the devastated interior— blackened streamers of wallpaper, a porcelain stove toppled on its side, an iron bed, fire-twisted and obscene. But the next building, a wooden shed noisy with barnyard fowl, was untouched.

Access to the fields and pastures beyond was possible through an outside door in one of the barns, offering us a quick and almost safe route to positions from which we could observe the German tanks in the hay shed, two hundred yards away. I concentrated the squad at that vital corner and we dug in as quietly as possible.

About nine P.M. Torrey called the squad leaders together at the C.P. He gave us the bad news tersely: the C.O. had ordered him to send out a combat patrol to knock out those two tanks. A sweet little sonofabitch of an assignment, and our respective hearts hit bottom. We drew cards for it, high man to go. (That was a favorite custom in our outfit: I don't know whether other outfits used it. Our ranking noncoms hated to select men for an unpleasant job, so we always drew for the chance to be a hero. I wasn't very fond of the system: I am phenomenally unlucky at cards, and ill luck had tapped me for most of the night patrols we'd done during the winter.)

We drew: Shorty, Greg Luecke, and I—high man to take the mission. I drew first and my card was a jack. My heart flapped miserably against my boot soles, but I struggled for a poker face and tried to look unconcerned. I fooled nobody. Greg drew next and pulled a queen. I tried a new expression this time: gentle sympathy. Again I fooled nobody. Then it was Shorty's turn. An ace! Greg and I didn't dare look at Shorty.

No definite hour had been assigned for the job: Shorty could go when he chose. We talked it over and decided that Shorty's team should be composed of men drawn from all three squads. We settled on two A.M. as the best hour because the moon would have set by then. The patrol would set out from my positions at the corner of the barn.

Returning to my squad, I inquired about any recent activity of the tanks and received contradictory answers. All of the men had heard ominous rumbles from the hay shed, but none could agree on their meaning. Some said the tanks had just been warming up; others asserted they'd pulled out. A few swore that more tanks had arrived to join the two at the crossroads. There was no way to check these conflicting reports: the moon had set, and a heavy ground mist cut visibility to less than fifty feet. The men were jittery, suspecting thousands of Germans creeping up under cover of the mist.

Shorty and I discussed the problem once more and decided it would be best to go far out on the flank and approach the tanks circuitously in order to hit their rear ends. However, when we laid our plan before the men who were to make up the patrol, they rejected it emphatically and said in effect, "If you please, sir—*no!*" And they meant it. (Who said the army wasn't democratic?) We held a kind of loose-jointed town meeting and finally agreed on a revised plan: they would crawl into the field at such an angle that their fire could be directed against the sides of the tanks.

One at a time they crept over the lip of our defenses and slipped silently into the mist—Shorty, three bazooka teams, one rifle team. Our intent had been to stagger the teams across the field, the first team to fire first, then the second, finally the third—all in rapid succession and each team streaking for home immediately upon discharging its rocket.

The last man had hardly crawled out of sight when some nervous character loused up the operation by firing his rocket. The other teams were not yet in position, of course, but the ill-timed shot forced them to fire also, and in a few seconds the entire patrol was back in the hole, the men tumbling over themselves in their anxiety to reach safety.

Of the three rockets fired, two exploded harmlessly in the field beyond the hay shed. The third hit something that rang metallically—we decided later it must have been one of the steel posts of the shed—but failed to explode. The mission had been a flop, and it was even more aggravating to learn the following morning that the tanks had gone from the hay shed several hours before our patrol set out. A neighboring unit saw them leave. The long torment of the night had been needless: the tension of waiting to see who would be chosen for the patrol, the worse tension of waiting for zero hour.

Shorty was too downhearted to want to report to Torrey on the mission, so I walked to the C.P. and delivered a somewhat puffed-up account. It was deliciously warm in the cellar, and Torrey invited me to sleep there, but I felt restless away from the squad and refused. I went back to the barn, made a pallet of hay, and covered myself with a German overcoat I'd found. Half an hour later I was awakened by someone who told me to rush to the C.P.: Torrey wanted me. When I reached there, still rubbing sleep from my eyes, the cellar was full of smoke and hysteria, and Torrey was no longer there. And I was the platoon leader.

My decision to sleep near my squad had been fortunate. Torrey, the German girl, and one of the male civilians had stretched out on the luxurious bed in the small storeroom—Torrey on one side, the girl on the other, the civilian in the middle between them. (They didn't trust us even when we were tired, these fleshwise Europeans.) During the night the fire smoldering in the ruins above had burned a hole in the thick floor, and a mass of burning coals had funneled down upon Torrey. His life was saved by the quick action of Howie Dettman, the medic, who pulled him out before the fast-growing pile had reached his face. His hands and arms were fearfully burned, however. The girl was untouched, and the civilian sleeping in the middle had been burnt only slightly. Torrey was rushed to the battalion aid station, but before he left, he designated me as platoon leader. (He never rejoined the outfit: his burns had been so severe that he was evacuated to England and spent the duration in a hospital there.)

There was no more sleep for me that night. Dettman and I sat on the potato bin and talked until dawn, making plans and eating apples.

The cellar was crowded now. More civilians drifted in, like the old woman who had arrived the day before. We saw her coming through the orchard, a bent figure with a large suitcase in one hand, a heavy bundle wrapped in a red and white table-cloth in the other. She reeled with weariness and stopped every few yards to rest, leaning her stubborn old body against the broken trees, tilting her shawled head upward to struggle for breath. Ten staggering yards at a time, and we watched her in silence, with pity. One man wanted to go to her, take her bundles and help her in. Wordlessly I voted him a Bronze Star for humanity, but had to refuse his request: a lurking sniper might not fire on an old German woman, but a fresh young American was a different target altogether.

She reached us finally, and two men helped her to the cellar. Returning to the house some hours later, I found her sitting at the bottom of the cellar stairs, her belongings piled around her. Angered, I asked the civilians if they could not offer her a better place to sit. They muttered that they did not know her, she had come from another village, the cellar was very crowded, there was no room for her, and please, when would I get the ambulance for their father? I damned them for their coldness, told them their father could wait, and stomped into their living quarters, trailed by bleats of protest. It *was* crowded, the old man *was* suffering, but I cleared a chair and went back for the old woman. No good: I couldn't budge her. Whether she was so dulled by exhaustion that she could not comprehend, or whether her pride would not permit her to accept hospitality thus churlishly doled out by her countrymen, I could not tell. She sat there all the long night, brushed by the knees of all who passed. And as I lay on the potato bin, talking to Dettman, my eyes turned again and again to the bent figure in shapeless black, the nodding head, the sudden starts into wakefulness each time the sagging body began to slip from the narrow step. I could offer her nothing more—all I had was a bin of potatoes.

At dawn I crept up to Shorty's position. (Not that it matters, but the date was March 22.) From his observation post it was evident that no tanks remained in the hay shed, but we decided to burn the shed to prevent it being so used again. We fired a white phosphorus rocket into the hay and in five minutes the shed was flame and quick ashes. We flushed no Jerries.

Returning to my late squad, I learned that a German shell had just scored a hit on the corner of the barn, wounding "Red" Hull slightly.

Immediately after noon chow we pushed off, our company in reserve. (That is, E and F companies were forward and G company followed, to be committed to action only if necessary.) Our objective was the little town of Nieder-kümpel

Ober, which sat precariously on a high hill overlooking the Sieg River. It was a helluva hike, uphill and down, dodging German shells all the way. We assembled for the assault in the woods on a neighboring hill and lay doggo there for two hours while the artillery worked the town over. It was peaceful in the wood, and the barrage was a remote phenomenon of unpleasant sound. We were tired, and content to lie quietly in the sparse grass, and five curious deer tiptoed daintily to the edge of the clearing and studied us gravely for a long time. When they were gone, I leaned my back against a tree and read a paperback mystery swiped from an unwary tank destroyer crew some days before.

Finally the assault! Pulse pounding in my throat, I watched the other companies take off. Our turn now, and at a nod from Captain Wirt, I started—my first day as a platoon leader and my platoon was leading the company! Holding my rifle at a fiercely-assault angle and shouting something in the knightly tradition—heaven forgive me, but it might even have been "Follow me, men!"—I gallantly hurdled a barbed wire fence, thoroughly conscious of the captain's eyes upon me. Three steps more and WHAM! I made a one-point landing on my chin, scattering my equipment for yards. A trailing end of that damned barbed wire had snagged my trousers, throwing me ass over teakettle before the captain's eyes. And me in the middle of an intrepid charge!

Picking myself up, I started off again, this time without any clarion call to the men, most of whom were already ahead of me anyway. All the long way to the village my ears burned with shame, and I was unconscious of fatigue and unaware of the bloody gash in my hand.

We passed many dead and wounded. I recall a hazardous trail through a gorge and a glimpse of a familiar pietà on the rock-strewn floor of the ravine far below: a medic cradling the head of a wounded man on his knees.

Nieder-kümpel Ober was blazing, and the civilians were fighting the flames with stirrup pumps and buckets of water. Three teenage girls spelled each other on the long handle of the town pump, the only source of water in the village. Old women and children staggered under the weight of water-filled pails hanging from yokes on their necks. A few feet from me two young women and a man labored to save their home. They worked in silence, spending words only to point out new danger spots, new small tongues of flame, but their faces were strained and desperate, shining with sweat. They worked swiftly.

I saw no tears, not even from children ... no tears at all until a house was given up for lost and surrendered entirely to the flames. Then the defeated stood back and watched with dull eyes, watched while all their yesterdays flamed up briefly and died to gray ash. Yesterday, today, and even tomorrow gone before the sweat had dried on their bodies. They watched quietly and wept only when it was irrevocable, when the dear familiar walls and doors blurred under the curling flames, began to dissolve and crumble. Then the men hunched their shoulders, their faces working, and the women covered their heads with their aprons.

Bill Bowerman, now leader of my old squad, had collapsed from exhaustion on the long uphill race to the village, and I had sent him to the battalion aid station in the rear. The platoon had no other casualties.

From our defense line on the crest of the hill we could see Siegburg, an important industrial center on the Sieg River. It looked big.

As the men lifted the last weary shovels of earth from their newly completed foxholes, the C.O. walked over and told me to move the platoon to another sector. I was ashamed to look at the men when I ordered them to pack up. They were so tired they could barely move.

Located on the edge of the village, as we were, and with many civilians moving about, we could not resort to our usual unashamed toilet expediency, a simple slit trench. (The American soldier's modesty about the functions of the body was a constant surprise to Europeans, accustomed to the sight of their own men casually unbuttoning at the side of any road.)

Some of the men, embarrassed by their needs and reluctant to relieve themselves before the staring civilians, came to me and shyly inquired about "a toilet." I scouted around and finally located one.

There was no plumbing of any sort in the village, and shell and flame had taken a heavy toll of all buildings . . . even little ones. The one I found was in pretty good shape—all it lacked was a door. That refinement lay on the ground nearby, apparently torn from its hinges by concussion. The doorless one-holer faced the rear of the largest and busiest building in the village, which housed our company C.P. as well as a score of civilians. It was a little public.

While I hesitated, uncertain whether to search further, an old woman wearily crossed the yard, heading for the little house. She paused for a moment and regarded the broken door. Then calmly hoisting her skirts, she did what she had to do and departed, her aplomb not at all shaken by the stares of the soldiers nearby. After several other civilians of either sex had followed suit, a watching soldier strode purposefully across the yard, beating a middle-aged woman to the throne by a neck. I turned on my heel, went back to the platoon, and told them where the toilet was.

We moved a thousand yards up the road to a cluster of buildings—it might have been a village—and I established my C.P. in the main house. The men dug more foxholes, and then orders came to send out a twelve-man reconnaissance patrol to sweep the sector for lurking Jerries. I accompanied the patrol. I was new at my job and self-conscious, and I didn't want to start off with the reputation of sitting on my fat can while everyone else worked. The patrol took two hours, and we waded through swamps and beat the fields and woods without spotting a single enemy. Returning home, I heated water on the kitchen stove and washed my feet before hitting the sack. Beatific . . . blissful . . . the "benison of hot water" . . . I soaked for an hour, wriggling my toes and murmuring pleasant words to myself, comfortable rich phrases.

Now, on the morning of March 23, I write this while seated in a warm kitchen. Only four hours' sleep last night, but I feel good.

Captain Wirt called me on the phone this morning and said, grinning, "Gantter, do you approve your promotion to staff sergeant?"

I gulped audibly and replied, "Yes sir, I sure do."

He laughed and said, "Okay, I put you in for it."

So I feel good now. And early this morning Leo Allen raided the chicken house and came back with forty-two eggs. *Fresh* eggs, not forty-two eggs' worth of powder! I had nine fried eggs for breakfast and four more, soft-boiled, a little later. So I feel pretty good.

An unhappy casualty last night—Herrington, the dark-haired, quiet-spoken Tennessean, shot himself in the foot while on outpost guard duty. I was sternly questioned by HQ as to whether it was accidental or deliberate. I'm convinced it was accidental, and I said so in my report. Herrington is a levelheaded and dependable guy, and his account of the accident is corroborated by the man who shared the outpost with him. They'd discovered that they could sit down while on guard and still have perfect observation. Herrington propped his feet on the rim of the hole, his rifle between his toes. While shifting his position, the muzzle slipped against his foot and the gun went off. I didn't see him last night before he was evacuated, but I'm confident his story is true.

It's going to be a day of leisure today. Leisure and eggs. Allen just came in with twenty-eight more in his helmet. Let's see . . . how will I have 'em this time?

Later in the afternoon.

I was wrong about the leisure. We shove off tonight. I've just come from a briefing at HQ. Our objective is the town of Geisbach, located on a tributary of the Sieg River. The plan of assault is a little complex, but I'll try to explain it.

My platoon moves out at eleven tonight, takes the minute village of Edgoven, near Geisbach, then waits. The remainder of the company jumps off at one-thirty A.M. and heads directly for Geisbach, entering the town from the south. When they've secured a toehold in the village, they'll send up a flare—a great star cluster—upon which signal I jump off from Edgoven, push into the north end of Geisbach, send up an answering flare when *our* first group of buildings has been secured, and then work south through the village to meet the rest of the company as it works north. There is one real difficulty in my assignment: I must cross a deep, swift creek to get from Edgoven into Geisbach.

So that's the story, and we've been making preparations ever since I returned from the briefing. I'm a little panicky at the responsibility of this assignment when I'm so damn green at this job, but I conceal my personal qualms and pretend a great confidence.

We've made plans for one last tremendous banquet of eggs tonight. All these eggs and no ———! Well, that energy *must* be good for something else!

CHAPTER TEN

"The road was the dividing line: on one side . . . the known, and on the other side—"

March 28.

I'm fumbling through a mist of hangover as though after a four-day drinking bout. No ordinary carousing, however, but an intoxication of color and movement and violent sound. I'm very tired.

We jumped off for Edgoven according to plan at eleven P.M. on March 23. With a vagrant moon to light our way, we moved swiftly along the road. There was one freezing moment when we rounded a turn and confronted a German tank looming grimly from a distance of less than fifty yards. We dropped like stones . . . waited five sweating minutes . . . made cautious reconnaissance and discovered that it was a dead tank inhabited by the dead, a smashed and burned-out iron shell, still warm to the touch.

Edgoven presented no difficulties. Not a shot was fired. The buildings were dark and quiet and the civilians innocently asleep. I established my C.P. in a tiny farmhouse inhabited by an ancient couple who listened to our quiet talking in the kitchen and shivered in their bed.

Leaving the rest of the platoon in Edgoven, four of us set out on a recon patrol, hoping to discover a means of crossing the creek that barred us from Geisbach. We'd progressed only a few yards through an orchard when we halted abruptly to examine the fresh spoor of a German tank. We moved cautiously after that, slipping quietly from tree to tree and hugging the bushes on the left bank of the creek as we approached Geisbach. We had not yet found a bridge, not even a footbridge. The two villages were not widely separated and soon we saw the buildings of the larger town, darker shadows against a dark sky, a stream's width away. A lumber mill stood on the bank directly across from us, and we crept forward until we could see the front of the building. At that moment the moon came out, and instantly we flattened ourselves in the mud and rank grass of the bank. We had all seen the motionless figure at the corner of the building, the glint of moonlight on rifle and belt buckle. Silently we slipped back to Edgoven to talk things over.

We had to cross the stream, had to get to the right bank in order to enter Geisbach—that much was clear. It was deeper and swifter and wider than we'd anticipated, but surely there was a bridge somewhere? How did the Edgovians, the Geisbachians, get across? Or didn't they fraternize? I sent out another patrol, with instructions to follow the stream in the opposite direction, and in a short time they reported back that they'd found a bridge. We could cross the creek all right, but there was an open field on the other side, an area naked of friendly trees or bushes for more than 150 yards. Well, we'd have to take that chance, even though the moon was now shining brilliantly and giving no indication of an early retirement. But supposing the Germans had mined the bridge? I rooted a civilian out of bed and questioned him. When had the German soldiers gone from Edgoven? Oh, several days ago. What was that field used for? For the cows, every day for the cows. Had the cows been in the field today? But yes, certainly. Had anyone walked on the bridge today? Only the cows, and the women who went after the cows. I led him to the bridge, told him to run across it, and when he reached the field on the other side, to turn around and run back again. If he kept on running when he reached the other side, we'd shoot him, and I pointed to the men standing nearby with ready rifles. Poor guy . . . his teeth were chattering, and not just from the skimpiness of his nightshirt. It was evident he couldn't understand why the crazy Americans wanted him to do such a senseless thing. Perhaps my method was brutal, but he was a healthy, middle-aged man, and I was damned if I'd risk any of my men on a bridge that might be mined when adult German males were available.

The test proved the bridge to be safe, and the terrified man skittered back to his bed, warned not to show his face again that night.

As two o'clock drew near, our tension mounted. We stared toward Geisbach, straining against the blackness to see a flicker of light. Shortly after two we heard the first popping of guns, and almost at once the heavy metallic booming of tank guns in reply. Our hearts sank a little: they weren't our tanks, and one of them sounded damn close.

The flare signal came at two-thirty and we pushed off. We were scared. Over the bridge and across the naked field on the double, one man at a time, scampering for the shelter of the nearest trees. And the moon pouring silver with reckless extravagance.

As soon as we'd crossed the bridge, we realized why one of the tanks sounded so near. It *was* near: it shared the field with us. Fortunately, its attentions were directed toward the lower end of town, and its crew members were so concerned with their job that we passed unnoticed.

We moved swiftly to the first building, the mill we'd approached while on recon patrol. We'd almost reached it when we saw the dark figure come around the corner of the building and sensed his quick suspicion. He shouted and fired, and other dark figures ran from nowhere and joined him. We hit the ground, firing as we fell, but the alarm had been given and now we had a fight on our hands.

The Jerries had us neatly, it seemed. We were pinned down, unable to move forward on the right side of the building because the enemy was waiting for us there, unable to pass on the left side because the mill had been built on the very edge of the stream. Leaving one squad to keep the Germans busy, the rest of us smashed into the rear of the building and went *through* it, our noisy stumbling over machinery, sawhorses, and piles of lumber lost in the greater racket outside.

It was over very quickly: we burst from the front door, the other squad rushed forward, and we had six prisoners, two of them wounded. Leaving a snuff-chewing southern boy to guard them, we headed for the schoolhouse across the road, our primary objective.

There ought to be a way to tell how it was from here on— how it had been exciting but familiar all the way from Soven to the road, from eleven o'clock last night to three o'clock that morning. The road was the marker: beyond it color flowed into movement, and sound had a smell, and the night had hands and a voice, and there were no dimensions, no rules. The road was the dividing line: on one side of it was the known, and on the other side—chaos, the negation of mathematics and all cool disciplines.

At the schoolhouse we took two more prisoners, whom I sent back to the mill to be kept with the others. I'd just given the order to fire the green flare that would inform the captain all was well when a flare rose from the lower end of the village and burst in slow green brilliance against the sky. What the hell! This wasn't according to plan! The captain had said he would answer my flare, but how could he be answering when we hadn't yet signaled him? Another thing, this was a green flare, but it was a parachute flare, not a star cluster!

Even as I gnawed my lips in angry indecision, another flare lighted the sky. A white star cluster! Then another—a red parachute flare! Another . . . then another! This was insane— these couldn't be our signals. We'd planned to use green star clusters because we didn't have anything else in the whole damn company. But maybe plans had been changed during the night, after I'd started for Edgoven; maybe we'd attached some other units and these were *their* signals?

(I learned later that the Germans, taking alarm from the captain's first flare, had surmised our pincer plan of attack and done their best to confuse us by themselves discharging a meaningless potpourri of flares. They'd done a good job. It sure as hell confused me.)

It seemed a futile gesture in view of the holiday colors already in the sky, but I told the grenadier to discharge our specified flare, according to our instructions. Then we started grimly into the town.

Somewhere in here the snuff-chewing southern boy—who'd been relieved of his prisoner guard detail—had an accident. He'd been given a spare flare against the possibility of the first grenadier having a misfire, and he was carefully instructed to carry the flare in his belt—*not* mounted on the launcher attached to his rifle. He'd also been cautioned to be sure the flare was not on the launcher if he had to use his rifle as a weapon, firing live rounds. (Flares are discharged by means of blank cartridges.) He forgot both warnings: he carried the flare on the launcher, then forgot it was there and tried to fire a live round. The speeding bullet exploded the flare only a rifle barrel's length from his face. But he was lucky: he escaped alive and wasn't even seriously injured, though his features were shifted around a little. He was evacuated and I never saw him again.

All hell broke loose before we'd moved fifty yards into the village. The firing we'd been hearing in the distance erupted violently upon us, and we were suddenly in a mess of fighting. I remember the chattering dialogue of bullets from rifles, machine guns, and burp guns, and the flares that blossomed endlessly in the dark sky. I remember a new and strange enemy weapon from which a tail of flame lashed malevolently, and my skin crawled because we'd never before faced a flamethrower. It turned out to be not a flamethrower but a bazooka. They were firing at us with bazookas, and this was a fantastic and outrageous thing, to fire bazookas at *men*. It wasn't according to the rules!

And there was shouting and many dark figures darting across the road and no way of knowing whether they were friends or enemies, and the sound of doors being battered down and the thin screaming of civilians, and unutterable confusion. And the new men in the platoon, lost and frightened and no one to show them how ... the new men huddling in little clusters and milling in pathetic bewilderment when I screamed at them and whipped them with my voice and the butt of my rifle. Green, green, they were so lost and green! Four of them would be sent to search a house, and in a moment they would be back, saying they couldn't get in because the doors were locked, and we'd yell at them, "For Chrissake, smash 'em, *smash 'em*, what've ya got a rifle butt for?" But I was sick at heart to use them so and drive them so: casualties would be high before the night was over.

And so through the village: fighting, smashing, terrorizing women and children ... more Hunlike than Attila. (Except that we didn't rape. There wasn't time for that.) The night was graying into dawn when we reached an important road junction in the north section of the village.

We'd been progressing steadily south along the main road, and the junction was formed where another road branched off to the east. A pretty little house sat on one of the corners of the fork, a picture-book house fronted by a neat little yard. The road to the east ran snugly beside it, so close to the house that a farmer in a wagon could shake hands with the hausfrau through a window.

We entered the house through a rear window that faced upon an apple orchard. After falling over a bicycle that some damn fool had parked in the dining room, I stumbled around in the dark until I found the cellar door. It was locked, and I pounded on it with my fist. Instantly, female screams of great intensity rose from the cellar. Two women, it sounded like, and they were yipping. *"Nicht schiessen, nicht schiessen!"* Don't shoot, don't shoot. In my bastard German I replied that we wouldn't shoot, but intended to find out who and what was down there, and how about opening the door? They yelled a little more at that and again wailed, *"Nicht schiessen,"* there were no *"Deutsches soldaten"* in the cellar. I pounded again, they yipped again, and then I heard footsteps on the stairs.

The steps mounted until I knew someone was standing on

the other side of the door, facing me beyond this thin wall of wood. There was a pause, and suddenly a new wail of fear— she'd forgotten the key! I heard her calling to the other woman to bring the key, and between her breathless phrases she kept moaning, *"Nicht schiessen!"* In a moment a new wail of terror rose from the cellar—the second woman couldn't find the key! At that, the one standing on the other side of the door let go with a series of really fine screeches, each one progressively louder in spite of my efforts to reassure her. I was about to give up the whole business in disgust when a howl of joy sounded from below. The key had been found! A moment later the door opened and a thoroughly frightened woman backed away, murmuring that monotonous phrase through fear-stiffened lips. I pitied her, but I was still going to search the cellar.

I started down the stairs and had taken only three steps when a calm, male voice said in perfect English, "I surrender!" and a German officer appeared at the foot of the stairs, his hands over his head. He was unarmed, and when I asked him for his pistol, he replied that it was in the cellar. Sending him off to join our growing collection of prisoners, I returned to the cellar and demanded the pistol. The women assumed round-eyed expressions of innocence, made extravagant play of searching in the most unlikely places for five minutes, and at last I found the pistol myself, demurely tucked away under a mattress.

The advance elements of the company reached us at dawn and were nearly mowed down when one of my trigger-happy infants, challenging the dim figures advancing through the mist, opened up with his BAR without waiting for an answer. Fortunately, he was so nervy that his first blast was wide of the mark, and he dropped his weapon when I yelled.

Three houses dominated the road that stretched eastward. Beyond them the land rolled in gentle swells, cresting to a ridge six hundred yards to the east. I sent two squads to clear the houses, and there was a brisk fight in the shadowy half dawn with Germans who were entrenched in a bunker before the farthest house.

Now, again, it is all confusion and blurred impressions. There was a ceaseless rain of bullets from the hills, from the bunker on the lawn, and from the windows of one of the houses. From somewhere a German machine gun sprayed the road, and interspersed with the vicious coughing of the gun we could hear the hoarse babble of German voices.

The platoon was spread thin. Most of the men were in the vicinity of the three houses, a few were in another building, and four of us—Shorty, Frank Eifler, a lad named Bowers, and myself—were still in the house on the corner, barred from joining the rest of the platoon by the mocking machine gun that dominated the road.

The back window of the house gave a clear view of the orchard, the hill beyond, and the road that curved over it. And as the half-light of dawn slid into full day, I heard the first warning rumble and saw the blunt pig snout of a German Tiger tank peer over the crest of the hill. It came down the road toward the junction, toward us, and I drew back from the window, sudden sweat making my rifle slimy. There was a flurry of movement across the road as the men caught sight of the tank and started for cover. The tank wasn't alone. A second followed it ... than another ... and now an endless stream of them poured heavily over the ridge. Self-propelled guns, too—mobile cannon that we called S.P.'s—and German infantry, gray shadows that moved furtively behind the iron giants. Some of the tanks and S.P.'s turned as they reached the orchard and swung toward the lower town, smashing through the apple trees. Some turned in the opposite direction, heading for the sawmill. A perfect pincer maneuver, and we were the nut. One medium tank continued along the road, coming our way, and I shrank back in the room, deep in the shadows, watching it. There was no escape for us: any attempt to leave the house would place us squarely before the guns of the tank. Now I could see the riflemen who walked behind the tank, peering over its protecting shoulders. Twenty-five yards to go ... twenty ... fifteen ... okay, our luck had worn thin, that's all. It was nearly up to the corner of the house now, slowing as it approached the junction, and there was a German rifleman close behind it, twenty feet from me. He hadn't seen me through the torn lace curtains, he didn't know we were there, and if we were already lost, there wasn't anything else to lose. I got him between the eyes, because how could I miss at twenty feet? No one saw him fall, no one but me saw a walking man become a smear of dingy gray-blue in the road, one leg doubled under him and his rifle fallen in the thick foulness of cow droppings.

This part is hard to write, as it was when I tried to tell about the dead German soldier in the field near Drove . . . the overcoat spread like blue wings against the pale stubble.

The man I'd shot had a comrade, another rifleman who'd gone on with the tank, unseeing. Suddenly becoming aware of his friend's absence, he turned and saw and hurried back to the dead man in the road. He knelt beside him . . . and I shot him. In that act of grace I killed him, and when he crumbled, the two bodies very close, their faces almost touching. And I cannot forget that he was kneeling, his body curved in sorrow over the body of his dead friend. If only he hadn't been kneeling.

It was quickly over, the last i dotted and every t crossed in the few seconds before the tank drew up beside the house. Even as I stared at the two figures in the road I became aware of silence. The tank had halted.

Through a broken window I could see the tank, could see the evil muzzle of the cannon pointing toward the junction. I could see the pet name painted in white on the barrel of the cannon: *Tutti!* in neat Gothic script, this black bitch at the window was called Tutti by those who loved her, and I could reach through the broken pane and pat Tutti on the nose. How the hell were we going to get out of here now?

Exit by the rear window was no dice: the rear end of the tank projected beyond the back of the house. As though that were not enough, the orchard seemed to be crawling with tanks, S.P.'s, and men in gray uniform. No exit by the front door, either: we'd have to run right under the nose of Tutti and her twin-sister machine guns.

There was no sound from the tank: no voices, no shots fired, no grating of machinery. We wondered what they were waiting for, and stationed ourselves by the doors and windows, prepared to welcome any guests.

Digging a package of gum from my pocket, I silently passed it around. Softening the gum with hasty chewing, we lodged the cuds between our teeth to hush their nervous clicking. Our breathing was loud and rasping to our ears and we tried to breathe slower, easing the air in and out gently through open mouths. So we waited, ten minutes . . . fifteen minutes . . . half an hour . . .

An elbow nudged me. Shorty. He held a white phosphorus grenade in his hand, the safety pin already removed. A few wisps of hay clinging to the side of the tank—obviously it had been hiding in a barn—had inspired him to try to set it afire. But now he was doubtful. Was there enough hay? Would the grenade land in the right place? If it failed to disable the tank, wouldn't Tutti swing around to breathe death against the house, against us? I was doubtful, too, and decided to wait a bit. We might get out of this yet.

Our situation was serious enough, but now there was an element of farce in it. I grinned at Shorty and he grinned back uncertainly, holding the grenade gingerly but with determination . . . a man with a handful of flypaper. He *had* to hang on. Once he let go, the handle would fly off, activating the fuse, and the grenade would burn within five seconds. And he couldn't replace the safety pin because he'd dropped it on the floor somewhere and couldn't find it. Choking with nervous giggles, we finally solved the dilemma by tying a strip of cloth over the release handle, and with a great sigh of relief Shorty tucked the grenade in his pack.

Still no sound from the tank. I crept into the side room, sword-dancing over the fragments of glass that littered the floor and crunched noisily underfoot. Concentrating on these small hazards, I forgot the shell holes in the wall and looked up to be instantly transfixed by the open eye slot of the tank regarding me grimly through a lath-shredded hole. For a freezing moment I stared at that iron eyelid, expecting death to blink at me. But nothing happened; nothing. Growing bolder, I looked through the hole and studied the entire length of the tank. Not a sound, not a person in sight. I crawled up the stairway to the second floor and looked down on the tank from a window. The turret top was open but there was no sign of a crew. Maybe the men in the houses across the road had knocked off the crew . . . maybe the crew had run away when their infantry escort fell . . . maybe they were just hiding, waiting.

We talked it over and decided to run for it. We left by the front door, closing it behind us quietly, and raced under Tutti's nose and across the road, fear snapping at our heels.

I flubbed badly on this deal by failing to disable Tutti. She was not a dead tank, only deserted, and I should have killed her. But we weren't anticipating a major counterattack; we couldn't know that Tutti would be recaptured and remanned by a German crew and used against us once more. Later that day—a hundred years later—I saw Tutti again, blackened and smoking, but dead at last. She had raised a lot of hell in the lower town before being knocked out finally.

The Jerries seemed to be under control for the moment, and there was a lull in the fighting, but Captain Wirt warned us to get set for another counterattack. My platoon was to stay in the north end of town and hold the vitally important junction.

I selected a house on the east road as my major strong point, since it was obvious that attack would come from the east and northeast. It was a large brick building with vast stables and barns, situated on a knoll that commanded a view of the ridge to the east. It was apparent we weren't going to have time to dig in: the enemy fire was growing steadily warmer.

There were a number of new men in the platoon, young and green but okay. That is, all okay but one. He'd been dubbed "the Combat Soldier" the day he joined us. (We wondered why the army had taken him: he had a wife and six children back in the States.) He'd been with us for only two days, and for two days he'd been irritating us with his swaggering, his windy assurances of fighting ability. Poor bastard—we knew he boasted because he was scared, but that didn't make us like him any better. Here in Geisbach, because I knew his windiness for what it concealed, I assigned him to the safest position I could find. A safe post but damned important because it overlooked the road down which the tanks had come. His position was the steps of the deep bunker on the lawn from which we'd evicted the Germans. It was the equivalent of a Grade-A foxhole. Hell, he could even sit down!

Ten minutes later, while I was trying to decide whether I should endanger a man's life by ordering him to a vital but unprotected position, I turned and found the Combat Soldier standing behind me. I tried to be calm as I asked him what he was doing there, why he wasn't at his post. (But the thing was, the blinding thing was, "This man deserted his post, endangering the lives of his own comrades!") His answer to my questions made me blow my stack completely: someone had fired at him out there—he'd heard the bullet go over his head—and he wanted "another post."

A counterattack was blowing our way and I was oppressed by the responsibility for other men's lives, but I let the war struggle along by itself for thirty seconds while I vented my own sickness and fear on the Combat Soldier. It was a merciless reaming.

The next counterattack hit us before we were prepared. A heavy shelling first, and then the tanks and S.P.'s began to roll, pouring over the crest of the hill and down the road. The earlier pattern was faithfully followed. Some of the tanks swung toward the lower town, some of them turned in the opposite direction. Infantry slipped like gray shadows over the hill, skulked behind the tanks. They were coming from the north, the northeast, and the east, and it was obvious they were forming a giant pincer to be slipped around us and squeezed shut.

Our house was taking a pounding. Tiny knife-edged fragments of brick whined through the air and many of the men were bleeding from myriad cuts. Running to the barn, I found the two men stationed there hugging the ground, nearly paralyzed by concussion. I moved them to a safer spot. The cattle in the stalls were bleeding from scores of small wounds, many of them in the head, and the scarlet drops clung to the white faces like tears of blood. During a brief lull I unchained several of them and tried to lead them from the doomed building, but they would not budge. In one stall a beautiful bay mare nuzzled with mute comfort the trembling, week-old colt huddled under the curve of her belly. She was chained to the stall and I could not free her.

With the three bazooka men, I climbed to the loft of the barn, hoping for a shot at a self-propelled gun in the field that was pounding the bejesus out of us. Only a hundred yards away, it offered a magnificent target, and convenient shell holes in the roof of the barn provided good firing positions. I told the three men to fire together on my signal so we could get out of the loft before the Germans returned the compliment. Three bazooka rockets emerging from a hayloft would surely invite the Jerries to belt hell out of the barn in reply.

Two of the men fired before I'd counted to three, and the third man fled in panic, neglecting to fire at all. In the race for the ladder, someone shoved me over the edge of the loft and I landed heavily on the barn floor below. There was no balm for my bruises in the discovery that we had only scratched the S.P., and it continued to fire at us with unflagging enthusiasm.

One of the bazooka men went back to the loft a little later. Shamed by the fiasco of the earlier attempt, he was determined to finish off the S.P. and from somewhere acquired another rocket for the purpose. He told no one of his plan—this was a private feud. The Germans, however, had been expecting another such attempt and were watching the hayloft closely. They got him before he had a chance to discharge his rocket, and we learned of his foolhardy and gallant gesture only when he staggered across the courtyard, his hands clasped to an ugly head wound and the blood streaming red rivers between his fingers.

We were in a little bitch of a spot. The artillery was pasting hell out of us, tanks and infantry were laying it on from three sides, and we had to lie there and take it. We fell back to the main road, to the solid comfort of a concrete wall. We were almost safe there, and we had a good field of fire. Again the platoon was split, most of the men huddling behind the wall and three men and myself in a muddy ditch on the other side of the road.

Maybe if I'd been a little more experienced at this business of leading a platoon I could have stopped what happened next. I was damn well conscious of my lack of experience, my lack of knowledge. I remember a moment when I grabbed Shorty's arm and my voice was shaking because I was shaking inside and I said, "Shorty . . . Christ, I'm too damn green . . . it's too short a time and I don't know what to do!"

It was decided for me. Across the road the platoon began to waver, the men calling out, asking why we didn't fall back farther. Helplessly, I watched the panic flare up like a sudden grass fire and I couldn't do anything, couldn't get across the road because the Germans were laying a carpet of lead between us.

They were good guys, most of them, but they couldn't stop this thing that was happening to them. And maybe it's unfair, but I blame one man in particular for our shame that day. He was a big guy, a former star basketball player and a large hunk of man, but his voice was the loudest of all in pleading for further retreat. Between bursts of fire I could hear him cajoling the others: "We *can't* hold out—they've got us nearly surrounded! We'll all be killed. Why should we stay and be killed?" And he yelled to me that we were suckers, we were holding the bag. "Headquarters and all the officers have pulled out!" (He was wrong.) "The weapons platoon took off!" (He was wrong. Most of the men in the weapons platoon were killed, wounded, or captured.) "The whole damn company's run out on us; they're taking off over that hill!" (He was wrong: a group of men from the lower town *had* taken off and fled to the safety of the hills, but the group was not large. The rest of the company stuck it out.)

I didn't know what to do . . . and this joker across the road could see the hills and I couldn't; he could see where the weapons platoon had been stationed and I couldn't. Maybe he was right, maybe we were deserted, maybe our stand was a futile and Quixotic gesture. I yelled to them to stay where they were until I returned, and I hightailed down the road toward the center of town, hoping to locate the captain and the rest of the company. I'd gone only a couple of hundred yards when I saw Rodney, the captain's radioman, placidly seated at the door of the barn that held our wounded. When I asked where the other platoons were, he replied laconically, "All mixed up and all f——d up! Some of 'em are here!" He pointed to the men lying on the bloody hay. "Some of 'em went over the hill, and I don't know where the hell the rest of 'em are!"

In this instance his use of the phrase "over the hill" was literal. The men who deserted in Geisbach did, in truth, go "over the hill." When they crawled back to us that night, shamefaced and voluble with explanations, they were met by a grim-faced captain who coldly informed them he intended to press court-martial charges against them. He did not—a wise and humane soldier, he gave them a chance to redeem themselves.

I went back to my platoon. It was in a bad way, and some of the men had already deserted the concrete wall and retreated to a walled courtyard. A few stubborn ones continued to fight, but most of them abandoned the job they were there for and devoted their energies to pleas for further withdrawal. Sick at heart, I gave the command for the platoon to fall back to the courtyard and we slipped across the road, a few men at a time.

I assigned new positions, but I had already made the big mistake I could not now undo. By yielding to their pleas, I'd given fresh impetus to their fears, had tacitly admitted the rightness of their desire to get as far as possible from the danger that threatened to overwhelm us. They continued to urge further retreat, and when two self-propelled guns appeared on our left flank, heading for the field behind us with obvious intent to cut us off, the panic was on. Without waiting for an order, the men began to run for the hills. When only four of us remained in the courtyard I said, "Okay, Shorty—let's go! Maybe we can build up a line at the creek." And we took off, leaving the courtyard just as another S.P. drew up in front of the house and began to fire point-blank into the lower town.

Reaching the creek, we lowered ourselves into it, standing knee-deep, waist-deep, throat-deep in the cold, muddy water. We were safe now, but we continued to look longingly at the hills behind us. They were so near . . . so damned easy. . . .

I couldn't find Shorty. No one had seen him arrive at the creek, and I decided, hopefully, that he must have cut straight across the fields and struck the creek farther down.

Defensively, we were in a good position. The twisting stream and the hills behind us made a flanking attack impossible, and two hundred yards of open field before us were adequate insurance that the enemy would not attempt a frontal assault. From my place on the end of the line I called to the man next to me and told him to pass along an order: we would hold the line here; we would move no more. I heard the words repeated as they passed from man to man, down the creek. But it didn't work; the men far downstream, seeing how seductively the creek curved toward the still secure heart of town, could not control their restless feet. It required only one man to start the new retreat: each man, seeing his neighbor departing, followed suit, and once begun there was no stopping. My commands, my futile rages, had no effect, and we moved farther and farther from the sector we'd been ordered to hold.

It was a treacherous passage, hazardous with sudden, deep potholes and the false solidity of slimy clay. Men floundered and went under, came sputtering to the surface with weapons dripping. But we dared not leave the stream: the Germans had found us out and were spraying the bank with bullets. Seeing the man before me up to his chin in water as he waded through a particularly deep pool, I rebelled at the prospect of ruining my camera (acquired in Soven) and my fine new pocket watch (a tribute from Aegidienburg). The rear bank seemed a few inches lower at that point, so I crossed the stream, snaked along the bank until I'd passed the pool, and slid back into the water once more. It was a foolish and stupid thing to do, and I was lucky. Another foolish and stupid man wasn't. I saw his body on the bank when I was still some distance from him, and the frozen absurdity of his position told me he was dead. He'd fallen on his knees and there balanced, the weight of his body resting on his face, his buttocks rounding skyward and his arms lolling brokenly under the arch of his body. A red neckerchief flamed incongruously about his neck. He lay on the bank nearest the enemy, dead because he'd deserted the slow safety of the creek. He couldn't have run very far.

I had pushed past, not really seeing him, when I remembered something and splashed back for another look. Only one man in the platoon had been wearing a red neckerchief; only one man had scoffed at warnings and insisted on wearing, in the guise of adornment, a target that only a color-blind sniper could miss. I looked sadly at the foolish dead face, the sightless eyes, the neat pattern of bloody holes stitched from neck to rump, and I remembered the boasting, the loud talk, the deserted post . . . the wife and six children at home. It was the Combat Soldier.

The aimless meandering of the stream resolved to a long curve that bent toward the town. We heard a shout, "Hey! Over here!" and saw a doggie beckoning from the corner of a shed fifty yards away. He seemed to us more beautiful than angels—we weren't alone in Geisbach after all. He told us that the company was still hanging on but taking a terrific beating. He pointed to a nearby farmhouse when I asked the whereabouts of the captain, and with a heart heavier than my water-soaked shoes, I set off to make my report. I found Captain Wirt bending over a map, and he looked calm and unhurried.

It's not easy for a man to bare the love and respect he feels for another man: the confession is somehow unmanly. And this stripping of self is doubly hard because Captain Charles Wirt was younger than I, younger and stronger, and it's not easy for me to admit to weakness and how I took strength from his strength.

He did not blame me for what happened that day; he never blamed me for it. When he saw me standing there, wet and shamed, his eyes seared me for a moment but he said simply, "What's the meaning of this?" He did not raise his voice. I answered, also simply—for how could I elaborate?—and my words were the measure of my degradation. "I couldn't hold them, sir."

For a moment he was silent. Then he said, "Go back and tell those men that they're going back up there. What's left of the company is in trouble and they need help."

Sometimes, at rare moments, the heroic action was matched by the language of heroism, though such felicity may seem unreal now. My reporting of this incident is accurate, however, and I've never forgotten the captain's words. They were right for the moment, and I was deeply moved by them.

I returned to the wet, shivering men. John Albert had an arm wound and could not go back with us; two others would not go back, pleading "battle nerves," and the captain contemptuously waved them to the rear. I never saw them again and I don't know what happened to them. Either they were captured when the Germans took our C.P. later that day, or they were quietly transferred out of the company when the day was over. I did not inquire about them.

The platoon now consisted of fourteen men, and I formed two squads of seven men each. The captain and I walked to the edge of the road and he pointed out where he wanted us to go. He talked easily and warmly, saying it was a dirty job but it had to be done, and the curse on my conscience lightened a little. I had the choice of returning by the road, risking fire from the enemy-occupied buildings, or going back the long way, up the creek. The road was the shorter route, and I chose that.

A last checkup of weapons and ammo and we were off, snaking from building to building and moving steadily back to the junction and the walled courtyard. It was a happy return: Shorty was there. He was in the cellar of the house with a weapons platoon survivor named Johns who was a helluva good Joe. It was good to see Shorty. En route to the creek he'd found his way blocked by the guns of an S.P. and he'd been forced to crawl back to the house. He and Johns had stuck it out alone there, almost entirely surrounded by Germans.

We maneuvered into position, a few men at this vital point, a few men at that. We were back at our old stand on the company's left flank. The remnant of the third platoon was on our right.

The hours that follow are blurred and lost. The things I remember are vivid with the clarity of nightmare, real enough in the physical terms of their expression but terrifying through distortion, twisted and hideous because some fundamental discipline had been violated. There was shelling and there were tanks and self-propelled guns, the rattling cough of machine guns and burp guns, the high staccato of rifles. These provided the orchestration for certain tableaux: dusty glimpses of gray uniforms, green uniforms . . . the flicker of movement in the window of the house across the street, and your hands swinging the rifle to your shoulder in a single fluid motion . . . the patient resistance of the trigger under your tightening finger, the sudden punch of recoil . . . the stone barn and the thorny hedge . . . the dead soldier who lay on his face in the ditch, his hand stretched to the gray stone, the blackthorn. His head was bare and he was very blond, very young . . . the nape of his neck as defenseless as a child's. On the edge of the road lay his bazooka . . . so near . . . only a grave's length away.

The Germans were all over: in the houses across the street, in the house next door, in the fields and orchards. They were sure of their victory now, and a little careless. Glancing up the road, I spied two Germans less than a hundred yards away. They were sprawled carelessly in the ditch near the junction, a light machine gun mounted beside them. They were smoking cigarettes with an air of indolent assurance. At my wave, Lieutenant Freeman joined me at the corner of the barn; we chose targets wordlessly and fired.

The enemy was now solidly entrenched in the houses across the road. A little below us the road bent sharply, curv-

ing into the heart of town, and the large building at the bend
in the road was infested with snipers. Peering around the
dung heap that sheltered me, I studied the windows of the
house, hoping for an incautious German to show himself.
Suddenly a German soldier ran from the courtyard, disappearing around the bend in the road before I could raise my
rifle. Cursing my slowness, I waited for another German to
make a move. Fifteen seconds later a second man sprinted
from the courtyard, and my finger was already tightening on
the trigger when I realized that this man was American. He
was empty-handed and his head was bare, and before he vanished around the bend in the road I recognized him as Weymeyer, a third platoon man. But what the hell . . . ? As I
blinked in startled wonder, another German darted from the
courtyard and after Weymeyer, and again I was caught with
my sights down.

I heard the story later: Weymeyer had been captured, dis-
armed, and ordered to follow the first German to the place
where American prisoners were being collected. Somewhere
beyond the bend in the road Weymeyer had overtaken the first
German. Seizing his erstwhile captor's rifle, he beat him to
death with it and escaped before the second guard reached the
scene. (Weymeyer was sent to OCS in Paris, and his boldness
became a company legend.)

Another incident of the day: a German tank rolled up to a
house where a few stubborn Americans still held out and
thrust the muzzle of its 88 in the front window. The tank commander stood in the open turret and in perfect English made a
speech to the doggies within, advising them in tones of good-
humored cajolery to come out and surrender peaceably "because you're already whipped and you'll only get killed if you
continue to fight." While he wooed them, they left quietly by a
rear window, crawled to the house next door, and shot him as
he harangued the empty building. (I talked with some of these
men later: they were cocky with triumph but still bristling at
the recollection of the German officer's arrogance. "The nerve
of that sonofabitch!" they said. "The nerve . . . !")

In one rush the Germans captured the barn where our wounded lay. Most of them we recovered before the day ended, but some did not return to us until long after the war was over. Some I never heard of again.

The full fury of the counterattack was now directed against the north end of town, and Captain Wirt joined us there. He told me to take a few men across that deadly main road and knock out an S.P. that was chasing us in circles.

We were about to start out on this mission when the captain ran up and halted us. He wanted my one remaining bazooka man, Frank Eifler, to take a crack at an S.P. who was prowling around in the lower field, and he and Frank hustled off. When Frank failed to return, I set out to look for him. As I crossed the yard toward the large farmhouse that had become Company HQ, an S.P. scored a direct hit on a nearby building. I ducked, but not quickly enough: debris pounded my shoulders and rattled on my helmet and I felt sudden sharp pain in my leg. I had time to think, This is it! and then something tremendous slammed me against the ground. I was out only a short time, I think, but I was shaken and dizzy when I sat up. God loves fools and great sinners, and obviously I am either well-damned or witless: a hasty checkup revealed only a cut elbow, a trouser leg slashed as though by a razor, and a small leg wound. The knockout blow had apparently been delivered by the two-foot slab of masonry lying beside me. (At least it hadn't been there before.) For two weeks my leg was to be a green and purple rhapsody, from knee to vital zone. Curiously, it was my inner thigh that had been hit: I had half turned and crouched when the shell struck. Blessed fortune—the family jewels were spared.

Shakily resuming my search, I found the captain in the cellar of the house, together with another officer, ten doggies, and twelve civilians. Learning that Eifler was in the nearby stone barn, I started off for him, but the captain told me to hold up: he'd ordered an artillery barrage, which would be starting at any moment. While I waited, I explored the kitchen, found a loaf of bread and a jar of jam, and ate. It had been a long time since I'd eaten.

The artillery barrage started, three battalions of it. I cannot describe it, but I never want to be that close to a barrage again. After observing the first several rounds, the captain ordered the range shortened, and presently the shells were dropping on the houses directly across the street. The barrage lasted over an hour. From within the cellar it felt like the rumbling and quivering of an earthquake, but I cannot imagine what it must have been like for the men who were in holes and shelters outside. With the barrage fingering so close to our own positions there were some short rounds, of course, but to my knowledge, none of our men were killed by our own shells.

(I saw some of the outside men when the barrage had ceased. They were gray with shock, and trembling so much they could neither light a cigarette nor hold it with their fingers. Eifler and the men in the barn with him had had a bad time of it. They shook uncontrollably, and their faces, their clothing—even their eyebrows were thickly white with plaster dust. They could not find words to tell of it—the explosions of sound that smashed at their eardrums like the sledgehammering of a lightning bolt, the reeling shock of concussion that turned heart and stomach to jelly.)

For a time I sat in the crowded cellar, wincing with each shell. There was no room to stretch out, and my legs were soon tormented by cramp. I wanted to go to sleep, tried to sleep and could not. Two-year-old Hildegarde, a pert minx for whom the barrage was only a loud thunderstorm, clambered over the intervening knees and settled on my lap, and I thought of my Sukey at home and felt worse ... or maybe I felt better for a while, I don't know. Still the barrage continued. After Hildegarde deserted my knees, I could bear the cellar no longer and I went upstairs to stand by a window, defying shrapnel and stone splinters.

Old buildings made of stone have a quality of permanence that is hard to define, particularly to Americans, who belong to a frame-house culture. The stone is solid and firm and untroubled, heavy with years and rooted to the earth. You lean against such houses and they have none of the frailty that goes with decaying wood. Stone houses are never sick, never ill-tempered in a thin-blooded, malicious fashion, never ailing with petulant disorders, like a woman too long virginal. Stone houses are broad-bottomed, lusty, male. Touching them, you know that nothing can shake or destroy them.

From a window in Geisbach I looked at houses like that, and scant seconds later watched them leap toward the sky in effortless, floating fragments, melt and disintegrate with the easy magic of soap bubbles . . . quickly gone, and only dust to mark the place where they'd been. And after the dust, the flames, and after the flames, nothing but blackened rubble. Destruction was a giant wind raging over the town, an evil and terrible thing to witness.

At last the guns stopped, and in the strange silence there was only the sound of flames, the dull grinding of falling walls. We came out and looked at what was left of Geisbach. The artillery had achieved violently what we'd been struggling with painful slowness to accomplish: force the enemy into the open. I got a stray Jerry as he came down the road, another as he crawled from the ruins of a building and started for the hills. Around me the rifles cracked with the bright impersonality of a shooting gallery, and the return fire was feeble and uncertain, a gesture of bravado.

A twelve-year-old boy tugged at my sleeve, saying that his grandfather wanted to talk to me. The old man, a white-bearded patriarch, indicated that he wanted to lead me into a nearby field and point out a wounded soldier. I demurred: I was damn certain that the soldier would be German. At any rate, I was not a medic, I could do nothing . . . and there had been so many deaths, so many wounded. But he persisted and I gave in, following him in weary patience.

I remember starting out with him, but I do not know how far we walked. At intervals I blanked out from weariness, continuing to move and even to talk, I think, but without aware-ness. The town had begun to crawl from the wreckage, and I remember flames and bodies and dust, smoking timbers and vast mounds of broken masonry. But the picture is kaleido-scopic, moving shadows seen through mist.

Two women stood beside a foxhole in the field, one of them tearing a sheet into strips of bandage with fierce energy. The other stood motionless, her face heavy and dull with shock, her nerveless hands limply holding a cup and saucer. A third woman bent over the young German soldier in the hole. His left leg had been fractured in two places and viciously torn by shrapnel, but he looked up at me and smiled weakly. For a moment I stared back without comprehension, and his smile faded, became tentative and very young. Then I prodded myself awake, spoke to him reassuringly, and told the women that the doctor would soon be there. (As soon as our men had been cared for, the medics would get to work on the German wounded.)

I walked back to the house with the old man. He'd been badly shaken by the sight of the wounded soldier and he was trembling. Presently I saw that tears were running soundlessly down his face, blinding him after a while so that he could not see the path, and he clutched my arm for help. He did not speak to me, but I heard him murmur over and over again, "The things that men do to each other! The things that men do to each other!" and the tears ran down the thin brown face and into the white foam of his beard. And I was weary of death and bone tired and I envied him his tears because he was old and could weep easily and without shame.

We cleaned up the town, taking listless potshots at the Germans who continued to crawl from the wreckage and scamper for the hills. The dead lay everywhere, grotesquely.

Finally our relief arrived: the tanks and tank destroyers and troops for which the captain had begged a few hours before. The town was securely in our hands by that time, but some odds and ends of resistance remained.

One of the tank destroyers pulled into the courtyard where the battered survivors of the first platoon had gathered. We grinned foolishly at the fresh-looking riflemen behind the T.D., looking at them with love because they'd come, but with something like contempt because they'd come so late and we'd survived without their help.

We were happy to turn the remaining jobs over to our relief. We pointed to a house a hundred yards away and watched with joy as the T.D. maneuvered into position and began to lay the wood to the sniper nest. We should have been smarter, we'd been in this business long enough to know better. But we stood in the open courtyard, exclaiming in silly excitement as the shells poured into the battered house; we stood there until the man next to me gurgled a little, clutched at his throat, and sank heavily to the ground. "Pop" Cunningham, fat, grinning Pop, who had just arrived with the relief company.

No one had heard the sniper's shot, but we looked dazedly at "Pop" and saw the blood gushing from his throat. In thirty seconds the courtyard was empty, the men racing for the safety of the cellar, pouring down the steps like water. I was too damn tired to react quickly and I forgot to run. And maybe in the back of what was left of my brain was the secret assurance that nothing could touch me; I'd lived through this day and nothing could touch me now. I was too tired to be very smart.

I yelled for the medic who was caring for the wounded in the cellar, and when he came to the doorway, I pointed wordlessly at Pop. He hadn't moved, but his right hand was clenching and slowly unclenching in a spasmodic appeal that was intolerable to watch. It appeared there was nothing that could be done for him, and the medic said yeah, it looked like it but he'd like to see, he'd like to get him in the cellar and try ... a helluva lot of blood, but maybe ... And he called out for someone to come and help us carry the wounded man.

No one came out, no one volunteered. The scared faces in the doorway drew back for a moment in shame, but no one came to help, no man from Pop's own company would help him. We waited, and I watched Pop and wished that slow hand would cease its blind groping. We bent over him, the medic at his shoulders and I at his heels, and we tried to lift him. A deep groan shuddered from the dying man, the fumbling hand clutched once more at the torn throat and blood, vomit, and saliva streamed from his mouth. The medic said, "No use ... he got it in the jugular." Gently, we lowered him again and stood there and watched him die. We couldn't leave him, not while he still lived; we couldn't turn our backs and go away and leave him to die alone. It didn't take long. In less than a minute he was still, and the blind hand uncurling for the last time. We left him then, and went into the cellar. I wasn't good for anything for a while. He'd been standing so close, and we were talking, and it had been so quick, so soon over. . . .

I established my C.P. in the remains of a nearby house. We found some canned fruit in the cupboard and ate greedy, dripping handfuls of it. A few moments later a Polish "slave" entered the kitchen. He was only a boy, not more than fourteen years old, but his eyes were shrewd and mature. He grinned boldly at our gluttony, placed a precautionary finger against his lips, and slipped down the cellar stairs. In a moment he was back, triumphantly brandishing two cans of cherries. We invited him to join us, and happily he dug in. When the civilian owner of the house suddenly appeared on the threshold, the boy started guiltily, heroically swallowed a mouthful of cherries, pits and all, and made a great show of sweeping up the kitchen, but as his "master" turned away, he grimaced slyly at us and patted his stomach.

Behind the house a little group of civilians stood silently over something on the ground that was covered with a black overcoat—an old man who had unwisely left his cellar during the bombardment. The civilians showed no emotion. Neither did we.

Shorty said he'd seen some camera film in the house next door, and we went after it. While he pawed in the cupboard, I opened the cellar door and idly glanced down. Some items of GI mess gear lay at the bottom of the steps, and I said, "Looks like the Jerries have been here," and started down to investigate. (During the day, many of us had discarded our packs, throwing them off because they impeded action. The loot-hungry Germans had searched every pack they found, seeking American cigarettes in particular, and men who later discovered their packs found they'd been stripped of everything valuable. The scattered gear in the cellar hinted that some doggie's pack had been brought here and looted.)

Halfway down the stairs I stopped short, my eyes on the foot of the bed I could see through the open door of a store-room. A bed in a cellar was a familiar sight, but a pair of unmistakably live feet in heavy German shoes gave this one a new twist. Gripping my rifle, I yipped, *"Komme si raus!"* and immediately five German soldiers meekly filed out of the room. One shamefacedly butted a Lucky Strike on the dirt floor before he started up the stairs. We marched them to the courtyard where prisoners were being collected and strolled back to our C.P., well pleased with ourselves.

We started to dig in against further counterattack, but no sooner had we begun than the captain ordered us to another sector at the opposite end of town. Wearily we trudged across town and wearily started to dig once again. At last the holes were finished and we made preparations for sleep, hoping that we would not move out until the morning. It took me a long time to get to sleep.

At two-thirty A.M. a light flashed in my eyes and someone was shaking me. "Report to the C.P." And I knew what that meant.

A couple of footnotes before we leave Geisbach. Our G-2 was a little late with the intelligence, but we finally got an explanation for the extreme violence of the late battle and the desperate intensity of the enemy counterattack. The Germans had selected Geisbach as the jumping-off point for a major offensive designed to sweep American troops from the entire Sieg River valley. To that end the German High Command had been marshaling forces for several days, and our sudden move into the town caught them by surprise. The German marshaling area was just over the ridge from where they swept down on us in such grim force, and though they were not fully prepared for the large-scale offensive they'd been planning, they threw against us— against a single company of infantry!—everything they had. Our bag for the day included four German tanks, four self-propelled guns, and an unestimated number of prisoners, many of them wounded. In addition, our colonel had counted 150 German dead as he strolled through the town. Then he stopped counting.

It cost us something, too.

A final note on Geisbach. During the day I had heard stories about a German girl wearing a Red Cross uniform who'd been shot by a German officer because she was treating American wounded. The stories were vague, and no one with whom I talked had seen the incident, although everyone knew someone else who had seen it. One of those things . . .

After some days I learned the story was true. The girl had emerged from her shelter to care for the wounded, German and American alike, and a German officer shot her when she ignored his repeated order to "Let the damn Americans die!" The story was confirmed, and it appeared that week in the New York papers. Incidentally, in the newspaper account of the battle, credit for the capture of Geisbach was given to a company that never set foot in it. Perhaps it was only a typographical error—although an officer who was not one of ours but with whom we were familiar was quoted in the story—but it sure as hell rankled in the collective breast of George Company. Geisbach belonged to us.

CHAPTER ELEVEN

"The news of the big push was good . . ."

March 25.

We left Geisbach at four A.M., first platoon spearheading. We headed east on the road down which the German tanks had trundled only a few hours before. Our destination was the town of Wingenshof, over the ridge.

It was dark but not dark enough, and I turned my head quickly when we passed the two soldiers I'd shot from the window of the corner house. But it was all right; they weren't real anymore. They had been crushed under the passing of many tanks, and their bodies were thin and flat, two-dimensional . . . paper dolls the size of men.

There was no moon. Behind us the night sky was sullen with the red glare of burning Geisbach, punctuated with the harsh yellow of exploding shells. The village was still being shelled, although with rather lazy indifference, by the enemy in the hills to the east.

We moved in weary silence, a column on each side of the road. As we neared the crest of the hill, two German shells screamed brief warning and landed in our ranks. We scattered instantly, fanning far out into the fields, but there were no more shells. Apparently these had been intended for Geisbach, and falling short, found us by evil accident. We waited a bit, then re-formed and moved ahead.

It was another hour before I learned that the shells had killed two men in my platoon. One of them, Cox, had been killed instantly. Bob Berthot was the other, and he died within the hour. No one else was injured. Cox and Berthot, incidentally, had been the sole remaining BAR men in the platoon.

There was no resistance in Wingenshof and we took it easily, and started at once for our next objective, Dondorf. We were to secure the main highway north of Dondorf, my platoon occupying the extreme left flank.

Our sector was a pushover, and the roused civilians who shivered in their night clothing vowed there were no German soldiers in the neighborhood. We picked up three prisoners: a machine gunner and two burp gunners we found sleeping behind a farmhouse. I set up a six-man outpost in a small house and selected a stone farmhouse, three hundred yards distant, for my C.P. Later in the morning the captain sent us a light tank, a mortar squad, and a machine-gun section. With the machine guns and mortar emplaced and the tank snuggled discreetly in the shadow of the barn, we had a real strong point. Leo Allen, now attached to the communications squad, ran a phone line to us, and we felt warmly secure against attack.

Notwithstanding our defenses, it was not a comfortable spot. We faced a deep valley, and the long, wooded hill across from us was thick with Germans. We were exposed to their direct fire, and they harassed us with a running commentary of rockets and mortars. (A rocket barrage, incidentally, is truly terrifying. The shells scream like a thousand violated banshees, a sound to turn the blood of strong men to sherbet.)

As Shorty and I stood in the orchard and discussed the location of his squad, a shower of mortar shells began to splash in the trees around us. We lunged desperately toward the corner of the house a dozen feet away, and though I made it unscathed, Shorty got a splinter of shrapnel in his leg. I helped him to the cellar and sat with him while the medic bandaged his thigh and the German hausfrau sewed the rip in his trousers made by the medic's knife.

Leaving him, I walked to a nearby cellar where a group of men rested between guard tricks. As I chatted with them, a German shell scored a hit on the thick wall of the cellar, smashing it in upon us. Four men were injured, and again I was stoned and powdered with plaster dust. But no wound, no lovely five points for me! I phoned for a jeep and trailer to come for the wounded and waved a mournful good-bye to Shorty, sitting erect beside the driver. I felt lost and alone and frightened—Luecke was gone (combat fatigue), Leo was with the headquarters company, and now Shorty was gone. Of the men who had come in with me, not one remained.

Lacking telephone communication with the six men in the outpost, I trotted down at frequent intervals to check on their welfare. The road was under constant enemy fire and I did not dally en route. Puffing up to the outpost at the end of one such run, I felt the curious stare of John Basile, who was digging a foxhole in the front lawn. Fifteen minutes later, as I prepared to start my run back to the C.P., John spoke up.

"Hey, Sarge! Do you go to church much?"

A little taken aback, I replied, "Well . . . uh, no, I guess not. Not very much."

"Uh-huh." He resumed his digging.

I waited for a puzzled moment, then inquired, "Why? I mean—why do you ask?"

He put down his shovel and looked up, a little surprised to find me still there. Then he said slowly, "Well, I don't know . . . guess it's just that whenever I see you gallopin' down the road with the Jerries throwin' that stuff over, I figure you don't go to church much!"

I loped off, confused by his logic. And as I thudded down the road, I thought, Now what the hell! Why didn't he reach exactly the opposite conclusion—that I'm a good Christian, that I'm safe and untouchable because I'm a loyal member of somebody's flock and safe in the arms of Jesus?

In the orchard behind my C.P. daffodils stood in sturdy golden clusters, and indoors a vase of them offered spring incense to a blue and scarlet image of the Blessed Virgin. I buried my face in the cool petals and sniffed mightily, and enjoyed the luxury of choking with a sudden fierce yearning for home and *our* garden and *our* daffodils.

* * *

Sometimes it seems there are no German civilians left in Germany. Most of the people we meet of late are "slaves," usually Polish or Russian, and young. Hundreds of them, thousands of them—the drudges who have kept the German machine running. They stand at the side of the road and cheer us and salute awkwardly and flash wide, radiant smiles. Many of them do not smile; many of them only stare with dull, vacant eyes. Our passing means nothing; it's an interruption of their toil, a chance to stand erect for a moment and ease aching muscles. Nothing more.

All slaves wear on their garments a label, marked P for Pole, OST for Russian. The labels are large and brightly colored for easy identification.

Average "pay," when they were paid at all, was about two and a half marks per month. This sum they were graciously permitted to squander on colored postcards extolling the Greater Reich, and they were allowed to send these cards to any relatives who might still be alive in their native villages. Postcards they could buy; all else was *Verboten* to slaves.

Ah, it's a wonderful empire Herr Hitler built! Here on either hand are the rich fields that were plowed and planted by slaves last spring, and here are those same slaves, their few possessions in cardboard valises or burlap bags, trekking painfully along these muddy roads, moving toward assembly points, repatriation depots ... going home. You look at the fields, smiling with the promise of fat crops, and you wonder, Who will weed you this year, and who will harvest you? With whose sweat, with how many slow drops of whose blood, will you be moistened this year? You look again at the dull faces of the slaves, the hopeless bodies, the bright labels ... you turn away, and for a moment you cannot see the fields, and you curse, "Starve, you German bastards, starve!"

The day was quiet after our wounded had been taken away. The shelling and sniping continued, but there was no violent action. Early in the afternoon we spied a long column of prisoners coming up the road from Dondorf, and we watched them and counted. There were 130 of them. They turned at the junction and moved slowly toward the crest of the hill that overlooked Geisbach. Then we saw something horrible and shocking: the Germans on the other side of the valley began shelling their captured comrades in arms. It was unmistakably deliberate: the gray-blue uniforms were apparent to the naked eye, and German artillery observers, using field glasses, could not possibly have mistaken them for Americans. No, it was deliberately done. And the orderly column of prisoners became an hysterical rout—we could hear the cries of panic and pain—and they broke and ran, clumsily, toward Geisbach and the haven of our stockade.

Further Note on How War Hardens the Tender Sensibilities (or Every Man a Killer): the death of Cox and Berthot had been a double, even a quadruple loss. We lost our only two BAR men and our only two BARs as well. No one had thought to pick up the weapons dropped by the two men when they were hit. We needed them badly, and I put in a call for a jeep to pick them up on his next trip out. When the jeep arrived, the driver handed me one BAR: the other had been damaged beyond hope of repair. It was Berthot's weapon, thick with young Bob's blood. I took it gingerly and passed it to the rifleman who had been Bob's assistant. He accepted it but held it stiffly at arm's length, his face twitching. For a moment he did not speak and I waited. Finally the words came and he said, not looking at me, "I can't—" He swallowed and tried again. "I can't clean this thing, Sarge." I didn't press him but took the gun from him and tried another man. Same result. And so it went through most of the platoon. Finally I returned the weapon to the jeep driver and asked him to take it back to Battalion HQ and bring us another gun.

These men were frontline troops, not old and seasoned, perhaps, but surely well-acquainted with blood. This was not enemy blood, however, or the blood of a stranger—it was the blood of Bob Berthot, gummy and cold on his own weapon. Most of us had eaten and talked with Bob only a few hours ago.

* * *

In the middle of the afternoon orders came to prepare to move into Dondorf. E and F companies, captors of the town, were moving out and we were to take over. However, *we* meant only the first platoon, not the entire company. "Oh, fine!" we thought miserably. It took two companies to capture the lousy town, and now one understrength platoon was supposed to hold it against a possible counterattack. Fine!

We started out, three or four men at a time, and with plenty of space between. The Jerries were blasting hell out of the road, using rockets, mortars, and tank guns. A heavy ground mist in our sector prevented the enemy from actually seeing us, but their guns were beautifully zeroed in on the road and they were obviously taking no chances on our movements. We covered the mile and a quarter to Dondorf in a series of convulsive leaps. We were running like a bat out of hell for a few yards, diving headlong into the nearest ditch when inbound shells screamed a warning, climbing back to the road when the shells had landed and you made sure you were still in one piece, running again, diving again ... and at last through the mist we saw the first houses of Dondorf and heard the welcoming challenge of the men standing guard there.

I saw something on that road that I cannot forget. Perhaps if I'd been less tired I would have passed it without comprehension, seeing but not seeing. But I was in the state of fatigue that is akin to a certain stage of drunkenness, a moment of suspension between worlds when, for an instant, the commonplace is illuminated and there's pain and all poetry in such things as the curve of an eyebrow, the turning of a woman's wrist, a shadow in a doorway.

As I jogged dully through the mist I saw the body of a dead German soldier on the road ahead. He lay on his back, his knees drawn up. His legs were toward Dondorf and they were naked. I was not immediately aware of the nakedness, that comprehension hit me several seconds later. It was the rude circumstance of his nudity that jarred me awake. He was, in fact, naked from the waist down. With the thin man's envy of the superbly muscled, I was intensely aware of the beauty of his body. His thighs were Grecian music, glimmering whitely against the dun-colored clay of the road like marble.

I took a last envious glance as I pounded past . . . then stumbled, choked for a moment with nausea. It was indeed an athlete's body and the legs were magnificent—what remained of them. They ended at the knee in jagged splinters of white, hung with red pulp. And although the outflung arms were strong and shapely and the torso beautiful even through the clumsy army clothing, the head was a crushed eggshell, the brains having squirted out savagely under the tread of a tank.

By the time we reached Dondorf, F Company had already gone and E Company was fretting with impatience. The town seemed alarmingly big and our tiny platoon was scattered across a wide front—three men in one house, four in another, two here . . . No one said much, but we were all saying the same thing under our breaths and saying it hard: "Don't let there be a counterattack . . . don't let it!"

Forty-four German prisoners, nine of whom were badly wounded, were being held in the *gasthaus* near my C.P. E Company turned them over to us, and I had to assign two men to that special guard duty. We added ten prisoners to the bag during the night.

The night was endless. My orders had been, "Stay in Dondorf until you are relieved by another unit. That should be sometime tonight." The captain had added that there was no telephone communication between his C.P. and Dondorf. We'd be strictly on our own.

Shortly after midnight the outfit that was to relieve us arrived, and our responsibility was over. We prepared at once to rejoin our waiting company, and when the platoon was assembled I turned to an officer of the relieving outfit—he was a first lieutenant—and said, "Sir, if you'll assign a couple of men to take over the prisoner guard in the *gasthaus*, I'll pick up my two guards and we'll take off."

His face assumed the expression of a dose of salts taking rapid effect and he said curtly, "Those prisoners are not *my*

responsibility. I haven't any men to spare for a prisoner guard.
You'll have to take them with you."

The sonofabitch. He had an entire company to do a job that
had been done all night long by a single pint-sized platoon,
and he couldn't spare two men for a guard detail!

But I was a buck sergeant and he was a first john, so I
replied, meekly, "Sir, they aren't my responsibility, either.
They were passed on to me by the two companies *we* relieved.
I'll be glad to take along all the prisoners who can walk, but
what about the nine litter cases in there?"

Upon which he looked as though the salts had taken effect
and he didn't like it and he snarled, "I don't care how you
handle them—but *you* take care of them. It's your worry!"

I ached with the bitterness of tears to be his equal in rank
for five minutes, just five minutes, Lord! But I held my
tongue and tried to think of new arguments. He'd obviously
decided the conversation was over, however, and stalked off
without waiting for my salute. I walked back to my platoon
slowly, pondering. I was still on my own in this damn town, I
couldn't contact the captain for advice, and the company was
waiting for us. Finally I reached a decision. I told the guards
to bring out all the prisoners who could walk but to leave the
litter cases, along with two German medics to care for them.
Then we took off. I'd like to have seen the face of that p——
of a first lieutenant when he discovered he had eleven prisoners on his hands, nine of whom would have to be moved by
ambulance.

And, oh yes—something I'd forgotten! During our brief
conversation he'd asked me if I'd checked the papers of all the
civilians in town. Figuring I'd already overworked this military courtesy business, I answered simply, no sir, I hadn't—
my concern was with men in uniform and it was not a part of
my job to quiz civilians, even if I'd had men enough and time
enough to do it. He'd glared at me in return but said nothing. I
wonder if the nine wounded Germans ever lived to see the
inside of a stockade or whether he "disposed" of them in more
terse fashion.

We walked up the road in weary silence—the rocket and

mortar barrage had stopped at last—and rejoined the impatient company. Then we started back to Geisbach. But we didn't stop there. We kept going, shortcutting through muddy fields and climbing steep hills that sapped our last remaining strength. Shortly before dawn we entered Soven once more, and stumbling into the first houses we came to, collapsed in exhausted sleep.

Our one souvenir of Dondorf: a couple of men raided the little chapel next to my C.P. and stole a four-foot holy candle, all gilded and painted and garnished with holy pictures. It was nearly two inches in diameter, and we cut it into foot-long lengths. Most of us were secretly shocked by this looting of a chapel, but candles were illumination and thus precious beyond rubies. So we took a backhanded slap at our consciences and reached greedily for a chunk of candle. Strange . . . most of the men are religious, many are good Catholics, and in civilian life such a theft would seem the most gross sacrilege to them. You can blame our amoral behavior on war . . . or weariness. Or both.

March 26.

We were awakened at seven-fifteen for chow, and immediately after breakfast everyone went back to bed. Everyone but me, that is: I spent the day working. Lacking a platoon guide, I had to do his work as well as my own. So I checked ammunition supplies, equipment, and so on, begged, borrowed, and stole what I needed from the supply sergeant, reorganized the squads, checked the roster—all the endless and petty details that are automatic "musts" when a unit is out of combat.

There were twelve men in my platoon. Twelve men in a rifle platoon, and only eight of them properly first platoon men. Our losses at Geisbach had been so great that Captain Wirt dissolved the poor remnant of the second platoon, sending the few survivors to the first and third platoons. We got four of those men, thus giving us a total of twelve, plus myself.

I'd barely finished the last of my petty jobs when word came that replacements were arriving, fifteen of whom had been assigned to me, and I was to send the second platoon men packing because their unit was going to be reorganized. My fifteen replacements were all new men, fresh from the States and dewy-eyed with wonder. But one outstanding bit of luck came my way. An "old man," Staff Sergeant Joe Hudziak, was assigned to me for platoon guide. More about Joe later—he was one of the finest men I knew in the army.

The job on which I'd worked since early morning now had to be done over, and the day turned into howling confusion. It was late afternoon before the mess was straightened up. At last it was done, and I looked yearningly at my mattress on the floor. No luck—orders came to pack up; we were taking off for a new sector.

We traveled in trucks for part of the way, and for the first time I began to rate some of the gravy that fell to ranking noncoms. As the top NCO of the platoon, I was entitled to ride with the driver in the cab of the truck. (Of course, if an officer is in charge of the platoon, *he* gets the gravy. But I was lucky on this deal—we had no officer.) I was warm and comfortable throughout the trip, and I could afford the luxury of feeling sorry for the underprivileged bastards bouncing on the unprotected wooden benches behind me.

It was well after dark when we detrucked—in another of those damned pine woods. There we waited . . . and waited . . . and waited. I spent the hours counting noses and trying to keep the green men from wandering off and getting lost in the dark. There was the usual preliminary boasting and promisory courage from the new arrivals, and the customary quiet smiles of understanding on the faces of the men who knew the score.

Finally we started off again, walking, and a long walk it was. We felt our way along a muddy road we were expected to occupy, slipping and falling, and reached our objective only to find another outfit in our positions. "Situation normal: all f——d up!"

That was a favorite phrase of the services, and from it came that colorful word so quickly and lovingly picked up by the civilians at home: "Snafu!" And therein lies a curious footnote. By the time I arrived overseas, the infantry had long since dropped "snafu" from its vocabulary, regarding it as a somewhat precious extravagance of speech. Civilian use had soured it; it had been private property and was so no longer. I heard it used only by very fresh infantry replacements and by Air Corps personnel. For a time we had a chaplain who larded his speech with it in hearty determination to be one of the boys, to our ill-concealed disgust. We usually said, simply, "Situation normal!" and loaded the two words with the most powerful overtones of irony at our command.

We had a long, cold wait in the woods while the captain attempted to contact Battalion HQ for new orders. Finally we walked a few more miles through the mud, ending up (O Tempora! O Mores!) in another woods. Naturally. I told the men to dig in, but I just curled up on the ground and closed my eyes.

March 27.

After breakfast we moved forward another three miles. The mud was only ankle deep. We had a few casualties from rocket and artillery fire, and once, our advance elements were briefly halted by a skirmish with twenty Volksturmers. This was our first encounter with Hitler's vaunted "People's Army," and we were not impressed. They had been preparing a hasty minefield as a welcome for us, but our untimely arrival scattered them before the job had been finished. The mines already planted—of the Teller variety—had been so amateurishly concealed that we spotted them instantly. Lieutenant Huch of E Company sat calmly on a fallen tree and directed a sweating Volksturmer who hadn't moved fast enough in the removal and disarming of the mines. It seemed a grisly but fitting retribution that one of the men responsible for planting the mines should now court death by digging them up again, and we grinned at Lieutenant Huch as we passed.

Half a mile later rifle and machine-gun fire burst on us from the woods and we took hasty shelter in the ditches to fight back against an enemy we could not see. Abruptly the green and scented woods were full of peril and the branches whispered in German. We flattened ourselves behind stumps and fallen trees and stared painfully at shadows, our skin crawling with the prescience of snipers.

Our situation was uncomfortable, but the actions of two of our green replacements lightened the atmosphere considerably. The platoon was split: half of us in one ditch, half in the other, and the empty road between us. And so we lay, our backs to the road. At a burst of fire from the woods across the road we started involuntarily, but we stayed as we were, confident that the men on the other side of the road could handle that situation. Two men lying near me, however, leaped spasmodically at the sound of the shots, made an about-face in midair and flopped down again, facing the woods across the road. Before I could order them to return to their original positions, a rattle of machine-gun fire from *our* woods spun them automatically to face this new danger. A few seconds later and they swung to face the road in response to fresh fire from the farther woods. And so the insane ring-around-the-rosy continued, in spite of orders and the hoarse advice of their neighbors to "get down and stay down you stupid bastards!" Their leapings, their whirls, became frenzied, and I rolled on the ground in helpless joy. I told myself this was wrong; this was the raw laughter of the Nazi bullyboys observing the humiliations of their victims. Self-admonition didn't help; we were tired, defenseless against hysteria, and we needed laughter.

After a while the firing tapered off and we started to dig in. Apparently the fight was over, but we were rigid with cold and the exercise would warm us. Finally the order came to re-form on the road and move ahead.

We trudged over the hills and into another century, a village so peaceful in the sunset, so unchanged by progress and war and similar modern improvements that we instinctively lowered our voices. No plumbing, no electricity, no mark of the twentieth century save us and the things we brought.

I took up quarters in the tiny home of an aged spinster. She lived alone, doing her own work and caring for a garden, two cows, three goats, and several score of chickens. She was gentle, kind, and frightened. When we went to bed that night, most of us slept on the floor. There was but one bedroom, and

I assured her that no one would rob her of it. She dragged from her room an enormous mattress filled with flax seed. When we stretched upon it, the seed slithered under our bodies like something live. But for all that, it was a luxurious bed, and we soon grew used to the sibilance of the whispering seeds. Four of us slept on it that night, and I had ten beautiful hours of sleep.

In the morning the old lady clucked distressfully over the hacking coughs of some of the men. She trotted into her bedroom and returned beaming, wielding a tablespoon and carrying a large bottle of a virulent-looking red syrup that she administered to the ailing men, all of whom had turned suddenly shy, scuffing their toes like schoolboys. I had a spoonful, too, and it was sweet and pungent and soothing to my raw throat. (I know, I know—back home the writers were screaming about the innocent American soldiers who died of poisoned food and drink proffered by kindly German civilians. And I guess it did happen. But you had to make a decision one way or another and then take your chances. It just happened that my decision was always, "This is an innocent gesture, well-meant. Accept it." And I guess I was right each time.)

We spent the day of March 28 resting. We sat in the timid sunlight and took the peaceful village into our bones and swapped rumors. The news of the big push was good and our hopes were burgeoning. I had leisure to reflect on Geisbach and wonder how I would ever sort the pieces of that jigsaw puzzle and fit them together to make a picture.

During the afternoon we became motorized infantry for a short time. Mounted on tanks, tank destroyers, and half-tracks, we roared through seven towns, sweeping the area for German stragglers. It was a cold and dusty ride. We took no prisoners, but it was an exciting afternoon. We were swift and invincible. Careening through the unobservant countryside, we assumed careless, rakish poses, but when we entered a village we stood martially erect, donning a stern demeanor and frowning the frown of conquerors on the sullen townspeople. It wasn't like Belgium or France—the women didn't smile and they didn't throw flowers at us and blow kisses. Only the kids were happy to see us. We were soldiers, we wore uniforms and carried guns, and that was enough for them. They stared at us, round-eyed, and scampered into doorways with happy squeals of terror.

We slept again that night at our gentle spinster's.

March 29.

We moved out and rode the armor to Holzhausen. A misty wet day, and yesterday's exhilaration was lacking. A brief pause in Holzhausen and on to Wurgendorf, arriving shortly after five. We set out at once for Wilgersdorf, this time on foot. The captain wanted to take our objective before dark.

The first platoon spearheaded, followed by the rest of the company and our escort of armor. Two miles out of Wurgen-dorf we hit a bad roadblock. It was a skillfully contrived double barrier: a roadblock followed by a mine field, then another roadblock and still another minefield. For more than two hundred yards the road was impassable.

Most of the roadblocks we encountered during the swift last weeks of the war were hasty affairs, feeble barriers thrown up in whimpering frenzy. But some of them were little bitches. The best ones were to be found in heavily wooded areas where the trees on both sides of the road could be felled—usually by dynamite belts—to form an interlacing barrier too massive for our tanks to smash. That was a *good* roadblock.

On the low end of the scale were the pathetic barricades erected against us at the gates of tiny villages—hand-hewn beams and heavy logs woven into a barrier that seemed medieval and a little silly when nudged by the steel snout of a tank.

I remember such a little town, such a barricade. The infantry climbed over the barriers, which blocked every entrance into the town, but the timbers were so stout, so well-emplaced, that our armored escort could not effect an entrance. The roadblock across the principal street was particularly effective, a solid wall of heavy timbers stretching between a house on one side of the road to a high bank of earth on the other. House, logs, high bank—it looked impregnable. I set a squad of men to work on the barricade and went on with the rest of the platoon to secure the town. Returning a little later, I found the men sweating and angry, and the roadblock still standing. The timbers had barely been scratched by our toylike hatchets, and a little group of civilians had gathered on the bank to watch. They murmured among themselves and smiled secretly.

The malice of their pleasure was an intolerable humiliation, and I went out to have a quiet word with the commander of the leading tank, an officer I knew. Firm and impregnable, huh? The officer accepted my whispered proposal as the proper solution to our difficulty, and I sent two men to clear all civilians from the house that anchored one end of the barrier. I nodded to the tank commander, he disappeared within the tank, and the turret slammed shut. There was an inexorable grinding of gears . . . then slowly, implacably, the tank moved forward, pushed the house gently with its steel nose . . . nudged a little harder, and now a crack leaped crazily up the pale plaster wall . . . harder now, harder . . . the crack widened, became a hole, and the tank lunged forward, smashed and crushed, tore at the hole with grim shoulders, snarled ironlike through a curtain of dust . . . disappeared from our sight. A moment longer we waited unmoving, hearing with our bones and our blood the sounds within the house. Suddenly, triumphantly, the tank appeared in the street. It was in the village, it was beyond the mocking, useless barrier.

Turning to strut into town, I glanced at the civilians on the bank, wanting them to see my pride. They had drawn together against the steel thrust of the machine, blindly seeking the ancient comfort of flesh. The secret smiles were gone now, and the malice, and the white faces were empty. There was no anger . . . not yet. Only shock and fear, a naked agony of bewilderment. I turned away and went into the town, feeling sick and angry, needing to do something useless and infuriating so that I would no longer see their faces.

The roadblock in the forest stalled our advance for nearly four hours. Regarding the dark forest and our tangle of men and machines, I reflected uneasily that this was a helluva good time for an ambush. But nothing happened, and eventually we moved forward again. After a while another platoon relieved us of point duty and we fell back to second place.

It was a weary march, mostly uphill. A second roadblock and an enemy machine-gun nest relieved the dullness briefly, but our tanks smashed through this barrier and knocked out the machine gunners, and we kept walking.

We had a lot of respect for armored outfits, respect well salted with envy. We envied them because we walked and they rode, because we were naked before the enemy and they had protection—or at least the *feeling* of protection. We had a particular regard for T.D. men. They were a hard-fighting, hellfire bunch, and they enjoyed hardly more protection than the infantry.

We had no quarrel with the High Brass strategy, which decreed: "It's easier to replace a company or two of infantry than to get a new tank." We were the expendables and we knew it, but we didn't blame the tankers for that. We *were* cheaper than a steel juggernaut that groaned dollar signs every time it warmed up. When we started out on a push and the order of march read: "A company of infantry spearheading, followed by two companies of infantry; tanks and tank destroyers attached"—we accepted the official wisdom and stepped out with wry-faced bravado, feeling naked in front but conscious of a sense of warm protection behind, like a hot water bottle on our backside.

But a few things were hard to take. With the bitter eyes of habit, for instance, we'd watch the tanks roll into the town we'd just stormed and taken, watch them roll in, whooping and hollering . . . and late. Dreary with exhaustion, we would stand at our guard posts, waiting for counterattack, and watch the tankers race from house to house in search of loot, watch them drink *our* wine and cognac and schnapps, watch and listen while they celebrated "their" conquest, and then—too damn many times!—watch the tanks roll out of town again, loaded with our loot, and the riotous crew members waving our bottles in drunken greeting as they passed.

But more than that, though we didn't forget the towns

where the tanks had saved our necks, we could not forget the occasions when we needed the tanks, when we asked their help and they crawfished. One tank outfit in particular drew our ire, because of what happened on that dark forest road near Wilgersdorf.

As I said, the machine gunners at the second roadblock had been "knocked out" by our tanks. In fact, we had to coax, beg, and implore before the tanks reluctantly went to the aid of the spearheading platoon that was pinned down. A short time later there was another machine-gun nest, and once again the column halted. I sent a runner to tell the tanks to pull up so I could direct them to the aid of the platoon ahead, but five minutes passed and the tanks remained silent and motionless. A runner came up from the beleaguered platoon with a message asking for help, and I walked back to the first tank.

In the thick darkness I could barely discern the figure of the tank commander standing in the open turret. I told him of the call for help and he listened without comment. When I finished, he said flatly that he wasn't going up. After a moment of strained silence I told him that it wasn't a *bad* ambush—only a couple of machine-gunners in the woods. He repeated that he was not going to risk his tanks and crews by leading them into a mess they "couldn't even see." (I refrained from pointing out that it was equally dark for the infantrymen up there.) He put an emphatic period to the conversation by withdrawing into the dark guts of the tank, and I heard the hatch cover slam shut.

Turning away, I encountered Captain Wirt, who was angrily swinging a German walking stick he'd lately affected. He was in a vicious temper and wanted to know whythehell the delay. I mentioned the enemy machine-gun nest and he started to ream my tail for not sending the tanks up to clean it out, but I interrupted and told him of my exchange with the tank commander. I didn't strain after polite phrases in my report, and I followed him hopefully when he turned and stomped toward the tank. Standing beside it, he called—at first softly, then louder, at last furiously. No response: the tank was buttoned up like a temperance worker. He rapped with his stick on the metal skin of the tank . . . tapped, then hammered, then pounded with such violence that it seemed doubtful whether even steel armorplate could withstand it. At last the hatch cover creaked open and a sleepy head appeared, yawning, "Whatsa matter?" I leaned forward expectantly, and was not disappointed: the reaming that followed was an example of prose so pungent, rank, and vigorous that my admiration for the captain rose to a new high.

The effect was immediate: the first tank moved forward, the others followed, the machine gunners joined their companions, and the column lurched ahead. Unfortunately for the repute of tankers, the story of the reluctant tank commander spread through the company and even infected the other companies in the battalion.

We arrived at Wilgersdorf shortly before dawn. There was a brief skirmish, prisoners taken, and the town was ours. I picked a good house for a C.P. and went to sleep.

March 30, Wilgersdorf.

Twice as I walked through the town today a sniper selected me for target practice, one shot splintering a slate shingle three inches above my head as I stepped through the doorway of my C.P. We searched the neighboring buildings with grim thoroughness but could not find him. He continued to fire at intervals throughout the day, but fortunately he was a poor shot and hit no one. Probably a civilian, but we wanted him, civilian or no. We weren't fond of snipers.

Late in the afternoon came the usual bad news: we were moving out. Although Wilgersdorf was our objective and we'd attained it, E Company had run into trouble and F Company was rushing to the rescue. That left F Company's objective still wanting, and we were the babies elected to take that and keep the battalion record spotless. So we started out for Gernsdorf, first platoon leading again.

Gernsdorf was some distance away, and Captain Wirt decided that our only chance of reaching it before dark was to go cross-country, through the mountains. Equipped with compass and maps, I stepped out with a brave show of self-assurance, but secretly I was a little shaky about the whole proposition. My bump of direction was hardly more than a bruise, and I felt uncomfortably ill-chosen for the role of trailblazer.

I soon made a discovery at which my uneasiness spiraled to the tizzy stage in no time flat. The maps I carried inside my jacket were copies of German maps of ten years ago. Since mountains and valleys change little in the space of ten years, that would seem to be small cause for alarm, but this was a country where forestry was akin to farming and trees were a cultivated crop, grown and harvested like corn and potatoes. Time after time my map would indicate coniferous trees when before me would be only an open, windswept space of scraggly undergrowth or harsh grass. In symbol language the map would vouchsafe, "This is grass, low shrubs," and a moment later I would spit out a mouthful of pine needles and close my eyes as I clawed through the tightly interlaced branches of pine trees taller than a man, muttering, "Buster, one of us is wrong!"

Anxious to reach our destination before night trapped us in the hills, we stepped up the pace. We saw no houses, no roads: only trees and, rarely, the grass-grown ruts of forgotten logging trails. The hills were bitterly steep, the woods so thick that sometimes we had to hack our way through with bayonets and entrenching tools. We had six miles to cover. If we failed to reach Gernsdorf before dusk, men would get lost in the dark, and the units of our task force would lose contact. (As it turned out, we did lose the third platoon for an hour, but they found our trail again and caught up with us. The weapons platoon we lost permanently. They wandered forlornly in the darkening woods for a while and finally retraced their footsteps to Wilgersdorf.)

By hook and by crook, by means of compass and map, the captain's help, the assistance of friendly angels, and simple dumb luck, we got there. And the precious minutes we'd wasted during our fumbling and erratic progress through the forest saved our hides: we reached the crest of the hill overlooking Gernsdorf just in time to see the Jerries leave the village, accompanied by tanks, self-propelled guns, and armored trucks. An hour earlier and we'd have walked smack into another Geisbach—three platoons of infantry against an incalculable weight of men and machines. Hidden in the deep shadows under the trees, we listened to the sounds in the village. We could hear the conversation of the enemy clearly, hear them shouting to each other, uttering the German equivalent of "Get the lead out of your tail!"

Lacking attack strength, the captain tried to contact Battalion HQ by radio to request an artillery barrage. This was mountain country, and HQ was many hills and valleys behind us, too distant for easy radio contact. We watched tensely, listened to the monotonous, low-voiced calling of our operator, and our lips moved in soundless, profane prayer: "Christ, we *gotta* have that artillery . . . if we don't get it, he'll send us in anyway . . . we *gotta* have it!" And at last Battalion answered, in thin, crackling syllables that wavered and died and rose again. We sagged in exquisite relief, trying to ignore the hollowness in our stomachs, which reminded us that this was only a reprieve. First platoon was to spearhead the attack on the town following the barrage.

From our private grandstand seats we watched the shells burst in the town below, and not *all* the sweat on our hands sprang from the spectacle of that bright flowering. We had to go in there in fifteen minutes, and we didn't know what might be waiting. Fifteen green men in the platoon, untried by combat, unfamiliar with the grim business of storming a town . . .

We moved in fast, and Joe and I out-Simoned Legree, whipping the men with the lash of our tongues, keeping them moving, preventing them from bunching up, jacking up the laggards, the timid, the looters who wanted to dawdle in the first house and search for diamonds instead of German soldiers. Without Joe Hudziak, the platoon would have fallen apart, but Joe whipped one end of the line forward while I snarled at the other.

We were lucky. The artillery barrage had sped the parting guests, and we had only to pick up the stragglers and the wounded. We got by without serious fighting and were very happy.

I split the platoon between four houses, and we sat down to wait for further orders. We were ravenous with hunger, but the captain said our chow truck would arrive in a couple of hours. That familiar refrain offered no satisfaction in our stomachs, and we started skonavishing. Howie Dettman found a basket of eggs; we built a fire in the kitchen stove, raided the cupboards for lard, bread, and canned fruit, and had a feast. It was three A.M. of March 31, and I slept for an hour.

The captain's runner woke me at four to give me fresh orders. We walked a mile to where trucks waited for us and drove back to Wilgersdorf. We had chow upon arrival—official GI this time, and not nearly so satisfying—and collapsed for two more hours of sleep.

Gernsdorf remains curiously dreamlike to me. We never saw the town in daylight, and the few hours we spent there were so frenzied, so packed with movement and sound and tension, that the place never seemed real at all. My memories are few, and sharply brief: I remember the muddy road down which we raced as we stormed the first buildings . . . a village street, cobbled, and smelling strongly of cow, and the tiny wooden bridge over the tiny creek that parted the town in the middle . . . the house that was my C.P.—white plaster gleaming silver in the moonlight, and the black cross beams, set at rakish tilts, which checkered the face of the house with bizarre lozenges and squares, a backdrop for the medieval caperings of Till Eulenspiegel. I remember the kitchen, crowded with men and shadows and warm with fire . . . the smoky sputtering of the solitary lamp on the kitchen table . . . the rich and satisfying smell of frying eggs, and someone striking a match in the dim room and leaning close over the stove to see if the eggs were done. That's all. Nothing else remains.

We slept for two hours in Wilgersdorf and were awakened at nine-thirty. An hour later we were on our way to Büren, 110 miles to the northeast, in Westphalia. We carried C rations, which we ate en route, and arrived at our destination at midnight. There was the usual waiting, wondering, stalling around for orders ("Situation Normal . . ."), and then we dumped our packs in the nearest houses and went to bed.

CHAPTER TWELVE

". . . weeping women, frightened children, the trembling bewildered aged."

April 1, Easter Sunday.

Our breakfast did not include hard-boiled eggs decorated in gay colors. As a matter of fact, our breakfast did not include eggs. Nor did we spend the forenoon hunting for goodies in the garden. We did, however, take an Easter Sunday drive. On tanks and tank destroyers we took the air to Geseke, a sizable community not many miles removed from Büren. Our short ride was like a royal progress. In civilian best, Sunday best, Easter best, the townspeople were abroad to see us go by. They smiled timid welcome, and the white flags hanging disconsolately from every house were banners of triumph to us. The kids on the street blew kisses and begged chocolate, and all faces were happy. Nearly all. It was a lovely day.

We stayed in Geseke for five days, helping to close the iron ring tightening around the remnants of the Wehrmacht in the Ruhr. We set roadblocks and paced weary hours of sentry duty but there was no fighting. So we ate and slept and accepted the easy surrender of tired enemy soldiers and flirted with the less stony-faced frauleins.

The last of my Christmas boxes reached me on Easter Sunday, the last of the packages Ree and my mother had so conscientiously mailed before September 30, 1944. The candy and cookies tasted fine. I had long since abandoned any hope of getting them, convinced that they'd vanished in the holocaust of the December breakthrough, when thousands of letters and boxes from home had been burned by our retreating forces to keep them from the hands of the advancing Germans.

From a letter home, dated April 2:

Last night Loeb and I glutted ourselves on pâté de foie gras, sent to him from New York by his wife. It's a screwball war—here we are, in the heart of Westphalia, home of those great-livered geese who supplied the noble pâté of Rabelaisian memory, pâté that's imported to expensive delicacy shops in New York City, where loving wives purchase it, wrap it carefully, and send it to their soldier husbands in Westphalia!

I found a piano today, and for an hour no one bothered me or wanted me to do something. So far it's been a good day.

Prisoners pass in unending numbers, even throughout the night. Last evening I picked up an ex–Luftwaffe pilot who, hands in pockets, sauntered unhurriedly down the road and surrendered without surprise. This is a swell way to run a war.

You ask about wounds and how we regard them, and you inquire specifically about Ketron. Our reaction to a wound is in direct ratio to the gravity of the injury. Ketron was badly wounded: his leg had been fractured and he'd been pretty well messed up by shrapnel. It was a serious wound and we liked him, so we grieved. But we were a little envious, too—he was going home and would probably be discharged. (He would, at any rate, be transferred from the infantry and assigned to duties more reposeful. A rifleman whose legs were unsolid was no good to a combat unit.)

A minor injury, such as Shorty's, we hail joyously as a "million dollar wound" . . . "a five-pointer"—the fervent wish of every Joe who is honest with himself. It means weeks, perhaps months, of pleasant hospital life, plus five points for the Purple Heart. Who could ask more?

You ask which is more frightening, artillery or snipers. Snipers are a cold fear, ghosts that walk every midnight street, lie in wait at every corner. It's like walking into a dark room and hearing the door close softly behind you and you didn't close it . . . the skin on your forearms telling you that someone, something, is in the room with you, watching you with eyes that never blink, never flicker away from you . . . something that listens to your breathing and the sound of your heart. Snipers are bad.

But I think you meant not "snipers" but "small arms," didn't you? Rifle and machine guns versus artillery? If I *have* to make a choice, I'll take small-arms fire. Rifles and machine guns are bad medicine, but they carry this small sugar coating: a hole in the ground, a hollow, even a tiny hummock of earth, offers reasonable protection against their bullets. Chances are you won't get hurt so long as you lie there. That is, not by small-arms fire. Artillery is something else again. Shrapnel cannot be denied by a hole in the ground, a hollow, or a little mound of dirt. You hear the shell screaming through the air, you estimate where it will fall and tense yourself. Then it hits, the earth bounds under you, trying to push you up, and the air is filled with the buzzing of maddened bumblebees. The hell with Ry-Krisp or lettuce-and-lemon diets—for ladies who would be swanlike I recommend a few hours under an artillery barrage.

My house in Geseke is one of a row of unimaginative buildings that rim the edge of the town, looking outward toward the "broad Westphalian plain." (How glibly that moldy phrase springs to my tongue! And why not? It *is* broad, it *is* a plain, and it is undeniably Westphalian.) Joe and I share a comfortable room. We have a bed, a table, a lamp, two chairs, and a stove.

It is a curious household. The building is inhabited by an indeterminate number of people, all of whom go about their tasks silently and never speak to us. Only one makes an effort to be friendly. She is a strikingly attractive young widow named Katherine Grebel. Occasionally she stops in our room to chat, but her visits are brief and furtive because the other civilians frown upon them and she is dependent on their bounty. Her story, though not uncommon, I suppose, is a pitiful one.

Her parents long dead, a brother now living in Miami

Beach, Florida, is her only living relative. He's a commercial photographer. In 1940 he sent passage money to her, urging her to come to the United States, but the German government refused to grant her a passport and (she says) denied her request to go to America as a tourist. A year later she married. Her physician husband was with the German army and for a time they lived in Posen. It was there that she made the acquaintance of an American woman, a Bostonian, who had been visiting relatives in Posen and was trapped by the outbreak of war. A few months after her husband's departure for North Africa, Katherine and her American friend were arrested by the Gestapo for conversing in English as they stood under the marquee of a cinema. She was held for several days and questioned. (She doesn't know what happened to the American woman.) Upon her release she fled to Berlin, a thoroughly frightened and unhappy young woman. There, her son was born, and two days before his birth she received the official notice of her husband's death in North Africa.

Alexander, her son, is now two years old, a pale, pindling child. When the Russian advance threatened the German capital, she fled once more, this time to Geseke and to these distant connections of her husband's family. She is nearly destitute, and her one hope is to join her brother in America someday. It cannot be pleasant for her in this house: the prosperous, comfortably fleshed peasants regard her poverty as a mark of personal weakness, and her sophistication and grace represent urban degeneracy to their stolid minds. We have grown so used to the sight of dowdy women, plain women, shapeless women, that slim, graceful Kathe in her furs, her turban, her silk stockings, is like a breath of home to us. When she has gone from the room, Joe and I sniff the air appreciatively and grin at each other in mutual, unspoken comment.

Today, at this moment and in this place, the war is a nightmare nearly forgotten. Not a gun can be heard, not a plane, not a shell. Somewhere in the house a baby is crying, a thin and far-off petulance, and here in my room a wood fire crackles intimately in the porcelain stove. There are no other sounds. From my window I can see pansies and daffodils in the garden, and this morning the cherry trees and the honeysuckle burst into flower.

One of the men in the platoon gave me a haircut today. My head looks a little odd: he'd never been a barber, but somewhere in his looting he acquired a barber's clippers. Now if I could only get a bath and some clean clothes! I've reached the stage where I can hardly endure my own smell—which, literally speaking, is really something rare!

April 7.

We left Geseke yesterday and trucked forty-two miles eastward to Brakel. We spent the night in a big house, one of the familiar courtyard establishments. This was a remarkably prosperous ménage, which included blooded horses, pedigreed cows—each with her name, pedigree, and milk record emblazoned on a shield over her stall!—and scores of pigs, geese, ducks, turkeys, chickens, and rabbits. Also, a large staff of Polish and Russian slave girls. I cannot understand why the slaves remain, why they continue to work, why they do not revolt and throw the masters out of the "big house," now that they are liberated. But they continue their serfdom, seemingly content.

Concerning slaves, our five days in indolence in Geseke apparently served to remind some of the men that they *are* men . . . or animals, if you insist. One of them, overcoming the language barriers in some mysterious fashion, was discovered this afternoon with one of the Polish slave girls in a dim corner of the barn. Unattractive as she was, and notwithstanding her evil-smelling boots and manure-smeared apron, she was bent casually backward against a conveniently placed barrel and they took their brief pleasure standing, with a bland disregard for anyone passing by. When they were discovered, he grinned over his shoulder and she smiled without embarrassment. And when it was done, he picked up his rifle and strolled away, and she, dropping her skirts, picked up her pitchfork once more and resumed her work.

We slept last night in the granary, using grain sacks and

flour bags for our beds. It's morning now and I'm sitting on my helmet in the courtyard, relishing the frail comfort of a watery sunshine. We shove off soon.

April 10.

Three days have passed since we left the house at Brakel. When we reached Amelunxen, we paused only long enough to eat, then rode on to Wehrden, on the banks of the Weser River. The initial crossing was to be made in assault boats by E Company, and we were to follow. Kickoff was scheduled for three P.M. Crouching behind the buildings of Wehrden, we watched the men of E Company prepare for the crossing. Across the river the thickly wooded hills looked menacing. We could see German troops plainly. There were a lot of them and they knew we were coming. They didn't seem excited.

Zero hour at last and the boats shoved off, the men crouching low and paddling with frantic energy. We watched the white boiling of the waves and fancied we could see the spurt of enemy bullets. And maybe we did—the Jerries threw a lot of lead at the boats. Miraculously, no boats were sunk, and the casualties were light for such a crossing.

After delivering E Company to the other side, the engineers manning the boats came back. Now it was our turn.

We were being signally honored: a photographer was to accompany us and take pictures of our landing. (I never saw the pictures.) Together we stood at the corner of a building, waiting for a signal from Captain Wirt. Together we raced for the riverside, threw ourselves into the boat and shoved off, hunching our shoulders in pathetic, instinctive defense. There were three engineers and nine riflemen per boat, and everyone paddled like hell except the photographer in our boat. He clutched his camera and looked excited and unhappy. Our boat was the first to land, and as we jumped ashore and streaked for the cover of the trees, the photographer threw himself on his stomach on the beach and leveled his camera at the boats coming in.

With the first platoon spearheading, we started for the village of Meinbrexen, hugging the protective shoulder of the bank on the left of the road. German rifles and machine guns chattered excitedly, and I winced when a sniper's bullet spanked the road a yard ahead of my moving feet. Soon the high bank that shielded us shrank and came to nothing and there was only an open field. We halted to consider. I sent word back to Captain Wirt, describing the conditions and saying we planned to continue along the road, on the double. While I waited for a reply from him, we took potshots at the German troops skulking in the hills.

The captain sent back an okay and we took off. Man, we really sweated! Here's a stretch of open road—grab your rifle, hang on to the hand grenades you clipped to your pockets (like a dope!) or they'll pull loose from the safety pin. Run, now! . . . run like a big-assed bird, your pack flopping up and down on your back, thumping hell out of your ribs . . . your helmet wobbling, slipping over your eyes and blinding you, your rifle suddenly weighing fifty, a hundred, five hundred pounds! Okay . . . here's a little embankment . . . slowly now, but not too slowly—there are men behind you, crowding up . . . keep moving, breathe deeply, regularly . . . try to catch your breath. Okay? Here's another open space, a long one. Okay, take off . . . crouch when you run and keep an eye on that patch of woods there . . . see something shining there? Ya sure? Funny . . . thought I did . . . maybe just a shred of that damn silver foil from our planes . . . run, you sonofabitch, I'm on your heels! Keep moving—two guys out here make a bigger target than one. . . . Okay, safe now . . . take it easy for a minute . . . *keep down, you dumb bastard!* You wanna walk into Meinbrexen minus a head? Awright, awright, wise guy . . . keep moving!

We made fast time. Suddenly we were nearly there, and we could see a church tower and now the red roofs of houses. The railroad embankment on our right hid us from watchers in the town, and we decided to follow the embankment until we reached the underpass indicated on my map.

We hesitated as we neared the underpass. The Germans surely knew of our advance, and they would expect us to enter the town by the underpass, the most logical approach. We'd

baffle 'em with some American illogic: we'd keep going and
enter the town from the rear, come in behind them.

Beyond the underpass the bank was higher, and even the
church tower could no longer be seen. One of the scouts
reported a large farmhouse on the other side of the tracks, and
we crouched below the rim of the embankment and studied
the buildings. We saw enemy soldiers in the courtyard and
fired upon them. Our fire was returned feebly, and we were
tempted to rush the farm and work into town from there. However, it was only an outpost, and we'd hold up the entire company if we stopped to slug it out. Whipping up a fresh burst of
speed, we rounded a bend in the road and there was the town,
fifty yards away. We were into the first buildings so fast there
was hardly time for dust to rise, so fast that the German soldier
walking down the nearby road was obviously unaware of our
presence. Rifle in hand, he was plodding steadily in the direction of the farmhouse we'd just passed. When we opened up
on him, he hit the ground like a sack of . . . well, he hit the
ground. We waited a moment and suddenly he was up again,
still clinging to his rifle and streaking for the farmhouse. We
fired again—a volley from at least six rifles, a BAR, and my
carbine—and he hit the ground again. Another minute. Again
he stood up—some shooting, hey?—but this time his hands
were empty and they were held high above his head. Two of
the newer men, trigger-happy and flushed with the triumph of
having a Jerry pinned between their sights for the first time,
instantly opened up on him. I yelled a blasphemous protest
and hastened to knock their rifles up in the air. Then, seeing
their stricken faces, I explained, "I'll tell you about it later."

My action was not because my personal ethics had been
violated. That was a part of it, sure, but there was a sound,
practical explanation, which I gave them later, soft-pedaling
the ethical side. I argued that when you fire at a man who's
prepared to surrender and has clearly indicated his intentions,
your bullets convince his fellow soldiers that the propaganda
is true—Americans *do* "always shoot their prisoners." They
tell themselves that if death is the only answer, they might as

well die fighting. And a fight means American deaths as well
as German.

We moved through Meinbrexen like a hot wind. The Germans fought back, but we knew they were frightened and
confused, whimpering inside, and the knowledge made us
swift and vigorous. When a group from the platoon behind
us stopped to argue about who was going to go in after a certain stubborn sniper, two other men, cocky with victory,
climbed through a window and took the sniper by surprise.
He surrendered quietly but with a look of arrogant contempt
for the victors. Young and well-built, he wore several important decorations and flaunted the hated SS insignia. I removed a tiny banner from his rifle, a small triangle of yellow
cloth decorated with a skull and crossbones in black. I learned
later that it was a marker for a German minefield.

The captain and I had an amiable argument—to which there
could be but one end, as I damn well knew!—concerning
whether the castle in the heart of the town would be the company C.P. (his) or—since it was in my defense sector—my
platoon C.P. It was an imposing hulk that stood proudly on a
tiny, exclusive island, surrounded by a moat. A real moat,
complete with water and swans. In the foyer of the castle were
two oversize armoires: one of carved ebony, the other of rose-
wood inlaid with silver and mother-of-pearl. The walls were
hung thickly with swords, daggers, and battle-axes, and in the
passages beyond I could see the gleam of armor and the rosy
warmth of tapestries. I never got beyond the foyer, but I'd
have relished a few hours of snooping, feeling with my eyes,
and trying to resist the temptation to look with my fingers.

After posting the men, I relaxed in the little *bier stube* that
was my C.P. and waited for chow. We'd been told that the
engineers were building a bridge across the Weser and that our
chow trucks would be the first vehicles to cross. Work on the
bridge had been started in the middle of the afternoon, and we
wouldn't have long to wait. So they told us. But our food
never did arrive. The engineers really loused up that job, one
officer countermanding another's orders, men getting in each
other's way, and everything confusion.

Captain Wirt later told me that a colonel and a lieutenant colonel had been relieved of their command because of their bungling at the Weser—not that a meal for G Company was so damned important, but the 3rd Armored had been forced to stall around in Wehrden on the other side of the river, losing precious time. Our hearts bled for the 3rd Armored, but we felt that the food failure in itself justified the use of a firing squad. We were hungry. Our only food for many hours had been the single swallow of milk ladled out to us that afternoon by a tearfully happy Meinbrexen frau.

The civilians who owned the *bier stube* were gentle, kind folk. They had given us several bottles of wine upon our arrival and asked, timidly, if we wanted food. Confident that our chow would not be long in arriving, we answered, "No, our food will soon be here." Their relief had been obvious, and they explained that they had little food left—the German High Command no longer provides food for the Wehrmacht, and the German soldiery is expected to live off the people.

A few hours later, seeing that our food had not yet arrived, they again asked if we wanted to eat, and again we declined. Around nine P.M. they inquired once more and we weakened and said, "Yes!" A boiled egg was prepared for each of us, and they gave us bread and ersatz coffee. Not much of a feast, but it covered the bottom of the most aching hollows.

We spent the night there, spelling each other at phone guard and sleeping on the big davenport that stretched across one end of the room. Theoretically, the building was steam-heated, and the pipes *did* hold a tepid warmth until midnight. We were almost comfortable, and there was a piano on which I fooled around softly for most of the night.

Monday, April 9.

No breakfast. No chow trucks. Our gentle hostess insisted on serving us with more boiled eggs, bread, butter, strawberry jam, and coffee. Eavesdropping on her murmured conversation with her young son, I learned that our meal included the last egg, the last morsel of butter, the last piece of bread in the house.

Shortly after breakfast the order came to pack up. We were moving on, and an engineer outfit, the same one, would take over the town. Presently a first lieutenant of engineers walked in and asked how soon we would be leaving. I told him any minute, and he said very well, he'd take the *bier stube* for his C.P. He waved an arrogant hand—well, maybe he didn't wave, but he sure as hell gave that impression—and a non-commissioned flunky hastened to nail a handsomely painted board on the front door, calling attention to the new status of the building. An indication of rear echelon decadence that amused us mightily.

What followed did not amuse us at all. He swaggered over to our elderly, sweet-faced hostess and brutally ordered her to be out of the building within two hours. Staggered, she lifted pleading eyes and asked, humbly, where they were to go. He answered that he didn't care: "That's your worry!" She came to me and asked if they really had to go, if I wouldn't intercede for them, and sadly I told them that he was an officer and I only an *unteroffizier* and I could do nothing. And though I ate humble pie and appealed to him, I *could* do nothing. He wanted them out, and that was the end of it.

The fourteen-year-old son, in faltering English, asked the lieutenant if they might please stay in one room—they would give up everything else. The *bier stube* had many rooms, he pleaded, and they would be very quiet. Before the boy had finished speaking, that brass-bound bastard had swung on his heel and walked away, not bothering to look back as he flung over his shoulder the single word "No!" And his ass-licking dog robber, having finished his sign-nailing, said savagely to the boy, "See how you like the same medicine you gave the Polocks!" (But damn it, damn it, *we* don't make war on the weak and the helpless! That's the theory, anyway.)

My heart was sick and I wanted to leave, fast. In my last glimpse of our hostess I saw her moving bravely down the hall to her kitchen, her back straight and her head held high. But her hands were pressed tight over her face.

All over the village it was like that—weeping women, frightened children, the trembling, bewildered aged. White-faced women hauling unwieldy carts to their doorsteps and loading food, bedding, small treasures, preparing to start out for—I don't know where. Some few civilians, those who lived in the smallest and most wretched houses, were spared. And the official brass edict was: "The civilians can double up and live together."

I reflected bitterly as we trudged out of town. Here was this goddamn bunch of engineers, and they came into a town we fought to take. While we slugged it out, they sat on their tails on the other side of the river. When it was all over they followed us in. They were more brutal, more ruthless in their treatment of civilians, than *we* were—and surely, if there is ever *any* justification for brutality (which I doubt) it is with the combat outfits, with the men who've seen their friends killed in the taking of towns such as this. But we have little desire to make the civilians suffer. Usually we treat them as considerately as we can and are grateful to them when they're kind. Now the women and the children had to leave this place, go to some other corner of this weary, God-forgotten land. Maybe someday they'd come home again and to a place they wouldn't recognize, their houses obscenely filthy, their furniture scarred and smashed and burned for kindling, their livestock devoured, their cupboards bare, and their wine cellars empty. So it's war, maybe, but there are degrees of war, as there are degrees of peace.

Assembling at the company C.P., we started the long march to Dernthal. Our chow trucks finally met us, and we ate happily and sprawled on the cool grass by the side of the road. In the house behind us lay a dead civilian, his body covered with a red-and-white-checked tablecloth. As we rested, a woman approached, leading a ten-year-old girl by the hand. With a cruelly faithful adherence to tribal custom, she uncovered the body and forced the child to look at her dead father, fixing the ugly sight forever on the terrified youngster's mind. Then, while the little girl wept hysterically, the woman rocked and moaned and told us—with an embarrassing implication that *we* were responsible—that this *kleine mädchon* was now an orphan. There was nothing we could say, and we rose with alacrity when the call came to move out.

Leaving Dernthal, we passed through a heavy woods along a road thick with roadblocks, most of them incomplete. Daily it became more evident that the Wehrmacht was crumbling. At one place every roadside tree for fifty yards wore a dynamite girdle, fused and wired and ready to be blown. The fleeing Germans had forgotten only the final step—pulling the switch.

We passed an enemy encampment in the woods that gave evidence of recent occupancy. It was a welter of tempting loot: new guns, cases of ammunition, an officer's jeep, a motorcycle, a staff car, helmets, uniforms, cases of food, boxes of cigars, *cases of champagne*! I found the cache of officers' supplies (the cigars and food and champagne) when I made a brief skonavish of the deserted camp—a stupid thing to do because the area might well have been booby-trapped. Before I ran back to the road to rejoin my platoon, I grabbed two bottles of champagne and thrust them inside my shirt. I told Lieutenant Krucas about the loot in the forest and he said, "The company will take care of it." His prediction was painfully accurate. Company HQ took the cream, naturally: the pistols, cameras, cigars, and twenty-seven bottles of champagne. But Headquarters was not niggardly, no indeed. Each platoon was graciously allotted three bottles of champagne. Pure white generosity *that* was! Three bottles per platoon—twenty to twenty-five men in a platoon—and that left fifteen bottles for the headquarters group (twelve men) to whack up.

Two kilometers from the village of Neuhaus we halted. An overturned wagon on the side of the road was my C.P., and we pawed busily in the spilled junk, finding such stray items as two superb saddles, several bags of oats, cigarettes, blankets, clothing, mess gear, shaving equipment, a bottle of cognac— hell, the list can stop there. Digging a three-man hole in the soft earth of the bank, we made it comfortable with the blankets from the wagon, divvied up the champagne, and drank our share on the spot. We saved the cognac for later.

We spent the night there. Joe Hudziak, Howie Dettman, and I spelled each other on phone guard through the night—I had set two outposts in the hills behind us—but it was an easy chore. We stayed under the blankets and propped the receiver beside us, each man merely handing it to his neighbor at the end of his trick. It was strangely sweet to lie there and regard the stars, exchanging sleepy comments with the men in the outposts. Our bellies were full and we were warm.

Something I just remembered. Several weeks ago we passed through a town that had been painstakingly, methodically, obliterated by our bombers. It was an old sight, and I walked in a dull haze of weariness, regarding without interest the familiar monotony of this destruction. Ahead of me a roadside sign caught my eye. KINDERGARTEN it said, and a black arrow pointed. I followed the arrow with my eyes, noting with pleasure the attractive modern building it indicated. It was low, rambling, many-windowed, built of white plaster and creamy brick. I glanced over my shoulder for a last look as we passed, and immediately the old churning started in the pit of my stomach. The building had been neatly bisected by a bomb, split as though a huge wedge had been driven through the snowy plaster with mathematical precision. Tumbling from the raw wound was a gay cataract of red, yellow, and blue blocks, multicolored beads, swirls and ripples of colored paper. The splintered wreckage of small desks . . . the diminutive tables and chairs that were exactly the right size for five-year-olds. I thought of Geoff and Sukey . . . Geoff and Sukey *here* . . . or the war and the bombs insanely transported *there*, where they are, to Edward Smith School in the city of Syracuse, New York.

A wrecked home, a blasted factory, even a ruined church—we've learned to accept them calmly or with only the smallest shudder. But a bomb-shattered school, a broken toy, a baby carriage torn by machine-gun bullets—we're shaken by these fresh reminders that not all the world is old and soiled and weary.

I thought about the kindergarten and wondered, Where did

it start to go wrong, this nation that so loves children? Because it *does* love them—German songs, German stories, German Christmas traditions offer rich proof. Even the word "kindergarten" is a testimonial of that love. And then I thought, But wait a minute! Love, yes, but a love that is often sickly and dishonest; a love that is too frequently only an arrogant, if sentimental, desire to mold the adult in miniature. Germans, ever mindful of tradition, believe in the fiction of "national" virtues, see themselves as the custodians of a great heritage, and ask nothing more of their children than that they mirror a mythical German "character"; Americans, having no real tradition, see their children not as carbon copies of themselves, but as the potentials of something better. Americans are secretly humble before the promise of their children; Germans are not.

The thing is, the children of continental Europe *work*, they are required to earn their right to exist. Children are a crop, a commodity, part of the basic livestock of a European farm. Only in America and England are children reared in the pleasant assumption that life ought to be fun for kids—and work is for adults only. Only in America and England are children given full freedom to experience the fragile miracle of youth, taste freely the subtleties that only the young palate can truly savor. Perhaps we baby our children too much, but I like it that way.

Most of our prisoners of late are pathetic, bottom-of-the-barrel specimens. The other day we picked up four whose respective ages were forty-two, forty-one, forty-three, and forty-five. They had been in the army four weeks. Yesterday we took three, one of whom was sixteen years old. He'd been in the army eight days. The Wehrmacht machine is worn out.

Tuesday, April 10.
We entered Neuhaus, and I had a stroke of luck: the building I took over for a C.P. had excellent beds.

Feeling unaccountably gay, we had a party, a real party. A raid on the cellar of our house netted all the wine we could possibly want—red, white, sparkling, dry, sweet. We used our bottle of cognac for chasers. Loeb came to call, bringing a box he'd just received from Sally, his wife. Sardines, crackers, olives, and a bottle of whiskey she'd contrived to smuggle through the mails. We drank nauseating combinations of wine, whiskey, and cognac and got satisfyingly drunk. We wound up the evening telling each other in loud and tearful accents how wonderful each of us thought the other was . . . what a swell guy . . . how dear to our hearts. . . .

April 11.

No hangover when I awoke, but a reaction infinitely more uncomfortable, which may have had no connection with the preceding night's revelry. The joints of my body, particularly my knees and hips, were swollen and aching, so painful it was a hardship to move at all, let alone start on a forced march. Which is what we did. Fortunately, we had to walk only a few miles, before being picked up by trucks and carried to the village of Imbshausen, thirty miles to the east. We spent the night in the home of some kindly old people. The grandmother, eighty-one years old, was terrified of us, and we had a helluva time convincing her that she was safe . . . no, we would *not* cut her throat while she slept.

On this day, one of the men found a German boot in the road, containing a foot and part of a leg. There was no trace of the rest of the body.

I spent the night almost comfortably on a red velvet sofa. Now, mid-morning, I sit by an open window, writing lazily and forgetting to write for minutes on end. I lean forward to meet spring, and the nagging, faint perfume of unseen flowers drifts through the open window. Brushing a deluded bee from my arm, I thought, Surely not even a spring-mad bee could mistake stale sweat for the scent of honeysuckle? Ah, it's spring, and time for me to be home! I'm tired of war, and tired of male smells. It's good to be sitting in a comfortable chair, a cushion at my back, the sunlight making patterns of peace on the green-dappled cobblestones of the street. It's good, but not altogether good. Under the placid surface of my content I'm restless, feeling the first stirrings of the dark surge of home-sickness that moves steadily upon me. It's always this way between actions; the only way to keep from brooding upon home is to keep fighting.

Why *won't* these bastards cry enough? Why do they continue to fight? Not because they still have faith in a final victory, surely! Nor can it be in the hope of winning a negotiated peace: they must know by now that they won't get it. Why *won't* they quit? They struggle now within the borders of their own land, seeing their own women and children frightened, hungry, and fearful of next year's starvation. (In these broad farm areas we make daily acquaintance with that fear, seeing women and old men each day confront the dry malevolence of empty fields and untilled soil.)

Tonight the woman of this house wept hard, painful tears as she told me of how desperately she and her aged mother must work for the little food that will keep them alive. They exist on a vegetable diet, enriched by an occasional egg or a rare morsel of cheese. They get no meat. I'd watched her in the garden, eighty-one years old and laboring most of the day in the vegetable patch. The younger woman told me of her father, dying last year at eighty-three, and how he'd worked like a beast of the field all his life, from small boyhood until the very day when a stroke cut him down and left him paralyzed and helpless for three months, when death was merciful. She said passionately that there ought to be more to life than this; more than eighty-three years of toil, and then death. And so there ought. Life is stunted and barren for people like this. It's easy to see how the figure of Hitler, blazing with tinsel glory and posturing heroically to the echo of Wagnerian horns, offered release to the festering turbulence of German emotion. But there's more to the picture than that: these people are hag-ridden by tradition and by an inbred, servile respect for authority. I think the people of Europe are never young—they're born old and they just grow older. They lack the hope and belief of Americans, qualities that are the rare prerogatives of the young.

Maybe this is what Germany is fighting for, the Lorelei

song that persuaded the young and hopeless to National Socialism: the fierce desire to *be* young, to make life more than a drudgery rounded with a death. They're working for it the wrong way, and that's why it's worth fighting them, but I begin to see a glimmer of the light that draws them, and the dark shadows from which they have attempted to flee. Poor strugglers . . . poor, blind runners.

April 12.

We traveled by truck on the first leg of an eighty-mile push to the east, reaching Herzberg at dusk. Our assignment was to clear the Harz Mountains. Last night we heard the good news that the 2nd Armored had crossed the Elbe and was sixty-eight miles from Berlin. We felt cocky with victory and our spirits were high, in spite of a weariness that teetered on the very brink of exhaustion.

Our house in Herzberg contains five civilians: an elderly couple, two daughters, and a three-week-old baby. Fearful at first, they became pathetically eager to please, once convinced that we intended no harm. But in spite of their friendliness, in spite of the fine piano in the living room, I'll be very happy to leave this house. Only the baby smiles and is content—the adults have been damp with tears from the moment we arrived. They spell each other; as soon as one stops crying, another starts, and the house is forever filled with the sound of weeping. That sounds flip, and I don't intend it to be. The tears are genuine, and we're not unsympathetic, but we cannot permit ourselves the dangerous luxury of emotion.

The weeping started when we answered their questions about Berlin. Had the Russians taken it yet? Did it still stand? Was anyone alive in Berlin? And when I told them, in all innocence (or was it deliberate cruelty?) about the success of the Russian push and the present condition of Berlin, they burst into tears, even the old man. There is a daughter—or there was—in Berlin. I was shown snapshots of her and her children, handsome, sunny-haired twins of five. Last summer the twins were there with the grandparents in Herzberg, but they'd been sent back to Berlin in the fall. There's been no word of them since, nor of their mother.

I tried to stem the flood of grief with glowing descriptions of the bomb-proof shelters that honeycomb Berlin, and with stout conviction I protested that "of course the kids are okay . . . why, sure they are . . . Gosh!" What else could I say! But it's an uncomfortable house, and I'm oppressed by the tear-stained faces that turn to me a dozen times a day for reassurances I cannot give.

April 13, a Friday.

Black Friday the thirteenth.

Someone shook me awake a little before dawn and told me the news—the President died last night. We cannot believe it . . . we cannot. At once everything is changed. The high spirits of yesterday are gone and the taste of victory has turned foul upon our tongues. The town looks the same—there are the same American faces and American uniforms, the same vigorous litter of GI equipment on the streets, but now it's a dead town. It belongs to the civilians today. No, we cannot believe it. It's a loss with such staggering implications that even the ancient superstitions common to the day become suddenly real, hold a threat of real menace. Now we're a little afraid of what else the day will visit upon us if we're required to go out on a mission.

We sat soberly at breakfast, talking in low voices . . . bitter, discouraged voices. We were convinced that one of the immediate effects of the President's death would be a redoubled resistance by the Germans, a last effort to win a negotiated peace while a grief-stricken America wrestled with confusion and disorganization. As for the peace table—a peace table with an empty chair to mark the place of the one man who could command any situation, resolve any disagreement—we could not bear to think of it.

This is Black Friday for the world.

CHAPTER THIRTEEN

"Where the hell are the canaries?"

April 14.

I write this in a ditch near burning St. Andreasberg. It's nearly midnight, but towers of flame from the burning town have turned night to high noon. The man next to me in the ditch is reading *Stars and Stripes*.

My fears of yesterday were realized—maybe not because Roosevelt had just died, and possibly witches' curses and moldy superstition had nothing to do with it either, but it was that sort of a day. Such a day that when night came, the night of Friday, April 13, I could not sleep. The conditions were right for sleep: I was tired, I had a comfortable bed in a warm room, and I was curled up in my blankets and ready for sleep well before midnight. But I could not sleep. I lay tense and shaking, so precariously balanced on the thin edge of hysteria that the ticking of the kitchen clock was an added and intolerable torment, and I got up and fumbled through the dark room to stop the pendulum with my hands.

First platoon lost seven men on Friday the thirteenth, three killed and four seriously wounded. Geisbach had been worse and more men had died there, but none with such unwarned suddenness.

Yesterday after lunch the captain summoned me to his C.P. We sat at the big table in the dining room and he gave me a map and told me what we had to do. E Company, attempting to take the town of Lohnau, which was three or four miles away, had encountered stiff resistance in the mountains and halted short of the objective. It now fell upon us to go out and take Lohnau, after which we would return to Herzberg.

We started off, the first platoon leading, one squad spearheading the platoon and the remaining two squads deployed on either side of the road. Tanks followed us, and behind them trudged the rest of the company.

A digression now, while I talk of charms and amulets and chewing gum. Men in combat acquire curious superstitions, even those who pride themselves on their incredulity. I was a little ashamed of my own pet charm, but it was no longer private and secret. From a platoon joke it had become a company gag, and whenever we moved out on a push, I'd be sure to hear someone yell, "Hey, Gantter! Got your battle gum?"

I don't know exactly when it started. I wish I could make this account as felicitous as fiction and say it began the first time I saw action, but it didn't. At any rate, early in my combat experience I learned the value of gum. When there was no food, or when there was food but no time to eat it, gum helped to dull the edge of hunger. And of thirst, too: combat was thirsty work, and you always ran out of water at a time when it was impossible to refill your canteen. Not a gum chewer in civilian life, I soon learned to provide myself with a cud every time we moved out.

As time went on, the habit took on a new significance. Probably it started only as a subconscious anxiety to protect myself against possible hunger and thirst, but as the months rolled by and I passed undamaged through scrape after scrape and saw my friends knocked off or wounded, my "battle gum" began to spell S-A-F-E-T-Y. I did not put my reluctant half belief to the test; I was never willing to go into an engagement *without* the gum to prove my intellectual scorn of superstition. I didn't have nerve enough to take that chance. Murmuring my special private prayer and tucking the gum solidly in the pouch of my cheek, I felt well-guarded and safe, armored against mischief. If I exhausted my own supply of gum, I borrowed, begged, or chiseled from anyone who could supply me. That's how my secret became common property: in a burst of gratitude I once confessed my private shame to the man who had just answered my cry for gum. And so it got around: "Hey, Gantter! Got your battle gum?"

As we left Herzberg I automatically explored my pockets, and then remembered that I had exhausted my gum supply two days ago. I asked Joe if he had any gum. "Nope." I asked Evans. "Nope." I asked Dettman. "Nope." Feeling the first shiver of panic, I asked everyone near me. "No gum!" was the answer. I told the man behind me to pass the word back, inquiring if *anyone* had any gum. The word went back . . . back . . . back . . . through the platoon and to the platoons following. Glancing anxiously over my shoulder from time to time, at last I saw a small something being passed up the line from hand to hand, and each man grinned and murmured a few words as he leaned toward the man ahead. When the gum reached the man behind me, he handed it to me with a mock courtly bow, saying, "Sergeant Gantter's battle gum . . . with the compliments of the third platoon!" I felt a little foolish, but I felt good, too. I had the gum and I was ready for the valley ahead. Spearmint never tasted so good. But I think my near miss on the battle gum was a bad omen for the day—it encouraged Loki and the evil gods to try new devices against us.

Herzberg was hardly a thousand yards behind us when we walked into an ambush. It was a little bitch of a spot in which to be caught: we were in a defile and the Germans were well-concealed on the hills around us. The next half hour was pretty bad. The Jerries had opened up as the platoon emerged from a little grove, and the men out in front were pinned down, unable to move forward and unable to crawl back to the shelter of the trees. Three hundred yards away, three hundred yards of open ground, was a thickly wooded hill. It was well-sprinkled with Germans, but we had no choice: we had to move forward, had to keep going.

Once again our tanks failed us. They hung back, made suddenly timid by the lone German bazooka shell that landed fifty feet from the lead tank. After some urging, however, the tanks were persuaded to come close enough to spray the hills with machine-gun bullets. Under cover of that fire, a blessed umbrella, we crawled forward until we crouched on the very fringe of the grove—that is, all except those who lay in the clearing ahead, their motionless bodies pressed flat against the ground. But the tanks would not keep pace with us. I'd order them up, and they'd move a grudging fifteen feet and stop.

I was scared. I knew we had to move out; the entire company was stalled behind us and Lohnau still lay ahead. As lead platoon, we had to get the hell out of there and in a forward direction.

On the left of the road was a shallow ditch, a fold in the ground that reached nearly to the foot of the hill ahead. Maybe that would do it . . . maybe. So we set out, crawling on our bellies in the shallow ditch and knowing that the Germans could see us, that portions of our anatomy were exposed. The top of my helmet protruded, and I knew it, and my tail was a quivering target, and I knew that, but I couldn't get either of them an inch lower and still be able to move at all. I saw other men get hit, saw them wince and stop moving . . . the wounded calling to me, calling for the medic . . . Charist, my first squad-leader, shuddering as the bullet struck him and I had to crawl past, rubbing against his body, and I gripped his shoulder as I went by and tried to tell him that the medics would be there soon, and he looked at me with wide, blank eyes, the sweat already standing in huge drops on his white face.

Huddled on the other side of the road was most of the second squad, under the leadership of a man named F. I'd named him squad leader only a few days earlier on the strength of his two and a half years' service in the Pacific Theater. (The Lohnau business proved that appointment to be a mistake, and I remedied it the next day.) F. and his men were safe from the raking hill fire because the meadow in which they lay was several feet lower than the road bed. From my position I could not see F., but I knew he was there and I called to him to "move ahead, get your men moving up!" His answer was, "I can't!" No matter how I yelled, that was his only answer. "I can't." And he didn't.

What was left of the first squad finally reached the shelter of the woods, and we kept going. Some of the Jerries on the hill had been knocked out; the others fled as we advanced. We crossed to the other side of the road after a while and waited for the third squad to catch up with us. The second squad, which was supposed to be out in front of the first and third, meekly brought up the rear.

We kept moving. I expected the tanks and the rest of the company to follow closely, but it was soon apparent we'd moved too fast. We were so far out in front that we'd lost contact with the company. I told the "300" man to contact the captain and inform him we'd lost physical contact with the company but were going to keep moving anyway. (A platoon runner is also the platoon's radioman, carrying a sort of "walkie-talkie," a small set we call a "536." The 536 has a limited range, and we'd long since outstretched the distance it could reach. However, on operations where units might tend to be widely separated, an extra radioman, carrying a larger set, called a "300," is attached to the forward elements. We had a 300 man from Headquarters Company with us, and when the 536 failed to reach the captain, I turned the job over to the 300.)

We followed the road, wading the icy mountain stream that bent and twisted across our path. Once we passed two dead doggies, lying at the side of the road, and I was struck anew by the ivory pallor of the recent dead. Their presence on this lonely road surprised me because I thought we were the first American troops to enter this sector, but I later learned that they'd been in a jeep that went on reconnaissance the day before and was ambushed. There was no sign of the jeep.

During a cigarette halt by the side of the stream, we spied a German soldier striding jauntily down the road toward us, and we crouched deep in the weeds to wait for him. He was badly shaken when we jumped up, surrounding him, and he babbled freely. He said there were no German soldiers remaining in Lohnau, but he sounded a little glib, a little insistent. He did "protest too much." I relieved him of a fine pistol and sent him to the rear under guard.

When the first buildings of Lohnau were but 150 yards away, I gave the men last-minute instructions and radioed the captain once more to tell him we were moving in. Then we swept upon the town—not quite a Mongol tide, perhaps, but doing our utmost to persuade the townspeople that we were. A brief skirmish or two, a sizable haul of prisoners, and the town was ours—the first platoon's town all the way. Lohnau was solidly in our possession before the rest of the company arrived, and we were intolerably vainglorious. I set up a strong defense post at the forward tip of the village and relaxed.

Presently, one of the guards rushed to me in great excitement to report that a car was approaching the village from the direction of the German lines. Hastily, I reinforced our guard positions, and we waited. Soon we heard it—the laborious chugging of a German civilian automobile. In a moment it came into sight—a miniature sedan, larger than an Austin but a helluva lot smaller than a Ford. We could distinguish three figures in it but could not tell whether they were civilians or enemy soldiers. As the little car drew nearer, we recognized the occupants as soldiers and tensed ourselves for the ambush. Waiting until the split second when the car was directly in front of my C.P., we swarmed from our hiding places and surrounded it. It came to a jerky halt and three astonished German faces stared at us, three faces frozen in—well, hell, forgive me, but it really was "stark consternation." Their surprise was so genuine, we grinned in spite of our best efforts to appear grim and implacable.

Booting them out of the car, we searched them and shooed them down the road toward the company C.P. and the prisoner cage. I climbed happily into the car and drove along behind them, honking the horn loudly and blowing extravagant kisses toward the grinning faces of my friends. I felt hilarious and damned cocky. The officers at the C.P. were adequately impressed by our prizes, but my personal triumph was short-lived—I was refused permission to drive the civilian car back to Herzberg because it was "against army orders." Later in the day I was to taste the bitterness of seeing one of our officers driving *my* car—back to Herzberg, naturally!

It was that kind of a day, all day. The battle gum, the ambush, the simpering timidity of our tanks when we needed them. The sourness of my regard for that tank outfit was not sweetened by their behavior after the danger was over. Long after Lohnau had fallen, the tanks rolled in with a roar of triumph, and we watched the tankers tear the town apart in search of loot. To hear their shouts and howls as they raced through the streets, it would seem that this was Rome and they were the Visigoths. They roistered and looted while we stood at dreary guard posts; then, clutching bottles of wine, they climbed into their tanks and returned to Herzberg. Watching the drift of dust that marked their passage, we bitterly concluded that they couldn't—or wouldn't—fight their way out of a paper bag, but they sure as hell were acting a tough war.

Late in the afternoon, E Company arrived to take over Lohnau, and we returned to Herzberg. And that night I couldn't sleep, couldn't unreel the piano-string tension of muscle and nerve, couldn't forget the seven men who had fallen that afternoon.

A footnote on the Lohnau casualties: one of them was a man named Allen. Not Leo Allen, the man from Watertown, New York—Leo was not a runner attached to company headquarters. *This* Allen was from North Carolina, a snuff-chewing southerner. North Carolina Allen was missing when we reached Lohnau and someone told me he'd been killed. Several weeks later Watertown Allen told me that *he* had been reported missing in action, and his wife so notified by the War Department. Fortunately for her peace of mind, on the day the official notice reached her, she also received a letter from Leo, a letter written on a date *later* than the one mentioned in the War Department telegram. The hope that there had been an official mistake sustained her through some very trying hours, and presently the War Department notified her that through a regrettable error it seemed that her husband was not dead after all.

But the real denouement to this story didn't come until nearly a month later, some hundreds of miles from Lohnau. We were in a mountain town where I had acquired a pleasant little house for my C.P. Planning on a bath, I dragged an ancient copper bathtub from the cellar, filled it with pails of warm water heated on the stove, and popped myself in. As I soaped myself in a luxury of comfort there was a knock on the door and I yelled, "Come in!"

The door swung silently open to reveal a specter, the sight of which turned my steaming bath to a glacial pool. The grinning face at the threshold belonged to a man who was supposed to be dead and buried and food for German worms. Without further greeting he plunged at once into the matter that seemed most urgent to him: "What squad am I in, sir? Where do I report?" It was North Carolina Allen, and the flesh on his bones looked healthy.

Through suddenly nervous teeth I quavered, "How come? Why aren't you dead?"

His story added the last ironic twist to the tangled tale of the two Allens. North Carolina Allen had been wounded in the valley of Lohnau, a head wound that looked nasty but wasn't. When Watertown Allen was discovered alive and unhurt after having been reported missing in action, it was decided that by hell *someone* named Allen was missing or dead and no one knew the whereabouts of North Carolina Allen so it must be he. North Carolina regained consciousness in a rear area hospital and learned that he'd looked so dead on the field that he was now officially listed as KIA; killed in action. It had taken him nearly a month to convince assorted clerks and brass hats that the paper reports were wrong and the flesh was right, and when could he go back to his outfit?

Every day, Captain Wirt reveals another facet of his character that enlarges my respect for him. The Richard Rodgers song "Blue Moon" is his favorite tune, a choice that I, perforce, salute.

The first platoon of G Company has acquired a reputation.

(Since this is a highly personal document, vanity has a rightful place in it.) We have so frequently spearheaded hazardous operations that when we do *not* lead off, there's a ribald comment from the rest of the company: "Whaddya doin' back *here*? The war over?... Must be nothin' but a coupla dead cows in front of us today.... Hey, get out in front! Ya layin' down on us?... Whatsa matter, ya nervous in the service? Crackin' up from shackin' up?"

We puff ourselves on this rough tribute, and maybe our stride gets a little too cocky, but it's a good thing to look at the men of the first platoon and see the confidence on their faces, the unhurried, easy sureness of their movements. It's a good thing to see.

Another and less comfortable reflection: the civilians inform us that the 1st Division is called the "American SS." They say it's because we are like the true SS—the same savagery in combat, the same rapacity in looting!

Before dawn on April 14 we were in trucks and on the road to a place called Sieber. By noon Sieber was far behind us and we were high in the Harz Mountains, en route to St. Andreasberg. Our course was cross-country and through the mountains, up slopes so sheer that we had to pull ourselves up, bleeding fingers clawing desperately for the frail security of tree roots and outcroppings of rock. The thick cushion of pine needles underfoot made a treachery of the most tentative movement, and once a man started to slide, he was fortunate indeed if he could bring himself to a halt before skidding to the bottom, let alone knocking a dozen others into the gully below.

The roughest lot fell to the men of the weapons platoon, toting their heavy burdens of machine guns and mortars. The bazooka men in the rifle platoons were hard-pressed, too. I watched one of them, a thirty-eight-year-old Texan in my platoon, as he fought upward to reach a brief shelf of rock. When he gained it, he fell on his face and could not get up again, his body shuddering with convulsive sobs. After a moment he turned over and lay on his back for several minutes, his face the color of old cheese and the sweat standing on it in thick, greasy drops. When the sobs that racked his body had subsided, he grinned painfully at me and said, "Guess I'm not as young as I thought I was." But he would not permit me to take the bazooka from him or assign it to a younger man. He just kept going. And he got there. When I watched him take off again, moving only because he would not permit himself to quit, and when I looked at little Albert, 114 pounds of skinny persistence, staggering under the load of a full BAR belt and a sack of grenades, I wondered bitterly how many people at home were still bitching about cigarette shortages, gas rationing, cuffless trousers, and the high cost of living.

At the top of each mountain, we were rewarded with a brief moment of rest, a pause that lasted just long enough for our hot, sweat-drenched clothing to cool, turning to icy shrouds. When the last murmur of conversation and commiseration had died in humorless misery, and chattering teeth made the only sound, we'd shove off again. A slipping, sliding, daredevil descent, a stream of ice water to ford when we reached the bottom, and lo! Before us another mountain to climb!

We ran a gauntlet of sniper fire in one mountain pass. And in the heart of the mountains we stumbled smack into a horse-drawn convoy and an entire company of Germans, eager to surrender, almost as though they'd been waiting for us. They were smiling and cheerful, happy to throw down their arms and march off to prison camp. Having no stockade for captive horses, we turned the animals loose to forage for themselves in the forest. There were scores of them, from fine saddle horses to heavily muscled Percherons. The convoy yielded an impressive quantity of loot, but I ended up disconsolately juggling two cans of meat, a loaf of bread, and a leather map case, while all around me happy doggies exclaimed over their new German pistols. (It isn't that I don't *try*—it's just that I get there too late, or I look in the wrong places.)

It was nearly midnight when we reached St. Andreasberg. We were hungry, having had no food all day except what we'd taken from the convoy. And the night was cold. For several hours we lay in the ditches and on damp ground on the outskirts of town, hungry, cold, and aching with fatigue, but hypnotized by the spectacle of the burning buildings. St. Andreasberg was burning to the ground, and the night was so bright that I could record my impressions on the spot. When at last we moved upon the town, it was in a grimly bizarre processional. Hooded, armed figures, we walked a blazing gauntlet along the cobbled streets, the houses on either hand so wildly burning that our hair singed and men instinctively shielded their ammunition from the intense heat. At an intersection where the buildings on all four corners were ablaze, we crouched low under an arch of flames and ran, to plunge knee-deep through the torrent of icy water gushing from a broken main. A town burning to the ground, and water wasting between our feet! We watched the old houses dissolve, watched roofs crumble in showers of sparks, and exclaimed over the lacy skeletons of blazing rafters. Standing as near a burning building as safety permitted, we watched St. Andreasberg disappear and felt the warmth on our backs and faces and liked it. And the civilians . . . the children, the stubborn women, the home-loyal old men who would have fled to the cellars when the shells started dropping on St. Andreasberg—how many were now imprisoned in these cellars, watching with unbelieving eyes the slow puffing and crisping of their own flesh, strangling in this evil smoke . . . perhaps (the last bitter irony!) drowning in the water that filled these streets and lapped at the low sills of steel-barred cellar windows. . . . Who is that, beating with bloody fists against a door that will not open?

These were questions to push away, to refuse. So we forced our minds blank and stood near the flames, thinking only of how good it was to feel the warmth.

The first platoon took over four houses, and by one A.M., April 15, the last squad was settled and I was back in my C.P. I'd barely made myself comfortable near the stove when a runner appeared. "Report to the captain at the C.P." I groaned and put my shoes back on.

The captain grinned apologetically at me and said, "Sergeant, if you had one guess as to why I sent for you, what would it be?"

Twisting my tired face into a phony smile, I replied, "Well, sir, the possibilities are limitless, but I'll damn well bet it's something unpleasant!" I thought my answer was pretty cute. I remember it because I was tired enough at the time to feel a little smug over what seemed to me some pretty sharp repartee.

The captain must have been tired, too, because he yocked appreciatively. Then, sobering, he said, "I'm afraid you're right," and he went on to say he'd just received new orders from Battalion to extend the company lines beyond the original plan, and the first platoon had been selected for the job.

So we packed up and wearily moved another three thousand yards to a tiny village. I stationed one squad in a small hospital, which was staffed by kindly nuns and filled with sick and homeless civilians. I sent another squad on a reconnaissance patrol, and the third I assigned to an outpost in a nearby farmhouse. Then I selected a C.P., a good one, and by then it was four-thirty A.M. I stretched gratefully on the floor and slept for two hours. The kitchen was nearly warm.

The women in the house I chose for a C.P. were a good cross section of the civilians we encountered as we moved deeper into Germany. They were, respectively: an elderly widow who owned the house, and two refugees from Cologne—another widow and her fourteen-year-old son—who rented a portion of the second floor. They shrank from us in shivering terror when we entered the house. (They had timorously unlocked the door, but not until we'd become disgusted by the lack of response to our polite knocking for admittance and begun to smash the door open.) When I said simply that all we wanted was a couple of rooms where the men could sleep and get warm, the women looked at me in a fearful wonder and said uncertainly, "Nicht . . . ?" and drew their forefingers suggestively across their throats. Incredulous at first, I stammered, "You thought . . . ?" and drew my forefinger across my own throat, slowly. They nodded dumbly, their eyes pleading, still not trusting, not quite daring to believe. And when I said in violent, sick rage that we had no war with *frauen und kinder* and that our concern was with *soldaten* only, they burst into the most torrential weeping I'd ever seen. It was an intolerably painful moment. One of the women, crying so hard she could not see, kept stroking my dirty, stubble-covered cheek timidly and sobbing, *"Du bist ein gut mann . . . gut mann!"* When they learned that we were American—at first they supposed us to be British—there was a brief resurgence of their fear. They asked, tremulously, if many *"schwarz soldaten"* had come with us. And again the forefinger drawn suggestively across the naked throat.

What had they been told about us? What did they expect? We were angry and disturbed to discover that the Germans, these "beasts, sadists, and monsters," believed with equal assurance that *we* were "beasts, sadists, and monsters." What was going on here?

I was awakened at dawn by one of the women stumbling over my feet as she entered the kitchen to start breakfast. She brewed a pot of tasteless ersatz coffee and invited me to join her. Over our coffee cups I mentioned that my father was German-born, and I added casually that I'd been a tourist in Germany in 1932 and visited relatives in Baden-Baden. I watched her face stretch with amazement, her glance drop to my uniform and the wonder in her eyes change to horror, and at last only sadness remained, a comprehension old as time . . . the eyes of Eve when she looked at Cain. She shook her head slowly from side to side and said no more. We finished our coffee in silence.

An observation plane is called an "Oscar." No one seems to know why. And the German observation plane that buzzes our lines regularly each night is hailed, for obvious reasons, as "Bed-Check Charlie."

One of the new men in the platoon is an Italian-born American named Adorno. He's lived in America only six years. Somewhere in Italy there is a Mrs. Adorno, but he seems not greatly interested in her whereabouts or welfare. He's a pleasant guy, but it's not the beauty of his soul that has won him the affection of the platoon—it's the mayhem he commits daily on the English language. He assaults the problem of communication with the fierce intensity and bumbling ineffectiveness of a puppy attacking a rubber bone.

A few days ago our chow wagons arrived to set up their stand in a town that had become ours only after a reasonably stiff fight. The muddy water in the cobbled gutters was still tinged with red, and the bodies of dead Germans lay in the street. A few yards from the chow truck a dead German sprawled in a small pool of thickening blood, his face hidden under the overcoat thrown carelessly over him. Limp and curiously flattened, the legs protruded from the shapeless huddle, the heavy shoes turned out and lying flat against the stones. The narrow street was choked with debris, and men returning with their chow had to step over the dead man. I saw Adorno turn away from the head of the line, his mess tin piled high with food. As he approached the dead body, he looked down and accepted the corpse without surprise. Then, pausing for a moment, he considered gravely, and at last, beaming with pride, uttered one word in tones of satisfaction and finality: "Snafu!" And walked on, ignoring the laughter of the men who had observed the scene.

April 15.

We resumed our trek through the Harz Mountains. More gut-straining labor, more sweating, more wet feet. And where the hell were the canaries?

We spent the night on the summit of a singularly inhospitable mountain, but not by choice. We'd just reached the top, a bleak, windswept space of rough boulders and scrubby ground pine, when a shower of mortar shells rained down upon us. From the neighboring mountains the Jerries zeroed us in, and they were engaged in a vigorous game of pitch-toss. We scrambled for shelter, and when things had quieted down a bit, we discovered: (a) German tanks were standing grim guard over two of the three roads that girdled the base of the mountain; (b) German troops were throwing heavy roadblocks across the one road that offered a possibility of escape from our predicament; (c) on the hills around us the Germans were clearly visible, thick as fleas in summer. We seemed to be surrounded, and the question was: Would they rush us? Would they assault, try to clean us out? We tarried not for a possible answer but made feverish haste to dig in.

On the very rim of the table-flat mountaintop we set up a defense line. Far below us the German tanks waited, motionless as toys that had run down, and we could see the enemy troops at work on the roadblocks, hear their voices and the sound of their axes.

Digging in was no fun. Underneath the thin skin of leaf mold and pine needles, the damn mountain was solid rock. Evans, Joe, and I scratched away for several hours, giving up when we struck what seemed to be bedrock. At its deepest point our hole was less than three feet deep, no security at all against mortar bursts. We puttered endlessly, building a towering and shaky wall of rock and sod on the side of the hole facing the enemy, padding the lumpy interior of the hole with pine branches and long grass. What the hell, we didn't have anything else to do ... just keep an eye on the Jerries and make ourselves as comfortable as the situation allowed. It didn't allow much comfort—we'd been traveling light because we were traveling fast, and none of us had blankets, overcoats, or warm clothing. Or rations. Further, the mountain winds were knife-edged and we dared not build a fire. We wrapped our featherweight ponchos tightly around us and grimly sat through the night.

Unaccountably, the Germans pulled out during the night, and we started off again shortly after dawn. Our objective was a road junction in the heart of the forest, called simply Point 69. Before we reached it, we ran into a vicious but short-lived firefight. At Point 69 we dug in, taking positions that would secure the road junction against attack from any quarter.

Late in the afternoon of April 16 our bedrolls were delivered to us and the chow truck arrived. The night was quiet—only a sullen sputtering of fire on the flanks, a few prisoners taken, and the familiar tension of guard duty in a forest. Trees at night are fearful things. We slept warm and with our bellies full at last.

April 17.

Our prize capture today was a German field hospital. Escorted by American guards, the Germans came through our positions in a horse-drawn convoy. Every conceivable type of unmotored rolling stock was represented in the grotesque caravan: crude farm wagons, buggies, landaus, Victorias, covered wagons that evoked nostalgic memories of the early De Mille movies, horse-drawn trucks and buses—even pony carts and wicker pony baskets! The commanding general, elegant in fitted overcoat and monocle, sat erect in a gleaming landau, his aide-de-camp at his side. Behind the carriage trotted the general's saddle horse, the reins held loosely by the aide-de-camp. A captured general was always good camera bait, but it was the sight of the horse that made me race for my camera. She was a thing of such quick and vibrant beauty that my throat ached with helpless love at first glance. A bay mare with the small head, the dainty feet, of Arabian blood, she moved like a princess, like a flame quivering in that dark wood. And a kind of sigh went through the silent, watching men when she disappeared down the muddy road.

I was ordered to move my platoon—the rest of the company sat tight—to new positions four miles away, a railroad station in the forest at a place where three dirt roads converged upon the railroad. A sizable enemy unit had recently been encamped in that corner of the woods, perhaps the very hospital outfit we'd so recently observed. The bivouac area was a litter of miscellaneous equipment: discarded clothing, ammunition, personal belongings, and an impressive scattering of German contraceptives. We examined the latter with great scientific interest, and I pocketed several for the curious examination of my friends at home. Since the U.S. government with an almost morbid persistence continued to press familiar-name American contraceptives upon us in embarrassing profusion—we accepted this tribute to our prowess with pleased smirks, but made frequent, bitter comment on the plenitude of means and the dearth of opportunity!—we were curious to discover how Germany cared for *her* warriors. The German products were of reprocessed or "ersatz" rubber, a discreet pinkish-brown in color. While ready to concede the aesthetic advantages of the color, we were frankly dubious about the functional efficiency of the German product. Just another thing to make us glad we'd been born Americans. (Incidentally, so far as I know, German troops were not issued anything comparable to our "Pro-Kit," a handy little gadget that was a minor miracle of planning and packaging. Evidently, the German High Command took the position that "protection before" was the end of official responsibility: "protection after" was the man's private headache.)

If I seem to refer to the subject of sex too frequently, remember that it gave army life, war life, a peculiar quality. There was either too much of it or too little—rarely was it held in simple balance, accepted and unquestioned, as in normal civilian life.

I have sometimes thought that the one real flaw in the reporting of the many fine war correspondents was a sin of omission and that was prescribed and obligatory, a stricture imposed on them by the nature of their media, press and radio. Felicitous and sensitive as their reporting was, it was meant for the family trade, and thus incomplete because it was so chastely reticent. It was good because you *can* write of war in terms of guns and tanks and planes and battles; it was bad because you cannot write of war in terms of men without also discussing sex and what its absence or abuse did.

Having satisfied our junkman's interest in the rubble at the crossroads, we examined our position. Dense forest surrounded us on all sides, but behind the station house a narrow road disappeared in the green depths of a gorge. Assigning two squads to positions near the station house, I sent the third into the gorge. When we discovered several bicycles hidden in the ferny undergrowth, life became at once very gay. It seemed suddenly necessary to make frequent inspection trips to the squad in the gorge—it was a helluva long walk back up the hill, but the ride down was filled with a thrilling uncertainty. Hairpin curves, sudden dips and twists, and a final exciting hazard at the bottom—a wickedly sharp curve and the challenge to essay it at full speed. If you missed, you were rewarded with a cold bath in the black pond that lipped the outer perimeter of the road. Twice I got my feet wet but was spared the full bath. However, two of the men, unblessed by a childhood lived on the saddle of a bicycle, spilled ass over teakettle into the pond and had to be spooned out.

Late in the afternoon we were relieved and taken to the town of Hohegeiss for the night. We were billeted in houses, we were fed, we slept in warmth. The infantry asks no more of heaven.

April 18.

Up early and setting out on another leg of our forced march through the Harz Mountains. The mountains were easier here, but not for me. I was sick, and I felt like hell.

We moved along at a good clip, but soon came upon evidence of recent enemy troops and slowed down, became more wary. As the scouts rounded a curve in the road, I saw them pause, their bodies rigid with surprise, then they turned and raced back to us. Going forward to verify their excited report, I was dumbfounded by the most massive, most skilfully devised roadblock we had yet encountered. On the left was a precipitous hillside, on the right a deep mountain stream, and on the road curving between these two natural obstacles the Germans had topped thirty-two trees, each one a giant, and so cunningly felled that they interlaced in a network that seemed impenetrable. Since they were too heavy to be pushed from the road, the trees would have to be cut into manageable lengths, one at a time—a slow, time-consuming business. If we climbed over the trees and moved ahead, leaving our armor behind, there was the double hazard of an ambush prepared for us beyond the roadblock, or a sudden attack on our undefended tanks and tank destroyers, immobile and helpless because they'd jammed the road and could neither go forward nor turn back.

The enemy resolved our quandary by opening fire on us from the hill. It was hot for a few minutes. Then, while the third platoon drew the Germans' interest, my platoon slipped quietly down the valley under the cover of trees more friendly than those in the road and made a flanking assault on the German-held hill. Score: three dead Germans, one prisoner. The others fled through the woods and escaped.

Everyone pitched in on the road-clearing job, and it didn't take as long as we'd feared. We reached our objective, the village of Rothehutte, at nine P.M. The town made little fuss and we cleared it easily and quickly. The lucky ones who weren't assigned to guard duty were in bed by eleven, including me.

April 19.

Up early and on the move, this time riding the tanks and T.D.'s, we careened into Rübeland, a lovely and picturesque town that lies deeply cupped in a fold of the mountains. Two glacial boulders, each as large as a small cottage, guarded the entry into the village, and on one of the boulders stood the upright figure of a bear, the symbol and seal of the mountain town.

A river bisects Rübeland—a real river, not an adolescent brook. In two places it was nearly choked by the automobiles, army and civilian, that the retreating Germans pushed into the water to keep them from our hands. A futile bit of tongue-sticking. We were lousy with vehicles—what did we want with charcoal burners?

War hadn't scarred Rübeland, and the houses looked clean and comfortable. I drew two decent houses for the platoon and then settled down in my own with a groan of comfort. The air was clean and sweet and scented with pine. I had a warm house, a good bed, and I could hear the sleepy gossiping of chickens behind the house. I resolved that I would have fresh eggs for breakfast or, b'gosh, I'd have chicken for dinner!

April 20.

After breakfast we started on a long jaunt to sweep the neighboring woods for stray Germans. The second platoon in position at the roadblock, the first and third did the woods-sweeping, each taking a different route.

Notwithstanding the job, there was a gaiety to the expedition, a picnic atmosphere. We were like summer campers on a hike. It was a wonderful day—fresh and clean and full of spring, and the sun came out. We moved through the woods, aware of violets and edelweiss, the glimmer of tiny white star flowers, the green shimmer of new moss. Mountain streams, choked with April, murmured drunkenly between spongy banks and offered icy sweetness for the courtesy of a bended knee. Once, hearing a cry from a scout and looking in sudden stiff alarm where he pointed, we saw—not the enemy, not gray-green uniforms and scowling machine guns—nine deer on a mountainside, staring at us in wonder. In an instant every sportsman in the platoon had his rifle to his shoulder, and I shouted a hasty "No shooting!" I made lame excuses as the rifles were reluctantly lowered: "We don't want to scare off every Jerry within hearing," and, "Sure I'd like some venison, too, but howthehell ya gonna get it back to town, on your back?" And all the time I knew that the real reason for my order was something else: it seemed wrong, somehow, to kill these deer only for the sake of killing. It was spring and they were quick and alive and there had been so much killing. It seemed wrong in a way I could not explain to myself to use these rifles, so frequently employed for the killing of men, against these gentler beasts. Kill men? Yes. Hunt deer? No.

I apologize to all sportsmen.

We came home with a bag of seven wretched prisoners, deserters from the collapsing Wehrmacht. Most of them were young and tearful. For many days they'd been creeping through the woods and mountains of central Germany, trying to reach their home villages before the debacle of final surrender. One of them had only seven more miles to go when we captured him. Seven miles from his wife and children. He hadn't seen them in three years. And we had to seize him thus rudely at the very threshold of his particular paradise and send him off to a prison camp. I wonder how many more months will pass before he finally reaches home. And what manner of greeting he will receive.

At dusk we were sent out to relieve the second platoon at the roadblock. We spent a quiet but chilly night in the woods, picked up three prisoners, and returned to Rübeland the following morning.

April 23.

The past two days have been placid. I've eaten well, slept well, written a lot of letters, and read two books. Yesterday I saw a movie, and the night before last I had a hot bath in a wooden laundry tub.

The war is far removed from Rübeland. Each afternoon the German girls appear, usually in couples, and stroll slowly through the town, twitching their rumps provocatively when they pass a group of soldiers. Giggling and whispering, they loiter on the bridges that span the river and spend long hours leaning on the iron rail in studious inspection of the swirling brown water they've known all their lives. They pretend a careless unconcern for the men who pause hopefully, but it's obvious they're not unmindful of the nudging of American elbows, the hinting pressure of American thighs and buttocks.

It is difficult to imagine the thunder of battle now taking place in Berlin and Leipzig. Here in this remote village the war is tapering off, a phonograph that's winding down and the record not yet played out. Rumors are thick: "The Russians are in Berlin" ... "The First Army is through fighting" ... "We're going to be pulled back for a long rest."

If peace came now, I think there would be little hilarity here. At this moment an announcement of peace would seem a feeble anticlimax, a third act "curtain" after the audience had fallen asleep.

Rumors, hopes, prophecies too warm for belief—all I *know*, all I am certain of, is my own sick heart. Let it be the end, let it be now! Let us go home!

From a letter, written April 23:

Thanks for the summary of that recent magazine article concerning the attitude of German civilians. You ask if the article seems accurate, if its claims stack up with my own observations. My answer is yes, for the most part. Joy *is* the first reaction of the civilians, wild and hysterical joy because our coming means there will be no more bombs, nor more shells. That is reason enough for celebration and we don't despise them for it. Today Dettman bandaged the hip and thigh of a six-year-old girl who had been injured by flying masonry. From hip to ankle her leg was a single livid bruise, and high on her thigh was an ugly open wound. Although Dettman's hands were gentle, the child wept bitterly, a bowel-twisting misery of sound, and we hated ourselves and could not talk after she had gone.

I cannot tell how much of the anti-Nazi talk is truly sincere and how much a matter of simple expediency. I think that there has been a large-scale reversal of feeling toward the Nazi hierarchy of late, and many civilians seem honest in their protestations of repugnance. But—and this is the clincher!—if the Nazi chieftains are now tribal outcasts, it is only because they continue to hold Germany to the waging of a war already lost. I have heard no one speak out against the ideology of National Socialism; I have met no one who reflects an intellectual rebirth, no one whose eyes admittedly see Nazism for the thing it is. Whatever this revulsion of feeling, it springs from the sensible reluctance of the German people to suffer further hardships for the sake of a war already conceded.

Even those who profess the most intense hate for the Nazis are uncomfortably aware that our eyes have taken note of the cleft stick in which they wriggle. Everyone in Germany has a husband, a son, a brother, or some other male connection in the army, possibly still fighting. And so they dissemble. And, with the exception of the children (who succumb to gum and candy) and frauleins (who succumb to soap, chocolate, cigarettes, and healthy male flesh), they do not like us. Why, indeed, should they? We are devastation. Where we have passed, little remains—no cameras, no pistols, no watches, very little jewelry, and damn few virgins. We leave behind us a spoor of broken dishes, emptied fruit jars, and plundered, dirty houses. And our general attitude (which I am inclined to share) is: So you wanted total war? You believed in it, boasted of it? Well, this is it!

CHAPTER FOURTEEN

"I want to go home . . . I want to go home . . ."

April 24.

We are in Beyernaumburg, sixty miles from Rübeland, near the Czech border. The house in which I have my C.P. is a very small, very poor affair consisting of a kitchen and a bedroom. That's all. The bathroom is a one-holer on the far side of the courtyard. We share the house with five civilians: a young woman, her three sons, aged from three to six, and a middle-aged aunt who is a refugee from Breslau.

The situation here is damn uncomfortable and I'm not happy. We live better when we capture a town and just grab a house that looks good. When a town has been secured before we move into it, as this one was, that ol' army SOP takes over and everything is done according to a system. And no one is happy.

The advance detail that preceded us into Beyernaumburg was required to examine the houses, divvy up the town, and guide each arriving unit to the sector assigned to it. G Company drew the poorest portion, a sector in which all the houses are small and wretched, many of them damaged by shells, and every building overflowing with civilians.

To add a new woe, the current nonfraternization policy, as defined by Division Order, prohibits German civilians and GIs from sharing the same building. If the army wants a certain house, the inhabitants must leave. The civilians were still in possession of their homes when we arrived in Beyernaumburg, and it became our painful duty to evict them, a task that should have been handled by the advance detail. It's a brutal business, a misery of tears and desperate pleading. For me the job is always double pain because my German, though crude—and mostly sign language anyway—is still the best in the platoon, and I'm forced to do the dirty work for each squad. When the civilians pathetically assure me that they will be no bother to us, my fumbling German is not equal to the task of explaining why their promises can make no difference and they must go in any case. (Yeah, I know: "You don't explain, Sergeant, you just order!")

It was like that today—tears and more tears, particularly in the house next door. Besieged by the sobs of its inhabitants, I pleaded with the captain and finally won his permission to let the civilians stay—*if* there was room and *if* they didn't crowd us. To the three civilians already living there, I added the five from my own house—making a total of eight people who were to sleep in one room!—told them they could use our kitchen for cooking, and settled back with a sigh of relief. But it remains an uncomfortable situation, and I don't like it. A minor irritation is their serene assumption that I understand their language perfectly, even though I speak it with something less than the purity of Schiller. They pound me with questions and will not cease fire. I have no peace. And the men in the platoon—who stoutly refuse to learn a word of "this bitchin' language"—delight in making remarks to the civilians in English, knowing I will be asked to interpret, and I *can't* explain, and—like Br'er Rabbit and the Tar Baby—the harder I struggle, the more I am held.

For example, today we carried our full mess kits from the chow line, planning to eat in comfort in our house. As we finished eating, the mother of the three boys put their lunch on the table. It was boiled rice. Just that, boiled rice, flavored with a few grains of beet sugar and a dash of cinnamon. The kids toyed disinterestedly with their food: their appetites had been blunted by tidbits from our own lavish meal, plus the candy with which we'd been stuffing them all morning. As their elderly aunt salvaged the scarcely touched plates, Dettman, knowing damn well that she wouldn't understand, said that the kids had eaten too much candy to have any appetite for lunch. Inquiringly she turned to me, and in sign language and bad German I tried to say that "their eyes were bigger than their appetites." Pointing to the kids, I rolled my eyes dramatically, patted my stomach, and made what I thought were appropriate German sounds. To my dismay, the old lady's eyes filled with tears and a look of mortal hurt came over her face. Five painful minutes later I understood from her sobbed remarks that it wasn't nice of me to criticize her niece for having three children! And their father a soldier, too!

While Dettman and Joe rolled on the floor in heartless laughter, I squirmed in this morass of misunderstanding, getting in deeper and deeper. For fifteen minutes I sweated and stammered, with the old lady getting angrier and bolder, sputtering at me like a wet firecracker. I doubt that she ever understood my original statement, but I finally made it clear that I was *not* suggesting that her beloved nephew ought to cut it off!

Amusing, huh? But maddening, too. They won't let me alone. I can have no rest, no peace, no place of retreat. Even when I sit down to write a letter, someone is sure to burst in and pelt me with idiomatic German.

Incidentally, the citizens of Beyernaumburg were horror-struck to learn that the Russians are in Berlin. They had been hoping the Americans would capture it and thus save it from being a Russian prize.

From a letter home, written April 25:

Do you remember the letter in which I commented gloomily on the unexploded shells, the forgotten land mines that lie scattered over this doomed continent or hide half buried in the earth? I made morbid prediction of kids not yet born who would be maimed by the explosion of rusty grenades long after the men who threw them had died of old age, farmers whose plows would stir sleeping mines from a long nap. Today we saw the first bitter coming-to-pass of that prediction. I was writing a letter in the kitchen when I heard the unmistakable BLAM of an exploding grenade. It sounded very near, and I leaped out the window and raced up the lane behind the house. I didn't have to run far. Two small boys had been playing in the lane near the house. One was about eight years old, the other hardly six. Their toy was an American hand grenade they found somewhere, and one of them had succeeded in pulling the pin. We carried the smaller one away, but he was dying, his head and chest sieved by shrapnel. There was no need to pick up the other child. A quiet village lane spattered with the bright blood of children . . . so much blood from such small bodies.

The village women hung over their fences and moaned as one of the men ran down the hill to the battalion aid station, the bloody body of the dying child in his arms. We threw a blanket over the small huddle in the sticky grass.

We're oppressed by a sense of guilt, but surely we are not to blame? Who *is* to blame? Where does blame start? We tell ourselves that *we* are innocent: war swept through this village long before we arrived, and no matter how painstakingly we police the area, we cannot possibly clean up all the dregs of earlier violence. We say, "Accidents like this are going to happen for years to come, and kids will die like this—in Germany and in France, Belgium, Holland, Luxembourg, Italy, England, Poland, and Russia." But such assurances are small comfort. I turn away, wincing, from the too bright vision of Geoff struggling with the ring of a hand grenade, sleeping death in his hands, and on his face the serious "this is man's work" expression that turns my heart.

I hope we leave here soon. I want to be moving again. The men are restless and so am I. There's too much time, too many free minutes, free hours, and the old litanies start again: "When will it end? When will it end? I want to go home . . . go home . . . April twenty-fifth . . . when will it end I want to go home . . ." A dreary song . . . no cadences, no resolutions—it gets nowhere. Like hillbilly music, banal and nerve-grating. Gray in color . . . muddy gray and dingy brown. No meter changes and only one chord. Endless and eternal and no intermissions.

* * *

Peacetime noises bother me. The familiar accompaniment of shell and bullet being absent from my daily routine, I am disturbed and irritated by the ticking of clocks, the simmering of a teakettle, the chirping of a courageous cricket in the wall, the distant hum of the generator at the company C.P. How will it be when I get home—the sound of cars, voices on the street at night, radios blaring, cats howling, dogs barking? Will it be all right with you (and the neighbors) if, the first few nights I'm home, I get up at two A.M. and do a little target practice in the backyard, light a few giant firecrackers? You don't want me to be homesick, do you?

April 26.

We've begun a rear area training schedule: manual of arms, drilling, instructions in the proper way to salute, and so on. A helluva way to spend the hours, but better than brooding, I guess.

Looks like I'm being put in for a field commission. Today as I worked the platoon on the drill field, Captain Wirt and Major Smith, the battalion executive officer, approached and stood for a moment, watching. Then Captain Wirt came over to me and said the major wanted to talk to me. As we walked toward the senior officer the captain grinned sideways at me and said out of the corner of his mouth, "Put your best foot forward now, Gantter." The first few questions from Major Smith illuminated this puzzling directive, and excitement made me fumble-tongued and awkward. Perhaps I should be scornful of the whole business, mask my pride with the common soldier's traditional contempt for the officer caste, but some fundamental strength is obviously lacking in my character because I am openly puffed up about it, ready to burst my buttons. Snob value? I suppose so. But it's more than that, too. If this commission really happens, the manner of its occurrence will give me courage for the rest of my life in situations where I'll need courage, will stiffen my backbone in the moments when I'm most oppressed by the sense of my own weakness. Because it came this way. I'm glad it came this way. I feel honest about it as I never could had it been the customary diploma from OCS. And there's a special bittersweet satisfaction because my rejection for OCS at Camp Wheeler on the basis of poor eyesight has always rankled. I have a thoroughly sophomoric impulse to return to Camp Wheeler one day, waggle my fingers, and say, "Look, you sonsabitches! So I can't *see* good enough, huh?"

Peace ... peace, Sergeant Gantter—you're still wearing stripes on your sleeve!

April 27.

We left Beyernaumburg in trucks and rode 141 miles to Selb, near the Czech border. We hovered on the outskirts of Selb until the following morning, but my only memory of the city involves a certain Gypsy caravan, three or four gaily painted wagons that stood in the little park opposite the houses where we'd taken refuge from the rain. Several Hungarian Gypsy women were visible, and they eyed us with frank, measuring interest. Two were handsome in a slatternly, bright-colored fashion, and soon they left the wagons and strolled over to the house occupied by some of our officers. They disappeared within the house and that was that. We saw no more of them and that's all I remember about Selb, except that it was big.

April 28.

We crossed the border into Czechoslovakia and walked to Rossenreuth. We are there now. It's raining and cold and miserable, but I have a warm house and am content. My setup is a happy one: the second and third platoons and the company C.P. are in Rossenreuth proper, but my platoon is a thousand yards from them in a tiny village that appears to have no name. I am king of this small domain, consisting of half a dozen farmhouses and their attendant outbuildings. The captain said, "This is your town, Sergeant, and you're the burgomeister. Whatever you say is the law. See that they understand that!" So, by royal edict and in keeping with the prerogatives of my imperial state, I have a fine room in the biggest house, which contains two double beds, a desk, and a magnificent porcelain stove. I have commanded that the room be kept warm at all times, and every time I snap my fingers, an anxious female trots up with another armful of wood, a pail of briquets, or a hat filled with fresh eggs. I'm toying with the idea of restoring the ancient custom of *jus primae noctis*.

We live in a constant delicious tremor of anticipation. Every news report, every rumor, pumps fresh hope into us that it's all over. We've heard that the Italian front has disintegrated, that Mussolini and the beautiful Clara have been executed by Italian partisans, that Hitler is ill, that Berlin is toppling. Our usual crude humor has an added edge of hysteria: we kid each other with a savage license akin to drunkenness, and every witticism and practical joke seems uproariously funny.

Captain Wirt related an anecdote the other day that's worth passing on. I'll give you the grim bones of the story first, saving the lighthearted sequel for a chaser.

The story concerns one of our better-liked, high-ranking officers who recently paid a visit to a neighboring unit, thereby meeting several Americans lately released from German prison camps. Freed by the Russians, these ex-prisoners had had an opportunity to see our allies in action. According to their report, the Russians are *really* rough, tough, and nasty, and the famed 1st Division, by comparison, as gently mannered as Girl Guides on a summer outing. The Russians loot, then burn every German house that falls into their hands, and say simply, "So it was done to us!"

Two American officers gave a vivid firsthand report of Russian reprisals. Freeing the American and British prisoners in a newly captured town, the Russians said to them, "Here is a street. From this corner to that corner is yours, and the houses on both sides of the street. But stay here! Do not go from here to another part of the town!" And when the Russians had finished their grim business, the buildings that had been assigned to the ex-prisoners were all that remained of the town. Nothing else.

Concerning women, the Russians are reputedly a shade

more delicate in their approach than were the Germans in Russia two years ago. The Russians *do* ask first, *"Komme sie hier und schlaffen!"* Sometimes they even say, *"Willst du?"* Freedom of choice remains, you see. Of course, if a flat *"Nein!"* is the answer, the Russian has the last word . . . and a pistol slug puts the final unanswerable period to further reluctant bargaining.

That's the story, now for the denouement! Our officer, listening to these accounts of Russian vigor, reflected upon the soft way *we* handle civilians, and the comparison made him angry and self-conscious. Riding back to his own headquarters, he considered further, and his anger mounted. Passing a German farmhouse, he suddenly ordered his driver to pull up, and puffed with firm resolution, the officer jumped from the jeep. Studying the farmhouse for a moment, he tilted his helmet and strode up the path. (Incidentally, he stands five feet three and weighs a generous 115 pounds.) He pounded roughly on the door, and when it swung open, he pushed past the cowering frau and walked in. Then, fixing the frightened woman with a stern eye, he stomped his foot, stretched an imperious hand, and said firmly, "Twelve eggs!"

Postscript: He returned to Battalion a little comforted by the discovery that there wasn't so much to this business of being tough. Why, hell, she handed over the eggs just like that!

April 30.

Last night it was officially reported that Hitler is dead. The platoon took the news very quietly, with no great show of rejoicing. We might have celebrated his demise properly if there'd been anything to drink. Other platoons, more fortunate than we, noted the occasion with some hilarity. Hitler is dead, that's fine . . . swell! But it's not what we're waiting for. The news we want to hear is the collapse of organized resistance by the German armies, the end of the war, the acceptance of defeat by the German people. Well, Hitler is dead—what's the delay? Why in God's name isn't it over?

* * *

I spent all yesterday at regimental headquarters, filling out questionnaires, taking a physical examination, answering questions and swearing oaths, yacketa, yacketa—all the little crap involved in this field commission. I chased from one office to another, being interviewed by this major, that colonel, this captain, that lieutenant. As I sat in an anteroom, waiting to see a particular VIP, I chatted with a certain tech sergeant, a male stenographer. His spotless, freshly pressed O.D.'s shamed me, and in self-defense I assumed a lofty disregard for my own uniform—the grease spots, the foulness of old sweat, the torn trousers mended with black thread because no other color had been available. For more than an hour this barracks soldier described in shuddering accents the rigors of life at regimental headquarters. Talcumed cheeks quivering with feeling, he assured me that the men on the front "just didn't *realize* how much work there was in rear echelon," and *honestly*, he got so *damn* tired and sometimes he just didn't *know* if he was coming or *going* and we just didn't *realize*! And I thought of the dirty, unshaven men up on the line, and I looked at the beautifully creased trousers on this character, the clean-shaven cheeks, the hint of talcum powder, and I wanted to get out of there fast, I wanted to go home, back to where the smells were honest. But I didn't leave. I smiled and nodded and murmured my sympathy, and we talked of books and Broadway plays and music.

One of the officers with whom I talked at Regiment dropped a bit of information that staggered me. He said a survey of our records indicated that less than three percent of the entire regiment, officers included, had better than a high school education. I don't know—maybe I shouldn't be surprised. Maybe that percentage is average; maybe it's comparable to the education record of any large, heterogeneous group of men—the personnel of a big industrial plant, for example. But the figure seemed alarmingly low to me, particularly in comparison to the high percentage of college men in the Air Corps.

[On the voyage home many months later I talked at length with a colonel who had served at division headquarters.

When I commented casually on the percentage of college men in my regiment, the colonel undammed a flood of bitter criticism against army policy that left me slack-jawed. I learned, among other things, that the Infantry traditionally gets the low-point men of each year's West Point crop; that army policy throughout the war had been to assign inductees with high IQs to the Air Corps, the Engineers, and the Artillery, in that order, and the Infantry gets what's left. I cannot vouch for these statements as proven fact, but the colonel presented them as such.

[He was particularly bitter because the Infantry was the dumping ground for the "culls," both officers and enlisted men. "You're the real expendables," he said. "The top brass still regards the Infantry as so much raw meat, easily replaced, and not worth the bother of special care. What the bastards don't realize is that there is no branch of service where so much depends on the split-second decisions of unit commanders, whether they're platoon leaders, company commanders, or battalion commanders. If they'd take a look at the casualty rate in the Infantry, they'd see how important it is to have *good* men always ready to step into responsible jobs at a minute's notice. The Infantry ought to get the *best* men, the cream, and what does it get? Always the dirty end of the stick!" He broke off bitterly, and I murmured, "The dirty end of the stick . . . maybe that's why they call us the 'Queen of Battles.' " He looked at me inquiringly and I amended, "Queen—spelled Q-U-E-A-N." He grinned, we shook hands in mock courtesy, and retired to his stateroom for a drink. I didn't need the drink—it was intoxication enough to discover someone who would appreciate my moments of pompous erudition.]

May 3.

We reluctantly emerged from our snug farmhouses and marched drearily through rain, snow, and sleet to Frantiskovy Lázne, Czechoslovakia—known as Franzensbad to the Germans, but I prefer the Czech. It's a resort town, like Saratoga—mineral springs, handsome villas, and ornate hotels and pensions. My C.P. is in one of the less handsome villas, but I'm comfortable. My sybaritic content is flawed only when I glance out the window and see cold, wet men standing guard in muddy foxholes.

Our rations have been erratic of late and I am running out of cigarettes. (I quail before the biting comments of home fronters who have been on short cigarette rations for months, but this is the first time the shortage has touched me. The Service of Supply did a bang-up job in keeping frontline troops in cigarettes, although near echelon units have been pinched for a long time.) At any rate, I have only six cigarettes on hand and that represents low ebb to me: my habit, up to now, has been to carry a reserve of two full cartons in my pack at all times.

As in all conquered towns, the civilians here have been warned to observe a curfew. The order reads: "All civilians off the streets by eight P.M." But Frantiskovy Lázne is a large town and there are occasional stragglers, sullen, reluctant dawdlers. There have been so many of these tardy, insolent civilians that, in order to emphasize the inflexibility of the curfew ruling, we have resorted to the happy practice of bouncing a bullet off the sidewalk or wall nearest them. They move then! And linger not to make their exits properly prideful and contemptuous, as befits the Super Race. Oh, these strutting, posturing Germans!

CHAPTER FIFTEEN

"Nothing remains of Germany but a great grief . . . and hatred."

May 5.

The news just came in, "It's all over in North Germany." So it's nearly done at last, nearly finished. Only Czechoslovakia to finish off and it's ended. I think the Czech business will not last long. The German armies trapped here are men without a country, without a leader, without purpose, without hope. And, on the practical side of the ledger, without supplies, without ammunition, without gasoline, without planes. What they may possess is hatred. But lacking hope, hatred becomes tired and turns to despair. And there is a great weariness in what was the German Reich.

So we know it will soon be over. The Volksturm, stripped of its cardboard and fustian, was a hopeful myth; the "Were-wolves" only the stinging of minor insects. And the "last ditch stand"? A boast of wind from an empty paper bag! It's over, it's over . . . and those who taught by the whip will now learn from the whip.

Still May 5.

It's ten-thirty P.M. and I'm on phone guard until midnight. I won't get much sleep tonight: we shove off at four-thirty A.M. on what we hope is the last push. It's raining, as it has been raining for a week, and the ground is a muddy sponge. We have a long way to go, and on foot. I've been studying the map the captain gave me and memorizing my orders. A *helluva* long way to go!

I feel edgy, ready to jump at strange sounds. The implications of the time, the place, and the situation hit me with brutal effect tonight, the equivalent of a rifle butt slamming into my groin. All day the radio chattered excitedly that the armistice is to be signed at noon tomorrow; the war is over in Europe. But we jump off at four-thirty, and our orders cannot be altered or postponed except through official channels. Official channels being what they are . . . !

I hope that a few days from now I'll be able to laugh at the weight of premonition pressing down upon me at this moment. Suddenly I remember a long-forgotten novel of the First World War, and the hero killed by a sniper's bullet in the very instant of the war's ending, scant seconds before the "cease fire" order was sounded down the line. The senseless tragedy and waste . . . men who must die because red tape, protocol, and official decorum demand that wars be concluded with a propriety utterly lacking in their prosecution. It is apparently agreeable that men should die, with or without dignity, but the funeral oration must be solemnly phrased and the orator properly hatted and gleaming for the ritual.

To die at such a moment, to die when there is no longer a meaning in the death, to know in that last lightning-shot moment that the blood you would once have offered hotly was now to be served up as a pale aperitif, proffered meaninglessly out of cold custom . . .

I attempt to persuade myself that I do not really feel such heavy foreshadows crouching on my spirit. But I am aware of a kind of unease, a subtle discomfort. And if it should be, if I should be so cheated—ah, there will be a restless spirit, a disconsolate ghost howling in the council chambers of the world through all eternity.

I hope all this will seem mighty silly to me a few days from now. As a matter of fact, it seems pretty silly right now.

Frantiskovy Lázne delights me. It is like Baden-Baden though not so old, not so famous, not so wealthy, not so beautiful. But it is a pretty town, with lovely parks and gardens and the elegantly lush architecture of the last century. It must have been pleasant and discreetly gay back in the eighties, bands playing in the pergolas and grimly convalescent elderly sinners seeking the cure for past evils in the vile waters that unaccountably make these spas famous. Most of the men in the platoon are convinced that 'tis more agreeable to die of a lingering illness than to drink these foul waters and bloom like a rose.

The other day I saw an elderly civilian emerge from one of the "drink" buildings, hugging a green bottle against his chest. A small grandson marched sedately beside him. A strolling GI halted the pair and I heard a greedy voice inquire if the bottle contained schnapps. The old man's reply was emphatic: *"Nein, nein! Wasser! Gut wasser!"* And he uncorked the bottle and extended it invitingly. One sniff, and the soldier backed away hastily, his mouth twisted with distaste. Watching, I grinned as the old man's face mirrored his astonishment at the strange behavior of these Americans. Then, shrugging philosophically, he tilted the bottle to his own lips and took a long swig. Patting his stomach in extravagant appreciation, he cooed, "Ahhh! Prima, prima!" and waddled away, small grandson trotting docilely beside.

From a letter, written May 5:

I think I will come home from the war almost unscarred inside. Not untouched, that is, but not shaken in my faiths, not bitter, not suspicious. In many curious ways I feel unmarked, almost innocent, and sometimes it bothers me that it should be so. There is something not quite decent in my inviolate state. I feel that I *should* be deeply changed, I *should* reflect some bitterness, some sickness of spirit. Surely one cannot walk on such troubled waters without even wetting his feet?

At this moment I'm still too close to predict with certainty, to analyze objectively and place an unerring finger on this spot and on that and say, "This will be different in me . . . this will be changed . . . this will be as you remembered." But *can* one chart the subtle discolorations of his own spirit?

One forewarning I can give you: knowing my own fondness for the dramatic tale, I am blandly aware that if my at-home audience listens to my stories and is properly pop-eyed, I will take dramatic fire from such flattery and stretch for new quaverings of emotion. So if you see me stare into space as though these horrors I see (and I *will* see them, you know, because I'm a good storyteller!) are with me always, haunting my every sleep—honey, you can discount a good fifty percent of my self-drama as malarkey! (You needn't publicize this pre-confession: I'm telling you and only you because I don't want you to torment yourself with unnecessary grief, languishing over a lacerated spirit that is not so sorely wounded as it will often appear to be.)

I seem to be bouncing back and forth between extremes: first too far in one direction, then too far in the other. But I think you will know what subtle middle ground I'm trying to find for your feet (and for my own). There will be memories I will never lose and never want to lose, deep scars that will always ache and throb a little. Thus far I am true to type, à la female magazine "returned vet." But I *am* healthy, I am *not* hag-ridden by remembered horrors. To my constant astonishment, I seem to have come out of this a better-balanced individual, a healthier human being than when I went in. Even the wounds I carry are an indication of sounder health because *these* were inflicted by the world without and not self-committed, not the festering, ugly sores that my twisted, shadowed, introspective self used to inflict with deliberation. Do you understand what I'm trying to say? I think I've gained a little in perspective, a little in stature, a little in balance. I think I am almost human enough to live with now. Almost.

May 6.

Today we walked twenty miles in an unfriendly rain. We hurdled creeks and waded them and fell in them. We crossed one stretch of swampland by walking the railroad track that spanned it, but we lost one of our attendant tanks when it tried to emulate us and succeeded only in trapping itself, spread-eagled on the track with the ends of the ties jammed tightly against the inner mechanism of the caterpillar treads. We lost another tank when it bogged down in the middle of a marshy field. (The crew members climbed topside on the half-submerged vehicle and calmly began heating C-rations for an early lunch.) We lost a third tank when it crashed through a flimsy wooden bridge and fell into the creek below. Meanwhile it continued to rain, and we wound up the day in a very damp blaze of glory.

Our destination was Maria-Kulm—or Chlum Sv Mari (I like the Czech better). No sooner had we arrived than I was ordered to take the platoon out on a contact patrol. My bed, finally achieved at a weary midnight, was in a damp, musty-smelling cellar.

Throughout Europe I have been dismayed by the shortness of the beds. Single beds, old-fashioned double beds, or twin beds—they're all too short. Damn it, I've *seen* tall Europeans. How the hell do *they* sleep? Maybe they curl up as in a womb and never really stretch out full length. (If these short beds were a uniquely German phenomenon, I'd hazard a Freudian guess and say, "No wonder the Germans are possessed by this dark frenzy for lebensraum! It would be cheaper for the world to give them longer beds!")

May 7.

So it's over. The news has just reached us. It will be final and official as soon as Eisenhower signs. And there will be no more guns, no more fear, and death that asks no questions no longer waiting around the next turn in the road. Night sounds will be innocent, and there will be no new corpses in the woods and in the ditches by the hedgerows. Now only the anguish and the tears and the slow cancerous grief . . . as it is in Germany on this May day, as it can be in no other nation in the world, because here there is no hope. Nothing remains of Germany but a great grief . . . and hatred. Sorrow and hate, hate and bitterness. It is significant that the hatred (all of it) seems to be directed against Russia exclusively. Always Russia—never America or England, or even France.

There is little rejoicing among the men in the platoon. We are too tired to celebrate, though it may be different tonight if we can acquire anything to drink. And the civilians, though happy it's over at last, weep fresh tears at the sharpened memory of husbands and sons who are dead or missing or prisoners of war. For the civilians the war has long been over. Today's announcement is more of an anticlimax for them than it is for us.

Here follows the account of the last day of the war for the first platoon of George Company, 16th Infantry Regiment:

We shoved off this morning (May 7) from Chlum Sv Mari, but never reached our final objective. We paused at one of the intermediate points, a town called Bukovany, and it was there that we saw the war creak and groan to a halt. We are still in Bukovany as I write.

The first platoon spearheaded on this final thrust. There was no fighting of any consequence en route, but we collected many prisoners. The Germans were eager captives.

This town, this day . . . I wonder if I will ever be able to make you see it the way it was. Our uneasy premonitions when we started out this morning . . . the reluctance of every step forward, the prickling sense of peril as we approached Bukovany and saw men in enemy uniform appear silently in the streets ahead. They faced us, unmoving and watchful, but they did not open fire, and I cautioned the men in the platoon not to fire first. Without slackening pace we moved steadily upon the town, and the figures in blue uniform retreated, slipped furtively between the houses and disappeared.

Our orders had been to move quickly through the town, turn right at the main square, and follow that turning to the village outskirts. There, we were to set up a perimeter of defense. The platoons following would similarly occupy other quarter sections of the town.

Turning at the square, we'd moved some distance along a pleasant street lined with attractive houses when one of the scouts raced back to me. "Hey, Sarge," he gasped, "there's something funny up ahead! Some big buildings with a barbed wire fence around 'em and a bunch of guys inside yelling their heads off!"

Halting the platoon, I went forward with the scout. Soon I could hear the sounds, the distant, confined yelling of many male voices. Jungle noises heard through a filter. A few steps more and we came upon the jungle itself. Not a jungle—a zoo . . . here were the cages and the animals. Several buildings, iron-barred, and faces pressing against the bars of the upper windows, scores of faces, a clotted mass of bearded, howling faces. As we came into view the yelling became a scream of triumph, picked up and echoed hollowly from the other buildings.

This was a stalag, a forced-labor camp (not a concentration camp) and these were the slaves. This was the "home" of the dispossessed, and this twelve-foot fence of barbed wire was the neighborly hedge that marked the boundaries of this country estate.

I called six men from the platoon and said, "Break the doors! Get 'em out!" The gates of the stockade were chained and locked, and we shot off the locks to the accompaniment of loud cheers from the faces. The first barrier. The heavy wooden doors were locked and we battered them down . . . the second barrier. Now we were within the building, but the slaves were confined on the second floor, behind still another locked door . . . the third barrier. We smashed it open and were instantly engulfed in a struggling mob of shouting, weeping, insanely happy men.

They loved us . . . they wanted to kiss us, and we blushed and resisted in a flapping sort of way and squealed like virgins in a haymow. (Forgive me if the flip tone seems in bad taste. I have tried and tried over again, yet I cannot write of this hour except awkwardly. Simple, direct language would capture some echo of that terrible joy, but I cannot find simple terms that do not also suggest the disciplines of selection and restraint. This was a pagan scene, a Pan-ic revel, with emotions too raw, too unashamedly naked, to be contained in the cool syllables of dignity.)

Even now, hours later, my throat aches and my eyes burn with unshed tears before the adoring respect that's spread like a carpet before our muddy feet. Tears and kisses and embraces, salutes proffered with the trembling intensity of worship. They are quiet now, content to bask and adore, consecrate themselves in the miracle of our presence, but only a few short hours ago they were expressing their happiness more vigorously. For the first (and surely the only!) time in my life, I have been carried on shoulders like a football hero. And I've been bounced. ("Bouncing" appears to be a boisterous Slavic way of expressing enthusiastic liking—a couple of strapping fellows seize the object of their affections and toss him high in the air, catching him as he comes down and heaving him upward in flight once more. As they tire, two more huskies take over the game and continue from there.) They "bounced" me in the building until my head ached from hitting the ceiling and I was powdered with fallen plaster dust. Then they carried me to the courtyard and bounced me some more. My pack fell off, I lost my helmet, I dropped my carbine—I couldn't make them stop, and everyone was having a good time but me. In a lull between bounces I grabbed desperately for my cigarettes and hastily began passing them out. That small gesture nearly finished me: I went down for the count under a fresh wave of kisses and impassioned bear hugs.

It was hilarious and exciting and heartwarming, and we were wrenched by the ardor of this joy. But the moment I cannot forget, the memory that still shakes me with pity and shame and the sorrow of knives, is the memory of the little man. He was middle-aged, I think, but slavery had stamped upon him and left the mark of eternity. He could have been thirty years old; he might have been sixty.

He followed me; wherever I went, he followed me. I'd turn and he'd be there, dog-like, his shoulders curved abjectly, his eyes shining with tears, a half smile, distant and dreaming, on his lips. He followed me because . . . he followed me because he wanted to kiss my sleeve, *to kiss my sleeve,* damn it! Oh, damn it, damn it! To kiss my sleeve in humility, to bend his head and kiss the filthy sleeve of my jacket as though I were Christ and he not worthy to touch my flesh. And I wanted to cry and to hit him to make him proud again, I wanted to hit something, I wanted to smash something because he was so broken and everything whole and perfect was an impiety.

I tried to get away. There was much to do and I rushed around in a fury of movement, trying to escape the whipped animal who shamed me with the reminder that he had been a man. But I could not lose him: whenever I paused, I would feel that slight pressure on my arm, sense that gentle, abject presence, and he'd be there, kissing my sleeve. You cannot know the raging humility, the angry degradation in being even for a little while another man's Messiah!

A sound of pounding and the muffled clamor of voices led us to investigate a long hallway in the building. When we smashed the locked door at the end of the hall, a new wave of men rolled over us, surging from a second stockade behind the building, and for a time it seemed we would not be able to control the screaming mob.

The German guards had deserted the stalag only a few minutes before we reached it. (We learned later that a hanging had been scheduled for that morning: a slave guilty of a minor infraction was to be strung up on the gallows in the rear stockade as an object lesson. By arriving in Bukovany sooner than the Germans had anticipated, we'd saved a life. The guards feared reprisals and decided to skip the morning's entertainment.)

Some of the guards, unable to get away, had sought hiding places in the vicinity of the stalag, and the slaves offered to smoke them out. I told them okay, go ahead. The manhunt that followed was a frightening thing to witness: the hunting pack of ragged, foul, wolfish men creeping upon a suspected hiding place, moving with a cushioned stealth that stirred dim, atavistic terrors and made the hair on the back of your neck suddenly bristle. And then the discovery! The cowering prey revealed, his body curled in pathetic weak defense . . . the howl of the pack, the animal howl of feast and delight!

We tried to save the wretched guards from hurt, but I

confess that we didn't try very hard. I wanted no murders,
but I rendered cold judgment and decided they had well
earned this guerdon of kicks and blows and the bitter spit of
hate. So we let the slaves beat them up a little before we res-
cued them. We had to fight to save one guard. A higher note
of hysteria from the crowd, and more piercing screams of
agony from the victim, warned us that this must be a special
case and we'd have to move fast. We had to use our rifle
butts roughly before we reached the skinny wretch in SS
uniform who writhed on the ground, trying to protect himself from the blows that fell upon him from every direction.
His face was covered with blood, his nose had been broken,
and the slaves were jumping on him with savage intent. We
lifted him to his feet and formed a chain of protection to get
him to the prisoner detail that waited in the road. His hands
shielding his bloody, ruined face, he ran through the cursing
mob and howled, a keening, animal sound.

The slaves were angry at our interference and explained
that he had been the officer in charge of their food rations.
Last winter, that bitter winter of 1944, he had enriched himself by selling their rations on the German black market.
Sometimes their day's food had consisted of one frozen
potato per man. I was almost sorry we'd saved him. And
when I made an inspection tour of the stalag, saw the
cramped and foul rooms where they had been confined, forty-
six men to a room . . . saw the four-decker bunks, so close
together that a man could get in bed only by sliding in flat,
and once in, had to sleep on his back or his stomach because
there was no shoulder space between the bunks in which
he could turn his body, when I saw the gallows and the
barbed wire, heard the accounts of whippings and other punishments . . . I saw the toilet and sanitation facilities . . . the
coal mines where they worked fourteen to eighteen hours a
day . . . when I *smelled* the place, the foul breath of it, I was
sorry we had saved *any* of the guards. (There was another
coal-mine stalag not far from Bukovany where the slaves had
been too strong for the American soldiers who freed them.
Seizing their former guards, the slaves made their own justice

and hurled the screaming, struggling wretches down the mine shafts.)

The hunt for the guards over, a new turbulence arose when the slaves broke into the kitchen and storehouses and began to gorge. I tried to halt this insane banquet, but only halfheartedly. There would be many sick men before the night was out, but I could not find it in my heart to take the food from them and put it under guard once more. They had been hungry so long . . . and the guarding of food, the withholding of food from the hungry, has always seemed to me the last cruelty, the ultimate perversion in a world of contradictions.

By late afternoon the camp had settled down and all was quiet. The nightmare of the past years had abruptly ended, and now the men were lazy and relaxed, in a trance state between sleep and waking. They didn't talk much, and then only in low murmurs. They sat in the sun, making faint markings in the dust with bits of wood, smiling secretly, remotely. Most of them would not sit in the courtyard, but chose the open road outside the stockade. Even with the gates torn off, the stockade was a prison still, a cage of daggered wire.

I do not know how many slaves had been held in the stalag. There were three groups—Russian, Polish, and French—each with its own elected leader or spokesman. The Russians and Poles greatly outnumbered the French. And hated them. It was easy to understand why. The Russians and Poles were truly slaves, having no rights, no privileges, no hope of deliverance except death. The French, however, enjoyed some of the privileges of free workers and comprised a distinct community, living in a separate part of the camp. They had less barbed wire and fewer guards; their food was better and more plentiful; they worked shorter hours, and they were even permitted a degree of intercourse with the civilians, including the freedom to go into town and purchase certain permitted articles at the shops. As a result, the French seemed healthier, more vigorous than the gray-faced skeletons whose labels identified them as Slav.

Wherever I walked, I was greeted with smiles of devotion and love, awkward salutes from hands that had nearly forgotten. Gravely I returned each salute and wished my supply of cigarettes had not run out. Presently, the room leader of one group approached and with simple dignity—and in English—invited me to be the guest of honor at a party his group was giving in their quarters. I accepted the invitation with a gravity and correctness that matched his own and we set out.

He snapped an order as we entered the room and the men seated at the long table jumped to their feet and saluted, holding the salute as I passed to the place of honor set for me at the head. I returned their salute and smiled foolishly when they continued to stand at rigid attention, studying me with grave eyes. And then, since I could not speak their language and did not know what I was to do, I collapsed helplessly in my chair. Instantly they completed their salute and sat down, moving in the perfect unison of military precision. Still they remained silent, watching me intently, not moving. In desperation, I turned to the leader and said, "Tell them to be happy . . . tell them to eat and be happy . . . that they will be going home soon!" He smiled, spoke rapidly in Polish, and the table came to life with a roar. They leaped to their feet again, offering toasts in water and bad coffee, and there were tears in their eyes and on their faces. There were tears on mine.

The meal was simple. We drank water and ersatz coffee. There was something called bread, and a red, sticky substance called marmalade. It had the consistency, the smell, and surely the taste, of old fish glue. But the main course was potatoes—raw, unpeeled potatoes, cut in thin slices that were slapped against the red-hot belly of the tiny stove at the lower end of the room. Sizzling on contact and making a delicious smoke, the raw potato slices would stick to the hot metal. When they'd been scorched brown on one side, the "cook" would pick them loose with his fingernails and turn them over. The room was filled with a nutty richness, and the men sniffed the good smell and grinned and pounded on the table, happily cursing the sweating "cook." I stayed for half an hour, but I was aware that my presence was a social burden and they could not entirely relax while I remained. Pleading the pressure of many duties, I begged their permission to leave, wished them "Godspeed" on a speedy return to their homes, and left. They rose and stood at attention until I passed from the room.

I have established my C.P. in the house next door, an attractive, well-furnished building. Only a high barbed-wire fence separates the rear yard from the exercise yard of the prison. The people in this house cannot help but have acquired a very intimate knowledge of the stalag—the work, the food, the living conditions, the punishments, the executions. It's apparent that their observations have not disturbed them: they are smugly placid and too damned healthy looking. Their normality under the circumstances offends and irritates me.

Since my major responsibility at the moment is the administration of the stalag, it was imperative that I establish my C.P. as near at hand as possible. Shortly after we freed the prisoners, I sent Dettman to tell the owners of this house that I required accommodations for four men. In a moment or two he was back to report, somewhat apologetically (he was a gentle guy), that there was no room for us. So the inhabitants had informed him.

Impatient with anger, I stomped over to the house and walked in. The civilians were waiting for me, servile enough on the surface but with arrogance showing in the tilt of their chins, indignation in their eyes. I regarded them coldly and told them what I wanted. At once they cringed, they whined, they cowered and complained. No room . . . there was hardly room for themselves . . . where would *they* sleep? . . . The woman who lived upstairs was ill . . . the house across the street was much, much larger . . . And so on. With every evasion that passed unchallenged, their arrogance rose a little more triumphantly, and now the contempt in their eyes was revealed nakedly and we saw how they despised us, how we seemed weak and soft to them because we did not brutally command and take.

A commotion at the rear of the house created a sudden diversion. A woman was screaming in anger, "No! No bread, you pig-dogs . . . not a bit, you dirt! Go away! Get out!" I ran through the house to the kitchen, followed by Dettman and the suddenly bleating civilians.

Two ragged men stood in the yard, released slaves from the stalag, and haranguing them from the half-closed door was an elderly harridan. Seizing her arm, I spun her around and bellowed, "Give them bread! Quickly!" All my rage and hate and inner sickness foamed up and I sputtered incoherently. "*You* are the dirt, not they! You! Du! *Du!*" Slack-jawed, her eyes frightened, she drew a loaf of bread from the cupboard and cut a thin slice with avaricious care. When she slowly offered the meager slice, I intercepted the reaching hands and took it from her, tossing it on the table and firmly removing the loaf under her arm. Giving that to the men, I told them to return to the stalag—there would be more food later. When they were gone, I turned without comment and walked back through the house to the front door.

I'd come to a decision by the time I reached the door. And so had the civilians—the incident had scared the pants off 'em. Picking up the equipment I had dropped in the vestibule, I told Joe, Howie, and Evans to get their stuff together—we'd take another house. I ignored the civilians.

As we turned to leave one of the women quavered, "Herr Lieutenant?"

Coldly I inquired, "Well?"

She gulped and made flutterings with her hands, pointing to the stalag. At last the words came: "Were all those . . . those over there . . . would they be released? Were they to be freed at once, free to leave the stockade and wander in the village?"

I nodded and said yes, they were free. My men would keep order as well as possible, but . . . of course, it was going to be difficult to control so many men, and unfortunately, I lacked sufficient guards . . . of course, there were sure to be regrettable incidents in the village, but they could rest assured that any who did wrong would be punished. That is, if we could *find* the guilty persons!

Long before I had finished, their wailing was a thing wondrous to hear, and I observed the temperature of their mounting hysteria with a coldly clinical eye. At that moment these smug bitches could be raped by every man in the stockade and I would not lift a finger to prevent it; "those over there" could take this bulbous and quivering German male out in the yard and slit his throat as they'd butcher a pig.

They begged, they entreated us to accept the hospitality of their home. Groveling at our feet, they implored us to regard their home as ours—they had fear! Man, I'll say they had fear!

I put on a great show of reluctance, indecision, made them squirm awhile longer. At last, still frigid in manner, I consented to establish my headquarters in their home. Then (and you will hardly believe this!) having won their point and thus regained some of their confidence, they had the cheek to propose that my three men and myself make the *kitchen* our quarters! A small room containing a stove, a table, two straight-backed wooden chairs, and a small couch. I stared silently at the civilians, and their glib chatter became abruptly feeble. Noticing a closed door in the far wall, I stepped across the kitchen and tried it. Locked. I glanced inquiringly at the civilians, but they studied the floor and made no move. So it was going to be that way, was it? I turned back to the locked door and lifted the butt of my rifle. One of the women whispered a little as the wood crashed and splintered, but no one said a word. The open door revealed a beautiful bedroom, set with modern blond furniture. Each of the twin beds was large enough for two men, and a porcelain stove filled one corner of the room. Flinging my muddy pack onto the nearest bed, I called to the waiting men over my shoulder, "Bring your things in here!" There was a hubbub of protest from the civilians, which ended when I turned to the German male and said firmly, "Build a fire in here, at once!" Then I walked into the bedroom and slammed the door. I was suddenly very tired of Germans.

So that was our V-E Day. If it *was* V-E Day. The radio had been proclaiming it throughout the day, but all commentators were careful to add that no official statement had yet been issued by Washington, London, or Moscow. That official pronouncement is expected tonight.

At any rate, the captain sent us a quarter barrel of beer, and we're going to celebrate. A quarter barrel isn't very much for thirty-one men: it will be token drinking only, unless we can acquire more from other sources. As for myself, it won't be V-E Day until I'm home, until I feel familiar arms around me, press my tired face against the satin of the young faces I have not seen for so many months.

I am beginning to realize how tired I am, a weariness that has been mounting imperceptibly for a long time rather than a simple physical exhaustion from the intensive pushing of the past week. V-E Day has been as I predicted some weeks ago. It brings only a great weariness of relief, the sense of a heavy load sliding from tired shoulders. I'm still alive—that's the important thing. Most of us feel this way—Christians who have crossed our particular Sloughs of Despond, our common Rivers of Death. And in the midst of our weariness, and even while the slow bubble of joy swells within us, we are sobered by the thought of the men in the Pacific Theater. For the first time we feel a kinship to that faraway war and a warm affection for the guys fighting it. So this is V-E Day.

CHAPTER SIXTEEN

"... the last parade ..."

May 10.

The day before yesterday we left Bukovany and moved to Goldorf, Czechoslovakia. We're stationed on the main highway outside the town, our roadblock serving as the first of a series of funnels through which the surrendering Germans must pass on their way to the vast P.W. enclosure a few miles to our rear. More than 100,000 German soldiers will pass through our lines before our task is completed.

We've been on duty here since six yesterday morning. It's now one-thirty A.M., and I write this while serving my tour of duty on the phone. The principal part of our job is to keep the prisoners moving as rapidly as possible without permitting a traffic jam to result.

The task has a strange unreality. There are so few of us and so many of them that we find it difficult to sustain the fiction that we're the victors here and they're our prisoners, no longer to be feared. There's the frightening sense of something gone askew, and we must resist the impulse to dive for the nearest ditch. It's like a bad dream. Confronted by the living shapes of our fears, we fumble nervously for the safety catches on our rifles, our uneasy hands seeking to complete the conditioned action.

All day and all night the Germans have passed. I hear them now on the road before this house, moving sullenly toward the barbed wire they have themselves loved so well. They pass in a bewildering variety of vehicles: vans, lorries, staff cars, half-tracks, buses, mobile kitchens, ambulances, motorcycles, wood-burning trucks, charcoal-burning civilian automobiles, horse-drawn wagons and buggies and farm carts. They come on bicycle, on horseback, on foot. It's not uncommon to see one car towing several others that have exhausted their fuel supply.

Most of the cars are benzine-powered, but many have been converted to wood or charcoal burners with great furnaces attached to side or rear. Frequently a converted vehicle will pull out of line and halt on the shoulder of the road while its occupants shovel in more fuel and wait for a fresh head of steam. Today I saw a German staff car that had familiar lines, in spite of the built-in wood burner in the rear. It turned out to be a 1938 Chevrolet.

All manner of prisoners: the wounded and the whole, German WACs, nurses, whores, wives and children, SS men, Luftwaffe, Panzer Grenadiers, snipers, medics, foot soldiers. High-ranking officers (I talked to a general yesterday). Boys of fourteen and fifteen in uniform (I saw one today who admitted he was twelve years old). And men of sixty. Some of them sullen, some of them arrogant still, many fawningly eager to sing whatever tune we choose to pipe, ready to swear with willing tears that they "never hated the Americans." All of them weary, most of them dirty—but not the officers! Even in this fallen moment the officers are polished, erect, clean-shaven, Prussian in their bearing whether their birthplace was Schleswig or Baden.

While I stood at the roadblock today, a traffic jam snarled up the road and I halted the moving line of prisoners until order could be restored. A car containing several company-grade German officers had halted only a few yards from me, and one of the young officers leaned from the car, an unlit cigarette in his mouth. He smiled in friendly fashion and pointed to the cigarette, saying, *"Bitte!"* I could not refuse him the small mercy of a light, and silently I handed him a paper book of matches. He lit up, puffed quietly for a moment, then commenced to talk. His ease of manner suggested that the late war had been a kind of football game or cricket match in which the German team had been the loser, but "let's shake hands like good sports, what?" He expressed his joy that the war was over at last and that once more "Germany and America could be friends." I was grimly unimpressed by his naive presumption, but he was not embarrassed. On the contrary, he had the monstrous arrogance to attempt a little proselytizing, saying carelessly, "It is a pity that you Americans do not see the Russians as *we* do. Ah, they are horrible! They are not even human! Like animals . . . !" Staggered by this insolence, I could only gape in reply. Then I turned on my heel and walked stiffly away.

All day they come in an endless swarm that shows no sign of lessening. Many are legitimately our prisoners, but a vast number are properly Russian prizes. They're throwing themselves into our hands rather than surrender to the Russians. How they fear the Russians!

The tragic note in this crowded scene is struck by the ragtag and bobbletail of civilians who seek to flee westward from the advancing Russians. Most of these civilians are residents of East Germany, now engulfed in the Russian flood, but many are refugees from Cologne, Aachen, Bonn, Munich, Frankfurt, homeless wanderers who fled to the then-safe east when the Allied forces broke through the Rhine barrier. Now they flee to the west again, running from the Russians. Today I talked to some refugees from Bonn, two women and two small children. For five months they have been walking: first fleeing eastward from Bonn, now trying to return to Bonn. The women pushed a four-wheeled cart piled mountainously high with luggage, a load weighing several hundred pounds.

The heartbreak for the civilians comes when they learn that this main road is a military highway from our roadblock onward, rigidly *Verboten* to civilian travel at the present time. Our orders are strict: under no circumstances will civilians be permitted on this road. They must be kept off, forced off if need be, and if they choose to continue westward, they must take to the woods and follow rough trails and paths.

A hike through these well-mannered forests would be no hardship for people traveling light. Unencumbered, they could move quickly and reach the sanctuary they seek. But they come pushing baby carriages, wheelbarrows, four-wheeled carts weighted with what precious household goods they'd been able to save, and the forest trails are rough and narrow, impassable for vehicles. They must abandon their bicycles, their carts and carriages, or turn back to the waiting arms of the Russians. There is no other choice.

And so we order the weeping women from the road and wince with the helpless knowledge of our own brutishness. The fields along the road have become an encampment of the stubborn, the hopeful, and the despairing—gray faces that lift imploringly and beg what we cannot grant, desolate shapes of grief weeping beside the treasures they must abandon and *know* they must abandon, yet cannot.

Surrendering German soldiers, dispossessed civilians . . . yet two other groups also pass along this road. They are the foreign laborers who were either lured to Germany with the promise of fat wages or were dragged forcibly from their homelands and put to work in German fields and factories. Now they're on their way home—Latvians, Poles, Russians, Frenchmen, Belgians, Italians, Spaniards, Dutchmen, Danes—an ambulant League of Nations. And there are the prisoners of war, freed now from German prison camps and forced labor camps. Hundreds and hundreds of them, most of them British.

Some have been imprisoned for as long as five years, working twelve, fourteen, sixteen hours a day for seven ounces of bread. This morning I waved hello to four British soldiers on bicycles, and they paused and swung into the drive. I gave them water and pressed cigarettes and chocolate on them. For twenty minutes they rested on the straw in the goat shed and answered my eager questions with weary indulgence. Although thin to emaciation, they were possessed of a lean and brittle strength, the kind of strength that is capable of short, fierce bursts of energy but lacks staying power. They felt they'd been luckier than many prisoners: the skilled factory work to which they had been assigned required strength and endurance, and the Germans had been forced to feed them reasonably well. Two had been prisoners for more than four years; the others for only two years. When they spoke of the

Germans, the dry and burning hate in their voices made the hair on my arms stir uneasily.

From them I heard stories that verified and amplified the charges of brutality that have been laid at the Nazi door. Stories about crewmen from fallen American planes who were mauled and beaten by SS men and then, bleeding and semi-conscious, delivered over to the cruelties of maddened civilian mobs. (The screaming German woman who fell upon one such beaten and half-conscious American flyer and castrated him with a paring knife while the mob and the SS men watched.) Stories about the floggings in the work camps, the cold, the disease ... the five thousand Jews who were marched from Sunday morning to Thursday night without pause, and those who collapsed dispatched on the spot by a bullet at the base of the skull ... the thirty Jews, selected carelessly—You ... you ... and you—and killed with exquisite slow cruelty, one at a time, and no explanation given to those who watched, horrified. ("Just an object lesson.") The special brutality accorded Russians and Poles. ("But a Russian is not quite human, he is not like other men! Oh, but our scientists have proved it: it is a scientific fact that the Slavic peoples have less sensitive flesh, fewer nerve endings. They do not feel pain the way human beings do!" Thus it was explained to me once by a young German prisoner. He believed it, too. And the unwelcome thought rose in my brain: by substituting the word "Negro" for the word "Russian" these same "scientific statements" parroted by a young German become, almost word for word, the "scientific statements" I once heard from a young American in the sovereign state of Georgia. Hello, Broadway—good-bye, Unter den Linden!)

Stories that made you want to shut your ears ... the blackest accusations ever leveled against a Christian nation. But you listened, and you entered them on one side of the ledger, and on the other side you recorded the sniveling complaints of the German civilians, the whines of *"keine brot, kein sucre, kein milch—alles kaput!"* (But never a "Mea culpa!") And when you totaled up the scores and compared them, you stopped thinking for a moment because you were blinded by the impulse to run with torch and sword among these savages, so good, so kind, so seemingly placid. You tried to tell yourself, "Maybe they were deluded, maybe they didn't know!" But you remembered the house next to the stalag in Bukovany, and you knew that all through Germany they had closed their eyes deliberately and would not see. The death camps—the quick-death camps for the unwanted, and the slow-death camps for the still useful—were scattered throughout Germany and German Europe, not concentrated in remote and guarded seclusion. They could not have been unknown to the civilians who lived nearby, the townspeople who closed their minds and their hearts. It was the easy, the safe way out—to learn to ignore the screams of men being whipped, the blood in the gutters, the miles of hasty graves, the smell of death and dirt and rotting food and fear.

So it passes . . . the last parade . . . a slow, inglorious review on this quiet road in the Sudeten. And we savor the throbbing triumph of this moment, the sight of the world's enemies inching their sullen way to the stockade. We take an additional and special pleasure in our task here: all Allied peoples, whether civilian or released P.W.'s, are given free and immediate passage through our roadblock. They take honored precedence over the surrendering enemy, and we delight in ordering the Germans to the side of the road in order to clear the way for a score of ragged former slaves.

And all day they come: the bemedaled, beribboned officers, the sullen men, the tired nurses, the flabby (but frequently beautiful) whores, the tattered, emaciated, exultant P.W.'s, the barefoot, painfully moving slaves, the frightened refugees, bewildered and lost. There should be motion-picture cameras to record this last parade. America ought to see this, and the whole world, and it should be required seeing for every school-child at home.

May 13.

It's time to quit this now. It was intended as a combat record, and the combat is done. Now we're engaged in a different kind of war, a war with many curious overtones and implications. Already there is restlessness, unhappiness, slovenly performance of duty, inefficiency, drunkenness, and crime among our own men. We are anxious to go home, and tired, and the careful bars of our disciplined restraint have been lowered.

And I am tired, too, and anxious to go home—sick of this whole dirty business, sick of writing about it, sick of everything in the world and wanting only to go home. Let it be soon . . . please, let it be soon!

Afterword

It was not soon. It was New Year's Day, 1946, when I landed at New York, and the months until then were the most unhappy I have ever known.

The final step in my commission was taken on May 26, 1945. The actual swearing in had been delayed by a snarl of red tape over the transfer of the division from 1st Army to 3rd Army jurisdiction. But finally it happened and I was a "sir" and suddenly separated from my old friends in the ranks by a thin but implacable barrier. We didn't feel any different—Shorty, Loeb, Joe, and Frank—but opportunities for friendly intercourse were difficult to arrange, and the old days of splitting a bottle together were over. I could not invite enlisted men to my quarters for a drink and a bull session, and though I visited them in their quarters several times, the presence of unfamiliar enlisted men who knew me only as a company officer was a restraint on our efforts to unbend. Notwithstanding pleasant company among the officers, I missed my old companions, and I resented the system that had suddenly made us part-time friends. My roots were in the ranks still, and there were patterns of thought and behavior in the officer group that I could not persuade myself to adopt.

MEN AND OFFICERS

I never shook off my enlisted man background, never felt completely an officer. Maybe it was because I'd been spared the slow tempering of Officer Candidate School, a processing some good Joes survived, to be good Joes still, but turned many others into prime bastards. At any rate, I continued to think like an enlisted man, even though I'd moved to the other side of the railroad tracks. And though I was fortunate enough to observe the workings of the army "caste system" from both sides, I know that my final judgments were colored by my earlier conditioning.

For that reason, the following paragraphs cannot be regarded as a fair exposition, cautiously developed, of the officer–enlisted man relationship. I cannot be completely objective: the pink underwear of my private prejudices peeps unashamed through the ragged lace of the dispassion I ought to be wearing. So let me briefly sum up my own position. When an officer was a *good* officer, his men were happy, efficient, and trustworthy, and (for the most part) decent and honorable in their behavior. The rub was that there were too many *poor* officers, poor in the sense of being morally ill-equipped to assume a true responsibility for the well-being of other men.

Just before he pinned on my bars, General Andrus, a brave and well-loved officer, inquired of me, "Sergeant, what would you say is the outstanding fault of many second lieutenants?" My embarrassment was acute. I could recall specific gripes against specific officers but nothing that I could label a *general* fault. I muffed the question and replied meekly, "Sir, I don't know."

He answered his own question. "They don't think of their men enough." Then, simply and with deep feeling, he spoke at length of an officer's primary responsibility—his men. When I left his headquarters half an hour later, I was proud and humble, conscious of a sense of dedication.

I think most officers of company grade *tried* to think of their men. But some tried only part of the time, and a few never tried at all. Many enlisted men endured needless suffering because their immediate leader considered his own comfort and safety before theirs. And the career boys, the reputation seekers, the eager beavers who sickened after medals and promotions add a bloody underscoring to that charge.

* * *

My first regimental officers' meeting was an exciting occasion for me. Dressed in borrowed clothing and insignia—I had as yet no officer's gear of my own—I entered the stately assembly room at regimental headquarters with a wildly beating heart. When I emerged an hour later, the bitter taste of vomit was in my throat, and my borrowed gauds burned like the mark of Cain.

During the meeting a high-ranking regimental officer had addressed us on "The Need for More Rigid Discipline in the Ranks." Fixing us with a pale eye and twirling the waxed ends of his mustache with manicured fingers, he spoke in slow and icy accents. "Gentlemen, [twirl] the rabble now in the ranks [twirl] . . . !" I didn't hear any more for a long time. Consumed with shame and impotent rage, I assumed an expression of respectful attention and gnawed my self-contempt, hating him for his polished boots and immaculately creased trousers, for the riding crop so casually disposed on the gleaming desk against which he leaned. And I hated the officers around me, and myself, for permitting this arrogance to go unchallenged. I wanted to strike poses, rise in bravado, thump my breast and say, "Listen, you sonofabitch, a week ago *I* belonged to that 'rabble in the ranks'—and I'm going right back to it!" I didn't say it; I didn't have the nerve. But I wish I had . . . I wish I had.

None of the officers whom I knew best felt this lofty contempt for the men in the ranks. I cannot believe that many infantry officers of company grade *did* feel that way: combat troops lived too intimately for the cultivation of such exquisite disdain. Not until I was on my way home did I encounter this exaggerated caste consciousness in a *group* of officers. And they were not of the infantry.

On a dreary, rainy day in November 1945 I sat in a tent in Camp Baltimore, France, and listened to the daily bull session. Each day a dozen officers gathered around the stove and exchanged boasts and gripes: the subject today was, "If I ever get back in this goddamned army, I'm gonna get me a job just as far away from enlisted men as I can get! A good desk job at regimental or division headquarters—but no enlisted men!"

Hearing only grunts of agreement with not a voice raised in

argument, I asked innocently, "Why? I mean—why *don't* you want anything to do with enlisted men?"

Heads jerked upward and they looked at me in sudden alarm, as though something not quite clean had crept into the tent. Finally one of them answered. "Why? Because I just don't like the bastards, that's why! All y'ever get is trouble. . . ." Then others joined in: "They're always looking for a chance to stick it into some officer and break it off . . . always bitching about something . . . they'd swipe the gold fillings from their mother's mouth . . . most of 'em are dumb bastards . . . !"

The chorus of indignation sputtered for several minutes, subsiding gradually to a litany of self-approval so familiar and so dear that my question was forgotten and they devoted themselves to a mutual masturbation of unexamined prejudices. Following an old pattern, they drifted to memories of those dear old days at OCS and one of them turned and inquired, "What was your class at Benning, Gantter?"

With superb timing (and ah, the relish with which I recall this noteworthy scene in the drama of my life!) I rose, drew on my gloves with what was surely a Chesterfieldian flourish, and drawled, "I never went to Benning, or to any OCS. I was an enlisted man, commissioned out of the ranks last spring. Anybody want to walk down to the library?" Quivering silence answered, and I rang down the curtain and walked alone in the teeming rain. It was a helluva good exit, and well worth a soaking.

On the long train ride to Marseilles a week later, I discussed the same subject at greater length and with greater passion. I shared a compartment with a certain captain, and the argument—it was never mild enough to be termed "discussion"—raged for several hours, subsided, and rose tumultuously again during the night, in the rattling blackness of the unlighted, unheated coach. Like the other officers in the group, the captain was violent in his contempt for the enlisted man, and I rose to do battle. We slugged each other joyously until he let go with a roundhouse swing that sent me gasping to the ropes: he mentioned casually that in civilian life he was a public school teacher. This officer who despised enlisted men, calling them inferior human beings ("Of course they were inferior—otherwise they'd be officers!"), was a schoolteacher, and the founder and director of a playground-and-activities project for underprivileged boys in his hometown! Reeling from the effort to reconcile these implications, I retired meekly to my corner of the carriage and could fight no more.

After we started occupation duty in Bamberg, Germany, we settled down to a garrison life, a spit-and-polish routine that even included a Saturday-morning inspection with the entire battalion drawn up on the parade ground. Frequently the inspecting officer was the "rabble in the ranks" officer I mentioned earlier, and it was his custom and pleasure to select several "whipping boys" from the ranks, and by his treatment of those unfortunates, cow the entire battalion into trembling submission.

My platoon was the unlucky object of his attentions one Saturday: he started his inspection with us and selected his victims from the first six men he scanned.

He was a skillful and subtle sadist and knew well the uses of his most potent instrument—a voice that could be as silky as the last faint moanings of flutes, as steely as a sword struck upon stone, as shattering as the full-throated bawl of a great bell or the explosive bark of a "Long Tom." He knew the evil power of his voice and enjoyed it, enjoyed the melodramatic magic of a whisper and the knowledge that a thousand men quivered and strained to hear, relished the sudden metal of his full voice, driving it like a mailed fist into the face of the wretch who trembled before him, expectant but never quite prepared.

The first man to suffer his attentions was given the full treatment: first, the cool, impersonal voice, then the silky whisper, and at last the full bellow, the open and undisguised contempt that published his shame to the world. And his sin, the crime so awful (such was the implication) that he was henceforth consigned to the company of sodomists, traitors, and matricides? The collar of his shirt was open (according to the order of dress) and the underdickey was neatly buttoned (again, as per order), but the poor guy was dark haired and endowed with a luxuriant growth of chest hair, a small tuft of which, like a dark shadow, peered exuberantly over the top of the buttoned dickey. For this offense against military order he shuddered under a raging contempt that was like a blow across the mouth, and the battalion, awed and pitying, witnessed his humiliation. He should have shaved it off!

The next man to meet the pale examination of those merciless eyes assumed the proper "Present Arms" position as the officer approached. Given the command to "Order Arms," he obeyed smartly. The officer started to walk on, paused, turned back, and faced the man once more. Again the soldier presented arms, and again the command, "Order Arms." He snapped the movements smartly and I could find no fault. But the inspecting officer was not easily satisfied. Stepping back a few paces, he studied the man, regarding him with an incredulous disgust, as though he were a monstrous aberration in the human race, an object strange and revolting and altogether horrible. He dropped his eyes to the soldier's boots and slowly examined him from toes to helmet, with scalpel precision cutting the garments from the shrinking body and stripping it naked—boots, socks, trousers, shirt, and underwear—and we saw, as he wanted us to see, the gooseflesh on arm and thigh, the quivering buttocks, the stomach strained tight with fear, the soldier's manhood shrunken and curling pitifully against the cold blast of this unloving disrobement.

Once again the sequence of commands was given, and again the officer watched in silence. Moving to the soldier's left side, he gave the commands once more. Still he made no comment, neither to the soldier, to me, nor to any of the other officers who stood with me.

He moved back to his former position: directly before the now trembling man. Silkily he gave the order: "Pre-sent ... ARMS!" and the man obeyed. Now he moved closer, standing so near that his nose almost touched the barrel of the rifle held so rigidly before him. In a voice that was the merest whisper, he said, "Now, soldier . . . do you know what 'Order Arms' means?"

We stood, a chorus in a Greek play, waiting for this principal to play out his scene, release us from the bondage of this tension and grant the mercy of catharsis.

The soldier gulped, and his eyes flickered toward the officer before he managed to say, "Yes, sir."

"DON'T LOOK AT ME! KEEP YOUR EYES WHERE THEY BELONG!" The voice rattled over the parade ground, and distant men who had forgotten to button a pocket shivered. "Didn't you have any better training than that?"

Again the man gulped. His eyes were wide and staring, fixed on a point in infinity. "Yes, sir," he said.

"Then demonstrate it!" A pause. Now the silky voice once more, filled with a kindliness that even a child would recognize as false, the prelude to a larger cruelty. "Now, soldier, show me again how you 'Order Arms.' "

At the familiar words, the distraught man made a convulsive movement, and immediately the voice lashed him across the face. "Did anyone give you the *command* to order arms! *Did I?*"

A long pause before the man could reply, "No . . . sir," he whispered.

"Then wait until you get it!" Pause. "Now! . . . Order . . . ARMS!"

For the first time the soldier fumbled in the ritual of movement, his fear-paralyzed hands refusing to obey. When the rifle came to rest at his heel, I saw that his knees were quivering uncontrollably. Sweat clung in shining drops to his forehead and his eyes were dark with tears. He was a good man, and nothing mattered now except that he *was* a good man and something vile was being done to him. I moved convulsively, taking a step toward the menacing back of the officer. The only important thing now was to end this, to stop it somehow by any means at all. But my good friend the captain silently grasped my arm and looked a warning at me, holding me with his eyes. He was my superior and my friend and I trusted him. And so I halted, and the fine edge of impulse dulled shamefully in me, and I froze to respectful attention again and watched a man flayed alive.

The torture continued . . . maybe five minutes more; it may have been ten. Over and over the shuddering man repeated the prescribed movements, and with every repetition his fumbling grew worse, his body at last reaching a point where it could no longer obey.

The one man who enjoyed this spectacle relished it with a pleasure that was obscenely sexual, lechery at its most vile. At last, satiated, he wearied of the sport, and turning, spoke to the silent group of officers at his back, spoke in a voice that carried over the parade ground, as he intended it should. "I can do nothing with this man. I hope he is not a fair sample of the intelligence represented here." To my superior he added: "Captain, I suggest that someone take him aside later and drill him. Drill him *and drill him*—until he learns that, at the 'Order Arms,' the thumb of the left hand lies along the seam of the left trouser leg! *And not a fraction of an inch away from it!*" He turned and completed his inspection of the battalion, sauntering through it carelessly because he was sated now, his orgasm complete.

When the inspection was over and the battalion had been dismissed, I followed my silent platoon to the barracks. I asked the platoon sergeant to assemble the men in one of the larger rooms, and when they'd gathered, I spoke to them. Feeling the bars on my shoulders burning like acid, I offered apology; out of my own shame and humility I apologized for the caste to which I had so recently sworn myself. They looked at me and listened gravely and without contempt and I respected them for that. But there was a barrier between us that had never been there before, and standing on opposite sides of it, we grieved for each other. Later I spoke privately to the two men who'd been singled out that day, and they listened to me with a dignity that was more awful than reproach.

Had my actions been made known to higher authority, I would have been severely censured. Maybe I'd have lost my bars. There were a few times when that would have seemed small loss.

* * *

During the summer of 1945 the regimental officers' club set up shop in an elaborate summer villa located on an island formed by the junction of the river and the canal. The villa became the scene of lavish swimming and garden parties: dancing—with frauleins, nurses, or Red Cross girls—good drinks, fine food, swimming, boating, or just plain dating. We swam in the canal, which flowed directly before the villa.

The river and the canal supplied Bamberg's water power, and not far downstream from our club were the locks that controlled the flow of water and thus the city's electricity. When the gates of the locks were open, the water level in the canal went down and we found little pleasure in swimming; when the gates were closed, the water was high and the swimming was good.

With the coming of the American Military Government (AMG) to Bamberg, certain responsibilities of our occupation duty were removed from our scope and placed under the jurisdiction of AMG. The control and administration of utilities was one of these lost responsibilities, and AMG took over the job of helping Bamberg industry to recover from its paralysis. An AMG lieutenant was stationed at the locks on the canal and required to observe a very rigid schedule governing the opening and closing of the gates. His orders came directly from AMG and not through regimental channels.

On a particularly golden Sunday in July a certain high-ranking regimental officer stepped from the clubhouse and strolled down the path toward the canal. His heart was filled with only the most tender regard for his fellow men. Had he not arranged a swimming party of such luxury that all previous parties would fade into muddy insignificance? Had he not invited his favorite officers (and their well-stacked girl-friends, of course), and were there not to be special guests in the persons of certain high-ranking officers from neighboring units (who would admire and envy)? Had he not ordered the preparation of the most elaborate buffet lunch ever served in South Germany, and had he not supplied his guests with fine wines and liquors? And had not the day cooperated by being exceptionally blue and golden?

Imagine, then, his consternation when his loving glance fell upon the swimming pool and discovered (Oh, the horror of it, the lèse-majesté!) an expanse of slimy, mud-covered bank growing ever broader above the descending face of the water. The lock gates were open, and the water level had gone down nearly two feet! It was still pleasant, of course, still swimmable, still a satisfactory picture, but that wasn't the point— the pool was not at its *best*! Howling with rage, he stormed into the club and ordered a trembling aide to call the unfortunate AMG lieutenant *at once*!

"I want the goddamn river up! Close or open the goddamn locks, but I want the goddamn river up three feet by four o'clock!" So went the imperial command, and angels trembled, second lieutenants wept tears of impotent anger, and two German civilians who worked in the kitchen went into the bathroom and tried to cut their wrists with the top of an old C-ration can.

The wheels of German progress moved slower that day, and German civilians balefully regarded their dim and flickering lights and wondered if the *verdammt Amerikanische* would ever get the electricity properly repaired. But the swimming was fine that day, the colonel smiled, and the party went down in history.

The following week the enlisted men were graciously permitted the freedom of the pool to have a party for *their* girls. But somehow the swimming didn't seem very good, and many a platoon sergeant wondered why his lieutenant had called it "the best place in Bamberg for a swim."

A few random notes:

Any officer, lowly company grade or exalted field grade, could buy drinks at the regimental club. But the Coca-Cola, cases of it, was reserved for the superior palates of "field grade officers only." Ho hum . . .

A certain colonel had the unpleasant drunken habit of buttonholing lesser officers and questioning them fiercely:

"You think I'm a sonofabitch, don' ya? *Don'* ya? Y'*always* think I'm a sonofabitch, don' ya?" (He was, of course, in many ways.) If the unfortunate buttonholee was *also* drunk and thus tempted to the admission, "You betcha . . . sir! Tha's *jus'* what you are—a sonofabitch!" his head rolled in the gutter on the morrow. Drunk or sober, the colonel remembered. And if the miserable victim squirmed and evaded and uttered feeble negative bleats, he was met with the fierce rejoinder, "Yer a liar! I say, *yer a goddamn liar!* 'Cause ya *do* think I'm a sonofabitch, don' ya?"

The code name for our battalion being "Dagwood White," our battalion C.P. was called "White C.P." In Bamberg there was a building known familiarly but quietly—it was supposed to be secret!—as the "*Black* C.P." In it lived the mistresses of certain officers who liked their sex life on a somewhat permanent basis. It was a kind of apartment house love nest for officers and their frauleins. Everyone in the battalion knew about it, of course, but I never heard an enlisted man criticize the situation or speak of it bitterly. After all, every enlisted man who so desired had a fraulein of his own. (Sex, at least, was not reserved "For Officers Only.") Maybe the enlisted man's girlfriend was not installed in a private apartment, but he didn't bitch or gripe because his officers enjoyed their sin a little more luxuriously. It was accepted, that's all, and I imply censure in no direction.

The point is, the Black C.P. was put on the list as a regular guard post! Enlisted men were required to perform their prescribed military duties as guards around a building containing nothing more valuable than the German mistresses of their commanding officers. And *that* created bitterness, hate, and distrust.

But the ultimate humiliation, the crowning contradiction in this bitter farce, was offered by a certain officer who, his German mistress smiling arrogantly at his side, gave orders to the guards that they were to "regard an order from her as coming from me!" And American men who a few months before had been conquering this country with blood and steel were now required to take orders from the enemy, to be at the beck and call of women who found the soft life of whoring to American appetites more agreeable than the stern barrenness of German hunger.

MEN AND MONEY

I have already written of looting during combat. And I said that officers as well as men were guilty—guilty of a greed that rivaled the Nazi rape of Poland, Greece, France. Here are a few more stories on looting, money hunger, corruption. Most of these accounts concern officers, but that's not to imply that enlisted men were less guilty. The opportunities merely varied in scope.

Shortly after our arrival in Bamberg, we were issued a weekly ration of cognac that was divided among the various officers' clubs, the NCO clubs, and the enlisted men. It wasn't always good cognac, but it was something to drink and it was cheap. Since the army controlled its manufacture—that is, we administered the German firms that made it, and even supplied them with the necessary sugar—and also handled its distribution (all of it went to the army: there was no cognac allotment for civilian use), it was, in theory, a nonprofit operation, and the liquor was supposed to be purchased at cost and sold at cost. (In our own officers' club we made a small profit over the bar because that helped defray other club expenses, but the warehouses and distilleries were supposed to supply our cognac at cost.)

As PX and liquor officer for the battalion, I drove to the warehouse for our allotments every week and unhesitatingly paid the sum demanded by the issuing officer. However, I began to wonder about the rising cost of living when the price inched upward each week, from an original five marks per bottle (a mark was worth ten cents) to eighteen marks a bottle. Quite by accident one day I learned the answer: the legitimate price was *still* five marks per bottle, and the other thirteen marks was being split three ways and disappearing into the capacious pockets of three high-ranking and well-known officers. This little graft lasted well over six months, and since my battalion—with a weekly allotment of 150 bottles—was only one of more than fifty units drawing their cognac ration from the same warehouse, you can get some idea of how much money was involved.

Officers lucky enough to be assigned to the right jobs made fabulous fortunes through dealings with goods-hungry civilians. The black market in gas, for one, made many officers and enlisted men rich. There was one of our officers who went home on leave, for instance, his duties during his absence assigned to other officers. His successor as steward of our quarters made an inspection tour of the building to discover the scope of his new duties. A locked room in the cellar aroused his curiosity, and when the door was broken open— the key had been unaccountably missing—an outrushing wave of gasoline fumes nearly knocked him out. Eighty-two five-gallon cans of gas were stored there, in an almost airtight room directly under our living quarters. Enough gas to blow us all sky-high. No one could account for the presence of the gasoline, but we began to remember the many after-dark excursions our former steward had taken in his jeep, and the many cans of gas he carried at all times "for emergency."

Officers in charge of civilian housing could also do well financially, and some of them did. Officers in charge of construction, or in charge of razing damaged buildings, could do very well indeed. And did. Many a civilian who needed bricks, tin roofing, gutter pipe, lumber, lead, roof tiles, or steel beams could get what he wanted if he had the proper wherewithal to offer in trade.

The dirtiest racket of them all, however, was run by American officers who victimized not the civilians but their own men, fellow soldiers, fellow Americans. A cute little scheme, it worked like this:

During combat, many enlisted men had acquired German cameras, which was permissible loot during the war. Some of those cameras were Leicas or of comparable quality, and good cameras fetched fabulous prices in certain markets—Paris,

London, the Riviera. Three officers of noble rank and ignoble spirit confiscated fine cameras from enlisted men on the street, using the pretext of an official order "from head-quarters" (*which* headquarters was left somewhat vague). The cameras were to be "examined and licensed" and then returned to the enlisted men who were the owners. But once he'd submitted his camera for "examination and licensing," it was the rare enlisted man who ever saw his possession again. It traveled southward the following week in a jeep or a trailer, along with other salable items destined for the Riviera trade.

Not all of the money was made by officers. I knew an enlisted man who averaged four hundred dollars a week for several months during the war. A fluent linguist, he served as the official interpreter in his outfit. With the agreeable connivance of two attendant guards, prisoners and civilians brought in for questioning were thoroughly searched and their money taken from them. Then, as soon as his outfit arrived in a town large enough to have a local bank, he would question the civilians until he discovered the hiding place of one of the bank executives. A private deal followed, and by threats, force, or merely the glibness of his tongue, he would arrange for the exchange of his stacks of marks for the English, French, or American bank notes that all banks had in their vault, or hidden away in some secret cache.

There was a constant traffic in army equipment, army supplies, army rations. Most officers wearily closed their eyes to the cigarette bartering, but the racket of stealing and selling GI blankets, to mention one item, reached staggering proportions and required stern official action to check it.

Across the road from our quarters in Bamberg was a vast rabbit warren of buildings, formerly a German barracks but now serving as an American "repple depple." An endless stream of men flowed through it, many of them in the process of being routed home on furlough, rotation, or to permanent civilian life. Occasionally a former 1st Division man came through. One day, an unfamiliar buck sergeant drifted into my office in the battalion C.P., identified himself as a former 16th Infantry man who had been wounded, hospitalized in England for several months, and finally reassigned to an outfit stationed in Berlin. He inquired about some of the old officers, and I directed him to their quarters. Several days later one of those officers told me that the sergeant had called on him and made a strange request: he offered to pay one hundred dollars for every additional hundred the officer would mail to the States for him! He had made a small fortune in Berlin, the man said, but now, because of the declaration of finances the army had recently required of every man in the European Theater, he was stuck with it, unable to mail home the thousands of dollars in American bills that he carried on his person, and unable to obtain money orders because he couldn't explain to a finance officer the source of so much money. A poker game or a crap game could always be blamed for a wad of several hundred dollars, but damn few poker games or crap games were of a scale that would enable a man to simper that he "won it" when the "it" happened to be twelve thousand dollars!

On the voyage home I heard about the enlisted man on board who had approached the officer in charge of his group and offered him a thousand dollars if the officer would appoint two men to act as his bodyguards during the voyage home. And he offered to pay each of the guards a hundred dollars a day. When the officer sardonically inquired what the hell he had that was so precious that it required the protection of guards, the man patted the swollen musette bag hanging at his side and said grimly, "The thirty thousand bucks I've got in here, sir." And he did!

Fantastic? Improbable? I don't know ... ask anyone who was there, and he'll tell you similar stories that he claims are true. And they are not beyond the realm of credulity if you can comprehend, even for a startled moment, the confusion that hung like shreds of storm cloud over Europe (and especially over Germany) in the last days of the war and the days immediately following, a confusion so great that the individual actions of individual men were obscured and lost in the frenzied teeming of millions. Europe was a fat corpse, white and naked and newly dead, and the ant hordes had found it. For the opportunist who was in the right place at the right time, for the ruthless—no matter where he might be—for the shrewdly dishonest who *made* opportunity where none existed, there were juicy pickings. And the marrow was so rich, the sprawled bones so heavy with fat, that the wonder is not that so many men were dishonest, but that so many men were not.

MEN AND WOMEN

Most men in the European Theater of Operations had one or more sexual adventures overseas. Some of these "adventures" were right and honest—right no matter how genuine the man's love for his wife at home, no matter how happy his normal civilian life. I've already written of this—of the deep need of flesh for flesh in the dark moments, the yearning and voiceless cry of the male for the promise of life implicit in the embracing of a woman, the solace of consummation and the restless godhead quiescent. There's no need to write further of this, nor of the days after the war when the longing for home was like a sickness in the bones, a malaise so desperate that for many men the long night hours were beyond endurance and the only opiates were liquor or women.

For many men, longing only for the familiar embrace of their wives, the choice was not easy. Hunger that made each day a fresh torment, or the agony of remorse? And there were so many opportunities, the girls were so available, the urging of the starved body so relentless . . . ("Ah, *she* wouldn't blame me . . . she'd understand . . . I've *got* to get some sleep tonight . . . she'd forgive me, she'd understand. . . .")

It was during the dreary months of occupation that many men, chaste till then, finally succumbed. One of them, a man who was young and vigorous, deeply in love with his wife, had been overseas for three years. Throughout all that time he'd been chaste, but the end of the war came and the long months of waiting followed, and there wasn't enough to do in the day-long, night-long hours. He began to drink, and one night he went home with a girl. It was one night only and never again, but he hated his body for its treachery.

Several days after his fall from grace he reported on sick call and asked the medic to check him for syphilis. The examination revealed no taint and he was sent back to his outfit. He reported on sick call again the following week and said, "Doc, I'm pretty sure I got syph. Will ya check me again?"

Another examination. Another report. "You're okay, soldier. Clean as a whistle!"

A few days passed and then one morning he was there again. Patiently the medic made another Wassermann, and patiently he talked to the soldier, attempting to persuade him from this incipient neurosis. The Wassermann proved negative, the effect of the talk was dubious, and the man returned to his outfit.

A week went by before he reappeared, his tormented face revealing the flame consuming him. He had a theory, a pathetic and desperate "out" for his agony: "But, Doc, this is a different kind of syph ... kind of a 'galloping syphilis'! It shows up every now and then, but after a while it goes away, and that's why you can't find it when I'm here!"

The amused but patient medic tried to explain the impossibility of this theory, tried to assure the man that he revealed no trace of *any* sex disease, but it was no go.

Then the whole story spilled out: the man had cheated on his wife, just once, and now he had enough points to go home and the captain said he'd probably be in the next shipment for the States, and supposing he had syphilis and went home and gave it to his wife, and he *did* have it, he *knew* he had it, and what in Christ's name was he going to do?

The medic kept him at the aid station that night and sent him to the regimental hospital in the morning. Calling the hospital, he explained the man's case history and recommended treatment by a psychiatrist. The soldier was kept at the hospital for a week, and a series of gravely conducted tests and examinations were made to lull his fears. The negative findings were shown to him and patiently explained in simple terms. The psychiatrist talked to him at length, and at the end of a week he was returned to his outfit, pronounced cured and his foolish fears at an end.

They were not ended, however—not until he himself put an end to them. The night he got back he put the muzzle of his M-1 in his mouth, pulled the trigger with his toe, and blew the top of his head off. "Better death than dishonor; better the grave than the death of love."

Sex behavior in Germany ranged from joyful cooperation to rape. The crime of rape seemed doubly bestial at this time and in this place: the frauleins (and fraus) were man-hungry and greedy for luxuries, and with so much easy stuff, so many pushovers, there appeared to be little excuse for unnatural or brutal sex behavior. Of the two most sordid cases I know, one concerned a nine-year-old girl who was raped and subjected to indignities by a soldier while his ever-lovin' buddy stood guard at the door of the barn to halt intruders. The criminal was caught and sentenced to death—later commuted to life imprisonment—and the man who stood guard was given ten years at hard labor.

The other case concerned a fifty-one-year-old woman who appeared at the local AMG office one morning, pointed to her toothless jaws, and asked a judgment of damages against a certain GI in order to get some new teeth. Assaulted and raped—a thing horrible to envision because, like all peasant women, she appeared even older than her years—she complained little of the act of rape. The loss of honor was small in comparison to the loss of the teeth the soldier had knocked out in his brutal attack. Sex she could take or leave alone, but she *had* to eat! (She got her new teeth and he got life.)

En route home, I listened to the raw laughter of a group of officers as they reminisced over their sex adventures in Germany. Two stories—two techniques, rather—struck me as a new low in mass male behavior. In the town where most of them had been stationed they devised a cunning scheme to secure a forever fresh supply of female flesh for the satisfaction of their appetites:

When a member of this inner circle noted an appetizing fraulein on the street, he would halt her and demand that she present her civilian papers for his inspection. Examining them, he would declare something out of order and cart her off to jail. That night he would return to the jail and offer to arrange her release if she would "put out." If she spurned his offer, she stayed in jail. Indefinitely. If she complied, she spent the night in his bed in full expectation of being released the next morning.

But ah, that's where the really subtle part comes in! The morning after her bedding down, she would be taken back to the jail with the promise that by noon she would receive the proper papers and be freed. All day she would wait, and that evening a new officer would come to the jail and regretfully inform her that the other officer had suddenly been transferred and *he* was now in charge, and what was she in jail for, anyway? Upon the recitation of her tearful story, he would make a proposal with a familiar ring—release on the following morning if she would put out. And so on through the ring, available to any officer interested until they wearied of her and of her tears and *did* release her.

Another device of this mob of gangsters was employed only once, on an exceptionally difficult case. A certain desirable fraulein had remained adamant to all offers and threats, and the frustrated officers determined to get her. Spurn the fair white bodies of Americans, would she? Hah!

They waited their time, and one day she appeared at the AMG office to apply for a wood ration card. Cold weather was at hand, and with no coal available either for cooking or heating, wood was a basic necessity in a German household. Particularly in hers, because she cared for an invalid mother and an aged father. The lieutenant in charge of the town's wood supply stalled and stalled and finally intimated that all the wood she could possibly burn would be forthcoming if she would "cooperate." Indignantly, she stormed from his office and for several days managed to get along on what scraps of fuel her neighbors could spare from their allotments. But that source was soon exhausted and she returned to the AMG office, to be met with the same smiling proposition. She begged, she wept and pleaded, but the proposition stood as before. Haunted by the vision of her ailing mother in an unheated room, she gave in at last, and the triumphant officer escorted her to his room.

The following morning he told her to call at his office in the afternoon and he would give her the requisition slip. But when she appeared, a strange officer was seated behind the desk. Blandly he informed her that *he* was the new officer in charge of the wood supply, and what was it she wanted?

Oh hell . . . finish it yourself!

Author's Note

So it's over, this one's over, and the next one may be ripening. All the blood, all the tears, all the pain and fear and dirt and madness to come again. . . .

That's the thing I've got to end on, that bleak note of what is mostly despair. Unlike Mr. Norman Corwin, I don't believe the war ended on a note of triumph. Because, although we were a little more aware of what we were fighting for *while* we were fighting, the old miasmas of greed and distrust obscured that fine clarity almost before the war was done. The web that held the Allies together was soon torn, and the gleaming, perfect tapestry that had been promised the world is already a tangle of raveled threads, dirty and unrecognizable. The rule of the fist and the lie threatens little people once more, faith has become a whore, and hope dies of malnutrition.

And America . . . once again America dithers in a soprano hysteria of suspicions and denials, charges and counter-charges, indecisive lunges first to the left and then to the right, political maneuvering and political opportunism. We know how to fight; we don't know how to make peace. And oh, my son, for whom this was written, I pray we learn the secret and the wisdom of peace before you're old enough to tote the gun and dig the foxhole that will be useless in the next war. And oh, my daughter, for whom also this was written, I pray we learn before you are old enough to wave good-bye to the man you love and see him go off to a cataclysm that could be prevented. Because if he does go, my dear, I doubt that you will see him come back.

IF YOU SURVIVE
by George Wilson

From the first penetration of the Siegfried Line to the Nazis' last desperate charge in the Battle of the Bulge, Wilson fought in the thickest action, helping to take the small towns of northern France and Belgium building by building. As the only member of Company F, 4th Infantry Division, to survive the war, Wilson bears heartbreaking testimony to the courage and honor of the men he fought with and the war they won.

Published by Ivy Books.
Available in bookstores everywhere.

PANZER BATTLES
A Study of the Employment of Armor in the Second World War
by
Major General F. W. von Mellenthin

It was the decisive victories of the German Panzer divisions in North Africa that taught the Allies the importance of an integrated combat team consisting of tanks, infantry, and artillery. PANZER BATTLES is a vivid account of the major armor campaigns of WW II, especially the legendary desert battles fought by Rommel.

Here is a model military history illustrating what the American military learned from the battles of WW II—experience that would be put to use by General Norman Schwarzkopf during the Gulf War.

Published by Ballantine Books.
Available in your local bookstore.

JG 26
TOP GUNS OF THE LUFTWAFFE
by Donald L. Caldwell

This is the story of the pilots and campaigns of
Luftwaffe fighter wing JG 26, known as the
Abbeville Kids. *JG 26* chronicles the rise and
fall of the famous fighter wing, from its found-
ing during Hitler's military buildup through
its glory days during the first years of the war,
when its bases in northern France were to be
avoided at all costs, right up to the grim final
hours of the Third Reich.

Published by Ivy Books.
Available in bookstores everywhere.

RANGERS IN WW II
by Robert W. Black

From the deadly shores of North Africa to the fierce jungle hell of the Pacific, the contribution of the World War II Ranger Battalions far outweighed their numbers. They were ordinary men on an extraordinary mission, whether spearheading a landing force or scouting deep behind enemy lines. With first-person interviews and in-depth research, author Robert Black, a Ranger himself, makes the battles of the greatest war the world has ever seen come to life as never before.

Published by Ivy Books.
Available in your local bookstore.

HEROES OF WW II
by Edward F. Murphy

Of the 13 million who served during World
War II, only 433 received the United States'
highest award for valor. And only 190 of those
brave men survived to receive their medals. In
this chronicle of their almost superhuman
feats of selfless courage, we witness the bombing of Pearl Harbor, the invasion of Normandy,
and other crucial battles as the history of
World War II unfolds in the heroic deeds of the
men who won the war.

Published by Ivy Books.
Available in bookstores everywhere.

THERE'S A WAR TO BE WON
THE UNITED STATES ARMY IN WORLD WAR II
by Geoffrey Perret

Here is a chronicle of the United States Army's dramatic mobilization and stunning march to victory in World War II. Geoffrey Perret shows how the army was drafted, armed, and led at every stage of the war. He offers vivid warts-and-all profiles of the commanders who would lead the way, men like MacArthur, Eisenhower, and Patton.

A must-read, major work of American military history.

Published by Ivy Books.
Available in your local bookstore.